D1643947

ROYAL HISTORICAL SOCIETY
STUDIES IN HISTORY
SERIES

No.45

SERVILITY AND SERVICE

The Life and Work of Sir John Coke

Recent volumes published in this series include

37	'Agrarians' and 'Aristocrats' Party Political Ideology in the United States, 1837-1846	*John Ashworth*
38	Caesar's Due: Loyalty and King Charles 1642-1646	*Joyce Lee Malcolm*
39	T.P. O'Connor and the Liverpool Irish	*L. W. Brady*
40	Law and Social Change in British History	*J. A. Guy & H. G. Beale (eds.)*
41	The Road to Sedan: The French Army 1866-70	*Richard Holmes*
42	The *Parlement* of Poitiers	*Roger G. Little*
43	Britain and Palestine during the Second World War	*Ronald W. Zweig*
44	The Right-Wing Press in the French Revolution	*W. J. Murray*

For a complete list of the series please see pp. 298

SERVILITY AND SERVICE
The Life and Work of Sir John Coke

Michael B. Young

Published by
The Boydell Press
for The Royal Historical Society
1986

First published 1986

Published by
The Boydell Press
an imprint of Boydell & Brewer Ltd
PO Box 9 Woodbridge Suffolk IP12 3DF
and 51 Washington Street Dover New Hampshire 03820 USA
for
The Royal Historical Society
University College London WC1

The Society records its gratitude to the following, whose generosity made possible the initiation of this series: The British Academy; The Pilgrim Trust; The Twenty-Seven Foundation; The United States Embassy bicentennial funds; The Wolfson Trust; several private donors.

ISBN 0 86193 202 1

Printed in Great Britain by Short Run Press Ltd, Exeter

To
Marcia and Heather
whose many sacrifices
made this book possible.

Sir John Coke
by Cornelius Jannsens

CONTENTS

ACKNOWLEDGEMENTS

I incurred many debts of gratitude while writing this book, and it is a profound pleasure to be able now to acknowledge them.

Two sets of documents lie at the heart of this study: the state papers located at the Public Record Office in London and Sir John Coke's personal papers, preserved since his own day at Melbourne Hall in Derbyshire. I am immensely grateful to the Marquess of Lothian, current owner of the Coke MSS., for permission to use and quote from them. I am equally grateful to Mrs. Kerr, Miss Dorehill, and Mrs. Leech, who gave me all the hospitality and assistance I could possibly have hoped for on my several visits to Melbourne. It was also through the kindness of Mrs. Kerr that I was able to visit Coke's ancestral home at Trusley. There I was graciously received by Mrs. R. Coke-Steel and Mr. David Coke-Steel who generously shared the 'Family Chronicle' and other papers with me. Of course I also worked at numerous public repositories, including the Public Record Office, county record offices, and the British Library. I am thankful to all the people who helped me at these places, but I would like to give special thanks to Mr. Lea for his unfailing and learned assistance in the Long Room of the Public Record Office. I am likewise indebted to librarians at several universities, including Harvard University, Yale University, the University of Illinois, Illinois State University, and Illinois Wesleyan University. I can only join the legion of other foreign scholars who have expressed their heartfelt appreciation of the Institute of Historical Research at the University of London. For patiently typing the drafts of my manuscript, I am grateful to Mrs. Glenna Schaab and several, long-suffering, departmental secretaries.

I hope my multitudinous footnotes give adequate acknowledgement to the work of previous authors, but I should particularly acknowledge my debt to A.P. McGowan, G.E. Aylmer, F.M.G. Evans, Ronald Rebholz, S.R. Gardiner, and, though my own work is intended to supersede hers, Dorothea Coke.

My work could not have proceeded without financial assistance which I was fortunate to receive from various sources at critical stages along the way. A Fulbright Fellowship financed my first year of research in England. In 1978 the National Endowment for the Humanities made possible a summer of study at Yale University, in particular at the Yale Center for Parliamentary History. In 1979 a grant from the Penrose fund of the American Philosophical Society enabled me to return to England. Throughout these years, I also shamelessly accepted innumerable contributions from my parents.

Nor could a project of this magnitude have been sustained without the assistance and encouragement of many friends and colleagues. Among the many to whom I am indebted are Saul and Kathleen Benjamin, Barbara and Cary Carson, Tom Cogswell, Linda Peck, Linda Popofsky, and several of my colleagues at Illinois Wesleyan University, most especially the other members of the History Department. Requiring fuller mention are the late J. Richard Jones of Moravian College, who was my mentor and oldest supporter; Caroline Hibbard, who has been a constant source of useful information and friendly advice, particularly relevant to chapter fourteen; William Bidwell and Maija Cole, who gave me remarkably free access to the Yale Center for Parliamentary History; Derek Hirst and Roy Schreiber, both of whom gave me valuable counsel.

W.K. Jordan and Joel Hurstfield supervised my first investigation of Coke's life in the form of a Ph.D. thesis completed in 1971. This book, however, is a vastly expanded and improved study begun in 1978, and it probably would not exist if I had not been fortunate to experience the great wisdom and sympathy of Conrad Russell and J.H. Hexter. Professor Russell did me the huge favour of reading the manuscript meticulously, and his copious comments showed me how to make many improvements. Professor Russell helped me in other ways, too, not least in sustaining my morale at a particularly dark moment. Of course there have also been bright moments in the history of this book, and among the very brightest was my first meeting with J.H. Hexter in 1978. Professor Hexter gave me the initial determination to embark on this project, and he has continued to be an incomparable source of support and inspiration. Words simply cannot express how much I appreciate what he has done for me.

In the end, still one more scholar – G.R. Elton – became supremely instrumental in assuring this book's publication. Without his efforts, the rest would all have been in vain. I am indebted even further to Professor Elton for his perceptive criticisms of style that have made this a more readable book.

The final and greatest debt I owe is to my wife Marcia. She made all the usual sacrifices that one spouse must make for the other to complete a project of this size, and for these alone she would deserve the dedication of this book. But Marcia was far more than a supportive bystander. She typed, transcribed, and researched for countless hours, especially in the Public Record Office. She patiently listened to my inchoate ideas, helped me to articulate what I already knew, and frequently pointed out what I had failed to see. I alone have written this book, but in all else I have had the benefit of a skilled historian by my side.

Michael B. Young
June 1984

AUTHOR'S NOTE

When quoting from manuscripts, I have modernized the spelling and capitalization. Where essential for clarity's sake, I have also modernized the punctuation. In dates the day of the month has not been changed from old to new style, but the year has been changed so as to begin on 1 January. References to parliamentary diaries for 1624 and 1626 are based on the typescripts at the Yale Center for Parliamentary History. References to the Coke MSS. are based on my own transcripts of the actual papers at Melbourne Hall, but the reader who wishes to can usually find reliable, printed transcripts of these same papers arranged by date in the *Cowper MSS.* published by the Historical Manuscripts Commission.

The portrait of Sir John Coke, by Cornelius Jannsens is reproduced by kind permission of the Marquess of Lothian.

M.B.Y.

ABBREVIATIONS

APC	*Acts of the Privy Council of England.*
BL	British Library.
CJ	*Journals of the House of Commons.*
Coke MSS.	Sir John Coke's papers, Melbourne Hall, Derbyshire.
Cowper MSS.	Historical Manuscripts Commission, *The Manuscripts of the Earl Cowper, K.G., Preserved at Melbourne Hall, Derbyshire* (twelfth report, appendixes I-III). These are the published transcripts of Coke's papers.
CSPD	*Calendar of State Papers Domestic.*
CSPV	*Calendar of State Papers Venetian.*
DNB	*Dictionary of National Biography.*
HMC	Historical Manuscripts Commission.
LJ	*Journals of the House of Lords.*
PRO	Public Record Office.
SP	State Papers, Public Record Office.

INTRODUCTION

What kind of man was Sir John Coke? Historians have often described him as if he were a faithful pet dog – not as bright or interesting as the people around him but singularly obedient and eager to please. S.R. Gardiner described Coke as 'a mere tool, ready to do anything or to say anything as he was bidden'.[1] Echoing this view, C.V. Wedgwood said that Coke was 'slow, old-fashioned in his ideas and rather obstinate'.[2] (It was apparently difficult to teach the old dog new tricks.) One historian, David H. Willson, began on a more positive note by conceding that Coke was 'an honest, faithful, and industrious bureaucrat', but he quickly added that Coke was 'without the slightest spark of imagination or originality, wholly intent upon obeying instructions'.[3] Willson concluded that Coke was 'essentially mediocre', and this judgment has been confirmed by G.E. Aylmer who called Coke one of Charles I's 'more humdrum' ministers.[4] Most unsympathetic of all, however, was Quentin Bone who relegated Coke to a footnote and declared that he 'displayed every characteristic of a toady'.[5]

Although there is much in Coke's life to support these impressions, there is much else that suggests he was a very different sort of person. For a supposedly dull man, Coke had a surprisingly interesting and successful career. Early in life he distinguished himself at Cambridge University and won the patronage of Sir Fulke Greville, the courtier and poet famous for his eulogistic life of Sir Philip Sidney. Indeed, after Sidney, Coke became Greville's closest lifelong friend – a fact especially difficult to reconcile with the conventional view of Coke.[6] By the end of Elizabeth's reign, Coke was Deputy-Treasurer of the Navy, but he was forced out of office shortly after James's accession. Coke's whole career under Elizabeth, his stinging defeat in 1604, and his alienation from the court during the next fourteen years have been largely ignored by historians. This ignorance of Coke's early career

[1] *A History of England under the Duke of Buckingham and Charles I, 1624-1628* (2 vols., London, 1875), I, 228.

[2] *The King's Peace, 1637-1641* (New York, 1956), p. 308.

[3] *The Privy Councillors in the House of Commons, 1604-1629* (Minneapolis, 1940), pp. 95-6.

[4] *The King's Servants: The Civil Service of Charles I, 1625-1642,* rev. ed. (London, 1974), p. 234.

[5] *Henrietta Maria: Queen of the Cavaliers* (Urbana, Illinois, 1972), p. 89 n. 73.

[6] Ronald Rebholz, *The Life of Fulke Greville, First Lord Brooke* (Oxford, 1971), p. 96. Rebholz says that Coke was 'without question' Greville's 'dearest friend after Sidney'.

has contributed to a superficial interpretation of his later career. It has also prevented historians from appreciating how truly remarkable his 'political comeback' was in 1618. Coke's work in the years immediately following 1618 has been much better understood and frequently, if grudgingly, praised. Although sometimes eclipsed by the more famous Lionel Cranfield, Coke contributed substantially to reform of the navy and planned similar reform in the ordnance office. He also impressed the duke of Buckingham, who became his new patron. Under Buckingham's patronage, Coke was made chief commissioner of the navy and in 1622 a Master of Requests. In 1625, at the age of sixty-two, Coke rose even higher to become Secretary of State, a post he would hold almost to the meeting of the Short Parliament. During the 1620s Coke was the one man in England most responsible for setting out the English fleets, and he was a major defender of the Crown's position in Parliament. If a man can be judged by the quality of his enemies, it should be remembered that Coke's bitterest opponent during this period was Sir John Eliot. And if a man can be judged by the quality of his friends, it should be remembered that during the 1630s one of Coke's closest supporters was the earl of Strafford, who said of Coke: 'I shall honour you all the Days of my Life.'[7] During the 1630s Coke also succeeded with Thomas Witherings in reforming the postal system, which has been hailed as 'one of the few authentic improvements achieved under the early Stuarts'.[8] Of course Coke's reputation has suffered from his fifteen years as Secretary to Charles I, and in some respects deservedly so. But Coke did not serve as Secretary under very enviable circumstances, and the strong bias of historians against the monarchy in those controversial years preceding the Civil War has hardly helped Coke to receive a fair evaluation. Even Coke's advanced age has made historians too quick to judge him unfavourably. In 1640, when Coke was seventy-six years old, he was forced at last to relinquish the Secretaryship. Shortly thereafter, while the Long Parliament was appraising the government of Charles I, Coke personally reappraised the part he had played in that government. He particularly reviewed in his mind all the reforming efforts he had participated in during the reigns of James I and Charles I. 'Now by all these and such other employments', he concluded, 'I have been taught that which the archbishop of Canterbury said often: that kings cannot be served against their wills.'[9]

[7]William Knowler, ed., *The Earl of Strafforde's Letters and Dispatches* (2 vols., London, 1734), I, 494.

[8]*The King's Servants,* p. 369. Conrad Russell informs me that the Coventry MSS. at Birmingham also show Coke as a co-founder of the passport office.

[9]Coke MSS., packet 65, Coke to his son John, [1641].

It is not easy, then, to characterize Sir John Coke's life in a single word or phrase. Two facts stand out, however. First there is Coke's obvious success. He began his career with little more than his native abilities but succeeded at court in acquiring office, influence, and wealth. Measured in these terms, he died a successful man. But then there is the second fact of Coke's life: his ultimate failure as an administrative reformer. Despite Coke's longevity at court, he left practically nothing behind him in the way of enduring administrative reform. There are numerous reasons for this failure, including Coke's own shortcomings, the incompetent management of James I and Charles I, and institutional defects such as the inadequate financial resources of the Crown. Perhaps more interesting, however, are the ways in which Coke's long-term failure as an administrator can be traced back to the very same factors that brought him success in the short run as a courtier. Coke's industry and ability went far toward advancing him in favour, but no less important were factionalism, patronage, and grovelling servility. And these factors which sometimes worked for Coke were equally capable of working against him, nullifying his ability and denying him success of a sort that would have been more lasting and significant. In this way, then, Coke was both a beneficiary and a victim of the court, who seems to have learned only at the very end of his career how great a price he had paid for his transitory success. Behind the superficial achievement of status and wealth lay the awful fact that Coke's talent and efforts dutifully expended over a lifetime of service to the Crown had been wasted. While it is true that Coke's daily labours were often humdrum, this larger interplay of success and failure overshadowing his work makes his life both fascinating and instructive.

A thorough and balanced reevaluation of Coke's life has long been needed. In 1937 one of his distant descendants, Dorothea Coke, published *The Last Elizabethan*. Though not without some value, this is inadequate, erroneous, and seriously flawed because of the author's uncritical admiration for her subject. The faults of the book were sufficient in themselves to warrant a new study. Moreover, recent historiographical trends have conspired in an uncanny way to make a reconsideration of Coke's life even more compelling and worthwhile. The gentry controversy has subsided, and historians have increasingly turned their attention back to the specific personalities and Parliaments that preceded the Civil War. In recent years, for example, biographies of at least a half dozen of Coke's associates have appeared. At the same time, the whole field of parliamentary history has been revitalized by revisionists who have asserted, among other things, that the dichotomy between court and country has been exaggerated, that an 'opposition' did not really exist in Parliament, that personal rivalries and local interests were more at work in these Parliaments than grand constitutional issues, and that the political crises of the period resulted chiefly from the government's particular inability to prosecute a foreign war. Coke's career, especially his work in Parliament and the navy, is intimately related to these revisionist claims. It is fortunate that the burgeoning debate over revisionism has coincided with the writing of this book, perhaps making it more interesting and certainly making it more balanced than it would otherwise have been. On the other hand, this book is not a partisan contribution to either side in that debate. My objective has been instead to write an account that would be sound enough to outlive such historical vogues. Granted that no history can be entirely accurate and free from bias, I have tried to reconstruct Coke's life as much as possible in the way the evidence dictated.

What have been the results of that reconstruction? First, at the very least, Coke's life provides another example of the way in which power was won and lost, patronage was wielded, and royal government operated under the early Stuarts. It therefore augments the recent studies of Cottington, Portland, Buckingham, and other courtiers. Secondly, Coke's life illuminates particular areas of early Stuart government. Among these is the little understood office of Master of Requests. Of course the one area of government most prominent in Coke's life is the navy. A.P. McGowan and Roger Lockyer have done much to rehabilitate Buckingham's reputation as Lord Admiral, but it was Coke who ran the navy for Buckingham. He was, in Lockyer's words, 'the Samual Pepys of his day'.[10] Unlike Pepys, Coke did not keep a diary, but he did in his typically thorough fashion leave behind a marvellous collection of papers. These papers have never before been utilized to full advantage. If they have made the present book long enough to tax the patience of some readers, it is because they have made it possible to document the career of an early Stuart official with unusual detail and richness. Thirdly, Coke's career dramatically demonstrates the general incapacity of the early Stuart government to reform itself, not only in the navy but in the several departments where Coke's efforts repeatedly came to naught. Fourthly, a reconsideration of Coke's life necessarily impinges on the history of Parliament, especially in 1626 and 1628. With the notable exception of J.N. Ball, historians evaluating Coke's performance in Parliament have given too much credence to the hostile testimony of his personal enemy, Sir

[10]*Buckingham: The Life and Political Career of George Villiers, First Duke of Buckingham* (London, 1981), p. 76.

John Eliot. We will see that this is particularly true of David H. Willson's characterization of Coke in the Parliament of 1628. Fifthly, by examining Coke's role in the foreign affairs of the 1630s, using primary sources that have tended to be neglected, we come to a deeper understanding of court factionalism in that period. Sixthly, Coke's career raises the intriguing question why a man who slavishly worked for nearly thirty years under three monarchs, a man who was a devoted follower of Buckingham in the 1620s and a dutiful servant of Charles in the 1630s, did not support the king in the Civil War. That question underlies this whole book and is the sole concern of the final chapter. Finally, on the most fundamental and human level, what is revealed in the following pages is a man torn between choices that have changed little over the centuries. Coke was torn between scholarly contemplation and public action, between lofty political idealism and harsher political reality, between family and love on the one hand, and work, fame and fortune on the other. These were not easy choices between absolute right and wrong. As we shall see, they were painfully difficult choices that caused Coke much soul-searching and sometimes regret, not the least of which is captured in his reluctant conclusion that the lesson of his whole life's work amounted to this – 'that kings cannot be served against their wills'.

1

THE EARLY YEARS

John Coke was born on 5 March 1563. His family home was in rural Derbyshire, but he was born in London, and that fact curiously presaged a life that would bridge the worlds of 'court' and 'country'.[1] Coke's roots ran deep in the Midland countryside. He maintained his ties there and later in life established his own country seat only a few miles from the family lands. Yet, strong as his ties to the country were, the attractions of his birthplace proved stronger. Only at London and the court was he able to obtain what he wanted out of life, only there was he ever fully satisfied. The world of the country gentleman and the world of the courtier thus merged in Coke's life and character; and that is why this story of his career at London and the court must begin by briefly surveying the heritage of the country world he never truly left behind.

Coke's earliest known ancestors lived in the late middle ages near the border between Staffordshire and Derbyshire. In the fifteenth century the family settled at Trusley, a manor in Derbyshire only a few miles from the town of Derby. Trusley and the other family lands descended to Richard Coke in 1575. Richard Coke was an enterprising man who attended the Inner Temple, practiced law in the Midlands, and from 1564 to 1578 was Clerk of the Peace for Derbyshire.[2] Before inheriting Trusley, Richard Coke had already enlarged his estate by marrying Mary Sacheverell, a Nottinghamshire heiress. Our subject, John, was the third child out of eleven born to Richard and Mary, a number that seems only slightly smaller when we consider that Richard himself had been one of fifteen children.[3] It is not known exactly how much wealth John's parents possessed, but they were clearly prosperous members of the lesser gentry, and, in any case, the

[1] The 'Family Chronicle' at Trusley. Coke's father recorded the births of all eleven of his children but gave the place of birth only in John's case.

[2] *Students Admitted to the Inner Temple, 1547-1660* (London, 1877), p. 8. Edgar Stephens, *The Clerks of the Counties, 1360-1960* (Newport, 1961), p. 75. Letters from Richard Coke to the sixth earl of Shrewsbury on legal matters are in the Lambeth Palace Library, Shrewsbury MSS., vol. 707, fols. 4, 6, 128, 185.

[3] John T. Coke, *Coke of Trusley, in the County of Derby, and Branches Therefrom: A Family History* (London, 1880), pp. v-vii, 1-11. A pedigree of the Coke family from the British Library Harleian MSS. is printed in John J. Briggs, *The History of Melbourne in the County of Derby,* 2nd ed. (London, 1852), pp. 161-5.

fortunes of their family lay not so much in land as in the destinies of their sons.[4]

By 1582 both Richard and Mary Coke had died, leaving behind John and five other sons. The eldest was Francis, who inherited the family estate with instructions to pay an annuity of £6 13s 4d to each of his five younger brothers. Thus Francis was well provided for, while John and the other younger brothers received only small annuities, much smaller in fact than previously assumed.[5] These straitened circumstances in his youth may go far toward explaining John's lifelong caution and thriftiness.[6] Looking briefly at all six sons, two died too young to improve upon their fortunes: Philip died in 1599 while still a fellow of Trinity College, Cambridge, and Robert was killed at the Battle of Newport in 1600.[7] The four brothers who survived did well, however. Francis looked after his younger brothers in a responsible fashion, married an aunt of the Denzil Holles of later parliamentary fame, served as a collector of subsidies for both Elizabeth I and James I, and was knighted by James I at Tutbury in 1619.[8] Thomas went to St. John's College, Cambridge, where he was made a fellow and earned both the B.A. and M.A. degrees. Between his Cambridge days and his untimely death at Padua in 1621, he served as secretary to Gilbert Talbot, seventh earl of Shrewsbury.[9] George also earned his B.A. and M.A. at St. John's College, Cambridge, and was made a fellow of Pembroke. After his ordination in 1602, George rose through the church hierarchy to become a bishop, first of Bristol and later of Hereford.[10] Lastly there was John, who served three successive monarchs as Deputy-Treasurer of the Navy, commissioner of the navy, Master of Requests, and Secretary of State.

These sons of Richard and Mary Coke represented the beginning of a new era for the Coke family. Whatever was happening to the

[4] As might be expected, little is known of the daughters after their marriages. Letters to John from his sisters are in Coke MSS., packet 91.

[5] Prerogative Court of Canterbury, 36 Butts; *Cowper MSS.,* I, 52. The value of this annuity has been considerably over-estimated at £40. *DNB*, IV, 700; Dorothea Coke, *The Last Elizabethan: Sir John Coke, 1563-1644* (London, 1937), p. 6.

[6] David Mathew referred to Coke's 'early poverty'. *The Jacobean Age* (London, 1938), p. 284.

[7] Coke, *Coke of Trusley,* p. 8. The circumstances of Philip's and Robert's deaths are related in *Cowper MSS.,* I, 23 and 26, respectively.

[8] Coke, *Coke of Trusley*, p. 13.

[9] John and J.A. Venn, eds., *Alumni Cantabrigienses* (4 vols., Cambridge, 1922-7), pt. 1, vol. I, p. 387. Letters between the earl of Shrewsbury, his family, and Thomas Coke are scattered through the *Cowper MSS.*, vol. I, and the Shrewsbury papers at Lambeth Palace Library. For Thomas Coke's death, see Coke, *Coke of Trusley,* p. 8.

[10] Venn, *Alumni Cantabrigienses,* pt. 1, vol. I, p. 384.

gentry class in general, John Coke's family was rising, and this provides an important key to an understanding of his character. He was the outstanding member of the new generation, who sought his fortune at London and the court but never abandoned the austere values of his ancestors who had laboured for centuries in the Derbyshire countryside. Whatever his faults, both his critics and admirers agree that for a courtier he remained unusually frugal, sober, devout, and hard-working. Indeed, his constancy to these values provides a standard by which to judge the English court from the last decade of Elizabeth's reign to the eve of the Civil War.[11]

Another key to Coke's character is his education. As he described himself later in life: 'I was not bred in servile or illiberal trades; the university was my nurse.'[12] The university Coke referred to was Cambridge, where he matriculated as a pensioner from Trinity College in the Easter term of 1576. He received his B.A. in 1581 and his M.A. in 1584, in which year he was also incorporated M.A. at Oxford University.[13] There are several indications that Coke did very well at Trinity. For example, we know his position on the *Ordo Senioritatis,* a list of degree recipients. Originally the names on these lists were arranged according to seniority, but by Coke's time academic merit seems also to have been a factor, especially toward the top of the list. When Coke received his B.A., he was listed fifteenth out of 194 recipients; when he received his M.A., his position was slightly lower at twenty-sixth out of 113 recipients.[14] Furthermore, the financial records of Trinity reveal that Coke received a foundation scholarship beginning in 1580.[15] Finally, Coke became a fellow of Trinity. He was a minor fellow in 1583 and a major fellow upon receipt of his M.A. in 1584.

Coke's fellowship payments appear in the bursar's accounts through 1591, which means he stayed at Trinity for seven years after

[11]Compare Mathew, *The Jacobean Age,* p. 281.

[12]Coke MSS., packet 45, Coke to Buckingham, 12 Oct. 1622. It is likely that Coke attended Westminster School before going to Cambridge. Coke, *The Last Elizabethan*, p. 5. Unfortunately, this cannot be corroborated by the imperfect records of the school. Coke is not listed in G.F. Barker and Alan H. Stenning, *The Record of Old Westminsters* (London, 1928). The likelihood of Coke's having attended Westminster is increased by the fact that there was a close relationship between it and Trinity. H. McLeod Innes, *Fellows of Trinity College Cambridge* (Cambridge, 1941), p. 13.

[13]Venn, *Alumni Cantabrigienses,* pt. 1, vol. I, p. 384; Joseph Foster, ed., *Alumni Oxonienses* (4 vols., Oxford, 1891-2), I, 320.

[14]John Venn, ed., *Grace Book Delta Containing the Records of the University of Cambridge for the Years 1542-1589* (Cambridge, 1910), pp. viii-xi, 336-8, 377.

[15]*Cowper MSS.,* I, iii.

receiving his M.A., but what exactly did he do during this period?[16] In their later assessments of Coke, both the earl of Clarendon and Sir John Eliot agreed that Coke lingered for a long time at Cambridge and that this experience left an indelible mark on his personality, but neither man specified what Coke did during these additional years at Cambridge.[17] The most likely answer is that he was a lecturer in rhetoric. Two early writers whose lives overlapped with Coke's asserted not only that he was the university lecturer in rhetoric but also that he gained renown in this position.[18] Leaving aside the question of his renown, there is one known incident that supports at least the basic assumption that Coke held such an office: when his brother George was made rhetoric lecturer in 1602, he asked to use John's notes.[19]

Whatever Coke's achievement and employment during his years at Trinity College, these were ultimately no more important to him than the personal associations he formed while there. One important friend whom he met at Trinity was Robert Naunton. Coke and Naunton had remarkably similar careers.[20] Both were born in 1563, both were fellows of Trinity College, both were associated with the Essex circle under Elizabeth I, and both went on under the Stuarts to become Master of Requests and then Secretary of State. When the two men met at Trinity in the 1580s, of course, Coke could hardly have guessed that thirty years later Naunton would help to rescue him from premature retirement and revive his political career.

A more important friend than Naunton – indeed probably the most important friend Coke ever had – was Fulke Greville. Greville is famous as the friend and biographer of Sir Philip Sidney, but he was also a

[16]Innes, *Fellows of Trinity College,* p. 27; *Cowper MSS.,* I, iv; Venn, *Alumni Cantabrigienses,* pt. 1, vol. I, p. 384. I am grateful to Miss Rosemary Graham of the Trinity College Library who has confirmed this information for me.

[17]Edward Hyde, earl of Clarendon, *The History of the Rebellion and Civil Wars in England Begun in the Year 1641,* ed. W. Dunn Macray (6 vols., Oxford, 1888), I, 80; *An Apology for Socrates and Negotium Posterorum: By Sir John Eliot,* ed. Alexander B. Grosart (2 vols., London, 1881), I, 114. See also *Cowper MSS.*, II, 65.

[18]Thomas Fuller, *The History of the Worthies of England,* ed. P. Austin Nuttall (3 vols., London, 1840), I, 371; David Lloyd, *State Worthies* (2 vols., London, 1766), II, 262.

[19]*Cowper MSS.*, III, 132. George wrote: 'I pray you for your notes *Pro Archia,* if you have them, to help me.' He thus likened Coke to Cicero and himself to Aulus Licinius Archia, a minor Greek poet whom Cicero defended. C.T. Lewis and S. Short, eds., *Harper's Latin Dictionary* (New York, 1879), p. 154.

[20]Naunton matriculated pensioner in 1579, took up residence as a scholar in 1582, received his B.A. in 1583, was made a fellow in 1585, and received his M.A. in 1586. W.W. Rouse Ball and J.A. Venn, eds., *Admissions to Trinity College, Cambridge* (5 vols., London, 1911-16), II, 124.

poet in his own right and a skillful courtier who made an ideal patron for Coke. His strength at court rested on the queen's personal fondness for him, so much so that when Robert Naunton later reflected on Elizabeth's reign, he judged that Greville 'had the longest lease, and the smoothest time without rub, of any of her Favourites'.[21] There is no evidence to indicate precisely when or how Coke became acquainted with Greville.[22] They may have been brought together by George Talbot, sixth earl of Shrewsbury, who knew both Greville and Coke's family. Coke's father, as Clerk of the Peace, and his uncle, as a church rector, had probably benefited from the earl's patronage; Coke's brother Thomas, as mentioned earlier, became the seventh earl's personal secretary.[23] If Coke did not become acquainted with Greville through the earl of Shrewsbury, then it must have been through the earl of Essex and his circle of associates at Cambridge. Essex was at Trinity College from 1577 to 1581, while Coke was there, and they had at least one mutual acquaintance who can be identified: a fellow of King's College named Lionel Sharpe. About the year 1588 Sharpe left Cambridge in order to continue in the earl's circle as his chaplain.[24] Sometime afterward, he wrote to Coke, urging him to do the same, forsake the university and join the Essex circle. Sharpe noted that Coke had impressed both the earl's tutor and Greville. He said that Coke would enjoy the comradeship of learned gentlemen and, no less important, an annuity of £30, though it is not clear whether Essex or Greville would provide this sum.[25] Either this letter from Sharpe or other inducements persuaded Coke to leave

[21] *Fragmenta Regalia* (Westminster, 1895), p. 50.

[22] Coke was not related to Greville, as is sometimes claimed (e.g., in Coke, *Coke of Trusley,* p. 59). Sir John Eliot described Greville as the man 'under whom he [Coke] had had his education as a scholler'. Eliot, *Negotium Posterorum,* I, 113-14.

[23] Richard Coke's legal correspondence with Shrewsbury has already been cited. His brother John was rector of North Wingfield in Derbyshire. A letter from John to Shrewsbury can be found in Lambeth Palace Library, Shrewsbury MSS., vol. 710, fol. 19. For more about this John Coke, see Venn, *Alumni Cantabrigienses,* pt. 1, vol. I, p. 384.

[24] Venn, *Alumni Cantabrigienses*, pt. 1, vol. IV, p. 50; *DNB*, XVII, 1,349-50. Sharpe received his B.A. and M.A. in precisely the same years as Coke. His fellowship continued to 1589, but he was reported to be in Essex's company as his chaplain in 1588.

[25] Coke MSS., packet 66, an undated letter addressed to 'Mr. Cooke of Trinity College' and endorsed by Coke, 'Mr. Lionel Sharpe from the Court. Chaplain to the Earl of Essex. Latin.' For helping me to translate this intractable letter, I am grateful to John Freed, David MacDonald, and Harold Hungerford. Sharpe's meaning is never crystal clear in this letter, but he appears to have given Coke just seven days to make up his mind. Coke must have attached special significance to this letter because, unless others have been lost, it is one of very few papers he preserved from this period. I am assuming that the Mr. Wright referred to in Sharpe's letter was Robert Wright, Essex's tutor.

Cambridge. After fifteen years at the university, it must have been a difficult decision to make and one he would sometimes regret. Indeed, years later, he wistfully described himself as a 'man estranged and banished from the hopes and ambitions of learning'.[26] At the end of 1591 Coke set forth in pursuit of more worldly hopes and ambitions.

The two years immediately following Coke's departure from Cambridge constitute an enigmatic period in his otherwise well-documented career.[27] Several previous writers have assumed that during this period Coke held a post somehow related to naval finances, but these authors apparently had no basis for this conclusion except the fact that twenty papers among the Coke manuscripts date from this period and concern naval affairs.[28] Closer examination reveals, however, that Coke's name appears nowhere in these papers, and there is no indication how, when, or why they came into his possession. Furthermore, they begin as early as 1588, three years before Coke left Cambridge, and continue through two years, 1594 and 1595, when he was out of the country. They therefore fail to prove that Coke worked in any capacity relative to naval finances between 1591 and 1593, and they are much more likely to have come into his possession years later when we know he did obtain a naval post.

More informative light is shed on this shadowy period by a financial account kept by John Powell, one of Fulke Greville's estate agents. Coke's name appears several places in this account, first as a collector of fines for Greville in October of 1590. Other references show that money was expended by Powell for Coke's lodgings, and several sums were delivered to Coke, the largest being £200 at the end of the account in Michaelmas term of 1591.[29] From this account it thus appears that Coke was helping to manage Greville's lands the year before he left Cambridge, and this probably continued to be his chief way of paying Greville for his keep after leaving the university. Although this form of work was less glamorous than the naval employment Coke is purported to have undertaken, it was an excellent way of creating a bond of mutual self-interest between a client and his patron. Coke made himself useful in the management of

[26] *Cowper MSS.,* I, 29.

[27] Before leaving Cambridge, Coke may have been employed by Lord Burghley in 1587 and 1588 in some capacity related to Burghley's Lord Lieutenancy of Lincolnshire. *DNB,* IV, 700; *Cowper MSS.*, I, iv, 2.

[28] Coke, *The Last Elizabethan,* p. 9; *Cowper MSS.,* I, iv; *DNB*, IV, 700; *Cowper MSS.,* I, 9-18.

[29] BL, Add. MS. 37,482, fols. 66, 68-9. This document was brought to my attention by Robholz, *Fulke Greville,* p. 96 n. 25.

Greville's estate in one way or another for most of the next twenty-five years, and he was amply rewarded.

The documentary record of Coke's life improves in the autumn of 1593, when he embarked on a four-year tour of the Continent that took him through the German states, Italy, Switzerland, and France.[30] Coke's travel roughly coincided with the earl of Essex's attempt to establish a network of agents throughout Europe, and it has been implied that Coke belonged to this network.[31] During his years abroad, however, Coke sent his routine reports to Greville. Apart from the fact that he once used an agent of Essex to convey a letter, the only direct link between Coke and Essex is the solitary surviving letter he wrote to the earl.[32] In it Coke said: 'I have not presumed as yet to write unto your lordship because in the ordinary course of my travel I found nothing worthy [of] your Honour's special information. Notwithstanding, to perform my duty from time to time I have written to Mr. Greville all I observed in these parts, and doubt not but he hath informed your lordship if anything therein were worth the notice.' Having observed the Diet of the Holy Roman Empire, Coke explained: 'I have now ventured according to your commandment to acquaint your Honour with these proceedings.' The fact that Coke tactfully referred to 'my duty' and 'your commandment' is probably not as significant as the fact that he had waited at least half a year to write this letter, communicating in the meantime through Greville. Whatever his relationship to Essex, Coke's true patron at court was Greville. This was demonstrated at a later point in Coke's travels when Greville informed him: 'I have showed your letter to the queen', who was 'in great good liking of it.' Greville further reported how he had seized this opportunity to recommend Coke's services to the queen: 'I told her if she would bestow you worthily, her service was both my ambition and yours, but otherwise I would forsake your company for no second person living.'[33]

[30]Coke's itinerary is based on his correspondence and a note of his financial arrangements in *Cowper MSS.,* I, 15-20, 51.

[31]Walter B. Devereux, *Lives and Letters of the Devereux, Earls of Essex* (2 vols., London, 1853), I, 278-95; Robholz, *Fulke Greville,* p. 96; Coke, *The Last Elizabethan,* p. 10.

[32]Coke MSS., packet 69, Coke to Greville, 13 Feb. 1594; Coke MSS., packet 69, Coke to Essex, *ca.* July 1594. This draft does not indicate who the intended recipient was. I have resolved that it was Essex on the basis of a letter from Thomas North to Essex in which North states, 'For such matters as were handled at the Parliament at Regensburg Mr. Cooke I am sure will not fail to acquaint your honour therewith, for I conferred with him thereof.' Hatfield, Cecil MSS., LIII, 65.

[33]Coke MSS., packet 69, Greville to Coke, 30 Sept. [1596?].

While on the Continent, Coke is supposed to have said 'that he came to learn and not to teach'.[34] Some of what he learned is evident in his report entitled 'A Letter and Treatise Concerning Staples in England.'[35] Coke was impressed by the trading centres of Europe and downright envious of the Low Countries. The problem he addressed in his treatise was 'how to divert the traffic of the Low Countries' to England, and the solutions he offered were mercantilist in nature. He advised the English government to build facilities, induce foreign merchants to settle in England, and foster domestic production of goods at present produced only on the Continent. These activities would benefit the English monarch, he said, because: 'The mightiness of a king is not territory but people; their many arms are his strength, and many purses his wealth.' Beyond these minor proposals, Coke made a major proposal regarding the Dutch. He conceded that the Low Countries had earned at least some of their prosperity, but the real boon to Dutch trade, he believed, had been the war between England and Spain. 'The Spanish trade', he said, 'they got from us by the wars.' Much as the Dutch disliked the Spanish, they did not hesitate to cultivate Spanish trade. According to this analysis, there was one obvious way for England to supplant the Dutch. As Coke succinctly put it: 'The Spanish trade as it was lost by war so it may be recovered by peace.' Coke was an ardent Protestant with a reputation in later years for his zealousness against Spain. It is surprising to find him thinking of peace at this point, less than a decade after the Armada, especially in view of the fact that neither the Essex nor Cecil faction favoured peace at this early date.[36]

The treatise on staples was probably written in 1595. Ironically, while Coke weighed the benefits of peace with Spain, Hawkins and Drake both died leading their last expedition against the Spanish colonies in the West Indies. Coke stood to profit from this calamity because the death of Hawkins on 12 November 1595 left the Treasurership of the Navy vacant.[37] A leading competitor and the eventual successor to that post was Fulke Greville. It may even have been Greville's anticipation of this new office that prompted Coke's return to England in the spring or summer of 1597.[38] At least another

[34]Briggs, *History of Melbourne*, p. 79, citing the 1679 edition of Lloyd's *State Worthies*, p. 945. The 1766 edition misprints 'teach' as 'search'.

[35]Coke MSS., packet 69 [1595?]. The nine-page treatise is endorsed by Coke: 'This was the occasion of a larger treatise written after my return home.'

[36]Rebholz, *Fulke Greville*, pp. 95, 114.

[37]Michael Oppenheim, *A History of the Administration of the Royal Navy and of Merchant Shipping in relation to the Navy* (London, 1896), p. 148.

[38]Coke's brother Francis addressed a letter to Coke at Essex House on 29 July 1597.

year and a half elapsed, however, before Greville was actually able to secure the office. Much as he tried to remain neutral, Greville was caught up in the rivalry between Essex, with whom he was closely associated, and the Cecils, who distrusted him because of that association.[39] While Greville pursued the Treasurership, Coke anxiously waited by his side. Letters sent to Coke during this period were variously addressed to him at Greville's lodgings in Essex House or at the court in Greville's company.[40] This waiting eventually proved worthwhile when, on 22 December 1598, Greville's patent as Treasurer of the Navy was enrolled.[41] Coke had as much reason as Greville to celebrate because he now stood on the threshold of a new career as Deputy-Treasurer of the Navy.[42]

The letter contains an account of how Francis managed his brother's money during the tour. *Cowper MSS.*, I, 19.

[39]Rebholz, *Fulke Greville,* pp. 99, 109-16.

[40]*Cowper MSS.,* I, 19-20.

[41]*CSPD,* 1598-1601, pp. 95, 134; Oppenheim, *Royal Navy,* p. 149 n. 2.

[42]There was no formal office of Deputy-Treasurer, but contemporaries addressed Coke as Deputy-Treasurer (*Cowper MSS.*, I, 23, 26), the *DNB* (IV, 700) employs the title, and I have retained it because it most accurately represents the capacity in which he functioned.

2

DEPUTY-TREASURER OF THE NAVY

Coke was Deputy-Treasurer of the Navy from 1599 to 1604. With the obvious exception of the death of Queen Elizabeth, the most astounding political event of that period was the fall of the earl of Essex. Coke had two reasons to be concerned about the earl's fortunes. One was Greville's close relationship to Essex; another was the fact that Coke's friend from Cambridge days, Robert Naunton, had become one of Essex's followers. In 1595, Naunton had left Cambridge to travel on the Continent.[1] Unlike Coke, Naunton reported frequently to Essex and seems to have been employed directly by him.[2] After Coke's return to England, Naunton relied heavily on him for news of occurrences at the English court, especially how Essex was faring. 'Send me a little of your light to clear these mists', Naunton said on one occasion when he heard Essex was losing ground.[3] At the beginning of 1599, when Greville and Coke had finally achieved office, Essex was preparing for his disastrous expedition to Ireland, and Naunton was contemplating whether to return to England and join him. Coke strongly argued against this course, telling Naunton to 'settle yourself in France till the weather clears'. If Naunton positively insisted on returning, Coke warned him to 'remember you bring no other desire with you but to be private and desire nothing'.[4] This is the course Naunton took. He stayed clear of the storm engulfing Essex by returning to Cambridge so inconspicuously that we can only guess it was sometime during 1599.[5] Through the twists of fate, nearly two decades later Naunton would be in a position to help Coke by bringing him to the attention of the court.

Meanwhile Coke saw the Essex tragedy played through to the end. He and Greville apparently sympathized with Essex but not with

[1]Robert Naunton, *Fragmenta Regalia. . . A New Edition* (London, 1824), p. v.

[2]*DNB,* XIV, 126. Some of the correspondence between Naunton and Essex is printed in Thomas Birch, ed., *Memoirs of the Reign of Queen Elizabeth* (2 vols., London, 1754), I, 359ff.

[3]*Cowper MSS.,* I, 25. Internal evidence indicates this letter from Naunton to Coke was written in 1597, not 1599 as suggested by the editors. From its opening lines it is apparent that Naunton and Coke corresponded frequently.

[4]Coke MSS., packet 69, Coke to Naunton, *ca.* January-March, 1599.

[5]The *DNB* (XIV, 127) speculated that Naunton returned 'about 1600', but Naunton's biographer believes that 1599 is more accurate. I am grateful to Roy Schreiber for this point.

his rebellion.[6] On 8 February 1601, Greville participated in the siege of Essex House, where he had formerly lodged with the earl. On 16 February, Greville, using Coke as his messenger, sent word to the earl of Shrewsbury not to miss Essex's arraignment.[7] On 19 February, Greville and evidently Coke were spectators at Essex's trial. Coke's own twenty-four-page account of the event is preserved today among his manuscripts, accompanied by an anonymous account of Essex's execution at the Tower on 25 February 1601.[8] Although Greville had managed to dissociate himself from Essex's rebellion, the earl's execution left him in a weakened position. His strength at court rested even more precariously now on the personal fondness of an aged queen. How vulnerable this made Greville and Coke would only appear in time, however. For the time being, they – like Naunton – had escaped the full fury of the storm.

At the time of Essex's execution, Coke had served under Greville as Deputy-Treasurer of the Navy for a little more than two years. Only weeks before the earl's rebellion, Francis Coke had written to his brother: 'I find now that you have obtained that which you have always courted, namely, great and continual business'.[9] Coke was not as important as this compliment suggests, but he was indeed busy.

Coke's work as Deputy-Treasurer was largely one of bookkeeping or accounting. This work was complicated by the fact that not all of it could be done in one place. After vacating Essex House, Greville established a London residence in Austin Friars, not far from St Paul's.[10] Coke was often required to be at the Austin Friars residence,

[6] Greville wrote, 'Myself, his kinsman, and while I remained about the Queen, a kind of *Remora,* staying the violent course of that fatal ship. . . abruptly sent away to guard a figurative Fleet. . . at Rochester, till his head was off.' Alexander B. Grosart, ed., *The Friend of Sir Philip Sidney* (Chicago, 1894), p. 35. One of Coke's former students (Roger Manners, fifth earl of Rutland) took part in the Essex uprising. *Cowper MSS.,* I, 35, 44, 59; II, 65; *DNB,* XII, 940-1. In a letter written about a month after Essex's execution, Coke referred to 'the echo of our tragedies'. Coke MSS., reordered packet 2, draft of Coke to Sir William Godolphin, 1 April 1601. As late as 11 July 1606, Naunton wrote to Coke about 'a busy practizer against our late E [Earl]'. Coke MSS., packet 1. The definitive analysis of Greville's role in these events is Rebholz, *Fulke Greville,* pp. 121-40.

[7] Lambeth Palace Library, Shrewsbury MSS., vol. 702, fol. 5. The calendar incorrectly indentifies the messenger as Thomas Coke, who was John's brother and secretary to Shrewsbury. C. Jamison, *A Calendar of the Shrewsbury and Talbot Papers in the Lambeth Palace Library* (London, 1966), I, 90.

[8] Coke MSS., packet 1.

[9] Coke MSS., reordered packet 2, 23 January 1601.

[10] Elizabeth ordered Greville and other notable occupants to vacate Essex House in March 1600. Arthur Collins, ed., *Letters and Memorials of State* (2 vols., London, 1746), II, 179. The first letters addressed to Coke at Greville's house in Austin Friars occur in late 1601. *Cowper MSS.,* I, 32-3. See also Rebholz, *Fulke Greville,* p. 123.

but he worked mainly at a naval office farther down the Thames at Deptford where Greville had placed him in charge of the whole household.[11] In addition to these two central locations, Coke frequently had to visit such places as Chatham, Portsmouth, and Gravesend.[12] At times he also had to travel between government officials to expedite the cumbersome naval administration, especially to extract money from the obdurate Treasury. This was the case, for example, in October of 1600 when he needed an order for money to discharge three ships at Portsmouth, and Lord Treasurer Buckhurst recorded: 'At my coming to my house I found Mr. Coke, deputy to Mr. Fulke Greville, attending for me.'[13]

Greville employed three lesser clerks to keep his daily accounts, but Coke supervised the accounts, calculated the monthly totals, and compiled the yearly abstracts.[14] He also prepared estimates when required and assisted in making the necessary financial arrangements for the outfitting and dispatching of the navy's ships.[15] His work was characterized by thoroughness and a careful attention to detail. In regard to his housekeeping duties at Deptford, for example, it was typical of Coke to complain to Greville that 'your pigeons grow upon you to a great multitude, and so a great and weekly charge'.[16] With regard to more serious matters, it was characteristic of Coke to advise Greville, 'I beseech you, urge Mr. Trevor to procure my lord's resolution in writing. . . that you may have authentical records for all your payments.'[17]

Greville obviously delegated a great deal of his authority to Coke. He even trusted him sufficiently to send a signed warrant with the comment, 'you may add or diminish as you find convenient'.[18] On another occasion, Greville demonstrated his reliance on Coke when

[11]The housekeeping bills from Deptford for the years 1599 to 1604 are preserved among the miscellaneous papers of the Coke MSS. in the muniments room.

[12]Coke MSS., packet 128, a small notebook for the period 1600-2 written by Coke and endorsed by him, 'Travelling Charges'.

[13]Hatfield, Cecil MSS., CCL, 33.

[14]Coke MSS., packet 128: (1) 'Money delivered into the office for ordinary and extraordinary charges upon account since Easter day being the 23 March 1589.' This endorsement and about half the entries are in Coke's hand. The receipts listed run through 1604, and all totals are calculated by Coke. (2) 'An Abstract of the Account of Fulke Greville, Treasurer of the Navy.' This abstract was compiled entirely by Coke and covers the years 1602 and 1603.

[15]*Cowper MSS.,* I, 30.

[16]*Ibid.*

[17]Coke MSS., reordered packet 4, Coke to Greville, 9 Sept. [1600].

[18]*Cowper MSS.,* I, 30.

he wrote that he had lain awake most of the night for lack of Coke's advice on a problem that was troubling him. As he explained, 'without you I conclude nothing and therefore refer all till we meet'.[19] Greville also grew increasingly reliant upon Coke for advice in the management of his lands.[20] In this area, too, Greville personally testified to his dependence on Coke. My estate, he said, 'both in *esse* and in expectancy is known to you and all the healths and diseases of it'.[21] In many ways, then, Coke cultivated the bonds of affection and obligation between himself and his patron. In return, Greville appreciatively vowed: 'I do very much thank you for the care and pains you have taken in all my businesses and presume they will prosper much the better when they are overseen with honest and wise eyes as I hold yours to be. If we live, we will perish or prosper together.'[22]

The Treasurer and his deputy prospered for only five years. During those years, their work was repeatedly undermined by what Coke variously called 'disorders', 'abuses', and 'corruptions'. The navy afforded innumerable opportunities for personal gain, and most of those opportunities had been exploited during the three years that the Treasurership was vacant between the death of Hawkins and Greville's appointment.[23] Thus Greville and Coke inherited a bad situation. They suffered through it for several years, then mounted an effort to reform the whole naval administration, and were promptly expelled from office.

What exactly were the practices that Coke and Greville objected to? The more minor of these were described in a paper Coke wrote during the first year of Greville's Treasurership entitled 'Allowances not warrantable in the navy'.[24] Here Coke was concerned with the fact that naval officers and shipwrights employed more assistants and paid them more money than their patents allowed. Coke understood that

[19]Coke MSS., packet 15, Greville to Coke, 4 January 1602.

[20]G. Bullough, 'Fulke Greville, First Lord Brooke', *Modern Language Review,* 28 (Jan. 1933), 10.

[21]Coke MSS., packet 69, Greville to [Coke], *ca.* 1600.

[22]*Ibid.*

[23]BL, Harleian MS. 306 appears to me to date from this period. It explains how the Surveyor of the Navy, in the absence of a strong Treasurer, corrupted the whole administration. Even Hawkins had not escaped charges of corruption. An official investigation in 1583, however, cleared his name. BL, Add. MS. 35, 831. Robert W. Kenny, *Elizabeth's Admiral: The Political Career of Charles Howard, Earl of Nottingham, 1536-1624* (Baltimore, 1970), pp. 28-9.

[24]Coke MSS., reordered packet 5, six pages in Coke's hand, endorsed '1599. Allowances not warrantable in the navy'.

there was some justification for these extra employees on the queen's payroll, but there were two circumstances under which he could not condone them. One was when they were used as substitutes in the 'absence of those chief ministers to whom of right the service belongeth'. Coke found the shipwrights particularly guilty of this practice. Because shipwrights were absent from their jobs and delegated their work to inferior assistants, Coke concluded that 'the queen is both worse served and more charged than she ought [to be]'. The second circumstance Coke considered unjustifiable was when men were employed simply because of 'mere favour without respect of merit'. Coke thought that these 'favours without merit' were the 'chief scandals', and in a flush of optimism, he declared, 'all to be abrogated'.

During the ensuing years, nothing was abrogated. Instead, Coke's list of abuses grew longer and longer. He saw barrels of gunpowder opened which were adulterated with sand.[25] He caught several men claiming seamen's wages with false papers. The next day he discovered that his vigilance had prompted someone to cut a whole page out of the crew's book. That page almost certainly had contained a list of fictitious names that would have been used to collect what were known as 'dead pays' for some enterprising schemer. Coke also listened to informants explaining how workers sold provisions out of the shipyards and how naval officers used both the queen's supplies and her workmen to construct their own buildings.[26] The worst offender in this respect as in many others was the Surveyor of the Navy, John Trevor. Coke described the chamber Trevor had made for himself at Chatham: 'The chamber was repaired, new wainscotted, new windows, tables, presses, and all other necessaries belonging to carpentry, joiners', or masons' work made at the queen's charge; and for the furnishing thereof with bed, stools, chairs, and such like provisions £30 was delivered'. This last example comes from Coke's most impressive list of all, a notebook thirty-three pages long.[27] One might argue that since there was no office space provided at the government's expense, Trevor should not be judged too harshly. But other examples from Coke's notebook cannot be so easily explained away. A painter, for example, told Coke that when he and an associate submitted a bill for painting one of the queen's ships, they 'could not get it dispatched by Mr. Surveyor till they had made an

[25]Coke MSS., reordered packet 5, a note in Coke's hand, 2 Feb. 1602.

[26]Coke MSS., reordered packet 5, examinations of Mr. Baylie and John Danbie in Coke's hand, Feb. and March 1602.

[27]Coke MSS., reordered packet 5.

agreement with his man, Edw. Faulkener, who demanded twenty pounds or more, and at length was contented with ten pounds'. Faulkener was Trevor's right-hand man, apparently employed chiefly in the collection of bribes. According to Coke's notebook, Faulkener collected from one purser 'near £40 in one year'. When Greville appointed a messenger for the navy, Trevor protested and tried to put his own man in the place, whereupon Coke wearily observed: 'For my part I am so much troubled with the sloth and corruption of one Faulkener that I pray God deliver us from another of his consorts.'[28]

Trevor's great partner was Lord Admiral Nottingham. Together they had made all the places in the navy available for a price. As Coke described it: 'The Lord Admiral hath drawn into his hands not only the appointments of captains and commanders but of all clerks of the check, masters, boatswains, pursers, stewards, cooks, smiths, joiners, carpenters, sailmakers, and all manner of workmen.'[29] Coke knew of a joiner, for example, who had paid £60 for his place, and a purser who had paid £100.[30] This buying and selling of offices was the fountain-head from which all the tributaries of venal exploitation flowed throughout the navy. Men who had paid dearly for their places naturally exploited those offices in every way possible to regain their investment. Nor were the people who had sold the offices, namely Trevor and Nottingham, in any position to demand honesty from the purchasers. As Coke explained: 'The same power which gave the places, perhaps at dear rates, must give toleration to improve them to a proportionable advantage, as hath appeared manifestly by the examples of diverse [persons] displaced by the officers for notorious corruptions, and [afterward] restored by the Lord Admiral in this only respect.'[31] The most blatant example Coke gave of this vicious cycle involved a purser named Duffeld. Duffeld had been caught trying to collect £24 in seamen's wages for seamen who in fact had run away before their ship sailed. However, by paying £40 to Trevor and Nottingham, Duffeld obtained a personal letter from the Lord Admiral asking the officers of the navy, of whom Trevor himself was one, to forgive Duffeld. The officers dutifully reinstated Duffeld and wrote Coke a letter, instructing him to pay the purser his back wages and all other money that had been withheld from him. Nearly 400

[28]Coke MSS., reordered packet 4, Coke to Greville, 9 Sept. [1600].

[29]Coke MSS., reordered packet 5, a three-page paper in Coke's hand entitled 'The principal and original causes of all disorders in the navy are these four which follow.'

[30]Coke MSS., reordered packet 5, Coke's thirty-three-page notebook.

[31]Coke MSS., reordered packet 5, Coke's three-page paper of 'The principal and original causes'.

years later we can still feel Coke's righteous indignation captured in his terse notation: 'This letter I have.' So outraged was Coke that he still refused to pay anything to Duffeld 'till it be further considered whether a fault so notoriously scandalous and confessed may be thus remitted'. In the end, however, he had no choice. His final notation reads: 'In conclusion, my Lord Admiral by his peremptory letters forgave this fault to the purser and restored him to his place.'[32]

Some of what Coke found wrong with the naval administration should be described as waste, inefficiency, and petty negligence, but much else, even from the perspective of the seventeenth century, was corruption.[33] When Trevor and Nottingham filled naval offices on the basis of their own profit without regard to the merit of the purchaser, when they built the queen's ships with faulty materials from which they had profited, when they purloined materials from the shipyards, when they allowed forgery and embezzlement to go unchecked, when, as in the case of Duffeld, they accepted a bribe to retain a known thief in the queen's service, they were corrupt. A minimal definition of corruption is the sacrifice of the public interest for the sake of private gain. Of course one might argue that a man cannot be accused of sacrificing the public interest for the sake of private gain if the very concept of a public interest is unknown to him and his contemporaries, but it was not unknown to Coke and Greville. To be sure, at this early point in their careers they had not yet learned to distinguish between the public's interest and the monarch's interest, but they knew the difference between these and purely private gain. They felt an obligation to administer the navy as economically and efficiently as possible, to discharge their duties honestly, responsibly, and conscientiously. And they would not follow or condone practices which they knew to be, in Coke's words, 'unjust in themselves, unprofitable for the queen, and so scandalous to the office of the navy'.[34]

[32]Coke MSS., reordered packet 5, Coke's thirty-three-page notebook.

[33]I do not believe this is an unfair application of twentieth-century standards to sixteenth and seventeenth-century practices. Compare J. Hurstfield, *Freedom, Corruption and Government in Elizabethan England* (London, 1973), pp. 159-62; Linda Peck, 'Corruption at the Court of James I: The Undermining of Legitimacy' in Barbara C. Malament, ed., *After the Reformation: Essays in Honor of J.H. Hexter* (Philadelphia, 1980), pp. 75-7; G.E. Aylmer, *The State's Servants: The Civil Service of the English Republic 1649-1660* (London, 1973), pp. 139-40; Howell A. Lloyd, 'Corruption and Sir John Trevor', *The Transactions of the Honourable Society of Cymmrodorion* (1975), pp. 97-102; Arnold J. Heidenheimer, *Political Corruption: Readings in Comparative Analysis* (New York, 1970), pp. 5-7, 54, 58-9.

[34]Coke MSS., reordered packet 2, Coke to Greville, 7 Aug. 1600.

Reprehensible as Coke found the actions of men like Nottingham and Trevor, he understood that there were also impersonal, structural reasons for the problems of the navy that needed to be remedied. As mentioned, Coke identified the buying and selling of offices, concentrated in the hands of the Lord Admiral, as the principal cause of the navy's problems. Because of this practice, Coke said, 'no man is preferred for merit but by means only', and venal exploitation of office was encouraged from the top to the bottom of the naval hierarchy.[35] Coke therefore thought that Nottingham's monopoly of patronage should be broken and that naval offices should be awarded on the basis of merit. Of course the tendency to exploit office was inherent in a system where office was regarded as personal property and where official compensation was inadequate.[36] A further remedy, therefore, would have been to provide higher compensation to naval personnel. There is no evidence that Coke considered this remedy at this time, but we shall see him support higher salaries to foster greater honesty at a later date. A second cause of the navy's problems, as Coke saw it, was that naval officers did not have a sufficiently clear and compelling understanding of their official duties. Coke thought that better performance could be got from these officers if their official duties were spelled out more thoroughly and impressed upon them. Coke was a firm believer in what the modern manager calls 'job descriptions'. Looking at the naval officers at this time, Coke complained that 'there is neither place, time, order, nor means appointed for their meetings and counsels, nor any distinction made of their several offices'. Coke would have specified the duties of each officer, sorting out what each was uniquely responsible for doing. He would even have specified when and where and how they should hold official meetings to conduct their business. These may seem laughably rudimentary prescriptions, but Coke was dealing with a rudimentary bureaucracy, trying to make it perform in a professional manner. As much as thirty years later, he complained that the king rented a room for the naval officers to meet in but still could not get them to use it. This brings us to a third cause of the navy's problems identified by Coke: too little accountability. By spelling out the duties of the officers, one could hope not only to teach them their duties but also to hold them accountable for the performance of those duties. Through

[35] Quotations and Coke's diagnosis of the navy's problems in this paragraph come from his three-page paper of 'The principal and original causes' in Coke MSS., reordered packet 5.

[36] Hurstfield, *Freedom,* pp.151-8; Aylmer, *The King's Servants,* pp. 178-82; Conrad Russell, ed., *The Origins of the English Civil War* (New York, 1973), pp. 46-7.

his firm belief in the principle of accountability, Coke again resembles a modern manager. We will see Coke repeatedly call for exemplary punishment of wrongdoers and, above all, for better, stricter methods of financial accounting. This does not exhaust the problems of the navy or Coke's understanding of those problems, but not until Coke's second career (especially in chapters four and twelve) will these come more fully to light.

For several years, Coke and Greville did what they could to foster greater honesty and economy in the navy.[37] Coke told Greville that no man would dare 'to charge you that you seek your profit in this place'. And he claimed the same virtue for himself, vowing that 'if any man living can say I have directly or indirectly under what pretence soever gained any penny more than your allowance, I submit myself to the shame and punishment I shall deserve for it'. By this behaviour, Coke and Greville aroused the hostility of the other officers. As Coke warned his patron, 'the courses you take to husband things for the queen are found too straight'. The other officers of the navy, said Coke, 'lie in wait for all advantages to make you pliant perforce to that [which] you mislike'.[38] One might assume that the Treasurer, through his control of funds, could safely ignore the other officers' threats and persist in curbing abuses. In fact, however, the Treasurer could 'not possibly be safe if he will be honest and do the queen service'.[39] As the following explanation should make clear, the Treasurer was literally at the mercy of his colleagues. There were four 'principal officers' of the navy: the Treasurer, Surveyor, Comptroller, and Clerk. Throughout the year, the Treasurer disbursed funds for the expenses of the navy, and often he was forced by the urgency of the situation to make payments that had not yet been officially authorized. As Coke explained, 'in the infinite occasions which daily and hourly call for money, no mean way can possibly be found but either to make great payments without sufficient warrant, or else to let the service stand still till it may be procured'.[40] By the end of the year the Treasurer was deeply in 'debt' because he could be held personally accountable for all these unauthorized expenditures. Of course there was a procedure to release him from these debts. When the Treasurer of the Navy submitted his annual accounts, the payments he had made were

[37] A.P. McGowan, ed., *The Jacobean Commissions of Enquiry 1608 and 1618* (London, 1971), pp. 36, 57, 84, 118, 124, 132, 161-2, 166, 252; Rebholz, *Fulke Greville,* pp. 166-7.

[38] Coke MSS., reordered packet 2, Coke to Greville, 7 Aug. 1600.

[39] Coke MSS., packet 138, a draft by Coke of a letter, apparently from Greville to an unidentified recipient [*temp.* Elizabeth].

[40] Coke MSS., reordered packet 2, Coke to Greville, 7 Aug. 1600.

scrutinized and 'allowed', which meant that the Crown accepted responsibility for them. The insidious flaw in this procedure, however, was that the Naval Treasurer's accounts were not accepted and allowed unless they were first certified by the signatures of two of the other principal officers. This stipulation was no doubt intended to keep the Treasurer honest, but in actual practice it placed Greville at the mercy of his fellow officers, particularly Trevor. The Surveyor actually had it in his power to bankrupt the Treasurer. In Greville's first year as Naval Treasurer, for example, his total disbursements amounted to over £67,000.[41] Throughout the year the Surveyor could find innumerable items to haggle over amounting to thousands of pounds. By means of such intimidation the Treasurer could be forced to overlook the offences of his colleagues. Again as Coke explained, 'so long as the Treasurer's account is thus subject to the officers. . . either the Treasurer shall never pass his account, or else he shall be forced if the rest be corrupt to conspire with them'.[42] This is precisely the technique that Trevor resorted to. Coke summarized the problem, both in theory and practice, as he and Greville had experienced it at the hands of Trevor:

> If the Treasurer and his ministers [for example, Coke] bound themselves with conscience and honesty, there is no course or possibility for an assured discharge but that it will continually rest in the power of every officer. . . to make stay of his accounts so that if he buy not their favours or give way to their discretions, he shall spend the whole year casting up books and attending to satisfy them, to his trouble and charge without end, and the great hindrance of her Majesty's service, as by this year's example hath appeared too plain.[43]

Coke bore the brunt of Trevor's harrassment. On one occasion he complained of 'great wars' with the Surveyor.[44] On another occasion he lamented: 'I have used more care and pains to make clear satisfaction to the officers in all your payments than ever heretofore hath been used in this office. And yet yourself were witness what cavils were used at the last quarter pay at Chatham.'[45]

[41] PRO, E 351/2,237. These annual declared accounts are prefixed by a copy of Greville's patent. Included is the passage describing the requirement that two other officers sign the accounts to testify to their authenticity. Trevor and the Comptroller certified this account for 1599.

[42] Coke MSS., reordered packet 2, Coke to Greville, 7 Aug. 1600.

[43] Coke MSS., reordered packet 5, Coke's three-page paper of 'The principal and original causes'.

[44] Coke MSS., reordered packet 4, Coke to Greville, 9 Sept. *ca.* 1600.

[45] Coke MSS., reordered packet 2, Coke to Greville, 7 Aug. 1600.

Under these circumstances, the problems of the navy were not likely to be eradicated through sporadic and limited confrontations. What was needed was wholesale reform, and that is finally what Coke and Greville planned. Although the plans themselves have not survived, it appears that what Coke and Greville called their 'book' of proposals would have curtailed the patronage power of the Lord Admiral, stopped price-fixing and kick-backs on naval supplies, eliminated costly delays and abuses in the payment of captains and crews, and freed the Treasurer from his position of crippling dependence on the other officers.[46] These proposals were consistent with what we have seen was Coke's analysis of the navy's problems. There was also an additional proposal to reduce the routine operating costs of the navy. Too little evidence survives to judge the practicality of this latter proposal, but certainly it was typical of Coke to assume that economy could and should be achieved along with reform.

Coke and Greville advanced these proposals shortly after Elizabeth's death, but there is every reason to believe that they had been encouraged to formulate their plans before then. As early as August of 1600, Coke had said in a letter to Greville: 'I doubt not but her Majesty's intent is to reform these abuses.'[47] Coke was gathering evidence with special vigour in 1602.[48] This coincides with action on another front that indicates naval reform was seriously contemplated toward the end of Elizabeth's reign. A naval commander named Sir William Monson was instructed by Cecil 'at the latter end of the Queen's reign' to write a 'discourse how the then abuses might be taken away and a course settled for a reformation'. What survives of Monson's discourse is not very substantial or trustworthy. It complements the view of Coke and Greville because it is written from the perspective of a commander who was concerned about discipline, the quality of the seamen, the adequacy of supplies, and the soundness of the ships. Monson wrote his report under Elizabeth, showed it to James I, and then adroitly adjusted to the altered circumstances at court. He continued in later life to portray himself as a champion of reform, but it appears that he fared well in the early years of James's reign because he ingratiated himself with Lord Admiral Nottingham

[46] The only existing evidence of the project conceived by Coke and Greville is among Coke's papers. Some are published in the *Cowper MSS*., I, 41-2, 45, 50-5. The first account of the project appeared in Coke, *The Last Elizabethan,* pp. 23-9. A far superior account is now available in Rebholz, *Fulke Greville,* pp. 160-80, 344-51.

[47] Coke MSS., reordered packet 2, Coke to Greville, 7 Aug. 1600.

[48] *Cowper MSS.,* I, 41. I have already cited most of this material from Coke MSS., reordered packet 5.

and subordinated reform to self-interest.[49] Coke and Greville did not make the transition to James's reign so safely. For them, Elizabeth's death in March of 1603 could not possibly have been more untimely. It left them in a very vulnerable position as advocates of reform without powerful protection at court. Ever since the execution of Essex, Greville's sole source of support at court had been the personal friendship of the queen. When she died, Greville was forced to fall back on the support of Cecil, who, unfortunately, had never really forgiven Greville for his earlier association with Essex. Thus Greville's influence at court collapsed at a time when he needed it most.[50] With practically no power on their side, Greville and Coke might have been well advised to hold back their proposals, but they did not. Probably they had already committed themselves to reform beyond the point of return. One gets the distinct impression that they were playing out a hand which they knew deep down could not win. Perhaps they entertained the hope that reform would appeal to a new régime or to the competing courtiers who might be persuaded to seize upon it as an issue to gain a more secure footing for themselves in that régime. If so, this was a gross miscalculation. In any event, when the time came to attend the court and personally urge the Privy Council to consider their proposals, Greville delegated the chore to Coke.[51] This attendance at court, beginning in October of 1603, would make Coke a bitter man cast out of office and determined to retire to a private life.

When Coke arrived at Salisbury, where the court was slowly assembling, he discovered that the plan for naval reform was not the only plan afoot. There was a counter-plan to drive Greville out of office. Sir Robert Mansell, a minor naval commander related to the Lord Admiral, was conspiring with Trevor to replace Greville as Treasurer of the Navy. Their strategy, as Coke reported it to Greville, 'was first to get a reversion and then to weary you out by that power

[49]Michael Oppenheim, ed., *The Naval Tracts of Sir William Monson* (5 vols., London, 1902-14), I, xvii-xxxvi; II, 232-44.

[50]Two particularly pathetic letters from Greville to Cecil are printed in HMC, *Salisbury MSS.*, XV, 83, 128. By July of 1603 Greville was uninformed of the purpose for a fleet he was ordered to prepare. *Ibid.*, p. 165.

[51]One explanation for Greville's avoiding the court is given in Rebholz, *Fulke Greville,* p. 170: 'Greville, with his usual caution, feared immediate reprisals from his fellow officers if they knew the Treasurer himself was lobbying for reforms.' Other factors may have been involved. Greville complained of ill health at least twice in July. HMC, *Salisbury MSS.*, XV, 182; Alexander B. Grosart, ed., *The Works in Verse and Prose Complete of the Right Honourable Fulke Greville, Lord Brooke* (4 vols., Edinburgh, 1870), I, lviii. Greville may also have retreated from court because of a rumour that he was secretly married to the controversial Lady Arabella Stuart. *CSPD, 1601-1603*, p. 299.

which the officers have over your account'.[52] In other words, Mansell would obtain a reversion to Greville's office, then Greville would be forced to resign by incessant objections to his accounts. Here, indeed, was a danger of the first degree.

One man whom Greville and Coke were depending upon to support naval reform and to whom Coke now also turned for protection against Mansell's plot was Lord Chamberlain Suffolk, another member of the powerful Howard family. Suffolk studied the book of proposals Coke gave him. He was not entirely pleased with the restraint placed on the Lord Admiral in disposing of naval offices, but his major complaint was that the proposals did not promise great savings for the Crown. This objection gave Coke an opportunity to present Suffolk with a further proposal. As Coke related the interview to Greville: 'Then I showed him the draft for reforming the ordinary, which he liked very well; but withall I told him that you could in no wise bear the envy of that proposition till their lordships had cleared you out of the officers' hands.' If Greville could be freed from the 'exorbitant power' the other officers held over his accounts, Coke promised Suffolk in an obvious appeal to his self-interest, 'their lordships should have honour by a true reformation'.[53]

Another major obstacle to reform not so far mentioned was Lord Admiral Nottingham. In his report to Cecil, Monson had written, 'the first thing that must be obtained is, the consent and countenance of the Lord Admiral; for I have showed that these abuses are crept in by his permission, or at least his officers'.[54] Coke and Greville had come to the same conclusion. Curtailment of the Lord Admiral's patronage power was essential to any genuine reform, but the Lord Admiral himself would be its staunchest opponent. What encouraged Coke to hope for the best in this respect was Suffolk's assurance to him 'that my Lord Admiral doth not build his estate upon this office but purposeth to leave it, and therefore they doubt not to bring to pass what they find reasonable'. According to Suffolk, therefore, the Lord Admiral would be no problem. Quite the contrary, he would actually open the way to reform by resigning from his post. This bit of wishful thinking was, indeed, too good to be true. Regarding the more immediate threat of Trevor's and Mansell's plot to drive Greville from office, Suffolk promised with equally unfounded confidence, 'they should have power and would take care to prevent and cross it'. On the

[52]Coke MSS., packet 1, Coke to Greville, 23 Oct. 1603. A transcript of this letter is printed in Rebholz, *Fulke Greville,* pp. 345-8.

[53]*Ibid.*

[54]Oppenheim, *Naval Tracts of Sir William Monson,* II, 240.

surface, then, Suffolk's reassurances were encouraging. But Coke was already suspicious. He saw 'a ground laid for putting off', and he concluded in his report to Greville: 'What is like to fall out I know not . . . but I look for differing. . . God only is my hope, for all men are doubtful.'[55]

Coke had one reason to be hopeful. As Suffolk's frequent use of plural pronouns suggests, he did not expect to be alone in sponsoring reform. The other ally he and Coke apparently hoped for was Secretary Cecil.[56] Suffolk had told Coke, 'at my Lord Cecil's coming he would deal clearly'. In view of the fact that Cecil had ordered Monson's report, it would have been logical for him to authorize the project prepared by Greville and Coke. And with Cecil's support, the project would have had at least a chance of success. When Cecil arrived at court, Suffolk showed him the book of proposals. Suffolk reported back to Coke that the Secretary 'liked all well; only he doubted again how the Lord Admiral would brook his restraint in the giving of under-offices'.[57] Since Coke had nothing else to bargain with, he reluctantly surrendered on this point, saying it 'might be qualified at their discretions'. Having made this major concession, however, Coke discovered that Suffolk and Cecil were still at best half-hearted supporters. Though they claimed to like the plan, 'they found it not fit to be propounded by either of them at this time but rather by the Lord Treasurer'. If Greville did not approve of Lord Treasurer Buckhurst, they were willing to suggest someone else, but in no case would either Cecil or Suffolk publicly assume responsibility for the project. Moreover, they postponed any action till the term at Winchester. Finally, it was now evident that Lord Admiral Nottingham had no intention of resigning. Suffolk and Cecil admitted that they found it necessary to treat with Nottingham but assured Coke, 'they have already bound him with so many protestations and oaths to yield anything which they shall propound for reformation that they doubt not to bring him unto this'. Earlier discouragements were inconsequential compared to this one. Including the Lord Admiral in the project, Coke must have known, meant crippling compromise if not defeat. If the project were to fail, it need not necessarily have resulted in personal disaster for Greville. Suffolk had promised to keep Greville's name out of the reform project and to block Mansell's plot to seize the Naval

[55] Coke MSS., packet 1, Coke to Greville, 23 Oct. 1603.

[56] There was possibly a third promoter whom Coke refers to as 'the other lord that first gave his hand'. Coke MSS., packet 69, Coke to Greville [19 Jan. 1604]. This was probably Lord Henry Howard. Rebholz, *Fulke Greville*, p. 175.

[57] Coke MSS., packet 1, Coke to Greville, 31 Oct. 1603. All quotations from Coke to Greville in the next two paragraphs are taken from this letter.

Treasurership, but Coke had no faith in these promises. Recounting several of Suffolk's prevarications, Coke observed: 'My lord speaketh nobly but still his issues vary.' Coke even wondered if Suffolk was lying about Cecil. As Coke wrote: 'With my Lord Cecil I have not had so much as one word about this business. Neither can I tell whether he hath seen the book or will meddle in it, but by my lord of Suffolk's assertion.' This state of affairs left little reason to be optimistic. Coke acknowledged both the waning support for the project and the ruinous consequences of the Lord Admiral's inclusion when he told Greville: 'I must consider how to fashion our book for more eyes, and to take out of it what may sharpen or offend the Lord Admiral.'

As the outcome of the business grew increasingly doubtful, the true interests of the protagonists emerged more clearly, and Coke assessed them in the following manner: 'In this darkness I gather this construction. That it is true my lord of Suffolk hath an eye to the Admiralty. . . and that he is more desirous to shorten his way to it than my Lord Cecil is forward to hasten it, who proceedeth with caution and scruple.' Coke suspected, then, that Suffolk supported naval reform because of his own ambition to become Lord Admiral. This would also explain why Suffolk repeatedly objected to any curtailment of the Lord Admiral's patronage power. In the beginning Suffolk had hoped that Nottingham would resign the Lord Admiral's office voluntarily. When that did not happen, he continued to hope that with Cecil's support Nottingham might still be persuaded to resign. By this time, however, Cecil had grown reluctant, and for good reason. Nottingham was fighting back fiercely. He was no doubt collaborating with Trevor and Mansell in their plot to gain the Treasurership. More importantly, in September the sixty-eight-year-old Admiral had suddenly married a nineteen-year-old cousin of the king and thereby immeasurably improved his position at court. James was showering Nottingham with wedding presents in October, at precisely the time Coke was promoting naval reform.[58] As Coke lamented: 'The Admiral hath gotten at least an appearance of strength by his match and will not easily be drawn to relinquish without the stewardship or some other satisfaction in lieu thereof.' Suffolk and Cecil were hard pressed to 'win him or bind him'. Coke now understood how little Suffolk and Cecil were motivated by altruism. He gloomily observed, 'how far they will improve this reformation to their ends, so much hope have I in it, and no minute further'. In all this, Cecil appears to have been by far the shrewdest participant. If at first he favoured the project, he soon realized that it might cost more than it was worth. Nottingham's

[58]Kenny, *Elizabeth's Admiral,* pp. 272-5.

intransigence may not have been the only obstacle. The project was evidently conceived under Elizabeth, but James, who sought peace with Spain and neglected the navy, must have been far less interested in it. If Cecil continued to countenance reform, he firmly refused to promote it openly. While Cecil remained cautiously in the background, Suffolk attempted to salvage the project and the private hopes he had pinned on it, but the subsequent course of events was an exercise in futility.[59]

Suffolk and his wife made repeated attempts to win over the Lord Admiral, but all without success.[60] Meanwhile, Coke remained about the court in a humiliating effort to bring the business to a conclusion. It was soon January of 1604, and Coke complained: 'I do still wait in my lord of Suffolk's eye, but get not so much as one word from him.'[61] As for the treatment he received from Suffolk and his wife, Coke observed that 'respect and kindness never spared so few words as come from both of them'.[62] Discouraged by this course of events, Coke wearily resigned himself to making the best of a bad situation. 'I will proceed with them like one that hath a good cause and hopeth not in it', he wrote, 'and yet will show confidence both in it and them, to draw it either to a good issue or an honest surcease.' Since there is no further record of the business after January of 1604, it can only be assumed that Nottingham's opposition eventually forced Suffolk to let the plan for naval reform die.

Having failed in their effort to reform the navy, it only remained to be seen whether Coke and Greville could avoid being driven out of office altogether. Sir Robert Mansell, who sought to replace Greville as Treasurer of the Navy, had the backing of Lord Admiral Nottingham, to whom he was distantly related. Through the Lord Admiral's influence, Mansell had acquired experience at sea and been appointed Vice-Admiral of the Narrow Seas.[63] He was likely to advance further in the navy, but it was Coke's and Greville's effort at reform that ironically catapulted him into the Treasurer's office. The whole reform venture had been predicated rather unrealistically on

[59] The respective roles of Cecil and Suffolk are best revealed in two of Coke's letters. Coke MSS., packet 69. They are printed verbatim in *Cowper MSS.,* I, 52-3, though incorrecty dated 1604-5. Rebholz reasons that they were written on 19 and 20 January 1604. *Fulke Greville*, pp. 344-5.

[60] Coke MSS., packet 69, Coke to Greville, 17 and 18 Jan. [1604]. These two letters are printed nearly verbatim but incorrectly dated 1605 in *Cowper MSS.,* I, 53-4.

[61] Coke MSS., packet 69, Coke to Greville, 18 Jan. [1604].

[62] Coke MSS., packet 69, Coke to Greville, 17 Jan. [1604].

[63] *DNB*, XII, 973.

the Lord Admiral's resignation, or at least his acquiescence in the correction of abuses for which he himself was largely responsible. Nottingham, far from acquiescing, probably helped conceive Mansell's plot in order to avert reform. At the very least he must have abetted that plot once it was under way. The defeat of reform and the triumph of Mansell were therefore opposite faces of the same coin. When Coke reported in January of 1604 that there was little hope left for the reform project, he also reported a disheartening conversation with Mansell. Coke had asked Mansell how he was faring with the lords of the Council. Mansell 'answered that he doubted not to find free passage and would desire nothing from you', Coke told Greville, 'but your resignation, and, if need were, to signify that you desired that he should have it before another'.[64] In other words, Greville was being asked not only to resign the Treasurership but also to recommend Mansell as his successor. This presumption on Mansell's part was apparently justified because in late April a grant was prepared in his name, on the surrender of Greville, for the office of Treasurer of the Navy.[65] On 26 April 1604 Mansell's patent was enrolled and he embarked on one of the most corrupt careers in the history of the British navy.[66]

When Greville lost the Treasurership, Coke naturally lost his position as deputy, but his work was not quite finished. On leaving office, the accounts he had supervised for over five years had to be collected and put into the hands of the auditor. This was a matter of the utmost importance since Greville could be held personally liable for any sums not adequately accounted for. In the preparation of the accounts, Coke was assisted from time to time by Greville's three clerks and the other officers of the navy. This time the naval officers were unusually cooperative, but there were other obstacles. Lack of money in the Exchequer made it difficult for Coke to procure funds to settle the outstanding debts, although he observed lavish amounts being handed out to other suitors at court where 'every man findeth way for his ends'.[67] Coke personally attended or sent a messenger to Suffolk every day and lamented, 'though every hour we have promise of dispatch, yet can we not procure it by any possible means'. Despite these impediments, Coke was able to report to Greville on the sixth of

[64]Coke MSS., packet 69, Coke to Greville, 17 Jan. [1604].

[65]*CSPD,* 1603-1610, p. 98.

[66]Oppenheim, *Royal Navy,* pp. 189-94; Julian S. Corbett, *England in the Mediterranean* (2 vols., London, 1904), I, 70. Corbett said Mansell 'stands without a rival in our naval history for malversation in his office'.

[67]Coke MSS., packet 1, Coke to Greville, 29 July 1604.

August that 'all your books of accounts are signed and finished'. He was confident that delivering Greville's accounts to the auditors would 'make stoppage of all proceedings against you', but he was wrong.[68] Greville was refused allowance for £1,982 of his expenditures. Slightly over half this sum was later remitted, but he was still forced to pay £878 out of his own pocket.[69] One small gesture was made to placate Greville: in July of 1604 he received a grant from the Crown for Warwick Castle.[70] Considering that Greville was driven from his office and forced besides to pay nearly £900 on leaving it, Warwick Castle was small recompense.

Coke left London in the summer of 1604 a humiliated and embittered man. For months he had waited outside closed chamber doors and pleaded for help from people who looked down upon him, but prevarications and empty promises were all he received in return. In Elizabeth's reign he had written: 'I well understand the jealousies and indisposition of the times from change and reforming.'[71] In 1604 he learned that the temper of the court under James was even more unfavourable to men like himself. Looking back on this period years later, he ruefully observed that he had been judged 'opinionative and somewhat too low for preferment of note'.[72] Coke had no reasonable hope of returning to office while the Howards were ascendant. The plan for naval reform had been exploited by Suffolk and defeated by Nottingham, and the one had been no more genuinely interested in its implementation than the other. The third member of the family, Lord Henry Howard, now earl of Northampton, had dealt with Coke only briefly but nevertheless contemptuously.[73] Furthermore, the Howards were associated with Catholicism, whereas Coke and Greville were ardently Protestant. The only courtier capable of opposing the Howards was Cecil, but Cecil had never cared much for Greville and certainly would not support him at the expense of alienating other courtiers as powerful as the Howards. Under these circumstances, Greville chose to remain a hopeful suitor on the periphery of the court. Coke, by contrast, renounced his courtier's aspirations and retired to the country. There, for the next fourteen years, he waited and watched.

[68] Coke MSS., packet 1, Coke to Greville, 6 Aug. 1604.

[69] PRO, E 351/2,241. The account was cleared on 18 March 1605. Compare Rebholz, *Fulke Greville,* pp. 178-80.

[70] *CSPD,* 1603-1610, p. 128.

[71] Coke MSS., packet 138, Coke to [anonymous], *temp.* Elizabeth.

[72] Coke MSS., packet 45, Coke to the marquis of Buckingham, 12 Oct. 1622.

[73] Coke MSS., packet 1, Coke to Greville, 31 Oct. 1603.

3

PREMATURE RETIREMENT

Coke's future was not entirely bleak when he left the court in the summer of 1604 because a new home and new life awaited him at Preston in Herefordshire. Preston was the home of Marie Powell, daughter of John Powell, the estate agent who had recorded Coke's early work for Greville back in 1590. In 1604 Powell was Greville's deputy in several offices attached to the Council of the Welsh Marches.[1] We do not know exactly when Coke met Marie Powell, but by May of 1604 he was deeply in love with her. In his first extant letter to Marie, he bemoaned the fact that working on Greville's accounts was keeping them apart, and he promised that 'affection will whet my industry, and help my despatch'. After delivering Greville's accounts to the auditor, Coke apparently hastened to Preston to join his bride.[2]

Coke's retirement from public life falls into two phases. During the first phase, from 1604 through 1606, Marie continued to live with her parents at Preston while her husband made frequent trips to London at Greville's request. Though Coke had no hope of regaining public office, he did vent his resentment on one occasion by informing the Chancellor of the Exchequer that the navy could be run for £10,000 less each year than Mansell was requiring.[3] Apart from such petty satisfactions, however, being in London was not as pleasurable for Coke as it once had been. He came to agree with Marie's complaint 'that we are not in our own place whiles we are so far asunder'.[4] It was on one of his visits to London in June of 1606 that Coke first appears to have considered a more complete withdrawal from the political world. He vowed to Marie that he would devote 'all my thoughts and endeavours to a speedy contriving of such a course of

[1]Rebholz, *Fulke Greville*, pp. 89-90, 145 n. 23, 177, 197.

[2]In his letter addressed to Mistress Marie Powell on 8 May 1604, Coke asked for the measure of her finger, which was presumably for the purpose of buying a ring. On 14 September 1604, Greville wrote to Coke at Preston, referring to Marie as Coke's wife. It can only be assumed that Coke and Marie married in the interim. *Cowper MSS.,* I, 46, 50.

[3]BL, Lansdowne MSS., vol. 142, no. 74. Sir Julius Caesar had just become Chancellor of the Exchequer. On the cover of this document Caesar wrote: 'Out of this paper delivered me by Sir Rob. Mansell the rate of the Admiralty in the books of assignations was made which is £32,000-0-0. But note that by an estimate to me delivered by Mr. Coke the same is reduced to £22,320-6-8.'

[4]*Cowper MSS.,* I, 58.

life wherein we may continue together without these distractions'. He asked Marie to help him choose 'either by this foreign attendance and striving with the world to seek a better estate, or by a domestical frugality and united counsels and endeavours to improve that small condition which we have already'.[5] There can be little doubt which of the two alternatives Marie preferred. By this time their first child, Joseph, had been born.[6] Marie's letters to Coke poignantly express her loneliness. In one of these she wrote: 'My thoughts do many times make me earnestly desire your company, that we may spend this short life together as much as may be.' To this she touchingly added: 'Your son calleth often, "Dad, Dad", although you do not hear him.'[7]

At the same time Coke and Marie contemplated their future, Fulke Greville's father lay dying. His death in November of 1606 allowed Coke to enter the second, more uncompromising phase of his retirement. From the Greville home in Warwickshire where he was helping to settle the estate, Coke wrote hopefully to Marie: 'I find here as hearty and dear affection as ever I did in my life and besides am encouraged to hope for profit which I know how to obtain.'[8] Greville's inheritance, combined with what he already possessed, amounted to a large estate. He needed someone to keep track of his financial accounts, and the obvious choice was Coke who had already assisted him thus for many years. From 1607 till at least 1615, Coke worked for Greville in a capacity that is not perfectly clear but appears to have been basically that of an auditor.[9] Whatever the exact nature of the job, it required less time away from his family than previously. Apart from serving as a local collector of subsidies in 1610, this was Coke's only outside employment during these years.[10] The greater part of his

[5]Coke MSS., packet 80, Coke to Marie, 5 June 1606.

[6]Briggs, *History of Melbourne,* p. 164. Their first son, Joseph, was born in 1605. Their second son, John, was probably born near Christmas of 1607 since Margaret Verney at that time wished Marie a safe and speedy delivery. *Cowper MSS.,* I, 58, 63.

[7]Coke MSS., packet 80, Marie to Coke, 15 Nov. 1606. In another letter, she wrote: 'I want your companie many times to make me merie when I am apt to be sad.' Briggs, *History of Melbourne*, p. 86.

[8]Coke MSS., packet 80, Coke to Marie, 19 November 1606.

[9]Coke's audits of Greville's estate for 1607, part of 1608, and 1609 are printed in *Cowper MSS.,* I, 64-7, 69-70. These, along with similar audits and fragments through 1613, are preserved in Coke MSS., packet 117. Coke was clearly in charge of these yearly audits (*Cowper MSS.,* I, 72) and served in other administrative capacities for Greville till at least 1615 (*Cowper MSS.,* I, 85, 88). Coke's notes for Wedgnock included this interesting entry: 'Mr. Townsend & Shakespeare have the coppice & bushie close.' Coke MSS., packet 117.

[10]*Cowper MSS.,* I, 72; Coke MSS., packet 118. Dorothea Coke wrongly claimed that Coke sat in Parliament in 1614 and served as a commissioner for purveyance in this period. *The Last Elizabethan*, pp. 44-7. She was misled by erroneously dated documents. SP 14/77/13; *Cowper MSS.,* I, 75.

time and energy during this phase of his retirement was devoted to his family and the home they now built for themselves. Coke had considered purchasing land in his native county of Derbyshire as early as 1603, and his brother Francis had kept him informed of likely estates that came up for sale.[11] Then marriage changed Coke's perspective. It was probably sometime during 1607 that he bought a parcel of land not far from Marie's parents in Herefordshire.[12] By April of 1608 he was building a home on that site which he named Hall Court, and by June he was purchasing the livestock.[13] Coke had clearly abandoned his 'striving with the world' and chosen the alternative course of 'domestical frugality'. Thus in 1607 Coke returned to the occupation of his ancestors. For the next ten years his major concern was the good husbandry of his estate. He was resolved to stay as far removed from court politics as possible, so much so that even an offer of £200 per annum, a house for his family, and other inducements from Greville could not persuade him to alter that resolve.[14]

Greville was not the only person who attempted to draw Coke away from his country retreat. In fact, Greville was perhaps the most sympathetic of Coke's friends in this regard. In 1611, for example, when Coke refused for the first time to answer a call from Greville, his patron averred: 'My own friend John . . . since your marriage, I have been temperate and respectful ever to that vocation.'[15] Similarly, in 1613 Greville wrote: 'I know you love home so well as I freely remit your coming up this Michaelmas.'[16] Robert Naunton was much less understanding about his retirement.[17] It was Sir Edmund Lucy, however, who best expressed the sentiments of Coke's friends when he wrote, 'my hope is you will not live this retired life longer . . . for Mr. John Coke was not made only for a country life. The world will require more from him'.[18] Lucy was right in observing that Coke was not suited for just a country life. Although Coke made little outward acknowledgement of the fact, he was not altogether happy in his exile.

[11] *Cowper MSS.*, I, 43, 54, 56.

[12] The first notice of Hall Court is on 19 April 1608. *Cowper MSS.*, I, 64. There is no apparent evidence for the claim (*Cowper MSS.*, I, iv and *DNB*, IV, 700) that Coke bought the property in 1604 before his marriage.

[13] *Cowper MSS.*, I, 64, 66.

[14] Coke MSS., packet 45, Coke to the marquis of Buckingham, 12 Oct. 1622. Recounting the offer in 1622, Coke said it was made to him twelve years earlier.

[15] *Cowper MSS.*, I, 72.

[16] *Ibid.*, I, 79.

[17] Coke MSS., packet 1, Naunton to Coke, 20 Oct. [1605] and 18 Jan. 1613.

[18] Coke MSS., packet 1, Sir Edmund Lucy to Coke, 1605.

In 1615 he described himself as 'a man that now ten years hath lived out of the world'. For Coke, 'the world' far too long ago had become London and the court. If he remembered his final years at court with bitterness, he remembered them, too, with a touch of longing. Both his alienation and his suppressed hope are evident in the words he himself used to describe his situation: 'I am sent for hither by my friends that seek to draw me again into the world. But my ambition is cooled and my comfort is at home, and I find my ways and ends out of fashion. I dare not therefore resolve to change till I see more cause.'[19]

When speaking of the fashion at court, Coke had foremost in mind the kind of men being advanced to power and the values those men represented. In particular, he was thinking of Cecil and the Howards who had deserted and defeated the plan for naval reform and driven Greville out of office. As long as his old patron was isolated from the court by these men, Coke naturally saw little hope for himself. One of the first signs that the fashion at court was changing, therefore, was Greville's surprising return to power.[20] Unlike Coke, Greville had not abjectly accepted his loss of office. He was described as a 'vessel of wrath'.[21] For a while he turned his attention to writing and to the renovation of Warwick Castle.[22] In time, however, he insinuated himself back into the court.[23] He did this chiefly by befriending Robert Carr, the royal favourite who became earl of Somerset. As Greville regained strength, the earl of Suffolk also warmed to him again.[24] Meanwhile, two opponents, Cecil and Northampton, were eliminated by death.[25] Then, in October of 1614, presumably with the combined support of Suffolk and Somerset, Fulke Greville was named Chancellor of the Exchequer.[26] Ten years after his expulsion from the Treasurership of the Navy, at the age of sixty and to the great amazement of many who followed the court, Greville had succeeded in returning to office.[27]

[19] Coke MSS., packet 69, Coke to Dr. Richardson of Trinity College, [1615].

[20] Rebholz, *Fulke Greville*, pp. 183-99, 233-9.

[21] HMC, *Portland MSS.,* IX, 143.

[22] William Dugdale, *The Antiquities of Warwickshire*, 2nd ed. (2 vols., London, 1730), I, 427.

[23] HMC, *Portland MSS.,* IX, 143.

[24] *Ibid.*, IX, 39.

[25] Some thought Greville would succeed Cecil as Secretary. *CSPD*, 1611-1618, p. 158.

[26] S.R. Gardiner, *History of England from the Accession of James I to the Outbreak of Civil War, 1603-1642* (10 vols., London, 1883-4, 1894-6), II, 259-60; *CSPD*, 1611-1618, p. 527.

[27] John Chamberlain wrote, 'Many marvel that a man of his years, wealth, and retired life, should affect such a place; but every body hath a doting time, and ambition is

It is a measure of Coke's alienation from the court that he did not return with Greville in 1614. He had continued on good terms with his old patron. In fact, he was in London in connection with his estate work for Greville when the latter regained office.[28] But Greville's appointment as Chancellor of the Exchequer did not convince Coke that the fashion at court had definitely changed, and he continued in retirement at Hall Court. At first this did not discourage Greville in his attempts to lure Coke away from the country. He implored him: 'Come up to London with me for a while, I will fetch you there.'[29] And when Coke refused, he reproached him: 'If ever we meet again, you shall fully know what was in my power to have done for you.'[30] Coke's stubbornness finally did exasperate Greville, and tension developed between the two old friends.[31] Fortunately, Greville was at this time considering the establishment of a lectureship in history at Cambridge while concurrently drawing plans for a tomb in honour of his famous departed friend, Sir Philip Sidney. By way of a peace-offering, Greville wrote to Coke for his advice on both these projects, and through the subsequent exchange of opinions a reconciliation was evidently achieved.[32] In effect, the two men preserved their friendship by coming to an understanding: Greville would advance Coke when the proper time came, but Coke would be the sole judge of which time, if any, was the proper one.

What was Coke waiting for? Obviously he wanted greater assurance that he would not be hurt all over again as he had been in 1604. But there were two other criteria by which he continued to judge the court and to repudiate it: religion and, for want of a better word, integrity. As for religion, Coke believed that the menace of Roman Catholicism was resurgent in these years. He wanted to see the religious and foreign policies of Queen Elizabeth's later years restored. That is why, when Greville consulted him about establishing

blind.' Thomas Birch, ed., *The Court and Times of James the First*, ed. R.F. Williams (2 vols., London, 1848), I, 349. Sir John Holles discoursed at length on the injustice of appointing Greville 'who by sitting still hath gained a greater hire than they that have laboured the heat of the day'. HMC, *Portland MSS.*, IX, 140-3.

[28]*Cowper MSS.*, I, 85-6.

[29]Coke MSS., packet 15, Greville to Coke, March 1615.

[30]Coke MSS., packet 15, Greville to Coke, 4 Sept. 1615.

[31]In the two preceding letters Greville referred respectively to 'conspiracies of fortune' and 'misprisons of unkindness' between himself and Coke.

[32]Coke MSS., packet 15, Greville to Coke, 4 Sept. 1615 and Coke to Greville, 16 Sept. 1615; Joan Rees, 'Greville's Epitaph on Sir Philip Sydney', *Review of English Studies,* new series, 19 (Feb. 1968), 47-51; Norman Farmer, 'Fulke Greville and Sir John Coke: an Exchange of Letters on a History Lecture and Certain Latin Verses on Sir Philip Sydney', *Huntington Library Quarterly,* 32 (May 1970), 217-36.

the history lectureship at Cambridge, he complained that 'these times neither live nor govern by stories nor patterns of times past'. It is not certain which candidate Coke was asked to evaluate (apparently not Isaac Dorislaus who eventually got the post), and his evaluation is too ambiguous to be informative, but he left no doubt what he thought the historian's purpose should be: to fight the Catholic 'adversaries', to 'discover their ambition, covetousness, impostures, tyrannies, treacheries, and all the depths of hell in that Roman gulf . . . and so plainly expound the prophecies and revelations of Antichrist that the hearts of all men, specially of princes, shall be prepared for the ruin of that beast.' By including the words 'specially of princes' in this sentence, Coke was probably betraying his anxiety about King James. Coke did see some reason for optimism on this front. He referred approvingly to the work of Isaac Casaubon, the great, Protestant, classical scholar whom James had lured to the English court.[33] On the other front – integrity – Coke saw no cause for optimism, except of course in Greville's appointment. He still viewed the court as dominated by extravagant, self-seeking, and dishonest men. Of course, his vision of the court was coloured by religious bias and a simmering personal grudge, but many modern historians have seen the same deterioration in court ethics at this time.[34]

It would be a mistake to assume from Coke's continuing reticence that he had no desire at all to return to court. This is obvious from a letter he wrote to Greville in 1616. Writing to thank Greville for a favour, Coke made his usual avowal that 'my way and end be cast out of the world'. He also added, however, that his daily prayers were for Greville's integrity and industry to be so successful that 'this incorrupted and noble way may come in fashion in great places'.[35] By expressing this hope and by concluding with an acknowledgement that his own ambition depended on Greville's prosperity, Coke betrayed his innermost thoughts. If his hopes and ambitions were suppressed, they were, nevertheless, far from extinguished.

Coke required still more assurance that the court was changing for the better and that he would not meet with the same humiliation and rejection he had experienced in 1604. He soon found that assurance in the advancement to high office of another of his old friends, Robert

[33]Coke MSS., packet 15, Coke to Greville, 16 Sept. 1615. For Casaubon, see *DNB,* III, 1, 166-70.

[34]Hurstfield, *Freedom*, pp. 156, 162; H.R. Trevor-Roper, 'The General Crisis of the Seventeenth Century' in Trevor Aston, ed., *Crisis in Europe 1560-1660* (New York, 1965), pp. 80-5; Lawrence Stone, *Family and Fortune* (Oxford, 1973), p. 57.

[35]Coke MSS., packet 15, Coke to Greville, 13 Feb. 1616.

Naunton. We have seen that the careers of Naunton and Coke followed remarkably similar courses but rarely coincided in their timing. Thus James's accession to the throne had witnessed the end of Coke's career and the revival of Naunton's. In the absence of an open civil service system based on merit, Stuart aspirants to office often resembled present-day actors hoping to be discovered and elevated to stardom. This is what happened to James's two greatest favourites, Somerset and Buckingham, who were serving in menial positions in the king's proximity when James discovered their pretty faces and advanced them to the top of the court hierarchy; and so it is supposed to have been with Naunton. As public orator for Cambridge, Naunton addressed James in 1603 on the new king's journey from Scotland. Naunton's Latin oration was said to have made a favourable impression, and, so the story runs: 'The smiles of James brought him to court.'[36] In reality, however, Naunton's speech to the new king was probably not as important as the support of Secretary Cecil, and even this did not make Naunton a star over night.[37] It was not until later in James's reign through the assistance of the king's greatest favourite, the duke of Buckingham, that Naunton achieved stardom. He was then able to profit from his friendship with Buckingham's mother, with whom he became so influential that he was called her chancellor.[38] The former follower of Essex was soon referred to as 'Buckingham's creature'.[39] As Buckingham rose in power, Naunton was appointed Master of Requests, Surveyor of the Court of Wards, and eventually Secretary of State in 1618.[40]

Between the time of his return to Cambridge about 1599 and his promotion to the Secretaryship in 1618, Naunton maintained his close friendship with Coke.[41] In March of 1617, when Naunton was Master of Requests and Surveyor of the Court of Wards but had not yet attained the Secretaryship, Coke received the following report: 'No man can express more hearty and sincere affection to another's welfare than he [Naunton] doth to you, in truth you are extraordinarily beholding to him, he lamenteth your resolution . . . of discontinuing from

[36] George Dyer, *History of the University and Colleges of Cambridge* (2 vols., London, 1814), II, 295-6.

[37] Roy E. Schreiber, *The Political Career of Sir Robert Naunton 1589-1635* (London, 1981), p. 4.

[38] Birch, *The Court and Times of James the First*, I, 433.

[39] *CSPD,* 1611-1618, p. 492.

[40] Schreiber, *Naunton,* pp. 8-15; *DNB*, XIV, 127.

[41] For Naunton's correspondence with Coke during these years, see *Cowper MSS.,* I, 32-3, 44, 58, 62-3, 70-1, 77, 95.

hence as a man that truly desires conversation of honest men.'[42] Now that Naunton's influence at court had greatly increased, it would be more difficult to resist his importuning. Moreover, since Naunton was a staunch Protestant and a stern moralist of the same school as Coke, his rapid preferment must have further persuaded Coke to believe that the mood at court, and consequently his own prospects, might be genuinely improving. The pressures, in other words, were mounting. By the summer of 1617, the example of Naunton's success was evidently weakening Coke's determination to stay in retirement. When he learned that the king planned to visit Greville at Warwick Castle, Coke wrote to his old patron offering to attend at Warwick as one of his followers or to do any other service which might be required.[43] This is precisely the sort of event Coke would have avoided if he had still been resolute in his withdrawal from public life.

In January of 1618 when Naunton was finally appointed to the Secretaryship, he wrote to Coke before anyone else to inform him of the appointment. Naunton confided that there was no one he could truly rely upon at court. He would gladly have welcomed Coke's company, he said, for both the church and state suffered for lack of dedicated, honest, and able men. More specifically, Naunton's promotion had left vacant his former offices of Master of Requests and Surveyor of the Court of Wards. The new Secretary said that he would have preferred Coke above all other men living to succeed him in either of these posts if they had not already been disposed of beyond his control. Nevertheless, Naunton was hopeful of future opportunities. He urged Coke to abandon 'so contentful a retreat as you there have raised against a storm' and invited him to come 'a little nearer the sun, while it shall shine upon you and such as shall live and die your true friends'. Coke's powers, he promised, would flourish in the light of the court 'as in their proper tabernacle'.[44] Far from being in his 'proper tabernacle', Coke was preparing the annual feed accounts for swine and other livestock at Hall Court when he received Naunton's letter. He rejoiced in Naunton's appointment, proclaiming that it had 'opened a window of hope to all faithful subjects that church and commonwealth shall not only have planets but fixed stars' in places of power about the court. Coke saw Naunton's appointment as final

[42]Coke MSS., packet 1, Thomas Coke to John Coke, 1 March 1617.

[43]Coke MSS., packet 15, Coke to Greville, 7 July 1617. It is impossible to determine whether Coke did actually attend.

[44]Coke MSS., packet 1, Naunton to Coke, 11 Jan. 1618. Naunton declared at the opening of this letter: 'The first advertisement hereof that mine own pen hath given, is this to your self (whose fear of God, and love of his dear church, and of our dear country, my soul hath so long embraced).'

proof that the complexion and mood of the court were changing, and thereby Coke's own 'window of hope' was opened. He replied to Naunton: 'I will be ready to put myself to any trial you shall think fit for me.' With this statement, Coke declared that after nearly fourteen years in retirement, he was ready to reenter public life. But characteristically he added: 'I pray God from my heart I may not move from my retreat except it be for a better account of my life.'[45]

At the beginning of 1618, then, Coke openly aspired to return to the world of the court. Those aspirations would have been mere pipe dreams, of course, if he had not possessed strong patrons at court in the persons of Greville and Naunton. Nor would even their help necessarily have been sufficient if other circumstances had not been favourable. Coke's decision to return to public life may have been influenced by the fact that the court was being swept by a wave of reforming zeal in the last months of 1617 and early 1618. The foremost leaders of this movement were Sir Lionel Cranfield, whose reform of the Household in 1617 was widely acclaimed as a herculean achievement, and the marquis of Buckingham, the last and the greatest of the Jacobean favourites. When, in the summer of 1618, they turned their attention to the area in which Coke was an acknowledged expert – the navy – the stage was set for Coke's return.

Naval reform was long overdue. After Greville's expulsion from the Naval Treasurership, the incompetence of Lord Admiral Nottingham and the dishonesty of Sir Robert Mansell became notorious. Feeble and totally ineffective gestures had been made to reform the situation in 1608 and 1613.[46] The effort launched in 1618, however, was a far more determined one. The attack on naval abuses was heralded early in the spring of 1618 when the Privy Council began a rigorous investigation of Mansell's financial records.[47] With his own accounts

[45] Coke MSS., packet 69, Coke to Naunton, *ca.* Jan. 1618. This letter is drafted over a rough sheet of Hall Court feed accounts for the year. In keeping with his own character, Coke had only one piece of advice for Naunton, to 'follow not the times but his own disposition'.

[46] Oppenheim, *Royal Navy*, pp. 193-4; Linda Peck, 'Problems in Jacobean Administration: Was Henry Howard, Earl of Northampton, a Reformer?', *The Historical Journal*, 19 (1976), 835-40, 851-3.

[47] Naunton and Greville were among the five Council members who signed the letter to Mansell demanding a certificate of his accounts on 26 March 1618 (*APC,* 1618-1619, p. 84). The investigation proceeded through April (*CSPD*, 1611-1618, pp. 535, 537). In November the new commissioners of the navy complained about the grossly inadequate, uncertified abstracts submitted by Mansell instead of the full records he had promised. SP 14/103/104. As late as February of 1620, nearly two years after the investigation began, the naval commissioners presented a final report on Mansell's abuses as Treasurer. SP 14/112/101.

now called into question – the very device he himself had used against Greville in 1604 – Mansell hastily arranged a tactical retreat. Some authorities wrongly claim that he was dismissed or forced to resign.[48] In reality, before any action could be taken against him, he sold his office of Treasurer of the Navy to a prominent investor named Sir William Russell. One court gossip reported that if Russell paid Mansell as much as was rumoured, then 'it was more than two such offices are worth'. Nor did Mansell retreat in disgrace. Instead, he had himself appointed Vice-Admiral of England, a largely honorific post that was considered 'a place in these times of more name and credit than profit'.[49] It was, in other words, a pleasant harbour in which to weather the storm. Not that there would be any storm as far as Mansell was concerned: his grant of the Vice-Admiralship included the unusual provision that he could not be prosecuted or removed for any offences he may have committed in his former office.[50] Even considering the assistance he no doubt received from the old Lord Admiral, Mansell escaped on far more favourable terms than might have been expected.[51] This was a very deceptive beginning, however. With Mansell out of the way, the Council prepared early in June to initiate a sweeping, full-scale reform of the navy.

The Council first referred the matter of a comprehensive naval reform to Fulke Greville, who was probably chosen for the task because he was the only member of the Council, other than the Lord Admiral himself, who was experienced in naval affairs. On 4 June Greville was directed to call before him 'any such person as he shall thinke fitt to informe himself touching anything that concerneth the Navey'.[52] Since he and Coke had both paid dearly for attempting reform in 1604, it was only fitting that they should both share in this belated victory. On 12 June 1618 the Privy Council sent a letter to

[48] Oppenheim, *Royal Navy,* p. 191; Menna Prestwich, *Cranfield: Politics and Profits Under the Early Stuarts* (Oxford, 1966), p. 212.

[49] Norman McClure, ed., *The Letters of John Chamberlain* (2 vols., Philadelphia, 1939), II, 161.

[50] See *CSPD*, 1611-1618, pp. 540-1, for Russell's grant of the Navy Treasurership dated 10 May and Mansell's grant of the Vice-Admiralship dated 14 May. McGowan, *Jocobean Commissions,* p. xvii, writes: 'There is no evidence that Mansell had heard of an impending enquiry, but neither is there anything to suggest why he should suddenly have voluntarily surrendered a lucrative and important post that he had previously hazarded much to retain.'

[51] Anthony Weldon, 'The Court and Character of King James' in Walter Scott, ed., *The Secret History of the Court of King James the First* (2 vols., Edinburgh, 1811), I, 432-3. Weldon reported that Lord Admiral Nottingham was responsible for Mansell's appointment to the Vice-Admiralship. [William Sanderson's] *Aulicus Coquinariae* also states that Nottingham used his influence on behalf of Mansell. *Ibid.*, II, 264.

[52] *APC*, 1618-1619, p. 157.

Coke signed by thirteen lords of the Council, including Greville and Naunton. The letter required Coke's attendance in the king's service and informed him, 'out of speciall choice you are thought fitt amongst others to be imployed the rather in regard of your knowledg and long experience in those affaires'. This summons did not specify the nature of the service required of Coke but promised him, 'at your comeing you shall understand the business, and before your departure receive. . . allowance and reward for your paines and travaile'.[53]

By this time it had been decided that the best way to achieve naval reform was to appoint a twelve-man commission of inquiry.[54] This naval commission was basically a subcommission of the one Cranfield had headed in the reform of the Household. Consequently, it consisted of Cranfield and seven other members from the Household commission, who were joined in this case by a commercial magnate and three naval experts whose technical knowledge would be required.[55] It was undoubtedly through Greville's influence, and almost certainly with the support of Naunton, that Coke was named to this commission as one of the naval experts.

This appointment to the naval commission in June of 1618 was one of the few, genuine turning-points in Coke's life. Fourteen years of retirement lay behind him; twenty-two more years of civil employment lay before him. Much had happened since those dark days in the summer of 1604 when he delivered Greville's accounts to the auditor, turned his back on London, and rode into the country to begin a new life with Marie. For fourteen years Coke had waited at his retreat in Herefordshire and observed the changing mood at court. He had witnessed it in the appointments of Greville and Naunton to high office. He had witnessed it, too, in the deaths of Cecil in 1612 and Northampton in 1614. The two remaining Howards, Lord Admiral

[53] *Ibid.*, p. 167. When Coke received an allowance for his work in the navy in 1621, the grant specifically stated that 'he was called to the said services by the Lords of our Council'. *Cowper MSS.*, I, 114.

[54] There is no clue how, why, or by whom the decision was made to transfer responsibility for the naval investigation from Greville to this commission. Rebholz, *Fulke Greville*, p. 248; McGowan, *Jacobean Commissions*, pp. xvii-xx. The Council ordered the commission to be drawn up under the great seal on 18 June, and the patent was dated 23 June. *APC*, 1618-1619, p. 174; Gardiner, *History of England*, III, 204 n. 2.

[55] R.H. Tawney, *Business and Politics Under James I: Lionel Cranfield as Merchant and Minister* (Cambridge, 1958), p. 160; *APC*, 1618-1619, pp. 174, 179. The seven members from the Household commission in addition to Cranfield were Sir Richard Weston, Sir John Wolstenholme, Nicholas Fortescue, John Osborne, Francis Gofton, Richard Sutton, and William Pitt. The commercial magnate was the governor of the East India Company, Sir Thomas Smythe. The two naval experts besides Coke were Thomas Norreys and William Burrell.

Nottingham and Lord Treasurer Suffolk, were still in power in the early summer of 1618, but they, too, would soon be forced to step aside by the new favourites, Cranfield and Buckingham. Last of all, and perhaps most gratifying to Coke, Sir Robert Mansell had been forced to step down as Treasurer of the Navy. It had taken fourteen years, but the wheel of fortune had at last turned full circle. A whole generation of courtiers had come and gone while Coke waited in the countryside to serve another day. When that day finally came in 1618, Coke was fifty-five years old. By the standards of his time he was far from being a young man. Yet he was just now embarking on a new, second career that would last more than two decades. The man who had grown to adulthood at the time of Hawkins, Drake, and the Spanish Armada was destined in his old age to participate in the negotiations with the Scottish Covenanters. Anthony Esler has written a book about the generation to which Coke belonged, men born in the later 1550s and early 1560s. Coke fits Esler's description of the men belonging to this generation who were 'cast aside' at James's accession: 'This was a generation of Phoenixes: their careers began as romantic quests for unique honor and absolute supremacy – and ended all too often as a taste of ashes in the mouth . . . This was the pattern of the aspiring mind of the generation of 1560, arching towards the zenith to end in the dust.'[56] In Coke's case, however, there was one important difference. His career, like the Phoenix, rose again from the ashes in 1618.

[56] *The Aspiring Mind of the Elizabethan Younger Generation* (Durham, North Carolina, 1966), pp. xiv, 202, 206-7.

4

COMMISSIONER FOR SURVEY OF THE NAVY

Coke's appointment to the Commission for Survey of the Navy in June of 1618 provided him with a rare opportunity to pick up where he had left off and achieve the naval reform he had been forced to abandon in 1604. Not often in life does a man have such a second chance; the evidence shows that Coke made the best of his. The true extent to which Coke dominated the work of the naval commission has often been obscured by the overshadowing presence of Cranfield, but the simple fact is that Cranfield had neither the time nor the experience necessary to direct the reform of the navy.[1] There is, after all, a limit to what one man can do, and this was true even of the seemingly indefatigable Cranfield. Overburdened by the demands of the Household, Treasury, and Wardrobe, he had little time left to devote to the navy.[2] Even had he possessed the time, he was conspicuously lacking in naval experience. Coke, on the other hand, had the advantage of his experience in the Elizabethan navy. As Godfrey Goodman, bishop of Gloucester under Charles I, observed, Coke came to the task prepared with 'all the precedents and notes of former times'.[3] Goodman specifically excluded reform of the navy from Cranfield's achievements and attributed it to Coke instead.[4] Coke's contemporaries, then, were not unaware of the dominant role he played. Some even came to believe that the very purpose of the commission had been to advance him to power. John Holland, for example, began his naval career in the mid-1620s and concluded from what he saw of its results that: 'The Grand Commission in the year 1618 was nothing else but a design to crush the then officers of the

[1]The naval commission is sometimes referred to as the Cranfield commission. Geoffrey Marcus, *A Naval History of England* (Boston, 1961), p. 126; G.P.V. Akrigg, *Jacobean Pageant: The Court of King James I* (New York, 1967), p. 99. But compare Leslie Gardiner, *The British Admiralty* (London, 1968), p. 63. Cranfield's biographers are not responsible for this false impression. R.H. Tawney said that Coke was 'on all that concerned the Navy at once a fanatic and an expert'; and with respect to naval reform, 'chief credit for the result belongs to Coke'. *Business and Politics,* pp. 160, 170-2, 235. See also Prestwich, *Cranfield,* pp. 212-15.

[2]Gardiner, *History of England,* III, 203. Although he wrote about this subject only peripherally and before it had been studied more thoroughly by others, Gardiner produced a remarkably accurate account of the naval commission, in which he observed: 'Cranfield was a member, but. . . overburthened as he was with other business, the chief part of the labour fell upon Sir John Coke.'

[3]Godfrey Goodman, *The Court of King James the First,* ed. John S. Brewer (2 vols., London, 1839), I, 54.

[4]*Ibid.*, I, 308.

navy, and advance Sir John Coke.'[5] Finally, it is worth noting that on the one occasion when Cranfield is known to have claimed credit for the reform of the navy, he succeeded only in drawing upon himself the charge that 'he [being] not pryvye to those imployments havinge ben otherwise bredd, used the helpe of others, namely of Mr. Cooke, and at last assumed the wholl glory to himselfe'.[6]

As a relatively unknown outsider, Coke could not have been the dominant member of the commission at the start. He appears, instead, to have risen rapidly to leadership in the course of the commission's work. In this, he had the assistance of Greville and Naunton, but equally important were his own untiring industry and superior knowledge of the navy. All of these factors can be seen manifestly working in Coke's favour almost from the start.[7]

When the commission began its survey of the navy at Chatham on 6 July 1618, its earnestness was unmistakable. Phineas Pett, a principal shipwright of the period, noted that the commissioners arrived at Chatham in great state, caused their commission to be publicly read, and announced their orders for every ship in the navy to be examined.[8] This investigation had been under way for little more than one week when Greville wrote that he was communicating the contents of Coke's letters to the king. He reported that James was

[5]Joseph R. Tanner, ed., *Two Discourses of the Navy 1638 and 1659 by John Holland, Also A Discourse of the Navy 1660 by Sir Robert Slyngesbie* (London, 1896), p. 118. In his editorial commentary at the bottom of this page, Tanner concluded that 'Cranfield's share in this Commission was far less important than that of Coke.' Sir Robert Slyngesbie was only a boy in 1618, but his father was Comptroller of the Navy. In his naval discourse written after the fact, Robert explained the reform of 1618 this way. 'The Earl of Nottingham, then lord admiral, being very old, and the then Earl (afterwards Duke) of Buckingham, ambitious of that high command, to gratify that young favourite, Sir Fulke Greville, afterwards Lord Brooke, and Sir John Coke, afterwards secretary of state (the one having been formerly treasurer of the navy and the other his paymaster) projected to do great service to the King by introducing a new model of the office of the navy under that new admiral.' *Ibid.*, p. 333.

[6]S.R. Gardiner, ed., *Notes of the Debates in the House of Lords. . . 1624 and 1626* (Westminster, 1879), p. 86. The reply cited was that of the Lord Keeper, Bishop Williams, who blithely dismissed Cranfield's other achievements as mere acts of personal gain. What is most significant about the Lord Keeper's answer is not that he discredited Cranfield but that he singled out Coke for the true credit.

[7]There are several secondary accounts of the commission's work. Oppenheim, *Royal Navy,* pp. 194-8, is surprisingly muddled on this subject. Other brief but generally better accounts are: Gardiner, *History of England,* III, 203-6; Prestwich, *Cranfield,* pp. 212-18; Tawney, *Business and Politics,* pp. 159-62; Gardiner, *British Admiralty,* pp. 63-72; Corbett, *England in the Mediterranean,* I, 66-82. In most respects, all the foregoing have been superseded by A.P. McGowan's unpublished Ph.D. thesis, 'The Royal Navy under the First Duke of Buckingham, Lord High Admiral 1618-1628' (University of London, 1967). McGowan's work is summarized in his introduction to *Jacobean Commissions,* cited previously.

[8]W.G. Perrin, ed., *The Autobiography of Phineas Pett* (London, 1918), p. 119.

sensible of the navy's condition and relying upon Coke's 'faithful labours in this trust committed to you'. Greville was obviously working assiduously to advance his old friend in favour, and a measure of his success is his concluding promise: 'When we next meet. . . you shall find the sun hath not stood still.'[9] Meanwhile, Coke was himself far from idle. Within three weeks of his arrival at Chatham, he had written his own historical survey of the navy, documenting its decline in size and noting which existing ships were unserviceable.[10] The commissioners continued their examinations at Chatham through the month of July and well into August. By early September their investigation was nearly complete, and Cranfield was already confidently proclaiming: 'We have laid a foundation to bring the King's navy into as glorious an estate, both for strength and honour, as ever it was.'[11] Those were strikingly optimistic words in view of the appalling state of affairs about to be disclosed.

The commission formally submitted its findings and recommendations to the king and Council at Hampton Court on 29 September 1618.[12] Cranfield acted as the commission's spokesman on this occasion, but it is important to note that the report he read was drafted by Coke.[13] Although it is impossible to know precisely how much each member of the commission contributed to this report, there is reason to believe that the major contributor was Coke. In addition to his unequalled naval experience, his general penchant for administrative reform, his own preliminary survey of the navy, and the testimony of contemporaries already cited, there is above all else the outstanding fact that he was the original author of the report; and that fact should be firmly borne in mind when considering the content, reception, and consequences of the report.

[9]Coke MSS., packet 15, Greville to Coke, 15 July 1618.

[10]SP 14/98/42. This seven-page essay entirely in Coke's hand is endorsed by him: '1618. July. 24. The state of the navy royal from time to time.' After briefly tracing the development of the navy from the reign of Edward III, Coke found that it had declined since the death of Elizabeth by at least six major ships or 3,250 tons.

[11]Goodman, *Court of King James,* II, 164-7.

[12]*APC,* 1618-1619, p. 263.

[13]Tawney, *Business and Politics,* p. 160; Prestwich, *Cranfield,* p. 215. Coke's draft, at the Kent County Archives office among Cranfield's papers, is ON 4858/EN M1110. The final report is preserved in the Public Record Office (SP 14/vols. 100 and 101). The report is printed in full in John Charnock, *An History of Marine Architecture* (3 vols., London, 1800-2), II, 211-70 and McGowan, *Jacobean Commissions,* pp. 258-306. An interesting epilogue to the report's history occurred fifty years later when Samuel Pepys alluded to 'the books of Propositions, which did please me mightily to hear read, they being excellently writ and much to the purpose, and yet so as I think I shall make good use of his defence of our present constitution'. Henry B. Wheatley, ed., *The Diary of Samuel Pepys* (9 vols., London, 1893-9), VII, 260.

The commission's report was a shocking catalogue of waste and corruption. The specific abuses were much like those identified by Coke and Greville in the late Elizabethan navy, but the magnitude was much greater. The Crown was paying over £53,000 annually on the navy, but it received very little value for money. Captains and pursers used inflated crew lists to collect 'dead pays'. Naval officials regularly paid prices far above the market level for nearly everything they bought, but the goods they received were often of an inferior quality, and the scale used to weigh incoming goods favoured the merchants by more than one pound per hundred. The most excessive expenditure was for cordage: in nine years a preposterous £108,000 had been spent on this commodity. Other money was being wasted on superfluous expenditures while at the same time workers were not provided with materials necessary to keep the ships in good repair. During a four-year period, shipwrights and caulkers were paid over £17,000, but there was no visible improvement in the condition of the ships. For that sum, said the commissioners, eight new ships could have been built. Meanwhile, naval stores were used and workers employed to repair, enlarge, and construct buildings for private use. Moreover, there were too many officers in the navy, and too many of these delegated their work to incompetent deputies. Venality of offices was as much a cause of corruption as it had been in 1603. The commissioners' report condemned 'the selling of most places at such rates that the buyers profess openly they will not pay and work, and that they cannot live except they must steal'. Finally, the report complained that there were inadequate procedures to discourage corruption: 'neither due survey is taken of ought that cometh in nor orderly warrant given for most that goeth out, nor any particular account made nor now possible to be made of any one main work or service that is done'. It is no wonder, then, that the commissioners found that twelve of the navy's ships were not worth saving. Even the twenty-three that remained would require over £15,000 to be made seaworthy.[14]

The best that could be said in regard to this sorry state of affairs was that great abuse provided an opportunity for great reforms. What the commission proposed in the balance of its report was an ambitious, five-year programme designed to reform and restore the navy while simultaneously saving money. The commissioners argued that if waste and corruption were eliminated, the navy could be repaired and augmented by two new ships each year, and yet the annual cost could be reduced from £53,000 to an average of about

[14]McGowan, *Jacobean Commissions,* pp. 258-74.

£30,000. When this five-year improvement plan was complete, the navy could be maintained thereafter at an even lower cost of £20,000 per year. In order to achieve this phenomenal reform, the commissioners offered several 'Propositions for bettering the state and lessening the charge of the ships that now remain.' These included proposals to eliminate the notorious dead pays, to abolish unnecessary offices, to discharge the vessels that had been found unserviceable, and to establish regulations that would have to be followed in the purchase and use of naval supplies.[15]

These proposals raise several questions. First, was the saving they proposed realistic? They were proposing to run the English navy at an amount somewhere between a quarter and a third of what Spain was spending on a comparable or even smaller navy.[16] This makes their proposal seem wildly optimistic. But the answer to this objection is obvious: if extraordinary services are excluded, the navy was run during the next several years far better than it had been previously and at a cost very close to what the commissioners had estimated. In other words, what the commissioners said could be done was done. Secondly, it is a common argument that corrupt practices like dead pays and purloining naval supplies had sprung up as ways of supplementing inadequate wages. Curbing these practices, then, might have driven naval personnel to desert the service or find even more desperate means to supplement their wages. But again the fact is that the level of corrupt practices in the navy appears to have dropped dramatically after the report of 1618, and it increased again only later when extraordinary services put more money and materials into circulation. It is a simple fact that the fewer pieces of rope and timber there are in a dockyard, the more likely any one piece is to be missed if it disappears. Likewise, the less money handled, the higher the likelihood that one pound will be missed if it is pocketed. By spending less money, naval administrators would be better able to monitor what they spent, while providing other naval personnel with fewer temptations and opportunities for theft. Equally important, though, is the fact that the commissioners understood the relationship between low wages and high corruption. Perhaps the most remarkable feature of the 1618 report was its proposal to raise wages for this precise reason. The commissioners knew that a fundamental cause of corruption was 'poverty of wages'.[17] They also knew it was a convenient excuse for

[15] *Ibid.*, pp. 274-96.

[16] I.A.A. Thompson, *War and Government in Habsburg Spain 1560-1620* (London, 1976), pp. 197, 295, 303.

[17] McGowan, *Jacobean Commissions*, p. 274.

failing to punish wrongdoers. By raising wages, they hoped to take away both the motivation and the excuse, and so be able to hold naval personnel more accountable for their actions in the future. Raising the wages of boatswains, said the commissioners, would make it 'possible for them to live without stealth, and just for His Majesty's officers to punish their offences'. Similarly, the purpose of raising other wages, said the commissioners, was 'to encourage all that are or may be made honest, and to enable the governors to punish and reform all abuses hereafter'.[18] A third question raised by the commissioners' report is whether reform, no matter how carefully planned, could actually be achieved if the navy was left in the hands of the same men who had done so much to make reform necessary. Here the answer is simple: no.

The chief individuals responsible for the state of the navy were the Lord Admiral and the principal officers.[19] The commissioners were expressly forbidden to blame the Lord Admiral for any of the navy's problems, but the principal officers enjoyed no such immunity. Consequently, the commission's report concluded with an open attack on the principal officers. In contrast to the 'outward' manifestations of corruption described earlier in their report, the commissioners now named the principal officers as the 'true inward causes of decaying the navy'. In view of the fact that the officers had done much to cause the deplorable state of the navy, the commissioners concluded that the 'propositions for restoring the ships cannot possibly be' entrusted to them. The commissioners described their plan for reform as 'a body or image (as it were) that has neither life nor motion till it be given by His Majesty by establishing such a government in the navy whereby that which is profitably propounded may faithfully, understandingly and diligently be put in execution'. Surely this could not be expected of the principal officers. Instead, the commissioners boldly suggested that reform could only be achieved: 'By enlarging the Commission that already is on foot, giving power to the Commissioners to put in execution their propositions for restoring the navy.'[20] In other words, the commissioners were asking that they themselves be put in charge of the navy for the next five years to carry out their own proposals.

Cranfield's presentation of the commissioners' report, culminating in their request to be entrusted with the administration of the navy,

[18]*Ibid.*, p. 284.

[19]Recent preoccupation with the 'structural' weaknesses of early Stuart government does not seem to me to excuse the conduct of individual persons. Compare Hurstfield, *Freedom*, p. 161.

[20]McGowan, *Jacobean Commissions*, pp. 296-9.

must have made this 29 September meeting of the Privy Council an unusually dramatic one, especially when one remembers that King James and Lord Admiral Nottingham were both present. Several proposals regarding the discharge of unserviceable ships and repair of serviceable ships were approved either immediately at this meeting or shortly afterwards.[21] The more controversial proposals, especially regarding the future administration of the navy, were referred to the further consideration of an eleven-member committee of the Council. Two members of this committee were Naunton and Greville. For reasons that will soon become apparent, a third member was the marquis of Buckingham.[22]

Buckingham played a decisive role in the reform of the navy, for he alone was capable of winning and holding the irresolute king to the cause of reform.[23] Coke said that Buckingham deserved to be honoured as the 'patron' of naval reform; Cranfield and King James testified to the same effect.[24] Buckingham was present at the reading of the naval commission's report, and he was the most important member of the committee appointed to consider it.[25] This open involvement on his part strongly suggests that the ultimate disposition of the business had already been formulated. That formula, as we shall soon see, had two parts: the commission would be granted the administrative authority it asked for in order to implement its own proposals, and Buckingham would assume formal leadership of the whole project by replacing Nottingham as Lord Admiral.

The investigatory phase of the commission's work ended with the presentation of its report on 29 September 1618. For five weeks after that date, the commission continued to function but with ill-defined status. It was, after all, a commission of inquiry whose declared purpose had been merely to survey and propose, not actually to

[21] Several of these propositions are followed by 'Fiat', and in one place by 'all this agreed unto'. Charnock, *Marine Architecture,* II, 230-2, 238. It is also apparent that some proposals were quickly approved because steps toward implementing them began well before the Privy Council took further, official action on 2 November.

[22] *APC,* 1618-1619, p. 263. The committee was empowered to summon and take testimony from the principal officers, but there is no concrete evidence that such meetings occurred.

[23] McGowan, *Jacobean Commissions,* pp. xvii-xix; Lockyer, *Buckingham,* pp. 48-50.

[24] Coke MSS., packet 21, Coke to Buckingham, 17 October 1618; Goodman, *Court of King James,* II, 164-7; Kent County Archives, Cranfield MSS. ON 164/EN M1078; *LJ,* III, 343-4.

[25] *APC,* 1618-1619, p. 263. Buckingham's exceptionally rare attendance at this Council meeting and his appointment to the committee have gone unnoticed, even by McGowan. See his *Jacobean Commissions,* p. xxv n. 3.

reform. The fact that the commissioners were able to proceed in implementing many of their proposals even while the form of a permanent solution was still being debated can probably be attributed to the protection they received from Buckingham. In contrast to Buckingham's emergence as the major court proponent of the project, Cranfield gradually withdrew from active participation in the naval business after presenting the commission's report, presumably because he was occupied elsewhere by his many other projects, reform of the Wardrobe in particular.[26] The daily leadership of the commission was subsequently assumed by Coke, thus giving him an opportunity to implement the proposals he himself had drafted. With Buckingham now openly supporting and promoting the project at court and Coke directing the work in the harbours and the dockyards, naval reform became, in effect, their joint responsibility. This was the beginning of a mutually profitable relationship that was destined to last until Buckingham's violent death in 1628.

The two men did not meet at this particular time and place in history entirely by accident. Greville may have had something to do with bringing them together, but apparently more instrumental in this respect was Naunton, who, as Secretary of State, enjoyed readier access to the king and his favourite. Coke effusively thanked Naunton for 'drawing my name out of the dark, and freely recommending it to those places which the times have valued at so dear rates; besides in your entering of the lists for me, even in the hazardous inclination of great men against me'. In return for this, Coke gratefully acknowledged his 'tenure and homage' to Naunton.[27]

It was apparently through Naunton's influence, then, that Coke received his first sign of favour from Buckingham a few days after the commission submitted its report. The exact nature of that favour is not clear from the evidence, but Coke described it as 'beyond my expectation and merit'. This occasioned Coke's first letter to Buckingham, in which he professed himself 'unable by any valuable services, to express my thankfulness or answer the expectation (it seemeth) your Honour hath conceived of me'. These, of course, were not unnatural sentiments for a client to express to his new-found patron. More surprising is the fact that Coke refused to accept any monetary remuneration until he could prove he was worthy of it. It was evidently enough simply to have secured Buckingham as his benefactor. With

[26] Prestwich, *Cranfield,* p. 212; Tawney, *Business and Politics,* p. 162. Cranfield was granted the burdensome office of Keeper of the Great Wardrobe on 14 Sept. 1618. *CSPD,* 1611-1618, p. 570.

[27] Coke MSS., packet 21, draft of a letter from Coke to Naunton, 6 Dec. 1618.

that achieved, Coke could be sure that a little forbearance for the present would be amply rewarded in the future.[28]

The working relationship that developed between Buckingham and Coke is well illustrated by the near-comic episode of the three points. The three points were measures that Coke found necessary to eliminate dead ships and dead pays and to prepare for the following year's rebuilding programme. Coke first wrote to Buckingham suggesting that it was imperative to take action on these points.[29] Buckingham responded by sending a nearly verbatim copy of Coke's three suggestions to Naunton along with instructions to the effect that 'his Majesty hath commanded me to signify his pleasure unto you that you give order unto the lords that they put into practice these directions of his Majesty'.[30] Coke's three points were thus transmitted to Naunton in the form of royal instructions that he was directed to place before the Privy Council. Eventually, Coke received back his own recommendations in the form of orders issued to him from the Council. Nor was this the end. Soon afterward Fulke Greville wrote to Buckingham on behalf of the Council to report what had been done in the matter, but he employed Coke to draft the letter for him.[31] To summarize the steps in this episode, Coke told Buckingham what had to be done, Buckingham told the king, the king authorized Buckingham to tell the Council, and finally the Council told Coke what to do. This circuitous route was made necessary by two political facts: first that orders had to proceed downward from the top of the court hierarchy, and second that Coke, who alone knew what orders had to be given, was not at the top but the bottom. Coke's importance should not be

[28]Coke MSS., packet 21, letter in Coke's hand dated 7 Oct. 1618 and endorsed by him, 'The copy of my first letter to the Lord Marquis Buckingham.' Significantly, Coke was notified of Buckingham's favour by Naunton, whose role as intercessor is further indicated by the fact that Coke sent him a copy of this letter (Coke MSS., packet 1, 'Copy of my letter to the Lord Marquis Buckingham, delivered to Mr. Secretary.') The impression that Coke refused pay for his services is based on the following passage: 'Only be pleased (my good lord) to accept my poor service without stipulation. For though by your large offer you express the nobleness and greatness of your mind, yet if I make myself mercenary, I shall condemn myself as unworthy of so ingenuous a patron.' This interpretation is confirmed by a letter written by Coke to Buckingham in 1622. In that letter Coke was declining an offer of £500 per year, and he said 'Nay, ask yourself. . . whether near five years since, when I first had the honour to be known unto you, you did not propound a greater entertainment.' Coke MSS., packet 45, Coke to Buckingham [12 Oct. 1622].

[29]Coke MSS., packet 21. This letter is dated 17 Oct. 1618 and endorsed by Coke, 'Copy of my second letter to the Lord Marquis Buckingham.'

[30]*Cowper MSS.,* I, 101. Coke was evidently kept informed of each stage in the process since this undated letter is endorsed by him, 'Copy of the Lord Marquis Buckingham's letter to Mr. Secretary Naunton. Extracted per Sir Clement Edmonds.'

[31]Coke MSS., packet 21. This undated paper in Coke's hand is endorsed by him, 'Draft of Mr. Chancellor's letter to the Lord Marquis Buckingham.'

exaggerated, however, because the crucial link in the circle was Buckingham. He made the whole process possible by virtue of his influence over James, his willingness to accept Coke's advice, and his desire to appear knowledgeable and forward in reform of the navy.

In the weeks immediately following the commission's report, substantial progress was made in reducing costs, constructing a new dock, and preparing for the building of two new ships the next year.[32] Yet all Coke's work in the fleet would have been worthless if it had not been accompanied by equal progress at court in reforming the naval administration: Buckingham had to replace Lord Admiral Nottingham and the naval commissioners had to replace the principal officers. The first to go was Nottingham. Nearly a year before the naval investigation, it had been suggested that Buckingham might replace the old Lord Admiral, but Buckingham is supposed to have declined on that occasion, pleading his youth and inexperience.[33] If so, Buckingham may simply have thought it was wiser first to promote a full investigation of the navy, realizing that this would discredit the old Lord Admiral and thereby make his own assumption of the post seem more respectable. Certainly Buckingham was no longer tormented by feelings of inadequacy when the commission delivered its report. Although the commissioners scrupulously avoided any direct censure of the eighty-two-year-old Lord Admiral, it was obvious from the day of their report that he had to go, and Buckingham aggressively worked to succeed him. Coke, who was in a unique position to know the political realities of the situation, treated Buckingham as the real head of the navy from the very beginning of their relationship. Nottingham was more reluctant to acknowledge the new realities; he was not easily persuaded to relinquish the office that for thirty-two years had been his.[34] In early October the best that could be agreed upon between Buckingham and Nottingham was a compromise whereby the two would have shared the post as co-admirals, but that was clearly an unsatisfactory arrangement.[35] What finally moved the old Lord

[32]Coke MSS., packet 21. This draft of a letter by Coke to Buckingham is undated, but internal evidence indicates it was written sometime soon after 4 Dec. 1618. Coke's personal initiative is most apparent in his explanation of how he discharged extraneous seamen, persuading the Treasurer of the Navy to provide £5,000 for the purpose.

[33]McClure, *Chamberlain Letters,* II, 118. It was even rumoured that Buckingham had been created a marquis as compensation for declining the Lord Admiral's place. *CSPD,* 1611-1618, p. 511.

[34]I do not agree with the biographers of Nottingham and Buckingham, who imply that the old Lord Admiral left of his own volition. Kenny, *Elizabeth's Admiral,* p. 322; Lockyer, *Buckingham,* p. 50.

[35]*CSPD,* 1611-1618, p. 582; Birch, *The Court and Times of James the First,* II, 92.

Admiral to step down was money. By November he agreed to resign his office in return for an annual pension of £1,000 and an immediate payment of £3,000 in cash from Buckingham.[36] This did little to prevent Nottingham from dying penniless, but it allowed the old man to leave office with a modicum of honour.

Meanwhile Coke was promoting the idea that the naval commissioners should take the place of the principal officers. He was apparently acting as spokesman for the commissioners when he told Buckingham early in October that reform would prove impossible if left in the hands of the current naval officers.[37] He repeated this theme in the letter, already cited, that he drafted on Greville's behalf to Buckingham regarding the three points. In this letter, Coke emphasized: 'That the officers of the navy cannot be made fit instruments to put that in practice which discovereth their shame, and that it much concerneth his Majesty to be well resolved in this point.'[38]

The king's resolution of the issue was finally announced at a meeting of the Privy Council on 2 November, a meeting which must have been every bit as dramatic as the one five weeks earlier when the commissioners' report was initially submitted. The king, Prince Charles, Buckingham, Naunton, and Greville were among those present at the 2 November meeting. Nottingham was not there, but the commissioners and their antagonists, the principal officers, were. The committee of the Council that had been appointed to consider the commission's proposals now endorsed those proposals, and the king concurred. He issued orders that the principal officers 'shall not hence forward meddle any further in that service'. Sir William Russell, who had bought the Treasurership from Mansell, was allowed to remain in office, though his powers were circumscribed by the commission. The Surveyor, Comptroller, and Clerk were sequestered from their offices. This meant that technically they still held their offices because of their patents, but in practice they were forbidden to perform any of the functions of those offices. The actual authority to administer the

[36]*CSPD,* 1611-1618, p. 586; McClure, *Chamberlain Letters,* II, 173, 210; Birch, *The Court and Times of James the First*, II, 134. The figures given by court gossips varied. The ones I have used here were confirmed by later events. In 1626 the second article of impeachment brought against Buckingham by the Commons was that he had bought the office of Lord Admiral for these amounts. Buckingham did not dispute the accuracy of the figures but claimed they were merely voluntary gifts to Nottingham. John Rushworth, ed., *Historical Collections* (7 vols., London, 1659-1701), I, 306-7, 379.

[37]Coke MSS., packet 21, Coke to Buckingham, 17 Oct. 1618.

[38]Coke MSS., packet 21, Coke's draft of Greville's letter to Buckingham, [late October] 1618.

navy passed out of the hands of the principal officers and into the hands of the commissioners.[39]

After the 2 November meeting of the Council, the outcome still remained in some suspense until the king's pleasure could be translated into a legal, written form. Coke helped with the drafting of this commission.[40] It was a delicate matter because the duties and powers of the new commissioners had to be clearly defined without detracting in any way from Buckingham, who, as Lord Admiral, would be their superior. As Coke explained, 'the frame of our commission' should 'not be mistaken as derogatory from the Lord Admiral's power'.[41] By the beginning of December the new commission was drafted.[42] Further progress had also been made in retiring and repairing ships, building a new dock, and paying off unnecessary seamen. Coke sent a long progress report to Buckingham and asked permission to go home after a six-month absence to be with his family 'with purpose by God's favour to return in due time to proceed in this or any other business where my education and studies may make me more able to do his Majesty and your Honour service'.[43] This brief respite in the country came to an end when Buckingham's patent as Lord Admiral passed the seals late in January and he urgently summoned Coke to return.[44] With Buckingham confirmed in his place, etiquette now allowed the commissioners to be confirmed in theirs. On 12 February 1619, the new naval commission was finally issued.[45] By this act, the commissioners for survey of the navy were transformed from a board of inquiry into a board of governors. Now referred to simply as the commissioners of the navy, they had a shorter title but greater power. Taking the place of the sequestered principal officers, they became the navy's official administrators, under the

[39]*APC,* 1618-1619, pp. 288-9. Sir Francis Bacon and Sir Edward Coke were also ordered to examine the officers' patents, and the officers were forbidden to sell reversions to their offices. The terms of sequestration are spelled out in the subsequent commission for the navy. SP 14/105/94. Future officers, said James, would only hold their offices during pleasure, and no reversions would be granted.

[40]Coke MSS., packet 21, Coke to Naunton, Feb. 1619. The Solicitor General, the Attorney General, and Cranfield were also involved.

[41]Coke MSS., packet 21, Coke to Buckingham, 7 Nov. 1618.

[42]S.R. Gardiner, ed., *The Fortescue Papers* (London, 1871), pp. 61-2.

[43]Coke MSS., packet 21, Coke to Buckingham, [*ca.* 4 Dec. 1618].

[44]*Cowper MSS.,* I, 102-3. Coke MSS., packet 113, Greville to Coke, 15 Jan. 1619; packet 1, Edward Reed to Coke, 2 Jan. 1619; packet 21, a draft in Coke's hand endorsed by him: '1618/9. Feb. Copy of my letter to Mr. Secretary Naunton, showed to the king and thereupon I had access to his Majesty at Whitehall.' Buckingham's commission was issued on 28 Jan. *CSPD,* 1619-1623, p. 8.

[45]SP 14/105/94.

Lord Admiral of course, with full authority to implement their programme of reform. The names of the commissioners were listed in the new commission as they had been in the old one, Cranfield's name appearing first, and Coke's tenth. In practice, however, Coke was known to be the chief commissioner. Only eight months after emerging from retirement, Coke had become the principal administrator of the English navy.

Coke naturally took great pleasure in having returned to court so successfully. A few days after the new commission was passed, he wrote with obvious exhilaration to his wife: 'Since my coming, I have been many times with Mr. Secretary and as often with my lord marquis, and twice his lordship hath brought me privately to the king, who vouchsafed in the presence only of the prince, the lord marquis, and Mr Secretary to spend above half an hour with me in debating a matter of great weight.' This and other gestures of confidence gave Coke reason to hope for even further advancement. Buckingham himself bolstered those hopes by appointing Coke and Cranfield to survey his personal estate and advise him how to manage it better. More to the point, as Coke reported to Marie, 'for my better encouragement he hath promised my friends that I shall be one of the next he will endeavour to prefer and hath privately to my self nominated the place to which he designeth me'.[46]

Despite all these encouragements, Coke was destined to be no more than chief commissioner of the navy for the next four years. Whatever the other reasons for this were, the main fact was that he was most useful to Buckingham where he was. There is probably some truth in the story that Buckingham had originally declined to become Lord Admiral because of his inexperience; he did not assume the post until it became obvious that he could rely on Coke and the other commissioners for guidance. No matter how one judges Buckingham's personal performance as Lord Admiral, it must at least be admitted that he recognized the responsibilities of the office and delegated them to capable men. According to Sir Henry Wotten, this was typical of Buckingham, who 'had learned at court... to supply his own defects by the drawing or flowing unto him of the best instruments of experience and knowledge, from whom he had a sweet and attractive manner to suck what might be for the public or his own proper

[46]Coke MSS., packet 1, Coke to Marie, 18 Feb. 1619. Coke's estimate of Buckingham's estate is printed in *Cowper MSS.,* I, 103-4. Greville probably had something more than the naval commision in mind when he told Coke, 'believe me I am confident that he [Buckingham] will bestow you in a place fit for you'. Coke MSS., packet 15, Greville to Coke, [Nov.] 1618.

purpose'.[47] Moreover, both Buckingham and James admitted as much when they insisted in later Parliaments that the royal favourite had purposely compensated for his own lack of experience by relying upon the proved ability of the commissioners.[48] There seems little reason to challenge this explanation. Coke was a fifty-five-year-old veteran of naval affairs when Buckingham made him chief commissioner. In contrast, it is well to remember, as contemporaries did with some misgiving, that the new Lord High Admiral of England was himself only twenty-six years old.[49]

[47] Wotton, *Reliquiae Wottonianiae,* p. 21, quoted in David H. Willson, *King James VI and I* (London, 1956), p. 397.

[48] In 1621 King James told Parliament that 'many would have thought I would have chosen an old experienced soldier'. But Buckingham, said James, 'though himself had not so much experience, yet he chose such commissioners who by their skill and his own industry hath brought things to this good pass as they are'. Defending himself against impeachment in 1626, Buckingham said, 'he would not rely upon his judgement or ability, but of himself humbly besought his then Majesty to settle a Commission of fit and able persons for the Affairs of the Navy; by whose Council and assistance, he might mannage that weighty business with the best advantage for his Majesties Service; which Commission was granted, and yet continueth, and without the advice of those Commissioners, he hath never done any thing of moment'. Wallace Notestein *et al,* eds., *Commons Debates, 1621* (7 vols., New Haven, 1935), II, 9; Rushworth, *Historical Collections,* I, 379.

[49] The Venetian ambassador observed and shared in the general apprehension that attended Buckingham's assumption of the Lord Admiralship: 'His Majesty has deposed the old admiral and substituted for him, with full powers, the Marquis of Buckingham, a youth. . . whose personal beauty and spirit together with the King's favour render him the chief authority in everything, and the entire Court obeys his will. . . . Accordingly people speak variously about what results or what steadiness can be expected in carrying out such an important matter.' *CSPV,* XV, 486.

5

A SURVEY OF THE COMMISSIONER

This book began with a question: What sort of man was Sir John Coke? We have now seen enough of Coke to begin to answer that question, and pausing here to take some measure of the man will put us in a better position to understand the twenty-five years of his life that still lie ahead. Besides, the events of 1618 raise serious questions about the sort of man Coke was. How can the chief commissioner of the navy and eager client of Buckingham be the same man at heart who for fourteen years had forsaken and condemned the court? Did the country gentleman from Herefordshire reveal his true character by resuming the life of a courtier? Was he an opportunist, a hypocrite, a sycophant?

Coke's return to court readily lends itself to a cynical interpretation. In 1604 he was a bitter man expelled from office, and naturally he took a dim view of the victors while licking his wounds in Herefordshire. Then, in 1618, he looks very much like a man who settled the score with his old enemies and suddenly decided that the court was not such a bad place after all. But this interpretation is too cynical to represent all, or even the most important, truth. Coke's condemnation of the court arose from principle as well as spite. What made the triumph of men like Nottingham and Mansell so especially galling to him was the fact that it constituted a triumph for rapaciousness and neglect of the king's service. Coke never objected to the court itself but rather to the degenerate state into which he believed it had sunk in the hands of men like these. As we saw, he passed up opportunities to move nearer the court as long as he was convinced that the prevailing tenor of the court was unchanged. When the court did at last appear to be changing, Coke was able to return on his own terms. One might argue that 'reform' in 1618 was simply a pretext for the triumph of one faction over another or that, where Coke was concerned, the truly important difference between the Howards and Buckingham was simply that the former did not like him and the latter did. But from Coke's vantage point this was not the way it looked. Coke's industry, his attention to detail, his penchant for organizing and economizing — all qualities he had in common with Cranfield — finally seemed to be appreciated. Viewed this way, Coke did not have to compromise or abandon his principles to rejoin the court because now those very principles were at least temporarily in vogue.

One aspect of Coke's character accentuated by the events of

1618 was his ambition. Obviously he did not return to favour against his will. Even in his retirement he had harboured a suppressed desire to be back amid the power and excitement of the court; and once there, he clearly relished his new-found importance. Coke was ambitious, but, on the other hand, his ambition was seriously tempered by several factors. For one thing, experience had been a cruel teacher. He had good reason to reflect that 'all the things of this world, and especially matters of court, are most uncertain and subject daily to change, so as no settled foundation can be built upon them'.[1] Aware of those uncertainties, he protected himself by modifying his expectations against disappointment and limiting his trust to those things which he knew could be relied upon. Hall Court epitomized that attitude. It was Coke's refuge, a place where a man's own hard work might bring him a reasonable degree of security and happiness if he only learned not to expect or hope for too much. Naunton acknowledged this fact when, in a letter to Coke, he referred to Hall Court as 'so contentful a retreat as you there have raised against a storm'.[2] When Coke himself looked back over that period of seclusion, he characterized it in this way: 'My life of late years hath been retired. I have not much applied myself to the times, nor affected any higher stage, nor hoped for better opportunity to give account of myself than in a private fortune.'[3] The events of 1618 radically changed that modest way of life and reawakened Coke's ambition, but they could not alter his habits of mind. He remained, both by nature and experience, conservative, wary, and deeply distrustful of the ephemeral political world. Even after he became chief commissioner of the navy, he cautioned Marie: 'You know the state of my mind, that it is not easily transported by the appearances of the world. The same resolution I commend also to you, that whether we settle or change, our moderate desires may find a constant contentment.'[4]

Coke's ambition and his attitude toward the court were both affected by his more basic ethical convictions. There is no doubt about it, he was a stern moralist. His capacity for moral indignation is obvious in his condemnation of the court under the Howards, but it did not require transgressors on that scale to offend Coke's sensibilities. In smaller matters he complained just as strongly: 'I hear both in country and court that tobacco, wine, and good fellowship have so transported most students in our university [Cambridge] that her sister [Oxford]

[1]Coke MSS., packet 1, Coke to Marie, 18 Feb. 1619.

[2]Coke MSS., packet 1, Naunton to Coke, 11 Jan. 1618.

[3]Coke MSS., packet 21, Coke to Buckingham, 7 Oct. 1618.

[4]Coke MSS., packet 1, Coke to Marie, 18 Feb. 1619.

beginneth to get the start of reputation in the world.' To Coke — a Cambridge man all his life — this was a 'scandalous imputation'.[5] Not surprisingly, he had some strait-laced sentiments on the subject of swearing, too. As he once told his son, 'howsoever swearing be grown such a common vice that most men are tame unto it, yet I have ever esteemed it a great favour of God that it hath not gotten ground upon my house; and I shall both pray and do my best always to keep it out'.[6] Amid the multitude of temptations surrounding the court, Coke remained uncommonly pious, grave, and temperate to the end.[7]

Coke's ethical convictions extended beyond the realm of private morality and influenced his view of public service. He was a firm believer in the work-ethic; few things were more repugnant to him than laziness. Sloth and pride, he wrote, are 'the quicksands of young men's minds', but he found sloth particularly noxious because it was 'the mother of all vice'.[8] If distinguished by little else, Coke was eminently hard-working and diligent. Even Clarendon, who had little else good to say about him, conceded that: 'His cardinal perfection was industry.'[9] Such industry, if not possessed in great measure by the king and his favourites, was all the more valued in their followers. After all, someone had to do the routine work of government, and that fact alone accounts in large part for Coke's rise at court and longevity there. Coke's attitude toward his employment was more than the simple, negative concept that 'the Devil finds work for idle hands'. It also encompassed the more positive belief that work should in itself be a form of religious expression. Coke believed that God 'will require an account' for the talents he has given us.[10] And this accountability to God required more of man than formal worship confined to church or the sabbath. A man's faith, said Coke, should be evident in his 'love of good works and duties' and practised 'in his vocation and place of his charge'.[11] Coke also believed in the closely related concept of a 'calling'. Soon after returning to court, when his future had seemed promising but still uncertain, he told Naunton that 'it maketh me lift up mine eyes to God's hand who hath stirred you up to be the means,

[5]Coke MSS., packet 69, Coke to Dr Richardson of Trinity College [1615].

[6]Coke MSS., packet 83, Coke to son John [1637].

[7]David Lloyd (*State Worthies,* II, 262) observed, 'his contemporaries character him a grave and a prudent man in gate, apparel, and speech'.

[8]*Cowper MSS.,* I, 76.

[9]*History of the Rebellion,* I, 81. One of Coke's friends paid him the same compliment more quaintly in calling him 'thou sluggard of intelligence'. *Cowper MSS.,* I, 47.

[10]*Cowper MSS.,* I, 76.

[11]Coke MSS., packet 1, Coke to Marie, 1 July 1606.

either to draw me to some employment wherein by his power my weakness may yield some better fruit of my life, or else to assure me that without guiltiness I may possess the rest of my days where he hath planted me already in a contented estate. In either, how humbly I submit myself to his good will and pleasure, he only knoweth.'[12] Such was the quality of faith that underlay Coke's work and made malversation in office so abhorrent to him. This is not to say that Coke's own conduct was always above reproach. What cannot be denied him, however, is that he was an honest and devout man who sincerely believed that a place at court was, in his own words, 'a stage to do good'.[13]

Much of Coke's temperament can probably be traced to his prolonged and rigorous education. Clarendon suggested this when he described Coke as 'a man of a very narrow education, and a narrower nature; having continued long in the university of Cambridge, where he had gotten Latin learning enough'.[14] These words were really meant by Clarendon to imply that Coke stayed too long at Cambridge and got too much Latin learning, an opinion shared by Sir John Eliot, one of Coke's harshest critics, who observed that 'his conversation being with bookes, & that to teach not studie them, men & business were subiectes wch he knew not, & his expressions were more proper for a schoole, then for a State & councell'.[15] Eliot hated Coke for several reasons we shall see in time, and here perhaps he was speaking from envy because his own university education had been cut short by the death of his father.[16] Nevertheless, this particular criticism may contain some truth. Coke's prose and his speeches in Parliament have a studied, didactic quality about them. His mind, though not as obtuse as it is usually portrayed, was methodical. His behaviour, unlike Eliot's, was rarely spontaneous and never the least flamboyant. He was too deliberate to indulge in or understand the theatrical flair that Eliot employed so effectively. Coke also lacked boldness, observing instead his own maxim that: 'I ever held it safest in matters of government rather to improve the received ordinary ways than to adventure upon any innovation.'[17] It is true that he could be combative when required, but he was not by nature aggressive. At heart he was a mild man who

[12]Coke MSS., packet 21, Coke to Naunton, 6 Dec. 1618.

[13]Coke MSS., packet 69, Coke to Naunton [*ca.* Jan. 1618].

[14]*History of the Rebellion,* I, 80.

[15]*Negotium Posterorum,* I, 114.

[16]Harold Hulme, *The Life of Sir John Eliot, 1592-1632* (New York, 1957), pp. 22-5. I am grateful to Conrad Russell for the very perceptive point about Eliot's education.

[17]Coke MSS., packet 22, Coke to Buckingham, 30 July 1622.

preferred not to risk hurt or loss. One need only recall how profoundly the events of 1604 had dispirited him. And if the successes of 1618 made him a victorious naval reformer, beneath the surface he was still, in R.H. Tawney's words, a 'wrathful dove'.[18] Indeed, with his distaste for factionalism and intrigue, Coke sometimes seems too ingenuous, even gullible, to have survived at court. As a courtier, then, Coke was more remarkable for the qualities he lacked than for those he possessed. As Clarendon put it, he 'was a man rather unadorn'd with any parts of vigour and quickness, and unendow'd with any notable virtues, than notorious for any weakness or defect of understanding, or transported with any vicious inclinations'.[19] Coke thus displayed few attributes that were likely to make him either a great hero or a great villain in the pages of history. Instead, he was exceedingly industrious, deliberate, thorough, and methodical. These are probably the characteristics Eliot had most in mind, the mundane characteristics of a scholar-turned-bureaucrat.[20] They help to explain why Coke always excelled as a bookkeeper and administrator but was unable in his later years either to inspire Parliament or to prevent his own place at court from being reduced to that of a functionary.

All this does not lead inescapably to the conclusion that Coke was just a narrow-minded pedant. If Coke had not possessed finer qualities of mind and character, he would hardly have become Fulke Greville's dearest friend next to the famous Sir Philip Sidney. Nor would Greville have sought Coke's advice on the composition of his poetry, as we know in fact he did.[21] Eliot's charge that Coke was too much an academician can be countered in several ways. It is true that Coke attached great value to the world of learning. He did on one occasion admonish a wayward student to 'utterly abandon your town and field companions and converse more with the dead than the living'.[22] On another occasion, however, he advised a young man: 'I could wish you so to study your books that you neglect not rather to converse with men, but proportion your times for both, that the knowledge you get out of good authors may teach you rules to understand men, and the practice of men may store you with

[18]*Business and Politics,* p. 161.

[19]This quotation is taken from the 1707 edition of Clarendon's *History of the Rebellion,* vol. I, pt. 1, p. 64. Clarendon also said Coke 'never had quickness from his Cradle'. *Ibid*., p. 122.

[20]Compare Willson, *Privy Councillors,* pp. 95-6.

[21]Rebholz, *Fulke Greville,* pp. 65, 66 n. 37. Norman Farmer, Jr. ('Fulke Greville and Sir John Coke', p. 218) said Coke's 'performance as a literary critic proves as competent and sensitive as it is methodical and informed'.

[22]*Cowper MSS.*, I, 77.

examples for the rules of books. And as I advise you to study books and man, the one to make you learned and the other wise, so especially I exhort you to study your self.'[23] Coke's mind was not a prisoner to an ivory-tower world. He succeeded far too well at court and in business, both the Crown's and his own, to be as naive about these things as Eliot would have us believe. Finally, if Coke did think and express himself in ways that were more appropriate to the university than to the political bodies of his day, does that constitute a criticism of Coke or of those bodies? A fair reply to this question would have to balance the cold disdain of Eliot with the warm admiration of Dr Richardson, Master of Trinity College, who implored Coke to return to the university. 'Certainly you may be more useful to your country in these parts', Richardson told Coke, 'than in that barren Ithaca, whose smoke is not worthy the affection you bear unto it.'[24]

Turning now from Coke's overall character or temperament to his more formal views on religion and politics, it is important to remember that he lived the first forty years of his life in the reign of Elizabeth, and fifteen out of those forty years at Trinity College in the shadow of Archbishop Whitgift. This meant above all that church and state were inseparably linked in Coke's mind. Separation of church and state was unthinkable, he once declared, because 'to separate is to betray'.[25] Furthermore, unity between church and state was dependent upon unity within the church. If uniformity could not be enforced within the church, then Coke believed that religious controversy would lead inevitably to political controversy, and the stability of the state would be jeopardized. It was therefore Coke's indivisible allegiance to the established church and state that caused him to abhor what he called 'factious and scandalous separatists' and to denounce 'private conventicles' as part of a 'factious doctrine which the unseasoned zeal of some' had brought to England and which now threatened 'instead of reforming to ruin our church'.[26] At a later point in his career, when he drafted the instructions for England's new ambassador to the United Provinces, Coke was writing on behalf of the king, perhaps under the eye of Laud, but surely he agreed in stating that England's policy toward the Dutch should be 'to prevent all

[23] Coke MSS., packet 1, draft by Coke to Roger Manners, 5 May 1602. In another letter much later in his life, Coke again extolled 'the profit and pleasure that by a mixture of studies and employments may ensue'. Coke MSS., packet 81, Coke to his son John, 24 Aug. 1634.

[24] Coke MSS., packet 1, Dr John Richardson to Coke, 13 Nov. 1615.

[25] Coke MSS., packet 15, Coke to Greville, 16 Sept. 1615.

[26] SP 16/233/4; Coke MSS., packet 1, Coke to Marie, 1 July 1606.

occasions which might tend to their division, which for the most part maketh her entrance by the church'. In the same vein, he desired the Dutch 'to keep their profession entire and not to give way to disputations which may engender strife, nor promiscuously to allow all kinds of religions to the scandal of their government, and especially not to suffer our sectarie fugitives to plant themselves there and by scandalous pamphlets sent from thence to defame our church government'.[27] Coke had all the more reason to protect the established church government of England when, partly through his own influence, his brother became a bishop.

We know, then, that Coke ardently supported the Church of England, disliked 'scandalous separatists', and was wary of 'unseasoned zeal'. Yet Coke has sometimes been described as a puritan. How can this be? There are several grounds on which Coke could conceivably be called a puritan, all depending of course on how one chooses to define that slippery term. First there is the obvious fact that Coke's stern morality (his aversion to swearing, smoking, and drinking, for example) was in the loosest sense of the word 'puritanical'. But this is certainly too loose a definition; using the term thus might lead one to suspect that Charles I was a puritan.[28] Secondly, there is the fact that Coke's attitude toward work resembles the famous Protestant work-ethic. To be sure, Coke does part company with Charles on this score, but the work-ethic was hardly a monopoly of the puritans (or, for that matter, the Protestants). A third argument might seem more conclusive than the previous two: Coke was a Calvinist. Although Coke's austere morality and attitude toward work are not sufficient in themselves to establish his Calvinism, these can be augmented by the fact that he supported the Calvinist Synod of Dort; and the New Testament from which his children were taught at home was the Latin version by Theodore Beza, Calvin's successor.[29] But Coke could have been a Calvinist without being a puritan, especially if the Church of England's own doctrine was basically Calvinist.[30] This brings us, however, to a fourth argument that is closely related but more concrete: Coke appears to be a puritan because of his conduct at the York House conference in 1626. At this conference Coke allied with other supposed puritans to defend the doctrine of predestination against the Arminian doctrine of Richard Montague. His behaviour

[27] SP 84/144/fol. 164v.

[28] Richard Ollard, *The Image of the King: Charles I and Charles II* (New York, 1979), p. 40.

[29] *Cowper MSS.*, I, 132. For the Synod of Dort, see below regarding the York House conference.

[30] J.P. Kenyon, *Stuart England* (Harmondsworth, 1978), p. 24.

on this occasion has convinced some historians that he belonged to 'the Puritan party at court'.[31] It is true that the basic record of the York House conference does show him at one point speaking decisively against Montague's Arminianism.[32] Moreover, Coke continued during the 1630s to favour Montague's chief critic at the conference, Bishop Morton.[33] This evidence arising from the York House conference would indeed seem to make Coke a puritan — if the conference were not open to a different interpretation. But an alternative interpretation argues that the Arminians were the real innovators at the conference, and they tried to malign their opponents by branding them puritans. The Arminians wished to make it seem that anyone who advocated the doctrine of predestination was a puritan innovator, whereas in fact it was the Arminians themselves who were the innovators in a church that had officially embraced predestination during the previous sixty years.[34] If this interpretation is true, then Coke was no more a puritan than other traditional adherents to predestination and the Church of England (John Pym, for example) who suddenly found themselves on the defensive.[35] A fifth ground for considering Coke a puritan was his deep-seated hatred of Roman Catholicism. For Coke, the Pope was Antichrist, Jesuits were an ever — present menace, and Spain was a natural enemy. This cluster of biases can be called 'radical Protestantism', as has been done in the case of Sir Fulke Greville, and the description would seem to apply equally well to Coke.[36] Yet many of Coke's contemporaries, particularly Catholics, were quick to equate this cluster of biases with something else, namely puritanism.[37] Coke was fervently anti-Catholic throughout his life, but this fervour became more conspicuous by comparison with other courtiers in the 1630s. When viewed through the eyes of Catholic sources from the 1630s, he does appear to be 'the Puritan Secretary of State'.[38]

[31] Irvonwy Morgan, *Prince Charles's Puritan Chaplain* (London, 1957), pp. 26-7, 56-8, 60, 141, 160-2, 166, 186; Christopher Hill, *Puritanism and Revolution* (New York, 1958), p. 243.

[32] John Cosin, *The Works of the Right Reverend Father in God John Cosin, Lord Bishop of Durham,* ed. J. Sansom (5 vols., Oxford, 1843-55), II, 38, 47, 63.

[33] *Cowper MSS.,* I, 444; II, 84, 160, 245, 246, 249. Coke patronized a man approved by Morton as vicar of Melbourne. For Morton see *DNB,* XIII, 1057-62.

[34] Nicholas Tyacke, 'Puritanism, Arminianism and Counter-Revolution' in Russell, *Origins of the English Civil War,* pp. 130-4.

[35] Conrad Russell, 'The Parliamentary Career of John Pym, 1621-9' in Peter Clark *et al,* eds., *The English Commonwealth 1547-1640* (Leicester, 1979), pp. 159-65.

[36] Rebholz, *Fulke Greville,* pp. 19-20, 26-31.

[37] Christopher Hill, *Society and Puritanism in Pre-Revolutionary England* (New York, 1967), pp. 14-16.

[38] Gordon Albion, *Charles I and the Court of Rome* (Louvain, 1935), p. 163; Joseph Berington, ed., *The Memoirs of Gregorio Panzani* (Westmead, 1970), pp. 153-4.

There is too much about Coke's religious views that we do not know. We do not know his opinion on specific questions of ceremony and doctrine that would clarify his overall position. We do not know who his favourite preachers were.[39] We do not even have a last will and testament. This ignorance alone should caution us against attaching a label to Coke's name.[40] Moreover, any label, no matter how subtle, is a stereotype. And no stereotypical view of Coke is likely to do justice to the complex, real man that he was. Three aspects of his religion that are particularly apt to be overlooked are his moderation, his pragmatism, and his tolerance. Coke's moderation is evident on the subject of predestination. His belief in predestination was not of the extreme sort that led to haughty self-assurance. As we saw earlier, he still attached considerable importance to a 'love of good works and duties', believing that God 'will require an account', presumably even from the elect. Coke's moderation and pragmatism were both evident in his behaviour at court. He was never so obsessed by his faith that it blinded him to political considerations. Unlike some, he did not abandon Buckingham after the York House conference; and he continued to work harmoniously with Archbishop Laud throughout the 1630s even though, as Clarendon said, Coke 'loved the church well enough as it was twenty years before'.[41] Again we are reminded that Coke's view of religion and the world was shaped in the reign of Elizabeth. The darker side of that view was a hatred of Roman Catholicism, which for Coke, as for Elizabeth, constituted a simultaneous threat to both church and state. The brighter side was the hope of a broad-minded, comprehensive church that could accommodate all but the most malignant spirits. If Coke never stopped hating, neither did he stop hoping. This was particularly evident in 1634, when he spoke in the Court of Star Chamber at the trial of one of the most famous puritans, William Prynne. To Coke's way of thinking, Prynne was an extremist, a misanthrope with no charity for his fellow man. Coke compared Prynne to a 'fiery spirit' full of 'nothing but damnation and destruction'. By contrast, Coke preferred what he called 'a good Spirit that is meek, tempered with modesty and humility, with mildness and with equity. . . always tender, not to destroy, root up, overthrow, but to bind, repair and

[39]Of course Irvonwy Morgan would include John Preston among Coke's favourite preachers, and there is some evidence that Coke approved of William Bradshaw. Samuel Clarke, *Martyrologie* (London, 1652), appendix, p. 107.

[40]The subtlest label available is 'moderate puritan', devised by Peter Lake to explain people like Coke who 'defy classification according to the conventional labels'. 'Robert Some and the Ambiguities of Moderation', *Archive for Reformation History,* 71 (1980), 254.

[41]*History of the Rebellion,* I, 161.

preserve'. Throughout Coke's speech there ran one theme: toleration. Coke affirmed that 'there must be a toleration in all states', and he concluded, prophetically, that a state without some degree of toleration would destroy itself.[42]

Shifting the emphasis now from Coke's religious views to his political views, the two remain intimately related to one another, and the formative influence of Coke's forty years under Elizabeth is still evident. Politics and religion merged in Coke's mind to form what has been called 'the Elizabethan world picture'.[43] Shakespeare immortalized that world view in the famous speech of Ulysses:

> The heavens themselves, the planets, and this centre
> Observe degree, priority, and place,
> Insisture, course, proportion, season, form,
> Office, and custom, in all line of order.[44]

Ulysess asserted that the political world was intended by God to follow the same rules of harmony, order, and hierarchy as did the physical universe. And Coke would have agreed. He devoutly believed particularly in the principle of hierarchy and in the importance of deference toward that hierarchy. Coke came uncannily close to the sentiments of Ulysses when he wrote to Buckingham:

> That in bodies politic as well as natural, the parts must have a symmetry and proportion to the head. That this proportion in kingdoms requireth a subordination of officers and magistrates. . . and that therefore the Lord Admiral as a chief officer of state receiving his virtue and motion from the first mover, the king, must thereby move and guide all others contained in his orb.[45]

A political philosophy of this sort was plainly conservative and authoritarian. Subordination to one's superiors in a divinely ordained natural order of things left little room for criticism. Coke was trained to accept authority, even to revere it, but not to question it. All legitimate authority, he believed, derived from the king. Of course, no one would have agreed more with these sentiments than King James himself. Indeed, it would be difficult to distinguish between the political theory of King James and Coke's unequivocal declaration:

> This then we must build upon, as an axiom and fundamental rule of government: that all our laws and statutes are the king's laws. . .

[42] T.B. Howell, ed., *Cobbett's Complete Collection of State Trials* (33 vols., London, 1809-26), III, 580-2.

[43] E.M.W. Tillyard, *The Elizabethan World Picture* (London, 1943).

[44] *Troilus and Cressida,* act I, scene iii.

[45] Coke MSS., packet 21, Coke to Buckingham, 7 Nov. 1618.

> all courts of law or equity are properly the king's courts; all justice. . . all dignities, all degrees, all titles, arms, and orders, come originally from the king, as branches from the root. . . all corporations, societies, nay counties, provinces, and depending kingdoms, have all their jurisdictions and governments established by him; and by him (for public good) to be changed or dissolved.[46]

Coke's parenthetical reference to the 'public good' near the end of this passage is the only hint to the modern reader that this sweeping assertion of royal power was in any way qualified. Beneath his words lay the unspoken assumption that the king would govern within the bounds of law and tradition. In 1628, after Charles I had exceeded those bounds, we shall see that Coke did not waver in support of the king, but he did characterize the government's conduct as 'illegal', he did assure the Commons that 'our liberties are our birthrights', and he did describe the common law as 'our inheritance that does preserve us'.[47] More important, at the very end of his life, Coke even came to realize that the king's conduct could actually run counter to the public good.

Because Coke viewed the political order in such a hierarchical fashion, and because he occupied a station nearer the top than the bottom of that hierarchy, he was particularly concerned to prevent the draining away of power from the head to the lower members of the body politic. On the concrete level of daily action, this led Coke to consolidate and defend the power of his immediate master against the encroachment of subordinate officials. Of course political philosophy conveniently meshed here with personal gain. It was to their mutual advantage that Coke guarded the prerogatives of his patron jealously. Such personal loyalty had long underlain his relationship with Greville, and it quickly came to characterize his relationship with Buckingham. This was evident in his concern to draft the new naval commission in words that could not be interpreted as infringing the Lord Admiral's power. It was evident, too, when he urged Buckingham to prohibit the sale of offices and reversions in the navy, thereby giving the Lord Admiral exclusive control over all these offices. In support of this proposal, Coke asked Buckingham to consider that 'the Lord Admiral's greatness is not to have a market under him of base and unworthy people. . . but his true and real greatness is the power and greatness of the king, the confidence of his favour, the trust of his

[46] William Laud, *The Works of the Most Reverend Father in God, William Laud, Sometime Lord Archbishop of Canterbury,* ed. James Bliss and William Scott (7 vols., Oxford, 1847-60), vol. V, part 1, 127.

[47] See below, chapter eleven.

service, and the reputation and flourishing estate of the navy'.[48] As much as a year later Coke expressed his continued determination 'to restore the Lord Admiral's authority in disposing of all places of the navy to honest and able men'.[49] At the end of Elizabeth's reign, when Nottingham was still at the helm, Coke had called the Lord Admiral's monopoly of offices one of the 'principal and original causes of all disorders in the navy'. Does this mean that Coke objected to the Lord Admiral's monopoly of power only when the Lord Admiral was his enemy and that he praised this same concentration of power when the Lord Admiral was Buckingham, his ally and patron? In one respect, the answer to this question is no. As Coke saw it, what caused corruption was not just the concentration of all naval offices in the Lord Admiral's hands but, rather, that concentration combined with the practice of venality. Coke was consistent in opposing venality no matter who the Lord Admiral was. Yet in another sense, the answer to this question is yes. Coke had changed his position. He thought that Buckingham, unlike Nottingham, could be trusted to fill offices with 'honest and able men' on the basis of merit. Coke might seem naive in trusting in Buckingham this much, but it was not a wholly unreasonable thing to do in 1619, and, practically speaking, it was the only choice Coke had. Of course the long-term solution was to replace personal patronage with an impersonal merit system. And that solution would actually have been more in harmony with Coke's basic predisposition because he always preferred, where it was possible, to put his trust in rules instead of men.

Still, the extent to which Coke exalted his superiors, the servility that characterized his behaviour toward them, will strike most modern readers as repugnant. Why was Coke so obsequious? One reason Coke acted the way he did was that he knew the price of insubordination. The two most traumatic political events of his early life had been the execution of Essex and the expulsion of Greville from court. Coke must have learned from these two events that excommunication from the court or even death waited in ambush for the courtier who stepped too far out of line. Conversely, though his own experience in this respect was limited to his relationship with Greville, Coke must also have known how abundant were the rewards that lay in store for the courtier who practised compliance. When Coke returned to court in 1618, these lessons were not lost on him. Viewed this way, then, he became a sycophant because he had learned that only sycophancy

[48] Coke MSS., packet 21, Coke to Buckingham, 7 Nov. 1618.

[49] Coke MSS., packet 21, draft of a letter by Coke on behalf of the commissioners of the navy to Buckingham, 24 Oct. 1619.

would get him what he wanted. Because historians have generally been unaware of the stinging failure and rejection Coke experienced in 1604, they have not viewed his sycophancy in later life from this perspective. They have had little reason to suspect that he knew what he was doing, that he realized how tenuous was his hold on the court, and that he sedulously observed the stringent rules of court decorum because he uniquely understood that his political life depended upon it. This may not make Coke's sycophancy more palatable, but it does make it more intelligible. By the same token, Coke's sycophancy cannot be understood on its own terms if we insist on treating it from an uncompromisingly idealistic perspective, as if it were something totally contemptible and absent from our own lives. Of course sycophancy at the early Stuart court was carried to an extreme, but surely it was different only in degree from the flattery and abject loyalty expected in many modern businesses, political organizations, and, for that matter, universities. Few modern readers who are gainfully employed will find this behaviour altogether alien to their own experience. In this connection, it is interesting to note how S.R. Gardiner's opinion of Coke changed over time. Gardiner first described Coke as 'a mere tool, ready to do anything or to say anything as he was bidden'.[50] Years later in his famous *History of England,* Gardiner, perhaps made wise by his own experience, was slightly more charitable toward Coke. 'Honourable as he was in all the private relations of life', Gardiner wrote of Coke, 'he had early imbibed the official view that he was to obey orders, not to criticise them, and he was therefore ready to carry out any policy which approved itself to Buckingham and the King.'[51] Gardiner now understood servility was a mode of behaviour Coke had 'imbibed' from his surroundings rather than an inherent weakness of character. In other words, Coke was not born to servility; he was trained to it by masters who made it a condition of court office that their orders be obeyed, not criticized. This was the point missed entirely by C.H. Firth when he solemnly and Whiggishly observed of Coke: 'The servility which stains his public career was inseparable from the theory of absolutism which he professed.'[52] The real point is that without servility, Coke would have had no public career at all, stained or otherwise.

At least in part, then, Coke's servility was a product of necessity, a matter of expediency, adaptive behaviour he had learned from harsh

[50] *A History of England under the Duke of Buckingham and Charles I, 1624-1628,* I, 228.

[51] *History of England,* V, 370-1.

[52] *DNB,* IV, 702.

experience. He knew that if he gave his masters what they wanted (hard work, flattery, loyalty, and obedience), they in turn would give him what he wanted (status, wealth, power, and a sense of worth). But this, of course, is not the whole story. There is another, subtler, sense in which C.H. Firth's judgement of Coke contains a residue of insight: Coke's servility was in some measure related to what Firth called 'the theory of absolutism which he professed'. Usually Coke seems totally sincere in his flattery, no matter how effusive. This could be a tribute to his skill as a dissembler, but it is just as likely a tribute, as Firth suggests, to the tenacity of his faith. Coke was too much a realist to believe that the political world around him was perfect; certainly he had no such illusion while the Howard family dominated the court. He obviously objected to the performance of individual office-holders within the political structure, but he never questioned the legitimacy of that structure itself. Basically he wanted very much to believe in the established political structure. He was much more inclined to place his hope in that structure than to be critical of it, much more inclined to think the best rather than the worst of men like Buckingham, James I, and Charles I. Once his own self-interest became associated with the established political structure, Coke found it doubly difficult to view that structure critically. Then both his self-interest and his ideological biases combined to make him see his patron and his king in as favourable a light as possible. Numerous other Englishmen, not just Coke, viewed the political order in this same wishful fashion. Though a more empirical and cynical view of politics was emerging, to be sure, Englishmen at the beginning of the seventeenth century still tended to romanticize the established political order. It required perhaps more faith to idolize James I and Buckingham than to idolize Elizabeth I and Sir Philip Sidney, but the will to believe was far from extinguished. Coke was not alone in wanting to believe that his masters were worthy of the loyalty he gave them. Viewed this way, then, Coke's servility was not so much a product of crass pragmatism as of stubborn idealism. If Coke perceived the disparity between the real monarchy and the ideal that supported it, then he worked all the harder for the realization of that ideal. Only after thirty years of work under three different monarchs did Coke finally admit to himself 'that kings cannot be served against their wills', that the gulf could not be bridged between what he wanted to be true and what he knew to be true.[53]

[53] Coke MSS., packet 65, Coke to his son John [1641].

6

DOUBTFUL REFORMS: 1619-1622

When Coke became chief commissioner of the navy in 1619, he and the other commissioners had five years in which to achieve what they had promised – principally, to reduce the annual charge of the navy from over £50,000 to £30,000 while augmenting the fleet by two new ships each year. These were ambitious goals, but the same advantages that had made the commission's early success possible were still working in its favour. One great advantage enjoyed by the commissioners was the fact that they themselves were now in charge. The removal of Nottingham, Mansell, and the principal officers had been in itself a momentous improvement. Cranfield and Buckingham understood that reform could not be entrusted to the men who had made it necessary. Cranfield followed that principle when he became Master of the Wardrobe, and Buckingham adhered to it by making himself Lord Admiral, sequestering the principal officers, and placing naval administration in the hands of Coke and the other commissioners. A second advantage of the commission was Coke's leadership. Probably no other post he held during his long career was better suited to his knowledge and abilities. Certainly he was the commanding member and driving spirit of the commission, and no one appreciated that fact more than his opponents, one of whom ruefully observed, 'of their number the first & principall was Sr John Coke. . . the rest were but cyphers unto him'.[1] The third and greatest advantage of the commission was undoubtedly the support they continued to receive from Buckingham. Coke reminded the new Lord Admiral of his responsibility in this respect by recalling: 'What opposition we endured and what envy was cast upon us for our propositions. . . is best known to your lordship, by whose favour and protection we were encouraged to proceed.' Now that the commissioners had proceeded in their work, they were more than ever dependent on the marquis for protection. The problem, as Coke described it, was that 'our service is very distasteful, not only to the late officers and all their adherents, but to other dissolute and ill-disposed persons who in the former corruptions got their livings with more ease'.[2] The legion of parasites who had

[1]Eliot, *Negotium Posterorum,* II, 6-7. See also Tawney, *Business and Politics,* pp. 171-2; G.E. Aylmer, 'Attempts at Administrative Reform, 1625-40', *English Historical Review*, 72 (April 1957), 234; Oppenheim, *Royal Navy,* pp. 195-6. Coke spoke with full authority for the commission, often drafting its letters himself. See, for example, *Cowper MSS.,* I, 104, 106, 107, 110, 114-17.

[2]Coke MSS., packet 21, draft of a letter by Coke on behalf of the commissioners to Buckingham, 24 Oct. 1619.

formerly drawn their sustenance from the navy now seized every opportunity to attack and discredit the commission. For example, the commission's effort to reduce the size of crews was particularly opposed by the captains, who previously had profited from inflated allowances. Coke, who had to defend the commission's action to Buckingham, charged that the smaller crews would be more than adequate if only the captains would go aboard their ships and discharge their own duties more often.[3] Nor did the commission's opponents always confine themselves to a harmless exchange of arguments. One malcontent threatened to kill William Burrell, the commissioner and shipwright in charge of building the new ships.[4] Another, the expelled Comptroller of the Navy, reportedly instructed a servant to tell Coke 'that he hath done me wrong and that if he do me not right I will shoot him with a pistol'.[5] Obviously the commissioners were safe only so long as Buckingham stood between them and the wrath of their enemies. Coke spoke for the whole commission when he told the Lord Admiral, 'under your favourable aspect and government, [we] hope to bring the navy in short time to that flourishing estate that after ages shall take knowledge of your name by the honourable title. . . of the Restorer thereof'.[6]

Threats and opposition notwithstanding, the commission's programme proceeded according to schedule. In November of 1619, the

[3]Coke MSS., packet 21, draft of a letter by Coke on behalf of the commissioners to Buckingham, March 1619. Compare Coke's draft of a larger, fifteen-page defence signed by all the commissioners and delivered to Buckingham on 15 July 1619 (Coke MSS., packet 113). See also SP 14/109/139. The commission's proposal to reduce the size of crews was the one part of their programme that the Privy Council deferred for further consideration. *APC,* 1618-1619, p. 289. Sir Francis Bacon told Buckingham, 'the number allowed by the commissioners had in my judgement a little of the merchant'. James Spedding, ed., *The Letters and the Life of Francis Bacon* (6 vols., London, 1872) VI, 341. Still, the reduction seems to have been implemented. McGowan, *Jacobean Commissions,* p. xxvi.

[4]Coke MSS., packet 21, draft of Coke's letter on behalf of the commissioners to Buckingham, 24 Oct. 1619.

[5]SP 14/160/41. When interrogated about this charge, the former Comptroller, Sir Guildford Slingsby, explained that he had only said he 'doubted not but . . . [Coke] would have cause to repent it'. SP 14/160/42. Coke took the threat seriously enough to appeal to the Privy Council for protection. SP 14/160/43. Slingsby was frequently involved in violent quarrels and, in fact, on one occasion did shoot an associate with a pistol. *CSPD,* 1629-1631, p. 107.

[6]This is the conclusion of Coke's fifteen-page defence of the commission, dated 15 July 1619 (Coke MSS., packet 113). Coke similarly said in a letter to Naunton: 'My lord's noble favour maketh me wish unto him this honour, in the entrance of his office to raise the king's navy on the sudden and above expectation and to do it as his own act so as even the commissioners that perform the project shall not assume [credit for] . . . so much as the project, the carriage, or dispatch, but all that be his own.' Coke MSS., packet 21, Feb. 1619.

king went to Deptford in order to christen the first two ships built by the commission. One of these he named *The Reformation,* in honour of the naval reform achieved by the commission. The other he named *Buckingham's Entrance*, in honour of the new Lord Admiral (though psychohistorians may one day attach more significance to it). Delighted that all this had been accomplished at only half the expense of former years, James freely praised the commissioners and congratulated Buckingham for having chosen such able assistants.[7] Thus the first and the easiest year for the commission ended successfully. In the four remaining years, there would be greater difficulties and disruptions, but the commissioners consistently fulfilled at least their basic promise by reducing the annual ordinary charge of the navy by £20,000 while still producing two new ships each year.[8]

In a sense, the work of the commission was ultimately imperilled by its own success. If the navy had rotted at its moorings under Nottingham and Mansell, the pacific James had at least kept it out of war. Unfortunately, the reforms of the commissioners made it possible for the navy to be used more prominently as a tool in English foreign policy at the very moment when Europe was plunging headlong into the Thirty Years' War. For much of the next ten years, Coke's energies and talents were squandered in preparing and defending a sad succession of wasteful, ineffective fleets.

Coke's work as commissioner had been complicated by these foreign adventures from the very beginning. Throughout 1618 the English had been receiving reports of a huge fleet under preparation in Spain. The official explanation given by the Spanish was that they planned to attack Algiers, the headquarters of the Barbary pirates. It was widely rumoured, however, that the true objective of the Spanish was to conquer Venice and use it as a base from which to attack the Protestants in Bohemia. Another rumour maintained that the secret destination of the Spanish fleet was England itself. This Spanish mobilization may well have been at least part of the reason James and Buckingham supported the project for naval reform. As soon as reform was under way, plans were unveiled for the formation of an English fleet to consist of six royal and fourteen merchant ships. The admitted purpose of this fleet was to assist the Spanish in attacking the

[7] McClure, *Chamberlain Letters,* II, 271; *CSPD*, 1619-1623, p. 93; Perrin, *Phineas Pett,* p. 121. These names were soon changed to *Constant Reformation* and *Happy Entrance*. See Corbett, *England in the Mediterranean,* I, 85.

[8] For the commissioners' own report of their five years' work, see SP 14/156/12. McGowan, 'Royal Navy', pp. 80-2.

pirates at Algiers, but, equally important, the English fleet would be on hand to monitor the Spanish fleet and, if need be, to counter it.[9]

Coke tackled the preparation of the fleet with the enthusiasm of a crusader, vowing 'to further the preparation of the six ships and all other services to the uttermost of my power'. Through this show of English strength, he confidently predicted, 'his Majesty's sea forces shall have more reputation [and] foreign princes will with more respect proceed in their attempts'. Only one cloud darkened Coke's optimism. 'To speak plain', he confided in Naunton, 'we are twelve commissioners, all goers to the church and all good subjects (as I hope) yet not all of one faith.' Coke suspected that one of the commissioners was secretly sympathetic to the Catholic cause. If that suspicion proved true, he worriedly told Naunton, 'in this preparation against pirates it may be conceived the state hath some further design'. In other words, an untrustworthy commissioner might divulge the ulterior purpose of the fleet to the Spanish. To prevent this, Coke proposed that the Lord Admiral should issue his orders to only as many of the commissioners as was absolutely necessary.[10] Coke was by nature disinclined to share responsibility. Still, it was not a good sign that he distrusted even one of his fellow commissioners at this early date. There is no way of knowing what became of Coke's suggestion because the remaining history of the fleet is a mystery. Sometime in the late spring the English preparations were discontinued, though it is not clear why. Spanish opposition to the project or a slackening in Spain's own naval preparations may have been responsible.[11] In any case, the last notice we have of the English fleet in 1619 is provided by Buckingham, who wrote to Coke early in May: 'Though I returned no answer to your letters and discourse upon the intended voyage to Algiers (hoping ere now to have had time to speak with you and give you thanks for your pains and care) yet you see I have made good use of them and followed that way which you chalked out.'[12]

[9]Gardiner, *History of England*, III, 286-9. For the joyous Venetian response to the English decision, see Sir Henry Wotton's dispatch printed in S.R. Gardiner, ed., *Letters and Other Documents Illustrating the Relations Between England and Germany at the Commencement of the Thirty Years War* (2 vols., Westminster, 1865, 1868), I, 48-9. Compare Lockyer, *Buckingham*, p. 77.

[10]All the foregoing remarks by Coke are taken from a letter endorsed by him: '1618/9. Feb. Copy of my letter to Mr Secretary Naunton, showed to the king and thereupon I had access to his Majesty at Whitehall.' Coke MSS., packet 21.

[11]Corbett, *England in the Mediterranean*, I, 89-95. Gardiner, *History of England*, III, 300-1. The most specific date for the cessation of English preparations is 18 April 1619. On that day the Privy Council informed Lord Zouch that James had decided to postpone the expedition. *CSPD,* 1619-1623, p. 37.

[12]Coke MSS., packet 21, Buckingham to Coke, 6 May 1619.

Thus ended Coke's first experience of preparing a fleet for Buckingham. In some ways it resembled his later assignments, particularly in the way he bore the major burden. In two respects, however, this fleet sharply differed from subsequent ones. In the first place, it did not sail, which, considering the fate of its successors, might not have been a bad example to follow. In the second place, it had at least some marginal success. There is no doubt that it made the Spanish worry, perhaps even to the point of altering their plans. Unfortunately, this turned out to be a singularly exceptional success.

With the objectives for 1619 accomplished and preparations for the Algiers fleet discontinued, Coke obtained permission from Buckingham to go home for the holidays at the end of November.[13] Only one year earlier Coke had been spending the holidays with his family when he was suddenly called back to court to learn that Buckingham's patent was passed, the new commission for the navy was almost ready, and a fleet was required to attack Algiers. Now, in January of 1620, Coke was once more summoned away from his home.[14] The news this time was that the preparations for Algiers were to be resumed.

The Barbary pirate project was bound up in the complex diplomatic manoeuvring of the Thirty Years' War.[15] At the beginning of 1620 James apparently decided, though he would have done anything to avoid war, that an English fleet had to be present in the Mediterranean to engage the Barbary pirates and, presumably, to strengthen England's hand in dealing with Spain. The commissioners were ordered to draw up an estimate of the charge for such a fleet, which Coke duly drafted and submitted on their behalf, though actual preparations were not pursued very vigorously until April.[16] On 8 April, Coke wrote to Marie, apologizing for his inability to come home at Easter and explaining, 'we received a new commandment from the king to hasten his fleet, and his Majesty sent Mr. Chancellor [Greville] to me particularly about it'.[17] Coke was occupied with these preparations until late in the summer and then made his long-delayed visit home. He was at Hall Court in October when one of the other

[13]*Cowper MSS.*, I, 107.

[14]*Ibid*. Greville wrote to Coke, informing him of the order to return. The urgency of the matter is reflected in the fact that Coke was instructed to return immediately with the bearer of Greville's letter.

[15]The events leading up to the dispatch of this fleet in 1620 and its recall in 1621 can be closely followed in Gardiner's *History of England*, III, 322-75; IV, 224-7.

[16]*Cowper MSS.*, I, 110.

[17]Coke MSS., packet 1, Coke to Marie, 8 April 1620.

commissioners reported to him that the fleet had sailed. At the same time, the two new ships for 1620 were launched, a new dock was completed, and Buckingham was observed to be freer than usual in complimenting the commissioners.[18] Thus the second year of the commission appeared to end with much the same success as the first one had.

As it began its third year of service in 1621, the fate of the commission rested largely on the uncertain fortunes of the fleet it had dispatched to the Mediterranean. The major question was whether it would succeed in its mission against the Barbary pirates. Of little less concern to Coke and the other commissioners, however, was the immediate leadership of the fleet. Its commander was – of all people – Sir Robert Mansell. The former Treasurer of the Navy was still very much in favour despite the fact that the commissioners in general, and Coke in particular, had not relaxed their efforts to condemn him. Even while the fleet was being readied, they submitted a damning report of his abuses to the Council.[19] Coke's draft of the report ran to thirty-three pages, and the charges it contained were not inconsequential.[20] Mansell, however, far from confessing his peculation while Treasurer, had the effrontery to claim that the Crown still owed him £10,000 for expenses he had incurred in the office.[21] Coke retained a deep and abiding contempt for the man; Buckingham apparently had no special affection for him. Only one person protected Mansell, but he was the most powerful patron of all: the king. James's attitude toward Mansell was illuminated in a timely incident recorded by a court observer:

> . . . Sir Robert Mansell was the only valiant man he [King James] ever loved, and him he loved so intirely, that for all Buckinghams greatnesse with the king, and his hatred of Sir Robert Mansell, yet could not that alienate the kings affections from him; insomuch, as when. . . by Buckinghams procurement, the Spanish embassadour came with a great complaint against Sir Robert Mansell, than at Argiers [Algiers], . . . the king himself defended him in these words: 'My Lord Embassadour, I cannot beleeve this, for I made choyce my selfe of him, out of these reasons; I know him to be valiant, honest, and nobly descended . . . and will never beleeve a man thus qualified will do so base an act.'[22]

[18] *Cowper MSS.*, I, 109.

[19] SP 14/112/101. For Mansell's rebuttal see BL, Harleian MS. 12,504, fols. 5-32.

[20] Coke MSS., packet 138.

[21] *CSPD,* 1619-1623, p. 176.

[22] Sir Anthony Weldon, *The Court and Character of King James* in Scott's *Secret History*, II, 6-7. Mansell enjoyed other favours. He was a member of the controversial

It would carry us too far afield to examine the daily adventures of Mansell's fleet, which was called home in the autumn of 1621. The fleet had at least symbolic importance because it constituted England's first major incursion into the Mediterranean, but it achieved little in concrete terms. It was never employed against Spain, and its one ambitious attack on Algiers, although heroic, was fruitless. Mansell claimed that his supplies arrived too late, his ships were defective, his plans were upset by crippling logistical decisions in England, and he was reduced to completing his mission with too few ships and too few experienced captains. Even weather and disease conspired against him.[23] But the Algiers fleet was kept at sea for nearly a full year and at a considerable distance from England. If the fleet was not a success, neither was it an abysmal failure of the sort experienced later in the decade. One has to probe more deeply to understand why, from the point of view of the naval commissioners, the Algiers fleet was a calamity.

Where the navy was concerned, money was indeed the root of all evil. The commission's five-year programme had been planned without considering what would happen if extraordinary demands were made on the navy. Ideally, the commissioners would have been given additional funds to finance an additional undertaking like the Algiers fleet. In practice, however, there were always delays and difficulties that forced the commissioners to exhaust their ordinary funds, to postpone even urgent expenditures, and to live on credit while waiting for additional money. The Algiers voyage was the first harsh demonstration, as Coke expressed it, that 'our fear and danger cometh by extraordinary services'.[24]

glass monopoly (Gardiner, *History of England*, IV, 10); and when he married in 1616, James is said to have given him £10,000 as a wedding present (*CSPD*, 1611-1618, p. 406).

[23]Two standard accounts of the voyage are Corbett, *England in the Mediterranean,* I, 98-133 and Oppenheim, *Naval Tracts of Sir William Monson,* III, 94-116. Monson entitled his account 'The ill-managed Enterprise upon Algiers in the Reign of King James, and the Errors committed in it.' There is also a printed *Journal* by the fleet's rear-admiral, Sir Thomas Button. The copy of Button's *Journal* in the PRO (SP 14/122/106) contains highly critical notations written into the margin. Both Corbett and Oppenheim assumed these notations were written by Coke. Oppenheim (*Ibid*, p. 109) said: 'Button's *Journal* in the State Papers is enriched by MS. notes in the hand of Sir John Coke, which are, naturally, ill-natured, and also remarkably stupid.' My own examination of Button's *Journal* has led me to two conclusions. First, the marginal comments are not ill-natured and stupid. Secondly, they are not in Coke's hand, which is unfortunate, for if they were, they would shed valuable light on his opinions. For Mansell's view see Kent County Archives, Cranfield MSS. ON. 6755; BL, Add. MS. 36,445, fols. 64-7, 102-3, 132-3, 187, 207-8; BL, Harleian MS. 1,581, fols. 70-2.

[24]Coke MSS., reordered packet 10, Coke's draft of a letter from the commissioners of the navy to Buckingham, 10 April 1622.

Coke tried to anticipate and limit expenses wherever possible. When four of Mansell's ships were recalled in July of 1621, Coke asked for money 'to prevent the charge and danger of keeping near a thousand mariners unpaid and discontented'. Regarding the demands of the captains, Coke pleaded with Buckingham not 'to follow the excess used of late, when to the great prejudice of the state and service, almost every captain got admiral's pay, as we have shown in the examination of Sr. Rob. Mansell's accounts'.[25] The balance of the Algiers fleet returned to England in September of 1621. Seven months later Coke, writing on behalf of the naval commissioners, sent a desperate plea for money to Buckingham. Coke's plea is of interest in two respects. In the first place, it reveals how far Cranfield as Lord Treasurer had drifted away from the naval commission to which he still nominally belonged. Coke was actually using Buckingham in this instance to pressure Cranfield into releasing money for the navy. In a concurrent letter to Cranfield, Coke reiterated the commissioners' desperate need for money, and he explained: 'We know no other means but by address unto him under whose command and protection we serve. Yet considering the interest your Honour hath in this service, and the due respect we all bear unto you, we have thought fit to acquaint you with the letter we have written [to Buckingham].' Perhaps Coke informed Cranfield of the commissioners' letter to Buckingham, as he said, out of respect. Or perhaps he did so in order to increase the pressure on Cranfield. In any case, one can see in these letters the growing alienation between Cranfield, who as Lord Treasurer was still concerned to save money, and the naval commissioners, who were being increasingly required to spend it. In the second place, Coke's plea to Buckingham vividly documents the appalling cost of the Algiers fleet. Coke lamented that the commissioners had been 'forced to disburse £3,000 out of our ordinary monies'. Without additional funds, he warned, the commissioners 'shall be driven to our great grief and discouragement' to discharge workmen, to go without provisions, 'to suffer all the ships which served at Algiers to lie weather-beaten and unserviceable as they came home, and lastly, to endure the clamour and perhaps the mutiny' of mariners who were discharged without pay.[26]

[25] Coke MSS., packet 21, a letter endorsed by Coke: '1621. July 16: Copy of my letter to Lord Marquis Buckingham, Lord Admiral.'

[26] Coke's draft of these two letters dated 10 April 1622 from the commissioners of the navy to Buckingham and Cranfield are on the same sheet of paper. Coke MSS., reordered packet 10.

The total cost of the Algiers fleet was well over £30,000.[27] Nor was this all. In the course of the voyage, other expenses developed that had not been anticipated. Chief among these was the revelation that the *Prince Royal*, the pride of the English navy, was not seaworthy. First reports of her decay and rottenness were so incredible that Coke required the opinion of a second board of experts. Eventually he was forced to conclude, 'her weakness is so great that all we can do unto her at this time with above £500 charge will but make her ride afloat and be able to go to sea upon our coast rather for show than for service'. To make her strong and perfect, he estimated, would require at least £6,000. 'This', he told Buckingham, 'we write to your Honour with grief and some just indignation, seeing a ship which so lately cost his Majesty near £20,000 and was boasted to be of force to fight for a kingdom, so suddenly perish.'[28] All the defects of the *Prince* were directly traceable to the unfit timber with which she was built early in the reign during Mansell's Treasurership.[29] In the final analysis, these additional expenses resulting from the Algiers voyage need not by themselves have been disastrous. By excluding all extraordinary expenses from their calculations, the commissioners could still claim to have almost stayed within their budget.[30] The Algiers fleet raised more serious questions, however, regarding the extent and durability of reform in the navy.

Perhaps the most obvious question is raised by Mansell's command of this fleet. Was he any more honest now than he had been in his fourteen years as Treasurer of the Navy? Opinion is divided on this question. To be fair, there is not sufficient evidence to condemn Mansell or even, indeed, to know with certainty the precise nature of the allegations against him. It appears, however, that he returned to England with three captured prize ships in tow, some very questionable

[27] Oppenheim, *Royal Navy*, p. 197n. It cost about £24,000 to put and keep the fleet at sea. To this must be added over £9,000 for repairs after its return. See also McGowan, 'Royal Navy', pp. 80, 303.

[28] Coke MSS., packet 21, draft by Coke of a letter on behalf of the commissioners of the navy to Buckingham, concerning the defects of the *Prince*, 1621.

[29] Oppenheim, *Royal Navy*, pp. 203-4. The *Prince* was built by Phineas Pett, a lifelong friend and ally of Nottingham and Mansell. After 1618 the commissioners naturally excluded Pett from naval business as much as possible. Pett complained: 'I was sequestered from meddling with any business, and all employments and privileges taken from me . . . and I [was] forced to live as a slave under them the whole of the time of their Commission.' Through Mansell's influence with James, however, Pett was allowed to build two pinnaces for the Algiers voyage and command one of them at sea. Predictably, his charge for building the pinnaces ran far above the original estimate (*Cowper MSS.*, I, 109). Pett's lively but highly prejudiced autobiography contains several references to the 'malice' and 'spiteful aggravation' of Coke, who opposed Pett till the very end. See Perrin, *Phineas Pett*, pp. 119-26, 153-6, 165.

[30] Oppenheim, *Royal Navy*, p. 197; McGowan, 'Royal Navy', pp. 80-2.

financial accounts, and at least £3,000 in cash from selling slaves and merchandise and ransoming Jews he had liberated from the pirates.[31] Coke required little prompting from Buckingham to lead an inquiry into the matter. It was Coke's contention that Mansell had never been authorized to take this booty, but having taken it, he now had to account for every penny and then surrender it to the Lord Admiral, to whom it rightfully belonged as a perquisite of his office. If Coke had succeeded in pressing these charges, he would have reaped the double benefit of discrediting Mansell while at the same time gratifying Buckingham. The final outcome was therefore only a partial success, for Mansell escaped without blame but Buckingham got the spoils.

As Coke's letters reveal, the king himself intervened to protect Mansell. In all his years of dutiful compliance, Coke was never more visibly dissatisfied with the judgement of his royal master. Of course he did not dare openly challenge James, but he found it difficult not at least to express how deeply he resented Mansell's immunity. Struggling to draft his final report to Buckingham on this subject, Coke wrote, 'we have reviewed the accounts of Sir Robert Mansell and Captain Love, and (as we formerly certified) find in them many things differing from their instructions and the order of the office. Yet... we have... chiefly in reverence to his Majesty's most gracious inclination, and according to your Honour's directions, disposed with the manner, and for the matter give allowance to whatsoever we find really expended for his Majesty's service'.[32] But then Coke had some second thoughts about referring so directly to James's protection of Mansell. He crossed out the words 'chiefly in reverence to his Majesty's most gracious inclination'. After some third thoughts, he crossed out the entire letter and began a new one. Even so, Coke's final draft still asked Buckingham for 'a signification from your Honour by a word or two in writing that his Majesty is pleased to dispense for this time with the disorders'. Coke chose his words carefully because he believed, whatever the king's affections, that Mansell's actions, if not Mansell

[31] *Cowper MSS.*, I, 115-16. Mansell's ordinary accounts as well as those for the prize goods were evidently subjected to careful scrutiny by Coke and the other commissioners. These papers relating to the examination are tentatively attributed to 1621, but actually some were written during the autumn of 1622, which indicates the investigation lasted at least a year after the fleet had returned. Compare McGowan, 'Royal Navy', p. 77; Prestwich, *Cranfield,* p. 340.

[32] Coke MSS., packet 69, Coke to Buckingham [*ca*. Nov. 1622]. This is only the first of many examples which show how jealously Coke guarded the prerogatives of his patron and how enthusiastically he sought ways to enrich him. Coke further reported: 'And now (my good lord) I have no occasion of attendance here save only to receive your directions and take order accordingly for the payment of your monies, which, as I have carried the business, shall need neither petition to his Majesty nor any new privy seal or to trouble the Lord Treasurer for any payments out of the Exchequer.'

himself, had to be condemned in order to assure 'the preserving of order in the service'.[33] It was imperative to state clearly and publicly that Mansell had acted improperly, but that this time – and this time only – the improprieties were being excused. Under no circumstances should Mansell's actions be allowed to assume the cloak of legitimacy; under no circumstances should the irregularities of the Algiers voyage become a precedent.

Coke keenly sensed and feared the infectious nature of corruption. Although he was unable to vent his full outrage over the Algiers fleet, he did tactfully insinuate that future commanders should be chosen from men of more 'government and moderation'.[34] When the scandalous state of the *Prince Royal* had been discovered, Coke had similarly seized the opportunity to point out the lesson to Buckingham: 'His Majesty and your lordship may thereby understand how necessary it is to entertain and encourage such servants as are conformable to order and government and can keep within their bounds.' When Coke had it in his own power to mete out punishment, he did so. When, for example, he found a boatswain guilty of embezzling, he had him dismissed and urged the Lord Admiral to impose a more severe punishment 'because some exemplary justice is necessary to restrain the inveterate corruptions in the navy'.[35] The tenor, standards, and discipline of the entire naval administration were at stake here, and consequently, as Coke realized, so was the future of the whole reform programme. Coke believed firmly in the modern administrative principle of accountability. He fully understood how ruinous it was not to hold men like Mansell accountable for their actions.

All his life Coke was also a firm believer in the power of the rule book. Honesty and efficiency, he believed, might be maintained despite the imperfections of some men if there were adequate rules and regulations to govern all men's actions. During his career he drew up regulations for the better administration of the ordnance, the Wardrobe, and the postal system. Naturally, he had plans for the navy, too. As Coke himself explained: 'Great businesses and many trusts were never carried without particular errors. And this moved

[33]Coke MSS., packet 69, Coke to Buckingham, [*ca.* Nov. 1622]. This second draft was written by Coke on the back of the first one which he crossed out. Although this report has been tentatively attributed to 1621 (*Cowper MSS.*, I, 115-16), Coke's reference to another matter in the second draft clearly dates from about November 1622.

[34]*Ibid.* Here, too, Coke had difficulty with his wording, implying but not charging that unfit men had been chosen to command the Algiers enterprise.

[35]Coke MSS., packet 21, Coke to Buckingham concerning the defects of the *Prince*, 1621.

me in the first year of our service to propound a frame of government for the navy wherein by regular and continual accounts these errors might suddenly be discovered and reformed.'[36] By the time the Algiers fleet returned in 1621, Coke was more strongly than ever convinced of the need for such a plan. Renewing his efforts, he wrote to Buckingham to remind him of 'a book in your hands, which I offered long since to be examined first by the commissioners, and then by the lords, and if by them it were approved, that your lordship would cause it to be put in execution'. Until 'some such orders be established', said Coke, 'the navy will ever be in danger of relapse'.[37] As might be expected, the plan was never put into effect.

In Coke's efforts to reprimand Mansell, his attempt to strengthen discipline with an act of exemplary justice, his plan to introduce checks and regulations in the service – in all this – there is a new mood. Gone is the exuberant spirit and drive of the commission's early days. Instead, Coke now seems less on the offensive, more on the defensive. His actions suggest a sense of despair or, at the least, an awareness that he no longer has full control of the situation. Whether Buckingham had favoured Mansell or, as seems more likely, he had merely deferred to James, it was a rude awakening for Coke. He was not the sort of man to roar in protest against the judgement of his superiors, but that only makes his feeble intimations to Buckingham that naval reform was being jeopardized seem all the more significant. Certainly Coke still believed that Right was on his side, but hereafter he seems less confident of Might's support. He was, in fact, even suspicious of his fellow commissioners. At least two of them, he complained, had 'fallen into the same corruptions they condemned in others'. As Coke recalled:

> Till the Algiers voyage, nothing was discovered amongst us but strict and frugal husbanding of all things for his Majesty's best service. But then I began to suspect, that in the great mass of provisions then heaped in, some had uttered their own wares. Yet when I charged them privately therewith, they cleared themselves by great protestations, against which I had no proof. But ever

[36]SP 14/151/35. An undated note in Coke's hand (Coke MSS., packet 129) reveals his efforts to reduce naval administration to a state of order through books of rates and regulations: 'The proportions for sails changed 4 times. Remember to send for the book of proportions and require it to be perfected for the new ships, and to have a copy thereof ready for the use of the commission. Remember to have a book of rates for prices of all particulars to be also . . .[remanded?] to the public use of the commission . . . . A book to be made by Newman of all manner of rates allowed in the navy. The book of proportions to be written out.'

[37]Coke MSS., packet 21, Coke to Buckingham, 16 July 1621.

> since, I carried a watchful eye over them and employed fit persons to discover their dealings.[38]

These particular suspicions may not have been justified, but they demonstrate how far the resurgence of corrupt practices in conjunction with the Algiers voyage shattered Coke's confidence. For two brief years the heady optimism of the commission had held the field. Then, during 1621 and 1622, familiar symptoms of what Coke now dejectedly called the navy's 'inveterate corruptions' reappeared.

This brings us to the most disturbing question of all raised by the Algiers voyage: had the reform of 1618 been an illusion from the start? There is no doubt that the commissioners greatly reduced the operating costs of the navy, but did they ever really make much headway in eradicating corruption? Unfortunately, the Algiers voyage illustrates that the success of the commission was seriously limited in several respects. In the first place, although the commissioners had got rid of Nottingham and the principal officers, they were unable to eliminate Mansell, and of course it was impossible to remove the multitude of lower naval personnel whose attitudes toward their work had been critically shaped in the days of Nottingham and Mansell. These people, trained and accustomed to corruption years before the commissioners arrived on the scene, were a major impediment to reform.[39] Through these men, the ill effects of the previous régime continued, unseen but real, like the rotting timber beneath the decks of the *Prince Royal*. This explains why Mansell's appointment as commander of the Algiers fleet was the worst possible signal to naval personnel and why Coke was so determined to make an example of Mansell. Given the continuity in naval personnel, the

[38]SP 14/151/35, 35I. Coke suspected two commissioners in particular. The first was William Burrell, the master shipwright, whom he charged with profiting from the sale of naval materials. Coke wrote a thirty-eight-page indictment against Burrell primarily based on his accounts for the year 1622 (Coke MSS., packet 138). The second was Thomas Norreys, the Surveyor, whom he charged with abetting rather than suppressing the larceny of boatswains and shipwrights. The validity of these charges is questionable, but Coke was persistent in pressing them first in 1623 and again in 1627. See also G.E. Manwaring, ed., *The Life and Works of Sir Henry Mainwaring* (2 vols., London, 1920-2), I, 154-5 and McGowan, 'Royal Navy', pp. 220-2, 273-4.

[39]Despite all the recent attention to the 'structural' problems of early Stuart government, G.E. Aylmer understood 'the decisive importance of individuals'. As he wrote, the 'tone set, and the standards enforced from the top downwards, mattered immensely'. See his review of McGowan's *Jacobean Commissions* in the *English Historical Review*, 90 (April 1975), 441. Michael Oppenheim long ago explained, 'ships might be replaced and open peculation checked, but the deeper wounds of spirit and discipline caused by fourteen years of license among the higher officials, and fourteen years of heartless chicanery suffered by those more lowly placed were not so readily healed, and bore their fruits for long afterwards in the habitual dishonesty of officials and workmen'. *Royal Navy,* p. 215.

greatest hope of the commissioners had been to keep them honest by careful regulation and supervision, but Coke's plea to Buckingham cited earlier shows that the regulations which were supposed to control the flow of naval supplies had never been implemented. Indeed, Coke admitted that 'the king's stores are not yet brought to a due form of accounts'. A dispute over the reversion to the storekeeper's place had further prevented the commissioners from establishing 'an orderly account'.[40] Then, too, there remained the intangible obstacle that Coke battled throughout his career – the problem of men who were unaccustomed to 'order and government'. Regulations by themselves would be ineffectual until men had acquired the mental habit of following regulations, or until they could be forced to do so, which again explains why Coke was so insistent on exemplary punishments. Of course the 'carrot' of higher wages was supposed to work better than the 'stick' of exemplary punishments, and maybe it did. But Coke noted that the boatswain he caught embezzling had done so despite the fact that 'their wages were raised only to keep them honest'.[41] Finally, there was the problem of size. The commissioners were capable of monitoring, checking, and controlling work in the navy as long as it continued on a small scale. Extraordinary endeavours like the Algiers voyage put more money and supplies into circulation, thereby placing greater temptation in the way of naval workers while at the same time straining the supervisory capacity of the commissioners. One recalls, for example, that Coke was afraid other commissioners had succumbed to temptation because of 'the great mass of provisions then heaped in'. This did not augur well for the huge war fleets that would be required in the future.

On the other hand, the problems that surfaced with the Algiers fleet should not be exaggerated. Coke could be accused of being an alarmist, especially with regard to his fellow commissioners and perhaps even with regard to Mansell. The commissioners did continue to fulfil their basic promise by building two new ships each year and by running the navy at a cost, exclusive of extraordinary charges, not awfully much over £30,000. And even their greater promise of truly sustained honesty and efficiency in the navy might have come closer to fulfillment if England had steered clear of war.

Fortunately, after the Algiers fleet there was a temporary lull in naval activities. Coke's next, major naval assignment would be to prepare a fleet to retrieve Buckingham and Charles from their journey

[40]Coke MSS., packet 21, Coke to Buckingham, 16 July 1621.

[41]Coke MSS., packet 21, Coke to Buckingham concerning the defects of the *Prince*, 1621.

to Spain in 1623. Meanwhile Coke's fortunes did not depend solely on his work in the navy. Another department that occupied him in these years was the ordnance office. The naval commissioners had briefly looked into the ordnance in 1618 as part of their investigation of the navy, but they apparently postponed a full-scale scrutiny till later.[42] This took place in the spring of 1620, and Coke was clearly in charge of it. He told Marie in April that this work 'proveth very important', and he hoped that the commissioners would give 'the king and our country as good an account in that as we have done in the navy'.[43] Coke knew the ordnance well; one of his friends, Sir Robert Pye, said many years later in the Long Parliament 'that no man in England understood the Navy and Office of the Ordnance so well'.[44] In the ordnance investigation of 1620, Coke's hand is ubiquitous. It was he who wrote a detailed survey of ordnance supplies received and expended between 1609 and 1620.[45] It was he who drafted the ordnance report that was submitted in July of 1620.[46] Indeed, he was apparently the one who had originally conceived the propositions for ordnance reform because, in a letter to Buckingham, he referred to the propositions 'which I first offered to your lordship, and by your encouragement to the commissioners, and so to the lords'.[47] Furthermore, when the ordnance officers resisted implementation of these proposals, it was Coke who vigorously refuted their objections in detail.[48] As final proof of Coke's dominant role in the ordnance project, there is the corroborative testimony of Godfrey Goodman, bishop of Gloucester under Charles I. Summing up Lionel Cranfield's

[42]Kent County Archives, Cranfield MSS. ON 4852/EN M1045. *APC,* 1618-1619, p. 269. The 1618 report on the navy contained this statement: 'Besides what may bee further saved in the munition and victualls, for want of time wee have reserved to farther consideration.' Charnock, *Marine Architecture,* II, 258. There is an undated copy of the commission to survey the ordnance in the Melbourne Hall muniments room, box 1 of Coke's papers. Coke endorsed this commission '1619 March'. Assuming that Coke would have used the old style of dating, this would mean the ordnance survey was commissioned in March 1620. This would concur with a notation (BL, Lansdowne MSS., vol. 162, fol. 234, no. 44) suggesting the naval commissioners should survey the ordnance, which is dated January of 1619/20. This would also explain why the actual survey occurred in April and May 1620.

[43]Coke MSS., packet 1, Coke to Marie, 8 April 1620.

[44]*Cowper MSS.,* II, 270.

[45]SP 14/115/61.

[46]Melbourne Hall muniments room, box 2 of Coke's papers. The date is given in *LJ*, III, 300, 373. There are at least three extant copies of the ordnance report, all undated. One is in the Melbourne Hall muniments room, box 2 of Coke's papers. Another is BL, Add. MS. 36,777. The third in the PRO is AO 16/6/3.

[47]Coke MSS., packet 21, Coke to Buckingham, 16 July 1621.

[48]Yale University, Beinecke Library, Osborn shelves fb 18.

achievements, Goodman wrote, 'how many several places he did reform, as the King's Household, the Wardrobe, the Courts of Wards, the Treasurer's Office, shall appear, only the Royal Navy and the Tower of London [where the ordnance was located] excepted, which was the work of Secretary Cooke'.[49]

The propositions for ordnance reform submitted in July of 1620 have been outlined elsewhere.[50] Suffice it to say here that a saving of £10,000 was anticipated, partly through greater economy and efficiency in the office and chiefly through a profitable exploitation of the king's monopoly on the manufacture of gunpowder. Cranfield's biographers have attributed ordnance reform to him, but the fact is that there was no reform, and if there had been, it would have been, as Goodman said, more Coke's achievement than Cranfield's.[51] None of the proposals regarding economy and efficiency were implemented, and the plan to make money from the gunpowder monopoly broke down when the king could not even keep up his own payments to the powder manufacturer. The total collapse of the ordnance project is puzzling, especially the fact that all the proposals for reform were approved by the king and the Privy Council yet never actually implemented. Coke kept pressing for their implementation. As late as July of 1621, he complained to Buckingham about the failure to prosecute ordnance reform. How could the ordnance officers, unlike the naval officers of only two years earlier, have escaped reform so completely? Although we will probably never have an entirely satisfactory answer to this question, there is at least circumstantial evidence implicating Cranfield.[52] Just twelve days after Coke complained to Buckingham about the lack of action in the ordnance, Cranfield concluded a deal with the ordnance officers to acquire their rights to land he was interested in. Perhaps Cranfield showed no interest in forcing the ordnance officers to accept unpalatable reforms because he was more interested in getting this land away from them than in implementing proposals that Coke, not he, had devised in the first place.

Although the project for ordnance reform died in the summer of 1621, the memory would linger on and come back to haunt Cranfield in 1624. One of the impeachment charges against him in 1624 was

[49]Goodman, *Court of King James,* I, 308.

[50]See my own 'Illusions of Grandeur and Reform at the Jacobean Court: Cranfield and the Ordnance', *The Historical Journal,* 22 (1979), 59-60.

[51]Tawney, *Business and Politics*, pp. 171-2; Prestwich, *Cranfield*, pp. 218-19.

[52]Young, 'Illusions of Grandeur', pp. 64-8.

that he had failed to observe the so-called settlement of the ordnance office in 1620. Technically, this charge was unfair because in fact nothing was settled in 1620. Yet Cranfield was found guilty on this charge, and the chief evidence against him came from: 'The said Declaration of the Officers of the Ordnance, and the said Depositions of the said Mr *John Cooke*.' Thus the opponents of ordnance reform and the architect of that same reform would join in common cause against Cranfield in 1624. The ordnance officers had an obvious motive: by this time they knew that Cranfield had bilked them in the land deal. Coke had ulterior motives that we will see develop in the course of events, and of course he wanted to please Buckingham. But more relevant to the charge was the strong possibility that Cranfield had declined to support Coke's plans back in 1621. Even the scheme to make money from the king's monopoly on gunpowder, Coke testified, had failed because Cranfield, as Lord Treasurer, did not keep up the king's payments to the powder manufacturer.[53] And that scheme, as Coke must keenly have remembered, was all that survived of his plans to reform the ordnance in 1620-1.

Apart from the navy and the ordnance office, a third arena where Coke was able to serve the Crown in these years was Parliament. On 30 January 1621 King James addressed the opening session of his third Parliament. The recent economy drives at court provided him with evidence to assure the Commons that any monies they granted him would not be wasted. In addition to Cranfield's reform of the Household, James emphasized the savings he had already effected in the navy, the improved government of the navy under Buckingham and the commissioners, and the expectation (though never realized of course) that another £10,000 annually would soon be saved in the ordnance.[54] Coke had done much to make these claims possible. It was only fitting, therefore, that he was among those men who in 1621 sat in Parliament for the first time.[55]

Coke's participation in the Parliament of 1621 did not amount to much compared to his prominent role in later Parliaments. We know that he sat as a member for the borough of Warwick. This he no doubt owed, like so much else in his life, to Fulke Greville, who wielded

[53] *LJ*, III, 373-4. Sir Francis Nethersole told Sir Dudley Carleton that the heaviest charge against Cranfield was his failure to make these payments. *CSPD*, 1623-1625, p. 217.

[54] Notestein, *1621 Debates*, II, 8-9 n.14; Edward Nicholas, *Proceedings and Debates in the House of Commons in 1620 and 1621*, ed. T. Tyrwhitt (2 vols., Oxford, 1766), I, 7-8.

[55] *Returns of Members of Parliament* (2 vols., London, 1878), I, 454.

considerable influence in Warwickshire.[56] In the records of the Parliament, Coke appears most often as a committee member, and many of these committees dealt with relatively minor issues.[57] Some of the more important committees he belonged to were concerned with the need to survey all the business of the House, the charges against Sir Giles Mompesson, the practice of compounding for concealed Crown lands, the exportation of iron ordnance, and Irish affairs. Still, there is no way of knowing what Coke did on any of these committees, most of which included twenty or more other members. Coke did occasionally enter into the debates of the House. In most cases, however, his opinion is not particularly clear from the fragments that have survived.[58] Fortunately, there is an extant record of one occasion when Coke addressed the House at length on a topic of some importance. It may well have been his maiden address, and the topic was, appropriately enough, freedom of speech. What makes the speech especially interesting is that it conforms so perfectly with what we might expect of Coke. He readily acknowledged that: 'The freedom of this House is the freedom of the whole land.' But he saw no just cause for complaint. Surely, he said, it was fair to restrain exorbitant speeches which served no end but malice and divisiveness. In all other cases, he declared, 'we have a freedom of speech to speak what we think good for government either in church or commonweal and what are the grievances'. Having reaffirmed that right, he now urged the House to move on to more important matters. In general, the tone of Coke's speech was conciliatory and positive. Harmony, Coke implied, could be achieved through the classic formula of reason and moderation. As Coke put it, 'every man's discretion and wisdom must be a rule to himself that so he do not propound things unreasonable or out of order'. Coke further suggested: 'because many propose general propositions only, which makes us spend many days to no purpose. My advice is that every one that proposeth any business may likewise bring some project or model for it'.[59] One could hardly ask for a better illustration of the way in which Coke's mind functioned. His instinctive response to a

[56] Willson, *Privy Councillors,* p. 70.

[57] *CJ,* I, 518, 529, 530, 540-1, 548, 572, 583, 584, 592, 593, 607, 614. Notestein, *1621 Debates*, II, 171; IV, 126; VI, 32, 56, 100, 262, 305. References to John Coke can be distinguished from references to Sir Edward Coke. However, I am not certain that either I or the indexer of the *1621 Debates* were always successful in distinguishing between John Coke and Clement Coke. My comments in the text are confined to instances where I am certain the Coke involved was John.

[58] Notestein, *1621 Debates*, II, 56, 205; III, 198, 254, 278; IV, 143; V, 257, 287.

[59] The passages cited here from Coke's speech of 12 February are taken from Notestein, *1621 Debates*, II, 56-7. A less complete version is reproduced in *CJ*, I, 517.

problem was to draw up plans, regulations, or propositions, to construct a project or a model.

The few scraps of evidence we have, then, give the impression that Coke approached his work in the Parliament of 1621 in the same businesslike fashion as he approached his other work. We see the same love of harmony and order, the same penchant for rules and plans. We see also a genuine desire on Coke's part for goodwill to prevail. The speech by Coke cited here occurred near the very beginning of the first session of the first Parliament of the 1620s. In the Parliaments that followed throughout the decade, Coke would repeat these themes again and again, but in the end there would be precious little left of the goodwill he hoped for.

A final, especially tedious employment for Coke during these years extended from July through September of 1622 when he served as a commissioner compounding for purveyance and carriage. These feudal obligations to provide the king with free provisions and means of transportation were often complained of in Parliament. Some of them had already been commuted into monetary payments, but both the king and the subject were abused by the middle-men who collected the money and payments in kind. In the summer of 1622, the Crown sent commissioners into the counties to negotiate directly with local representatives and agree upon a mutually acceptable sum. This was expected to free everyone from the exploitation of middle-men while putting some sorely needed money into the king's coffers.

From a 'Journal' and other notes kept by Coke, it appears that the commissioners encountered difficulties.[60] The 'Journal' provides sums paid or agreed upon for only eight counties, and in those counties there were several instances of resistance. In Oxfordshire no one came to meet the commissioners, supposedly because the sheriff had forgotten to announce their coming. In Essex, Coke recalled that the commissioners debated with local notables, 'whereupon differing we brake'. In Derbyshire, Coke's own brother, Francis, wrote on behalf of the justices of the peace, demanding to see a copy of the commission and inquiring both how far their authority extended and what receipt or assurance they could give to guarantee their bargain. For Hertfordshire, Coke kept notes on the commodities in question, which included all sorts of grains, meats, poultry, wood, and carriages. The compounders, he wrote, 'alleged that they had not sufficient power from the country'. But they were willing to pay £1,500,

[60] The 'Journal' is printed in *Cowper MSS.*, I, 73-5, where it is incorrectly attributed to the year 1611.

provided that hawks and hounds were thrown in for good measure, and Coke was inclined to accept their offer.[61] Whatever its success, this was an arduous employment. Coke calculated the number of miles he rode through all but the northermost counties, and the total came to over one thousand.[62] In a letter written to Buckingham, which Coke later decided not to send, he complained of 'having followed no business of my own since February last, and travelled this summer a thousand miles at least in his Majesty's service'.[63]

By the time Coke returned to London, he had, typically, thought of ways to manage the project better. He was frustrated in his first attempt to voice these opinions 'by reason of their lordships' great businesses at that time which suffered them not to give us so free audience as was fit'. Undaunted, however, Coke appealed directly to the king. As he proudly reported to Marie: 'I for my particular drew an account in writing and therein gave advice what I thought necessary to be done for the expedition of the service. This I sent by an honourable person to the king, and his Majesty was so well satisfied with it that he sent the same lord to the Lord Treasurer and Lord Steward with commandment unto them to follow those directions.'[64] After the acceptance of Coke's proposals, he was required to stay on in London several more weeks to participate in the remaining negotiations. This must have been irksome to Coke who had already been forced to neglect his home and his family for so long. As it developed, however, these few weeks in the autumn of 1622 were among the most important in his life.

[61] *Cowper MSS.,* I, 119, 125-7.

[62] *Ibid.,* I, 75.

[63] Coke MSS., packet 45, Coke to Buckingham, 12 Oct. 1622. This letter is accompanied by a briefer one which Coke's endorsement tells us he sent in its place.

[64] Coke MSS., packet 45, Coke to Marie, 16 Oct. 1622.

7

MASTER OF REQUESTS

Coke was never wholly satisfied with being a mere commissioner of the navy. From the beginning, he had hoped for something more at the hands of his new patron. As early as November of 1618, Greville had assured him of Buckingham's intentions. 'In the mean season', Greville vowed, 'believe me, I am confident that he will bestow you in a place fit for you.'[1] When the naval commission was transformed into an administrative body and Coke assumed its leadership, he still hoped for greater preferment. We have already seen his optimistic letter to Marie, in which he boasted that Buckingham 'hath promised my friends that I shall be one of the next he will endeavour to prefer and hath privately to my self nominated the place to which he designeth me'.[2] It was either this place or, more likely, another one Greville had in mind when he wrote to Coke more than a year later, in June of 1620, 'the office we spoke of long since I doubt will not fall to your share. Notwithstanding, be confident better will come and that shortly, for I have seen both the king and my lord of Buckingham's mind clearly of you'.[3] This view was confirmed by another friend at court who also assured Coke that Buckingham had not forgotten him.[4]

Despite these verbal reassurances, the material fact was that Coke saw the years 1619 and 1620 pass by without any further promotion. More than that, his sources of influence appeared to be waning. Greville and Naunton, his closest friends and faithful patrons, were on their way out. Naunton's case was by far the more extreme of the two. As a zealous Protestant, he was not liked by Gondomar, the Spanish ambassador who was promoting the marriage between Prince Charles and the Spanish princess. In January of 1621, Naunton became entangled in a complicated plot involving the Spanish match. Apparently he was acting with James's connivance in a scheme to put pressure on the Spanish, but the scheme backfired. Gondomar confronted James and demanded that Naunton be punished. James found himself in the position of having to make Naunton a scapegoat to salvage the Spanish match. He suspended him from the Secretaryship and ordered him confined to his home.[5] Naunton retained formal

[1]Coke MSS., packet 15, Greville to Coke [Nov.] 1618.

[2]Coke MSS., packet 1, Coke to Marie, 18 Feb. 1619.

[3]Coke MSS., packet 15, Greville to Coke, June 1620.

[4]*Cowper MSS.,* I, 110.

[5]Schreiber, *Naunton,* pp. 68-83.

possession of the office for nearly two more years, but he was given little work and no real responsibility. His usefulness to Coke had certainly come to an end.[6] Greville's status at court was more ambiguous. Probably most alarming to Coke was Greville's removal from the Chancellorship of the Exchequer, which occurred in October of 1621.[7] Greville remained a Privy Councillor and was appointed to later committees, but his loss of office, advanced age, failing health, and diminished activity at court gave Coke substantial cause for anxiety. Coke had no way of knowing that Greville, unlike Naunton, could still be a valuable patron.

As these developments unfolded, Coke grew more impatient for an office at court. His dissatisfaction surfaced in the summer of 1621, several months after Naunton's disgrace and well after it was rumoured that Greville would be forced to resign. For nearly three years Coke had been neglecting his own estate in return for unfulfilled promises. Most recently, Buckingham had told him he would see an issue of his hopes when Parliament was adjourned. Coke did not fail to remind the Lord Admiral: 'Your late assurance that at this adjournment I should know his Majesty's pleasure gave me much comfort, and the sense of my estate and time spent make me now bold to put your lordship in remembrance thereof.'[8] Coke accompanied this appeal with the usual amount of fawning flattery, at one point inviting Buckingham to 'fashion me and set no stamp upon me but his Majesty's and your own'. The new and significant element in Coke's tone of voice, however, was the subtle insinuation that it was time for some concrete reward. 'Your Honour best knoweth', he wrote, 'whether I have been hitherto negligent or importune, or whether I have quietly and confidently relied upon the expression you have been pleased to make of your own goodness towards me.' The immediate result of this new entreaty was yet another promise, but this time from the king himself. Coke responded with appropriate gratitude, professing to Buckingham that: 'His Majesty's gracious promise. . . and your lordship's most ingenuous and rare descent, in expressing unto him a true sense of my estate. . . have given me much confidence and comfort.' In reality, though, even a promise from the lips of the king himself was nothing more than a few, bare words. James had made the act seem somewhat more convincing by naming Buckingham and Prince Charles as his witnesses and charging them to see to it that he

[6]After relinquishing the Secretaryship, Naunton was compensated by being appointed Master of the Court of Wards. He remained a strangely isolated figure at court till his death in 1635. Schreiber, *Naunton,* pp. 84-96, 122, 132-3.

[7]Rebholz, *Fulke Greville,* pp. 254-6, 266-8; *DNB,* VIII, 603.

[8]Coke MSS., packet 21, Coke to Buckingham, 6 June 1621.

honoured his word. Coke implored Buckingham to respect this obligation and betrayed his own continuing anxiety when he pleaded, 'since it hath pleased his Majesty to nominate the Prince's Highness and yourself to be his Remembrancers for me, let me not languish and grow older in the hands of so powerful angels, but. . . enable me some way to give his Majesty, his Highness, and yourself some account of my life'.[9]

In the summer of 1621, then, the best that Coke had been able to obtain was another promise, albeit from the king. Thus he returned to Hall Court as usual to attend to the harvesting and accounting with his position at court little changed. In September, however, he received what by now could not have been entirely unexpected — another summons from Greville: 'I am commanded by my lord of Buckingham to send for you. . . he assures me without further expectation you shall see an issue of your hopes. I pray you, therefore, fail not yourself but be here by the time appointed, and be confident you have and shall find me your constant loving friend.'[10] It is a curious fact that Coke did not immediately respond to this summons. Instead, he seems to have lingered at Hall Court. More than a week later, he received another letter, this one from Henry Vyner, a close friend who worked for Greville. Vyner was amazed that Coke had not returned to court immediately. He described the great changes taking place there. Cranfield was appointed the new Lord Treasurer. Sir Richard Weston was expected any day to replace Greville as Chancellor of the Exchequer. 'Now therefore', he told Coke, 'you shall quickly see what reward is intended for all your good service.' There should be no doubt in this point, he emphasized, because: 'The first messenger was sent by commandment from my Lord Admiral.' His concluding, urgent message to Coke was 'hasten hither'.[11] Despite the glowing optimism of Greville and Vyner, when Coke finally did arrive at court, he learned that he was still nothing more than a commissioner of the navy. But in the future he would at least be a better paid commissioner. On 8 November 1621 he received a grant from the king in the amount of £300 per year for his 'good services done unto us in the several Commisions for our marine causes and for the office of Our Ordnance'.[12] The grant acknowledged what Coke had often complained

[9]Coke MSS., packet 21, Coke to Buckingham, 16 July 1621.

[10]Coke MSS., packet 21, Greville to Coke, 24 Sept. 1621.

[11]Coke MSS., packet 1, Henry Vyner to Coke, 3 Oct. 1621. Conclusive internal evidence and Coke's own endorsement firmly establish the date of this letter. It was mistakenly attributed to the year 1622 in *Cowper MSS.*, I, 120.

[12]The grant is printed in *Cowper MSS.*, I, 114.

of, that he 'hath long attended the same far remote from his family and to his great charge'. There were several interesting features of the grant which warrant some comment. In the first place, it acknowledged Coke's frustrated efforts in the ordnance as well as his work in the navy. Secondly, though it is not absolutely certain, the grant does appear to have been retroactive. If so, the total for his three years of service would have amounted to quite a windfall. Finally, and most important, the text of the grant specifically stated that this was not intended as a final and adequate reward for Coke's services. This grant would help to repay Coke 'in the meantime' while the king continued to consider 'a fit reward for him'. It is hard to escape the conclusion that Buckingham and James were concerned to keep Coke working for them while they waited for the right court office to fall vacant. It also would seem that Coke had given them reason to be concerned.

Thus 1621 had yielded a small mark of favour. But Coke's status had actually changed little; and money for the present does not seem to have allayed his apprehensions for the future. At the beginning of 1622, he was where he still preferred to be, at home with his family. In mid-February, Greville wrote that the other naval commissioners resented his neglect of the navy, particularly in view of the fact that, unlike themselves, Coke now received a generous allowance.[13] Nearer the end of February, Sir Robert Pye, an auditor and financial adviser to Buckingham, sent Coke the same warning. 'I could wish you here', he wrote, 'for it is thought very much that you should have. . . £300 p[er] ann[um] and now leave the business.' Pye also asked Coke for the date of his intended return and promised to make excuses for him till then.[14] Finally, in March of 1622, Coke responded to the pleading of his friends, returned to court, and worked on naval affairs through the spring. With the advent of summer, he was called upon, as we have seen, to ride through all but northernmost England as a commissioner compounding for purveyance and carriage. Then, in the autumn of 1622, the issue of Coke's future reached a sudden and dramatic climax.

Coke's time was running out, and he knew it. The naval commission was scheduled to last only one more year. When it expired, he would be left with little to show for his five years of work

[13] *Ibid.*, I, 116.

[14] Coke MSS., packet 21, Sir Robert Pye to Coke, 25 Feb. 1622. Apart from the shipwright, Burrell, who also received £300 per annum, it is not clear what, if any, allowance the other commissioners received. Greville stated that they received no pay. *Cowper MSS.*, I, 114, 116; Oppenheim, *Royal Navy,* p. 195.

but a lot of empty promises. Even if Buckingham's favour continued, the likely prospect was a tenuous succession of occasional commissions and special employments, nothing certain, nothing permanent. What Coke wanted and needed was security — in other words, a court office. He was an old man with a family to support, he had worked as hard and as best he knew how, and now his patience was running thin. By the fall of 1622, he was ready to make the gambling pay off or stop playing the game.

Buckingham made the first move. Without yet spelling out the precise terms, he offered to employ Coke in his own personal service; but there would be no formal, court office. Coke would have no part of this. In fact, he suspected that it was a plot instigated by his rivals at court who knew he would offend the Lord Admiral by refusing the offer. In his letter to Buckingham declining the offer, Coke broadly hinted that one of those rivals was Cranfield.[15] He alluded to 'some that serve their turns with the labours of others'. He declared himself always ready to serve Buckingham 'with more faithfulness and affection and with more moderate desires than some others have done'. And in an apparent comparison of himself with the Lord Treasurer, he observed: 'I am conscious to myself that I have these four years, with neglect of my own estate, done his Majesty and your Honour not seeming but real service'. Coke then proceeded to explain his position to Buckingham: 'If I were young and without charge, I should gladly embrace any kind of noble dependence. But my poor reputation and my estate accord not with a court attendance at large without place.' Coke would not settle for less than a place at court, and so he made his counter-proposal: 'If by your favour I may have any convenient place in his Majesty's service whereby I may draw my family nearer and support myself with some credit and comfort, I will wholly and faithfully addict myself thereto.'

Buckingham responded by raising the ante. He offered, as Coke described it, 'to confirm the allowance I have out of the navy of £300 per annum and to give me more out of his own purse £200 a year'. In addition to this annual income totalling £500, Buckingham offered certain privileges, including 'diet at his table, and provision for my horses in his stable, and a lodging when I should attend at court, [and]. . . access to the king's presence and to himself at all times'.[16] But still there would be no court office, and still Coke refused. This time he specifically named Cranfield as his detractor.[17] In a long letter

[15]Coke MSS., packet 69, Coke to Buckingham [early Oct. 1622].

[16]Coke MSS., packet 45, Coke to Marie, 16 Oct. 1622.

[17]Coke MSS., packet 45, Coke to Buckingham [12 Oct. 1622].

intended for Buckingham, Coke reiterated his position at length. He began by recounting how he had patiently served for four years, not demanding or importuning for himself, but quietly relying at first on Buckingham's assurances, and, more recently, on the personal promise of the king himself made in the presence of Prince Charles and the Lord Admiral. 'But', Coke admitted, 'when all these hopes, and other later encouragements by my friends, determined [i.e., resulted] in a service at court without a place, I was (I confess) troubled a little.' Coke acknowledged that he had received Buckingham's latest offer by way of Greville. Then he proceeded to refuse the offer in no uncertain terms. Regarding the £300 allowance, he said, 'let it not offend your lordship if, for the king's honour and yours, I desire to have it continued no longer than my service in the navy shall require and deserve it and the commission stand on foot'. Regarding the additional £200 in 'wages', Coke observed that twelve years earlier he had refused the same amount when it was offered by Greville 'with a house for my family and other benefits besides'. Indeed, said Coke, 'ask yourself (my good lord) whether near five years since, when I first had the honour to be known unto you, you did not propound a greater entertainment'. Now, Coke concluded, being five years older, it would be even more unreasonable for him 'to dispose of my life for wages'.

Before Coke could send this letter, news reached him of a new development that radically changed his bargaining position. Coke was keenly interested in the vacant office of Master of Requests and had evidently broached the subject to Buckingham.[18] But the Lord Admiral had already promised the place to another suitor, Thomas Meautys. There seemed no way of satisfying both Coke and Meautys at the same time. Then Coke learned that an aged Clerk of the Council, Sir Clement Edmondes, had suddenly fallen ill and lay near death.[19] Coke himself was not interested in becoming Clerk of the Council, but Meautys might be persuaded to accept this place. If so, that would leave the way open for Coke to become Master of Requests. Coke therefore put aside the long letter of explanation he had been drafting to the Lord Admiral and sent, instead, a briefer, more positive message, with this proposal:

> . . . you were pleased to tell me that you would have bestowed me in the office of Requests if I had moved it before you were

[18]The Master of Requests office was left vacant by the death of Sir Christopher Perkins in late August or early September. *DNB,* XV, 980; McClure, *Chamberlain Letters,* II, 451.

[19]Edmondes died 12 or 13 October. *DNB,* VI, 390; McClure, *Chamberlain Letters,* II, 458.

> engaged to another [Meautys]. It now falleth out by God's hand that a worthy Clerk of the Council is in great extremity and (as it is said) beyond hope of recovery. And the reversion of that place, as it is of more worth, so doubtless will it be more welcome [to Meautys]. . . And then, if your lordship think me worthy of the Mastership of Requests which is now in your hands, your Honour shall both bind me and enable me. . . to serve your Honour in the navy, the ordnance, and all your own occasions to your full content, and that without charge.[20]

To continue the gambling analogy, Buckingham's hand had been called. It was the moment of reckoning, and Buckingham had only two choices left: either make Coke a Master of Requests or lose his services when the naval commission expired. There was no middle ground. Coke was going for broke, all or nothing, the Master of Requests place or a retired life in the country. If Buckingham genuinely valued his services, if he ever intended to honour the promises he had made over the past four years, this was his chance to prove it. And he did.

It was not easy for Buckingham to make the arrangements Coke proposed. Meautys had to be persuaded to relinquish his claim to the Master of Requests place. He apparently had a reversion to the office because Coke said it was 'already promised to another who had an ancient grant of the reversion thereof'. Buckingham planned to solve this problem by paying Meautys to wait for the next vacant Mastership of Requests. As Coke explained it, Buckingham would deal with Meautys 'to be contented with money for the present (which his lordship would give out of his own purse) and with the next reversion afterwards'.[21] It is doubtful, though, whether Buckingham had to dip into his own pocket. Meautys obtained a reversion in 1622 to the Writership of Star Chamber to the Great Seal, and this may have been one way of paying Meautys to leave the Requests office free for Coke.[22] The other way of manoeuvring Meautys out of the Requests place, as Coke had proposed, was to give him the Clerkship of the Council instead. This was an especially logical solution because Meautys had also coincidentally acquired a reversion to a Council Clerkship more

[20]Coke MSS., packet 45, Coke to Buckingham, 12 Oct. 1622. This letter is endorsed by Coke, 'Copy of the letter sent in place of the other'. This and the preceding letter bear the combined endorsement: '1622 Octob. 12. Copy of a letter sent to the Lord Marquis Buckingham and of another not sent. Both concerning his lordship's proposition to myself.'

[21]Coke MSS., packet 45, Coke to Marie, 16 Oct. 1622.

[22]Aylmer, *The King's Servants*, p. 292.

than three years earlier.[23] He did not get the Council Clerkship left vacant by the death of Sir Clement Edmondes, however. Instead he obtained another Council Clerkship which had been held for the past nine years by Francis Cottington. One reason Cottington was willing to part with his Clerkship at this particular time was that he had just secured a more advantageous place at court as Secretary to Prince Charles.[24] Another reason was money. Buckingham, who was negotiating among all these parties, told Meautys, 'because Mr. Cottington paid £450 for the place when he came to it', it is 'reasonable he should receive it again'. Buckingham thus instructed Meautys to pay Cottington £450 for the Clerkship, but he softened the blow by further explaining: 'I have, therefore, to show my care for you both, found out this expedient, that you pay him his money which you shall have again out of a baronet; and to that purpose would have you harken out some fit man for that title.'[25] In other words, Meautys would have to pay Cottington £450 for the Council Clerkship, but he could recoup at least part of that amount by selling a baronetcy which the Crown was putting at his disposal. Meautys may have figured out how to follow these instructions without letting yet another person enter the already crowded picture. There is no way of knowing for certain who got the baronetcy in question, but three months later one new holder of a baronetcy was none other than Cottington. Furthermore, Cottington did not buy his baronetcy; he somehow obtained it without paying the usual fees. The most plausible explanation for this is that Cottington and Meautys made a deal: Cottington accepted the baronetcy from Meautys in lieu of all or part of the £450 Meautys owed him for the Council Clerkship.[26]

These complicated negotiations, presided over by Buckingham, lasted nearly five weeks. And all that time Coke anxiously waited on the sidelines. At the outset he was optimistic. On 16 October he described for Marie the brighter future they could now look forward to: 'We shall have means to live together here, or in the country when we think fit, and in a better fashion than we have done heretofore. . .

[23]McClure, *Chamberlain Letters,* II, 216; Spedding, *The Letters and the Life of Francis Bacon,* VII, 390-1.

[24]Martin J. Havran, *Caroline Courtier: The Life of Lord Cottington* (London, 1973), pp. 42-3, 51, 65-9. The Clerkship that Edmondes had held went to John Dickinson. *CSPD,* 1619-1623, p. 460.

[25]SP 14/134/6.

[26]Compare Havran, *Caroline Courtier,* p. 70. Chamberlain mentioned this baronetcy in a letter dated 22 February. SP 14/138/59. Lawrence Stone has estimated that the price of a baronetcy in 1622 was between £220 and £250. 'The Inflation of Honours, 1558-1641', *Past and Present,* 14 (1958), 53.

and shall be also able to settle our children at the university, and you shall be freed from those drudgeries and domestical cares which now take up your time.'[27] Then more than a week went by without results, and Coke became concerned. On 27 October Buckingham wrote to him reassuringly: 'I must desire you to have a little patience and not to think I am forgetful of you that I have not yet given you an account of your business, the reason of which delay is only my desire so to contrive your satisfaction that it may be without the prejudice of others.'[28] Coke promptly apologized for his impatience and declared that: 'I now study nothing but how to be thankful.'[29] Nevertheless, the negotiations were far more protracted than Coke had expected. After the first week of November, Coke reported to Marie that he had met with the Lord Admiral, 'yet the other party who hath a promise of the place could not then be treated with, and therefore of necessity we must both of us follow the court this next week'. Coke regretted the delay but asked Marie to understand that it was 'more reasonable for me to tarry a few days and put his lordship to the performance of his engagement unto me than to lose so fair a hope and advantage by abandoning the opportunity'.[30] Then suddenly it was all over. On 18 November, after five suspenseful weeks, Coke had 'a warrant for the taking of my oath before the lords of the Council, and for drawing my letters patent'. As he proudly explained to Marie: 'I have now a real experience of my lord marquis's favour, by whose means his Majesty hath bestowed on me a place of good account in his service, and the manner of the giving doth also much amplify the gift.'[31] On 20 November 1622, at a meeting of the Privy Council, Coke was sworn in as Master of Requests.[32]

Coke's departure for Hall Court was delayed for several more weeks after his appointment. He apologetically told Marie: 'I was commanded a service by the king himself, and I have two or three businesses for the lord marquis.'[33] There was also the responsibility of his new office. 'Since I was sworn Master of Requests', Coke complained, 'I have had continual business.'[34] Another cause of delay

[27]Coke MSS., packet 45, Coke to Marie, 16 Oct. 1622.

[28]Coke MSS., packet 45, Buckingham to Coke, 27 Oct. 1622.

[29]Coke MSS., packet 45, Coke to Buckingham, 30 Oct. 1622.

[30]Coke MSS., packet 80, Coke to Marie [*ca.* 10 Nov.] 1622.

[31]Coke MSS., packet 80, a letter endorsed by Coke: '1622. Nov. 18. To my wife from London. Master of Requests place.'

[32]*APC,* 1621-1623, p. 356. Coke's name is incorrectly printed 'Cole'.

[33]Coke MSS., packet 80, Coke to Marie, 18 Nov. 1622.

[34]Coke MSS., packet 80, Coke to Marie [*ca.* 1 Dec.] 1622.

was the technical but important matter of seeing the bill for his new fee passed. The amount involved was £100 annually, and Coke became especially worried when the rumour began to circulate that he would have no fee at all. He anxiously wrote to Buckingham that 'some here have already said to my disadvantage that I am a Master of Requests sworn in ordinary without fee, which no man ever was before'.[35] He was no doubt greatly relieved when the bill was signed and passed by the second week of December.[36] Finally, Coke was now busily planning to abandon Hall Court and move his family to London. While searching for a suitable place to live, he described one place as 'a house that hath but little room and yet a great rent'.[37] With all these matters consuming his time, it was probably near the end of December before he was at last able to return home and spend the holidays with his family. The waiting, it would seem, had been worthwhile. Coke had got what he wanted. He went home secure in the fact that he was at last a man with an office at court.

Reflecting on the last months of 1622 which witnessed Coke's appointment as Master of Requests, there are several points worth emphasizing. One is the continuing importance of Greville, who was at least marginally involved in the affair at the beginning. His usefulness to Coke and influence with Buckingham were far from exhausted. Another is the fact that Coke did not buy his office. Seen in its seventeenth-century context, there is of course nothing particularly ethical or virtuous about this, but it is politically significant that Buckingham, in effect, bought the office for Coke. That brings us to a more important point: the fact that Buckingham actually did accede to Coke's request. He certainly did not have to. After all, he had made Coke a generous offer of his own, and Coke had neither the power nor the money to demand something better. It can only be assumed that Buckingham did place a high value on Coke's services. To be sure, Coke's loyalty and submissiveness counted for much, but so apparently did his industry and ability. James and Buckingham had been promising for four years that his work in the navy and the ordnance would not go unrewarded, and evidently they had meant it. Finally, and perhaps most important, Coke's attitude deserves attention. For behind the polite facade, he was driving a hard bargain. It is a plain fact that he spelled out his own terms to Buckingham and refused to settle for anything less. We glimpse in these negotiations a more independent and assertive Coke than is usually revealed to us,

[35]Coke MSS., packet 69, Coke to Buckingham [*ca.* 1 Dec.] 1622.

[36]*Cowper MSS.*, I, 123.

[37]Coke MSS., packet 80, Coke to Marie [*ca.* 1 Dec.] 1622.

and this should caution us against assuming that he was always quite as servile as his public expressions made him appear. Coke was rewarded for his hard work and servile behaviour not only because this is what his masters wanted from him but also because he positively insisted upon adequate reward. Of course Coke returned to his usual posture of subservience the moment Buckingham seemed ready to comply. A cynic would say this simply proves that all men have their price, and for Coke that price was an office at court.

In one respect there can be no doubt that gaining an office led Coke into more complete servitude. For the past four years, he had lived one life at his home in Herefordshire and another one at court. Although his interests were clearly divided between the two, his deeper loyalties and affections had seemed to belong to his home in the country. It had been his refuge for more than a decade prior to the naval investigation, and while the court remained uncertain, he seemed inclined to return there when the naval commission expired. Hall Court gave him an alternative, an option he could exercise if life at court turned sour again. But his appointment to the Mastership of Requests changed all that. It irrevocably reversed the decision he had made nearly sixteen years before; it turned the course of his life away from 'domestical frugality' and back again to 'striving with the world'. Thus, in winning himself an office, Coke had in a very real sense lost his independence. After disclaiming the court for fourteen years and resisting it for another four, Coke suddenly acquired what all the time he had really wanted: full-fledged membership in that select group. And once he became a part of the court, there was never again another place capable of competing for his loyalty. In December of 1622, he already seemed bent on deserting both a world and a way of life he so recently had cherished. He was, in fact, spending his last Christmas at Hall Court and his next-to-last with Marie.

While Coke was a Master of Requests from 1622 to 1625, this was not his only source of work or of influence. The navy still occupied a great deal of his time. As it turned out, the naval commission was not allowed to expire in 1623, and Coke continued to be the chief commissioner. Then, too, much of Coke's work during this period cannot be put strictly within the category of the navy or Requests. Buckingham continued to employ him in various additional capacities. Consequently much, or indeed most, of Coke's work during these years would be lost or misunderstood if he were thought of only as a Master of Requests. Having issued that caveat, however, we can proceed to examine the particular duties and advantages that were associated with Coke's work as Master of Requests.

There were four Masters of Requests, judges of the Court of Requests.[38] Compared to something like Chancery, the Court of Requests was relatively informal and popular. It had originated with the king's obligation to dispense justice to even the poorest of his subjects. To begin with, the petitions of poor suitors had been reviewed by the Council or any number of its members. Gradually, however, the task became too burdensome for a Council that had more important matters with which to occupy its time. The office of Master of Requests was therefore established to assume the responsibility for receiving, reviewing, and passing judgement on petitions from persons too poor to prosecute their cases in the common law courts. At first there were two ordinary Masters who travelled in the company of the king, then two extraordinary Masters were added to remain behind in London. By the time of Coke's appointment, all four Masters were given ordinary status and rotated the attendance at court on a monthly basis. Also by this time, the four Masters acted as judges dispensing justice during the law terms in a particular room at Westminster which had come to be known as the Court of Poor Men's Causes or more precisely as the Court of Requests. Thus, following a familiar course of development, the power or duty of the king, originally delegated to the Council, eventually evolved into a separate institution. The Court of Requests was therefore a prerogative court or court of equity dealing with civil cases analogous to the Court of Star Chamber, which was similarly descended from the Council but dealt with criminal cases. Requests, however, never acquired a statutory basis. In fact, the common lawyers had done everything possible to discredit Requests and nearly succeeded in eliminating it altogether late in Elizabeth's reign. Nevertheless, it survived these assaults, retained its popularity, and even experienced a renaissance of sorts in the decade or so preceding the Civil War. In addition to poor persons, it often attracted more prosperous litigants. All members of the royal Household were also entitled to use it.

The most self-evident function of a Master of Requests, then, was to serve as a judge on the Court of Requests. Though we know this much in general, it is exceedingly difficult to be more specific about how any particular Master performed this function. The records of the

[38]The Court of Requests, especially during the Stuart period, has been relatively neglected. Most accounts rely heavily on I.S. Leadem, ed., *Select Cases in the Court of Requests 1497-1569* (London, 1898). The most comprehensive study is the unpublished M.A. thesis by W.B.J. Allsebrook, 'The Court of Requests in the Reign of Elizabeth' (University of London, 1936). More recent is L.M. Hill's 'Introduction' to Sir Julius Caesar's *The Ancient State Authoritie, and Proceedings of the Court of Requests* (Cambridge, 1975).

Court of Requests are sparse and intractable. They yield very little information regarding the individual role of any one Master. It is understandable that the few biographies which have been written about men who served as Masters of Requests are very sketchy on this aspect of their subjects' careers.[39] We can do little better in Coke's case. The only salient point that can be discerned from the extant records concerns attendance. The initials of the Masters in attendance are given along with the daily orders and decrees of the Court. Allowing for the incomplete and sometimes decayed nature of these records, one generalization about Coke does appear valid: he was present less often than any other Master. All three of the other Masters attended Requests much more than Coke did during his three years as a Master. In fact, the Court's records indicate that Coke's first regular attendance did not occur until nearly a year after his appointment. Looked at another way, Coke was a Master during eleven full law terms, but apart from a few isolated appearances, he was in attendance only three out of those eleven terms. This contrasts most sharply with one of Coke's fellow Masters named Edward Powell, who was incidentally a cousin of Coke's father-in-law. Powell attended during all but one of those eleven terms. During Coke's first year especially, the other Masters carried most of his share of the load. During his second year something much closer to an equal distribution of work was achieved. But during the third year Coke was mostly absent again.[40] What can account for Coke's markedly infrequent attendance? Lack of legal training was evidently not the reason. Coke's successor in 1625 also had no legal training, but he immediately entered into the work of the Court on a roughly equal basis with the other three Masters.[41] Besides, during Coke's second year as a Master, he and Powell did most of the work of Requests for two consecutive terms. By this time Coke obviously knew how to do the job, but he dropped nearly out of sight again during his final year as Master. The real reason for Coke's infrequent attendance was probably his work in the navy. As we shall see, during his first year as Master he was preoccupied with the fleet required to retrieve Buckingham and Charles from Spain. During his last year he

[39]Menna Prestwich's incomparably thorough study of Cranfield contains only a few references to Cranfield as a Master of Requests. *Cranfield,* pp. 193-5, 254n., 257-8. Similarly, see Roy Schreiber's *Naunton,* pp. 9-10. The best consideration of an individual Master's work is in L.M. Hill's unpublished Ph.D. thesis, 'The Public Career of Sir Julius Caesar 1584-1614' (University of London, 1968), pp. 236-85.

[40]These conclusions are drawn from the order and decree books of the Court of Requests: PRO, REQ 1/31-2. The draft order books are much less substantial but lead to the same conclusions: REQ 1/56-8.

[41]REQ 1/32, 1/58. Coke's successor was Sir Thomas Aylesbury, who took his B.A. and M.A. at Oxford and was particularly interested in mathematics. *DNB,* I, 749.

was busy with ships loaned to the French government and with the first of the war fleets. These periods of increased naval activity coincide with Coke's absence from Requests. Buckingham had given Coke a place at court, but his primary motive in doing so was to insure his continued work for the navy.

In addition to serving as a judge on the Court of Requests, each Master had a second function which should be equally self-evident but is routinely ignored by historians.[42] As already mentioned, each Master took his turn on a monthly basis at court – not the judicial Court of Requests but the royal court. Here he was responsible for receiving and processing all sorts of requests, from rich and poor alike.[43] These requests came in the form of petitions for royal favour, and they fell roughly into two categories. By far the largest number were requests to the king for offices, land, or money. Less often they were legal appeals to the king for relief from creditors, remission of fines, or pardons for crimes committed. Both kinds of suits were settled without employing the formal machinery of the Court of Requests. The Master simply conferred with the king about each request and disposed of it according to the king's desire. Sometimes the king referred the request to an appropriate official, sometimes he appointed a committee to consider the request, and quite often he simply ruled on the request himself. The Master's function here was no less important and surely more lucrative than his work in the institutionalized Court of Requests.

Coke's turn for handling petitions at court fell in the months of January, May, and September.[44] In the January of 1623 immediately following his appointment as Master he was enjoying his long-delayed visit home to Hall Court. He had therefore arranged for Edward Powell to take his place, but through a letter from a friend Coke learned that another Master 'had possessed himself of this month's waiting' and thereby done him 'an injury'.[45] The injury was probably not so much a matter of etiquette as of fees. Fortunately, for several of the other months when Coke did attend at court, he kept the notes he made for the purpose. Those notes consist of lists of unsettled suits

[42]G.E. Aylmer is exceptional in his appreciation of the Master's work outside the Court of Requests. See *The King's Servants,* pp. 13-15, 153.

[43]The other court officers who received and processed petitions were the two Secretaries of State. Since Coke served in both offices, he received a great many petitions. There are approximately 300 among his extant papers, Coke MSS., muniments room, box 1.

[44]*Cowper MSS.,* I, 123, 125, 168. SP 16/5/108. This fact is also confirmed by the dating of Coke's notes soon to be discussed.

[45]Coke MSS., packet 45, Thomas Alured to Coke, 3 Jan. 1623.

and petitions to bring to the attention of the king. From Coke's endorsement on each list, it is evident that he presented each suit to the king in a personal audience with him. Coke then wrote in the margin beside each case such comments as 'refused', 'granted', 'recommended to the lords', 'recommended to the Lord Treasurer to inform his Majesty what he thinketh fit in this business', 'his Majesty will consider', and 'the king mindeth not'.[46] This was the essence of personal government, the king summarily dispensing justice and favours. This was also the essence of Coke's work as Master — receiving petitions from suitors, procuring the king's decision, and carrying out whatever instructions he received to give effect to the king's will.

It should be patently clear, then, that being a Master of Requests meant something more than sitting as a judge in a poor man's court. Most of the petitions that passed through Coke's hands were, indeed, from poor suitors. Widows and prisoners were among the most frequent of these.[47] In 1625, when James died, all the royal servants anxiously asked to be confirmed in their places, and Coke received petitions from Household employees as obscure as the Groom of the Crossbows and the Yeoman of the Great Bakehouse.[48] On the other hand, though the Court of Requests was usually limited to poor suitors, the process of petitioning was not. Consequently, among Coke's notes one also finds such people as the countess of Berkshire, the bishop of Exeter, Lord Stanhope, the earl of Somerset, and the earl of Suffolk.[49] Since the Master of Requests was a crucial link between suitors and the king, he was in a highly advantageous position. The Master was far more than a neutral messenger in the process. He could hasten, delay, obstruct, or facilitate the progress of a suit. More than that, he could represent the suit to the king in such a way as to encourage or discourage its favourable reception. This was the real source of the Master's power and influence, and it made his services worth paying for. Sir Edward Montagu found this out in 1604

[46]Portions of Coke's notes, usually omitting his marginal notations, are printed in *Cowper MSS.*, I, 148, 158-9, 163-4, 171-2, 184-5, 194-5, 197-9. The representative notations I have quoted are taken from Coke's audiences in Sept. 1623, Jan. 1624, and May 1625. Coke MSS., reordered packets 13 and 14 and old packet 25, respectively. Notebooks of a similar nature exist for at least two other Masters. Sir Thomas Aylesbury's notebook for part of 1638 is BL, Add. MS. 38,598. Another notebook with entries from the period 1613-17 is in the Coke MSS., muniments room, box 1. Those years coincide with the Mastership of John Daccombe, but there is no proof that it is his notebook.

[47]*Cowper MSS.*, I, 141, 165-7, 180.

[48]*Ibid.*, I, 198.

[49]*Ibid.*, I, 147-8, 158, 197.

when he sent a petition to the king by way of someone other than the Master of Requests. Montagu was required to resubmit his petition, this time through a Master. Montagu's brother subsequently reported from court: 'The King hath given answer to your petition now at length. . . he said when it was delivered him before he did not understand it; but when things are done by the ordinary officer then he can acquaint him with the matter and he will be ready to do them.' Montagu's brother pointedly added: 'I think the Master of Requests looks for a fee — I suppose some six angels will serve his turn.'[50] Lord Stanhope was even more explicit when he gave a petition to Coke and asked him to 'use your best help and furtherance by adding such motives as you shall find fit and behooveful by word of mouth to his Majesty for the obtaining thereof'. Stanhope added: 'For which your courtesy (the grant once procured) I will give you forty pieces.'[51] Another suitor of more modest means wrote to Coke: 'I have herewith sent you, Sir, five pieces as a remembrance of my thankfulness.'[52] One man who had a post in the navy worth £20 annually and desired a better post paying £40 told Coke: 'which first fruits of my increase of augmentation, I shall, good Sir, be ready to render upon the accomplishment hereof as a thankful remembrance and token of my unfeigned love for your great care and pains in my behalf'.[53] On another occasion, Coke received a note telling him that he would receive £10 from the late queen's Grooms of the Chamber as soon as they received the reward promised them by the king. On the bottom of this note, Coke wrote: 'Spenser to come tomorrow to bring money.'[54] The highest specific amount offered Coke that we know of was £150 for a pardon. But Coke's father-in-law, who conveyed this offer to him, said he knew Coke was not receptive to cases of this sort.[55] Gratuities were not always referred to in such blatant and specific terms. Lord Vaughan told Coke, 'what courtesy you have performed shall be requited'.[56] Another suitor similarly said, 'for which your great pains and care there shall be further requital'.[57] Even the very poor were constrained to make such promises. For example, when the

[50]HMC, *Buccleuch and Queensbury MSS.,* I, 237. Sidney, another of Montagu's brothers, was a Master of Requests at the same time as Coke.

[51]Coke MSS., packet 45, Charles, Lord Stanhope, to Coke, 23 Aug. 1623.

[52]Coke MSS., packet 45, Doctor F. Ryves to Coke, 10 Feb. 1624.

[53]Coke MSS., packet 24, Henry Goddard to Coke, 3 May 1625.

[54]Coke MSS., muniments room, miscellaneous papers removed to boxes 1 and 2 of Coke's papers.

[55]*Cowper MSS.,* I, 152.

[56]Coke MSS., reordered packet 15, John, Lord Vaughan to Coke, 28 Sept. 1624.

[57]Coke MSS., reordered packet 17, Henry Goldsmith to Coke, 13 Jan. 1625.

Solicitor General wrote to Coke about several persons imprisoned for debt who were seeking their freedom, he relayed this message: 'Out of their penury they have desired me to let you know that you shall have a very thankful acknowledgement before the petition part from your hands.'[58]

Put in its simplest terms, a Master of Requests was in a position to do favours and to expect favours, monetary or otherwise, in return. One party Coke especially favoured was his *alma mater,* Trinity College. Dr Richardson, the Master of Trinity, told Coke on one occasion, 'your power. . . in three hours space delivered me from a most deep, desperate, Machiavellian practice which had been these two or three years in hatching'.[59] At another time, Richardson wrote: 'You did me a very seasonable good turn when you stood in the breach and stayed the flood.'[60] Coke's services were equally appreciated by the Vice-Chancellor of Cambridge.[61] In return for these favours, Coke knew that his sons would be well received at Cambridge and that he could influence the election of a fellow when he wanted to.[62]

The annual fee of a Master of Requests was only £100, but the true rewards of the office were many times that amount. This made it one of the most avidly sought after offices at court, and one Master was said to have paid at least £3,000 for his place.[63] Furthermore, in addition to the financial rewards of the office, there was the incalculable advantage of close and frequent intercourse with the king. The Master who knew how to exploit this position of privileged proximity could use it as a stepping-stone to even higher office. In fact, three men succeeded in rising from Master of Requests under James I to Secretary of State, and one of those three was Coke.[64]

[58]Coke MSS., packet 45, Robert Heath to Coke, 16 May 1623.

[59]Coke MSS., reordered packet 13, 1 Oct. 1623.

[60]*Cowper MSS.,* I, 153.

[61]SP 14/185/29.

[62]*Cowper MSS.,* I, 150, 173.

[63]G.R. Elton, ed., *The Tudor Constitution: Documents and Commentary* (Cambridge, 1965), p. 185 n. 4; *Cowper MSS.,* II, 67.

[64]The other two former Masters who became Secretaries were Sir Ralph Winwood and Naunton.

8

OF LOVE AND WAR: 1623-1624

The abiding importance of the navy in Coke's career after his appointment as Master of Requests is demonstrated by the fact that his main task in 1623 was to prepare another fleet. Buckingham and Prince Charles had put on false beards, mounted their horses, and gone off secretly to Spain where they hoped to arrange the marriage of the Spanish princess to Charles. Whatever else one might say about their departure, it was cheap. Only one vessel had been required to sneak the prince and Lord Admiral across the Channel. By contrast, a whole fleet, richly equipped and burdened with a large entourage of gentlemen and servants, was required to bring them back.

Coke's primary associate in the preparation of this fleet requires an introduction. His name was Sir Edward Conway, and he replaced Naunton as one of the two Secretaries of State at the beginning of 1623.[1] Conway shared many of those same ties with Coke that Naunton had. Early in his life, Conway had been a follower of Essex, who knighted him at the sacking of Cadiz in 1596. Like Coke, Conway may have survived the fall of Essex because he enjoyed the additional support of Greville. In fact, Conway and Greville were cousins, and it was probably through this mutual relationship that Conway and Coke became acquainted. A good part of Conway's life had been spent in military service in the Netherlands as Lieutenant-Governor of the Brill.[2] The Netherlands appreciated a valuable Protestant supporter when they saw one and awarded Conway an annual pension of £500.[3] While at the Brill, Conway corresponded with Coke; and his surviving letters attest both to his friendship for Coke and the mutual regard of the two for Greville.[4] When Conway was appointed Secretary of State in 1623, he and Coke worked well

[1]For Conway see Florence Evans, *The Principal Secretary: A Survey of the Office from 1558 to 1680* (Manchester, 1923), pp. 79-85; Mathew, *The Jacobean Age,* pp. 257-80; R.E. Bonner, 'Administration and Public Service under the Early Stuarts: Edward Viscount Conway as Secretary of State, 1623-28' (unpublished Ph.D. thesis, University of Minnesota, 1968).

[2]Coke's brother, Robert, died fighting in the Netherlands, probably under Conway's command. It is commonly asserted that Conway was the Governor of the Brill, but in the letters between him and Coke it is clear that he was Lieutenant-Governor. *Cowper MSS.,* I, 22, 26.

[3]*DNB,* IV, 976.

[4]*Cowper MSS.,* I, 22, 43-5, 56-7; Coke MSS., packet 1, Conway to Coke, 25 July and 19 August 1603.

together from the outset. Indeed, they worked so well together that this may help to explain the gradual eclipse of the other Secretary, Sir George Calvert, a phenomenon that is usually attributed to his Catholic sympathies. While Conway threw himself into the duties of his new office with real industry and worked closely with Coke, Calvert seemed more reticent and on one occasion even obstructive.

Coke was given two particular responsibilities at this time. The first was to prepare the fleet for Spain; the other was to lead an investigation into piracy. Two English captains, Sir Henry Mervyn and Sir William St John, were charged with having seized a French ship and sold her cargo for their own profit.[5] A commission headed by Coke was appointed to look into these charges, which appear from Coke's papers to have been true.[6] For this business, as for the preparation of the fleet, Coke supervised the work in the field while Conway provided the communications and arrangements that were necessary at court. It should be added, too, that with Buckingham away in Spain, King James took an active interest in both businesses.

The idea of a fleet to convey the Infanta to England had been announced in early January of 1623.[7] What was new in February was not the idea of such a fleet but the fact that Charles and Buckingham, rather than being in England to direct its preparation, would be in Spain awaiting its arrival. Coke was not entirely straining the truth when he referred to 'my Lord Admiral's providence and directions before his departure', but, on the other hand, the very precipitate nature of that departure created acute demands that had not in any way been anticipated.[8] Buckingham and Charles had gone to Spain with little more than the shirts on their backs. Now they urgently called for servants, rich trappings, and jewels. James planned to send all this in a light pinnace, but was the pinnace he had in mind the most suitable one? This, Conway told Coke, 'his Majesty requires you (as one in whom he hath a particular confidence, with the rest of the commissioners for the navy) to judge and inform him'. Coke was instructed to 'advertise his Majesty of your opinions in all points very particularly'.[9] Coke's first opinion was that a light pinnace was not the right sort of vessel to employ. He reported directly to James that: 'I

[5] *Cowper MSS.*, I, 129; SP 14/139/173.

[6] The commission was formed at least partly in response to complaints from the French ambassador. *CSPD*, 1619-1623, pp. 495, 500-2, 507.

[7] Gardiner, *History of England*, IV, 409.

[8] SP 14/139/12.

[9] SP 14/138/95.

found no such pinnace fit for this service, but rather made choice of your Majesty's ship the *Adventure*. . . and gave present order for her.'[10] Coke was careful to say that he acted with the concurrence of Cranfield, Secretary Calvert, and the Chancellor of the Exchequer, Sir Richard Weston, but in Calvert's report of the matter to Conway it is clear that Coke acted first and obtained the concurrence of these other men only afterwards.[11]

Coke maintained his position of leadership throughout the preparations. Another example of this fact immediately arose because the captain of the *Adventure* was St John. As St John was currently under investigation at the insistence of the French ambassador, Coke judged that it would not be appropriate to employ him in such an affair of state. Indeed, Coke recommended that both St John and Mervyn be relieved of their commands, and he sent Conway drafts of two letters which would inform the suspect captains to that effect.[12] Coke further recommended that Sir Richard Bingley replace St John as captain of the *Adventure*. This was a charitable recommendation. Coke commended Bingley for his experience at sea and favoured him 'because his long suspension from his office in the navy hath brought him into want'.[13] Bingley was one of the former principal officers of the navy whom the commissioners had replaced in 1619. Responding to these suggestions, Conway reported to Coke that King James was still 'confident of your particular faith and industry' and likely to agree in the matter of the captains.[14] Subsequently, both Mervyn and St John were relieved of their commands, and Bingley was appointed captain of the *Adventure*.[15] Furthermore, when it came time to give Bingley his instructions, Coke told Conway: 'I have drawn his instructions, and showed them to the commissioners, and sent them to your Honour as our common act.'[16]

There is some reason to believe that the other commissioners resented this sort of domination. On at least one occasion, Conway seems to have warned Coke about his autocratic methods. Coke responded by thanking the Secretary for his 'good admonition, and

[10] SP 14/139/12.

[11] SP 14/139/10.

[12] SP 14/139/32, 73.

[13] SP 14/139/32.

[14] SP 14/139/45.

[15] *CSPD,* 1619-1623, pp. 514, 523.

[16] SP 14/140/6. Coke similarly drafted the instructions for other captains, masters, and pursers on the voyage. *Cowper MSS.,* I, 154 and Coke MSS., packet 130.

grave and friendly counsel, which I will follow with care'. But Coke was far from apologetic in explaining:

> . . . in his Majesty's service, I go not by myself but have desired the assistance of my fellow commissioners, as his Majesty well knoweth. Neither have I certified anything wherein they dissent. But where the pains and care of one man is rather required than the counsel of many, I confess I have been forward to discharge the special trust reposed in me, though I know that thereby, as also by the many addresses I receive from your Honour, I draw envy upon me, wherein my duty to his Majesty and my thankfulness to my lord make me neglect my own respect.[17]

Coke was one of those persons who believe that if you want a job done well, you must do it yourself. He was not going to delegate any more authority than necessary in a project for which he himself would be held responsible. Operating in this manner during peacetime, Coke did manage to get things done. Only later, during the war years, would it become apparent that this short-sighted approach failed to produce other men who were sufficiently experienced and trustworthy to assist in an undertaking that no man by himself could manage.

The primary problem in the preparation of this fleet was, as usual, money. In the beginning, it was difficult to limit the number of servants who went over on the *Adventure* with the jewels. James was painfully conscious of this cost. 'His majesty seems contented', Conway wrote, 'that the ship will carry few. And in my letter to the prince's officers, I have declared the king's pleasure that they regulate the number to as short a proportion as possibly they can.'[18] Notwithstanding this instruction, Coke later lamented that 'the number continue great'.[19] Of course the problem was multiplied in the case of the larger fleet. Again Conway voiced the king's concern: 'His Majesty thinks he can never put too much caution where two points so contrary as honour and frugality are at strife. . . but he sees not how 800 men passengers can come to be increased with the prince's train, or how there would be stowage for them.'[20] Coke was similarly dissatisfied with the first estimate of provisions required for the voyage.[21]

No one was more concerned to limit the cost of the voyage than Cranfield, who was now the Lord Treasurer and bore the title of earl of

[17]SP 14/139/109; Coke MSS., packet 45, draft of the same.

[18]SP 14/139/28.

[19]SP 14/139/41.

[20]SP 14/143/50.

[21]SP 14/143/29, 41, 83.

Middlesex. From Cranfield's point of view, the navy was a constant threat to his economy drive. Coke had run into difficulty getting adequate funds from the parsimonious Treasurer before. As if to assure Coke that this problem would not recur this time, Conway had written at the very beginning of the preparations: 'The Lord Treasurer (who can well judge of the necessity and importance of this occasion) will upon information of his Majesty's pleasure . . . prepare and furnish monies as shall be requisite.'[22] Cranfield was not all that cooperative, however. Coke reduced the demands for provisions to the point where they were 'moderated to near the half number propounded at first, and not much more than half the charge'. He firmly believed that 'they will not conveniently bear any abatement', but Cranfield was determined to reduce the cost even more. He believed that this could be achieved by giving the responsibility for victualling to the captain of each ship instead of administering it, as had been planned, through the Household officers. Coke thought this was a 'doubtful' course to follow, and he resented the delay Cranfield was causing. He told Buckingham: 'So that business stayeth only upon his lordship's resolution, and the whole fleet hath now no other cause of stay but that business.'[23] The issue was finally resolved in the Privy Council, where, as Coke reported to Buckingham, 'the lords of the Council found it not fit to trust the honour of the state, and of the prince and princess, into the hands of men inexperienced and unable [that is, the captains]'.[24] Thus Cranfield lost the argument, but Coke was still left with the memory of the opposition and delay. This episode reinforces the general impression that Coke looked upon Cranfield as a rival. Cranfield threatened Coke because he controlled the flow of funds that Coke desperately needed and because he offered competing advice. When Buckingham returned from Spain, he would set out to destroy the Lord Treasurer in Parliament. As we have already seen, Coke had many motives for assisting in Cranfield's impeachment. To these should be added his desire to remove not only an impediment to his work in the navy but also, and more simply, a competitor.

All efforts to prepare the fleet as swiftly and economically as possible were ultimately overturned by one factor: the uncertainty about the exact date when the fleet would be required to bring the prince and his new bride home to England. Coke was positively penalized for his efficiency. While the negotiations dragged on in Spain, the ships sat idly by waiting to be called. At the beginning of

[22]SP 14/138/95.

[23]SP 14/143/83.

[24]BL, Harleian MS. 1,580, no. 59, fol. 297: Coke to Buckingham, 2 May 1623.

May, Coke complained: 'All [the ships] are yet at Chatham, though there they put the king to no less charge than if they were at sea.'[25] By the end of July, when the fleet was finally ordered to sail, it had already consumed three-fifths of its provisions.[26] Unfortunately, this was not the last time that Coke would work frantically to prepare a fleet, then disconsolately stand by watching it deteriorate while his master delayed putting it to sea.

Most of the other major points of interest that emerge from Coke's work on the fleet are equally evident in his investigation of the two captains suspected of piracy, which continued through these same months. In this case, too, Coke dominated the commission appointed for the task.[27] His authority for doing so, however, may have been greater since he was ordered by James to conduct his own 'underhand' investigation.[28] He was instructed to report his findings weekly, he was deputed to deal personally with the complaints of the French ambassador, he employed his own informant or spy at Portsmouth, and, as we have seen, he recommended that the two captains be removed from their commands and even drafted the letters employed for this purpose.[29]

The most interesting feature of Coke's work during 1623 is the network of power or influence that lay beneath the surface. The immediate impression may be that Coke's position did not change very much with his appointment as Master of Requests. In particular, his principal employment was still related to the navy. On closer analysis, however, it is obvious that he had in a very real sense moved nearer the centre of power. As a member of the court, he acted with far greater initiative and authority than he had before; and he maintained surprisingly close and frequent communication with the king. This was no doubt partly due to Coke's new office and the special importance of the fleet he was supervising, but it owed something as well to his relationship with Conway. The two old friends formed a quick and lasting partnership, which was given formal recognition less

[25] *Ibid.*

[26] *CSPD,* 1623-1625, pp. 26-8; *Cowper MSS.,* I, 145.

[27] SP 14/139/32, 41.

[28] SP 14/139/29. In this letter of 3 March 1623, Conway repeated the king's instruction to Coke 'that you should make an underhand inquiry of the guiltiness of the two captains'.

[29] SP 14/139/12, 28, 41, 73, 108; 14/140/6, 18, 70; *CSPD,* 1619-1623, p. 507. The ultimate outcome of the investigation is uncertain. Charges were brought against Mervyn in the High Court of Admiralty. But according to an account written by Coke two years later, the proceedings lapsed because Cranfield refused to provide money to prosecute the case. SP 16/7/18.

than three years later, when Coke became Conway's official colleague as the other Secretary of State.

A corollary of the close cooperation between Conway and Coke was the limited participation of Secretary Calvert in these proceedings. This was probably due in part to his preoccupation with foreign affairs, but there were other possible reasons. Calvert had specific instructions to assist Coke in the naval preparations, but he obviously played little part in them.[30] The same was true of the piracy investigations. Here, in fact, Calvert was even a liability at times. Coke was disappointed in the first place when Calvert was unable to hasten the slow passage of the commission through the seals.[31] He was most distressed, however, when Calvert refused to issue a warrant to prevent one of the captains from escaping.[32] From Calvert's pointed defence of this delay, it appears he was strongly criticized for it.[33] Although he finally did issue this warrant, he transferred responsibility for another warrant in the same case directly to Coke.[34] To complicate the matter, Calvert later refused to allow the captain to be questioned by the commissioners. He argued that because the captain was now being held on a warrant from the Council, it would be an offence to the Council for anyone else to examine him. With a hint of sarcasm, Coke attributed this to 'Mr Secretary perhaps being not well informed'.[35] In both these instances, Calvert does not appear to have been wilfully obstructive. The problems arose more because he was extremely reluctant to take any action for which he felt he might not have adequate authority. In his own defence, he wrote: 'It is always safe for a man not to take to himself a greater latitude of discretion than is allowed him.'[36] The leading authority on the Secretary of State's office has said that Calvert's disfavour at court began in September of 1623, when his excessive caution caused a fatal delay in the Spanish marriage negotiations.[37] From what we have seen, this characteristic

[30]SP 14/138/95; *CSPD,* 1619-1623, p. 501.

[31]SP 14/139/32.

[32]SP 14/139/41, 73.

[33]SP 14/139/78.

[34]SP 14/139/79.

[35]SP 14/140/18.

[36]SP 14/139/78.

[37]Evans, *The Principal Secretary*, p. 83. According to Evans: 'The partnership [between Conway and Calvert] showed its first signs of strain in September 1623, when the Spanish marriage negotiations seemed on the point of completion. Some scruple of Calvert's due to no disagreement with the scheme but to a conscientious desire to perform his task thoroughly, caused a hitch in the proceedings and another of those delays which eventually proved fatal.'

caution was already working to Calvert's disadvantage earlier in 1623.

Another striking feature of this period is the extent to which King James relied upon Coke. Of course the fact that Buckingham was out of the country had something to do with this, as did the fact that the navy was Coke's acknowledged area of authority. But still it is surprising how often James asked for Coke's opinion, waited for his advice, and praised his reports.[38] Conway summed up this very situation when he told Coke that James 'gives good approbation of your proceedings, commends your care, and doth most graciously cherish that diligence and good affection which you show in all occasions of his'. In a more personal vein, Conway added: 'I take pleasure in presenting such things to his Majesty as come from you in regard of the good acceptance they find, and no less in giving you account what gracious testimonies his Majesty gives of your faith and diligence and how happy you are in his Majesty's good opinion.'[39]

As Conway and Coke worked through these first months together in their new court offices, their old friend and mutual patron, Fulke Greville, now Lord Brooke, was far from idle. In fact, he appears rather prominently in both the piracy investigation and the naval preparations.[40] The abiding ties between the three men and their common relationship to Buckingham were both expressed by Coke when he assured the Lord Admiral: 'The Lord Brooke carrieth a watchful eye for you, and to that end both attendeth the king's person and often visiteth the noble ladies your nearest friends. Of this good affection your lordship may do well to take knowledge. For that worthy and noble Secretary [Conway] I shall need to say no more but that he is yours as your own heart can wish.'[41] One could hardly find three more ardent Protestants at court than Greville, Conway, and Coke. The thought of a union with Spain must have been intensely repugnant to them. Yet they dutifully followed where Buckingham led because they were, above all, political animals guided by their sense of survival.

Of course the central figure in court politics, even during his absence in Spain, was the incomparable Buckingham. It is true that

[38]SP 14/138/95; SP 14/139/28, 29, 45; SP 14/143/36, 44; *CSPD*, 1619-1623, pp. 507, 536; *Cowper MSS.*, I, 130, 139, 148.

[39]Coke MSS., reordered packet 13, Conway to Coke, 17 Aug. 1623.

[40]*CSPD*, 1619-1623, pp. 507, 510, 512, 516, 547, 550, 560, 563, 565, 566, 569, 570, 572, 577; *Cowper MSS.*, I, 136-8, 148. See also Rebholz, *Fulke Greville*, p. 274.

[41]BL, Harleian MS. 1,581, no. 71, fol. 284; Coke to Buckingham, 4 May 1623.

something like a rival court faction began to take shape around Cranfield, but it is doubtful whether this ever constituted a very serious threat to Buckingham. While in Spain, Buckingham was elevated from a marquis to a duke through the continued affection of King James, and he gained a new ascendancy over Prince Charles that assured his eventual triumph over any would-be rivals.[42] Still, while the great favourite sojourned in Spain, there was a distinct increase in the anxiety level at the English court among those who feared, sought, enjoyed, or opposed his influence. The death of the Provost of Eton, for example, left several aspirants to this post hanging in suspense. The place could not be disposed of until the king of patronage returned from Spain. As Lord Keeper Williams, a key figure in the business, told Buckingham: 'It will rest wholly upon your lordship to name the man.'[43] The Provostship was not a particularly lucrative post, but its prestige and perquisites attracted a remarkable number of suitors. These men were afraid they would not get the post. Coke, by contrast, was afraid he would. Williams, preferring a man with an adequate university background, approached Coke to know if he would be interested in relinquishing his post as Master of Requests to become Provost of Eton. Alarmed by this overture, Coke reported to Buckingham: 'My answer was that in regard of my access and service to his Majesty and your Honour by that place, I would never be accessory to any such motion.' Greville had suggested to the Lord Keeper that Coke might be willing to trade his £300 yearly allowance in the navy for the Provostship. In his letter to Buckingham, Coke did not entirely close the door on this possibility. But Coke did not want to appear to be making a deal in Buckingham's absence, and his overriding concern was to cling, at all costs, to the Mastership of Requests.[44] Perhaps Coke had little chance of being appointed Provost. There is no further record of his being considered for the post. The incident is significant, however, because it prompted Coke to acknowledge in writing what he valued most about the Master of Requests place: that is, the enviable degree of access it gave him to

[42]Compare Conrad Russell, *Parliaments and English Politics 1621-1629* (Oxford, 1979), pp. 146-7.

[43]Isaac Walton, *The Lives of Dr. John Donne, Sir Henry Wotton,* ed. Thomas Zouch (York, 1796), p. 160. Sir Francis Bacon, Sir Dudley Carleton, and Sir William Beecher were among the most prominent aspirants, but the office was ultimately bestowed on Sir Henry Wotton. The anxious competition for the place can be followed in *CSPD,* 1619-1623, pp. 494, 538, 542, 559, 574, 580; 1623-1625, pp. 22, 70, 74, 91, 103, 106, 109, 125, 156, 184, 201, 207, 213, 297, 307. See also Mathew, *The Jacobean Age*, pp. 212-14.

[44]BL, Harleian MS. 1,581, no. 65, fol. 272: Coke to Buckingham, 11 April 1623. Cf. Harleian MS. 1,580, no. 29, fol. 90: Sir William Beecher to Buckingham, 29 March 1623.

Buckingham and the king. Indeed, Coke would not relinquish his Mastership of Requests until 1625, when he traded it for a Secretaryship of State, the only office at court that carried with it a guarantee of even greater access to Buckingham and the king. Meanwhile the escapade in Spain did nothing to diminish Coke's favour with Buckingham. From Madrid, the Lord Admiral wrote appreciatively to Coke: 'I know well the difference between naked obedience and that where affection is joined to it. The difference between those dispatches which pass your hands and others gives me good experience of it. You shall hereafter have the like of me, and the experience of a little more time shall better assure you how much I am your faithful friend and servant.'[45]

For all practical purposes the infatuation with the Spanish match ended when Buckingham and Charles finally left Spain in September. The story of their departure is well known, especially their ride to the Spanish coast and their joy at finding the English fleet waiting for them. When the bachelor prince returned to England, he met with a joyous welcome.[46] He and Buckingham temporarily made themselves popular by utterly failing in their negotiations and returning without a Spanish princess, a strange example of snatching victory from the jaws of defeat. The question of whether to continue pursuing the Spanish match was laid before the Parliament that assembled in February of 1624. In point of fact, however, despite James's resistance, Buckingham and Charles were already intent upon war.

Coke sat in the Parliament of 1624 as a member for the borough of St Germans.[47] He owed this seat to his brother-in-law, Valentine Carey, bishop of Exeter, who was traditionally allowed the privilege of nominating a burgess for St Germans.[48] Coke was appointed to numerous committees again, as he had been in 1621, and again it is impossible to know what role he played on them.[49] Among the most important were those which considered the Spanish treaties and the

[45]Coke MSS., packet 45, Buckingham to Coke, 28 May 1623.

[46]Gardiner, *History of England*, V, 128-9.

[47]*Returns of Members of Parliament,* I, 457.

[48]Carey's letter to Coke informing him of his nomination is printed in *Cowper MSS.,* I 157.

[49]*CJ,* I, 673, 676, 680, 681, 683, 686, 688, 717, 722, 728-32, 734, 737, 738, 745, 747, 753, 754, 760, 762, 764, 765. In the *Commons Journal*, knights are normally referred to by full name and title. For this reason Coke can probably be distinguished from Sir Edward Coke and Sir Robert Cooke, who also sat in this Parliament. But he cannot always be distinguished from Henry Coke, to whom consequently some of the preceding references may apply.

impeachment charges against Cranfield.[50] The work of these committees reflects the fact that Buckingham and Prince Charles effectively pursued two objectives in the Parliament of 1624. The first objective was to abandon the treaties with Spain and set England on a course for war; the second was to destroy Cranfield. Had Coke not been obliged to promote these objectives by virtue of his dependence on Buckingham, he would likely have done so just the same. For there could hardly have been a more perfect identity between his own personal views and those of his patron on these two subjects.

We have already alluded to Coke's role in the impeachment of Cranfield. The depositions of Coke and the ordnance officers were the chief instruments used in the Lords against the Lord Treasurer on the charge that he had ignored several attempted settlements of the ordnance office. Coke was perfectly truthful in his deposition, from which the Attorney General then selected only certain parts to read in order to make Cranfield's guilt appear more manifest. In the course of the impeachment proceedings, Cranfield recited his reforms to gain sympathy. This only served to draw upon him the accusation that he claimed the credit for other men's work, and it was on this occasion that Lord Keeper Williams made the remark previously cited that Cranfield had assumed the glory for naval reform but it was in truth the work of others, particularly Coke.[51] By cooperating in Cranfield's ruin, Coke eliminated a principal rival at court, and he gratified those feelings of jealousy, resentment, and frustration that had been accumulating since 1618. He also insinuated himself even further into Buckingham's favour. We should not allow this to obscure the fact, however, that Cranfield and Coke at heart were kindred spirits, both natural champions of reform and economy. In the years that followed, when Coke found himself overwhelmed by the unprecedented waste of war, there is no reason to believe that he ever realized how short-sighted it had been to remove Cranfield from the Lord Treasurership. So easily could personal antagonisms and the client-patron relationship subvert principle.

The treaties with Spain and the desirability of war were subjects that triggered a primal response in Coke. His passionate views are spelled out in what appears to be his draft for a speech in the Commons at the beginning of March, though it cannot be proved that

[50] *Ibid.*, I, 673, 683, 728, 729, 734, 754, 764.

[51] See my 'Illusions of Grandeur', pp. 68-73 and Robert E. Ruigh, *The Parliament of 1624* (Cambridge, Mass., 1971), pp. 236 n. 150, 322-3.

he actually delivered it.[52] Perhaps with Cranfield in mind, Coke began by arguing that financial necessity should not be used to justify accepting a Spanish dowry. 'And for our wants', Coke ironically said just weeks before testifying against Cranfield, 'neither Spain nor the riches of India shall be able to supply them till we regulate our expenses, and then we shall need none of their help.' Then Coke launched into rhetorical invective against the treacherous intrigues of the Spanish papists:

> . . . we deal not with babes but with a nation potent and wise, as much used to gain by our treaties as we have been to lose, and that by marriages hath ever prevailed more than by arms. And shall we think they will bind themselves for our ends and not bend us for theirs? Or will they not have power to do themselves right if we do them wrong? Is not the sword more ready in their hands than ours? And are we scarce able to right ourselves against them now. . . and shall we be more able to do them wrong when their spirits and all their recipes are within our bowels?

Coke concluded by admitting that conditions were not entirely ideal at home, but he argued that: 'There was yet no government ever so perfect that it could be free from just grievance and complaint. Even the wisdom of Solomon could not prevent it.' The king, he assured the House, was anxious to remove all just grounds for complaint. On the other hand, Coke typically added, the House should subordinate 'the humour of discontent' to 'what is good for our country and prince' and expect no more than 'a reasonable course' to 'satisfy all our moderate desires'.[53] Equally typical was the hope he expressed that Parliament would 'end with so good correspondence with his Majesty and such unity amongst ourselves that Rome and all our enemies may grieve to see [it]'.

On the question of breaking the treaties with Spain, the House achieved that unanimity which Coke hoped for. On the subject of war, their position was much more ambiguous. It can be argued that the Commons was very reluctant to enter into war of any kind. Certainly they did not want to give the king a supply adequate for war if there was a chance that no war would follow. Even if war could reasonably be expected to ensue, there was still the further, troublesome question of what kind of war it would be. There was serious concern about the

[52]SP 14/77/13. In the *CSPD* this document has been incorrectly attributed to 1614.

[53]The complaints Coke referred to were probably the dispute over privileges in the Parliament of 1621 and the arrest of several members after its dissolution. The lingering 'humour of discontent' had re-surfaced in the Parliament of 1624 just before the Spanish treaties were first debated on 1 March. Ruigh, *Parliament of 1624*, pp. 171-5.

cost of a war for the Palatinate which would be waged on the Continent against the Emperor. Those who advocated war were more enthusiastic about a revived Elizabethan naval war against Spain, which it was thought would be less costly. Coke addressed these questions when the debate on supply reached a climax on 20 March, and there are several accounts of his speech which one historian has called an 'ameliorative explanation'.[54] Coke argued firstly that the nature of the war was a question that had to be left to the king: 'Where the war shall be or what it shall be, this must proceed from the king.'[55] Secondly, however, Coke assured the House that what James expected was in fact a war with Spain. Coke said, 'the King's declaration hath a further extent than the Palatinate . . . the King doth not thereby confine us to a war in or for the Palatinate'.[56] Instead, as another account of Coke's speech declares, 'the general aim and the necessity is apparent to be a war with Spain'.[57]

The course adopted by the Commons at the end of the 20 March debate was consonant with Coke's speech. The House agreed upon a grant of three subsidies and three fifteenths amounting to £300,000. The preamble to the subsidy act declared that this money was intended 'for the maintenance of that war that may hereupon ensue, and more particularly for the defence of this your realm of England, the securing of your kingdom of Ireland, the assistance of your neighbours the States of the United Provinces and other your Majesty's friends and allies, and for the setting forth of your Royal Navy'.[58] The Commons were not promoting war, least of all an offensive, land war for the Palatinate. They were led to believe, though, that the breaking of the treaties with Spain might inevitably involve them in war, a naval war against Spain. Their grant was intended, as they said, 'for the maintenance of the war which may ensue thereupon'. The Commons were chiefly concerned with defensive preparations and only secondarily with offensive capability. If, upon the breaking of the treaties, Spain declared war upon England or James found it necessary to initiate war against Spain, then

[54]Ruigh, *Parliament of 1624*, p. 221.

[55]Spring diary, fol. 141v.

[56]Nicholas diary, fol. 96v. Nicholas confirms the speaker was John Coke rather than another Coke by referring to him as the Master of Requests.

[57]Spring diary, fol. 141v.

[58]J.P. Kenyon, *The Stuart Constitution* (Cambridge, 1969), pp. 76-7. For the origin of this wording, see S.L. Adams, 'Foreign Policy and the Parliaments of 1621 and 1624' in Kevin Sharpe, ed., *Faction and Parliament* (Oxford, 1978), pp. 165-71. Compare Russell, *Parliaments*, pp. 158-203; Ruigh, *Parliament of 1624,* pp. 166-234; Gardiner, *History of England*, V, 193-202.

Parliament could presumably be convened again to make further provisions as necessary. In the meantime, England would be prepared for whatever developed, and at a cost of only one-third of what James had said would be required for all-out war.

Coke was vitally affected by these decisions. Whether the navy became engaged in defensive or offensive operations, it was Coke who would have to supervise the naval preparations. This task would be complicated by the fact that a Council of War had been created which paradoxically included both Greville and Sir Robert Mansell.[59] This new Council would interfere with the clear lines of authority under which Coke was accustomed to work. More broadly speaking, in the spring of 1624 England stood poised on the brink of a new era of war abroad and discord at home. Coke's employments over the past six years – reform in the navy and ordnance, the Algiers fleets, the fleet to retrieve Buckingham and Charles from Spain, even the Parliaments of 1621 and 1624 – all these would seem rather timid and inconsequential compared to the tumultuous events in the years ahead. Although Coke came to regret the ensuing waste and disorder, he was also a dutiful follower of Buckingham and Charles, who devoted all his energies to implementing and defending their decisions. Coke was all the better able to devote himself wholeheartedly to the increased demands of this new period because in April of 1624 a personal era of his own came to a sad conclusion with the death of his wife, Marie.

Coke and Marie spent twenty years of married life together, and two particularly vivid impressions arise from those years. One is the fact that they were very much in love. This is apparent in their letters, where, beneath the restrained and perfectly proper surface, lay genuine tenderness and affection. Secondly, however, their relationship always seemed marred or threatened by Coke's preoccupation with the court. In the beginning, Coke was fleeing the court, and Marie offered him a new home and a new life. Soon they jointly decided that he should cease his fruitless attendance in London and devote all his attention to his home and family. Then this agreement was disrupted by the renewal of Coke's political career. In 1618 he still wrote that: 'I suffered enough by being [away] from home where I love to be, and at London where I never take pleasure.'[60] And in 1620 he vowed that: 'I will not be induced nor forced to live from you any longer, but will rather break away and abandon all the expectation of reward than neglect those real duties which I owe to yourself and my family.'[61] In

[59]*CSPD*, 1623-1625, p. 220.

[60]Coke MSS., reordered packet 9, Coke to Marie, 19 Sept. 1618.

[61]Coke MSS., packet 80, Coke to Marie, 21 April 1620.

truth, however, Hall Court was never so much a home as a refuge for Coke, and he readily abandoned that refuge when Buckingham gave him a secure position at court.

Between 1618 and 1622, while Coke was working in the navy and pursuing higher office, Marie was left with much of the burden of their home. Among other things, this meant bringing up their six children (Joseph, John, Thomas, Mary, Elizabeth, and Anne).[62] Coke hired a tutor named Mease to instruct the two oldest boys, but Marie was dissatisfied with him and assumed some of this responsibility too. As she explained to Coke: 'I doubt if John have not some more help of a master (but not Mr. Mease) or of a tutor he will never be a good Grecian. I do hear him construe half a chapter a day in the Greek Testament and I help him with Beza's Latin Testament and likewise Joseph.'[63] In another letter, Marie similarly said: 'And when I have quite finished all my housewifrie I will have time to write Latin.'[64]

In addition to her work as a mother, Marie supervised much of the daily farming operation at Hall Court. She shouldered these responsibilities despite the fact that she was not well. The first indication of her illness appeared in 1614, when Coke wrote to her: 'I am not quiet till I hear from you in regard of that indisposition wherein I left you. Write I pray you as often as you may, specially of your health, and how your sowing proceedeth.'[65] After Coke's return to court, most of his letters to Marie contain these same two elements: practical instructions regarding the management of Hall Court and an ominous, unrelenting anxiety about Marie's health. At Easter of 1620, for example, when business at court forced Coke to postpone his visit home, he advised Marie to 'send forth your wheat and your cheese', though he also said it was 'much against my heart that you should still trouble yourself with those services which are proper for your maids . . . sweet wife spare yourself rather than money'.[66] In October of 1622, Coke futilely speculated on the cause of 'that pain in your side', attributing it to breast-feeding their child, 'pensiveness and want of comfort in your solitary course of life', or 'the cares of our family and my absence'. Yet at the same time, he told Marie to 'thrash out and sell your wheat, if the markets be reasonable, and put as many of your oxen or kine to feeding as you may conveniently, and . . . also

[62]Briggs, *History of Melbourne*, p. 164.

[63]*Cowper MSS.*, I, 132.

[64]Coke, *The Last Elizabethan,* p. 38.

[65]Coke MSS., reordered packet 8, Coke to Marie, 19 Oct. 1614.

[66]Coke MSS., packet 1, Coke to Marie, 8 April 1620.

make haste to work up your hemp and flax'.[67] Shortly thereafter, when Coke proudly announced his appointment as Master of Requests, he advised Marie to consider 'how to sell away and set our provisions and grounds'. 'But chiefly', he added, 'take care of your health.' He complained, too, that he had received no letter from Marie to assure him that she was well.[68] When such a letter from Marie did arrive, Coke wrote in reply: 'I was so glad of your letter. . . that I willingly gave the deliverer a triple reward.' Anticipating the move to London, Coke further wrote, 'be careful to cherish yourself with good diet, and to use some stirring and exercise and now and then to take the air, that you may be fitter for a journey when time shall require to remove our family'. As usual, however, there was still work to be done, so Coke instructed his wife, 'if corn bear so good price, I hope you send good store to the market and thrash out apace to deceive the rats, for the killing whereof take what course you think fit'.[69] A long letter written by Marie in March of 1623 shows that she was left with much of the worry about disposing of their land and livestock and moving their possessions to London.[70]

On 19 July 1623, Coke and Marie left Hall Court.[71] As events would show, the move to London was both a real and symbolic break with the past. Marie now had less than one year left to live, much of it filled with pain and sorrow. Despite her failing health, she was pregnant again. In a cheerless letter to Coke, she wrote: 'I praise God I do endure, though I drive out the time wearily.'[72] In November, Coke and Marie sent their two oldest sons to Cambridge, where Dr Richardson greeted them as 'welcomest to me that ever came to the college'.[73] When the two boys returned home for their first Christmas in London, tragedy claimed its first victim. Joseph, the older of the two, contracted and died of spotted fever. In a letter to an acquaintance at this time, Coke referred to 'the affliction that we suffer, I by the breaking of the very staff of my age and my wife in her motherly affection'. January was Coke's month to attend at court. Because of his 'necessary absence at court', he explained, he was not able 'to

[67]Coke MSS., packet 45, Coke to Marie, 16 Oct. 1622.

[68]Coke MSS., packet 80, Coke to Marie, 18 Nov. 1622.

[69]Coke MSS., packet 80, Coke to Marie [Dec.] 1622.

[70]*Cowper MSS.,* I, 130-2.

[71]Coke MSS., muniments room, miscellaneous papers, a nine-page statement of accounts endorsed by Coke, '1623. July 19. Being the day of our remove from Hall Court.'

[72]*Cowper MSS.,* I, 120.

[73]Coke MSS., reordered packet 13, Richardson to Coke, 12 Nov. 1623.

comfort my family nor to support or assist a woman that is indeed very sensible of her loss'.[74] Marie was left to face much of the grief alone while Coke could only offer reassuring letters. In one of these he tried to be hopeful about the future. 'What know we', he asked, 'whether God hath not blessings in store for us?'[75] In another letter, he expressed his love with special tenderness, vowing, 'you are dailie in my hearte and dearest affection . . . I esteeme you as myself . . . no woman shall have more cause to be confident in the love, care, and tenderness of a husband than you shall finde whilst I live'. Trying again to direct Marie's thoughts to the future, he added, 'doubt not sweete harte, that God hath still his mercie in store for us, and that you and I by his goodness shall see better daies'.[76] But Coke was cruelly deceived in these hopes when, two months later, while giving birth to twins who barely outlived her, Marie died.[77]

Coke's marriage to Marie lasted about as long as the average marriage of his day. In other, more interesting ways it deviated from what is supposed to have been the norm.[78] At forty-one, Coke was older than the average when he married Marie. As a fellow at Cambridge, he had been prohibited by the terms of his fellowship from marrying. After leaving Cambridge, he would have been discouraged from marrying until he had sufficient means to support a family. Yet this does not seem to have been the fundamental reason why Coke married so late. If financial security had been the chief impediment, he would hardly have married at precisely the time that he lost his office in the navy. Nor was Coke's marriage arranged for him; his parents had both died more than twenty years earlier. Coke, in fact, chose to marry a woman far removed from his family ties in Derbyshire. We might theorize that he was finally brought to that decision because he wished to establish his own family line before it was too late or because he was experiencing a 'mid-life crisis' exacerbated by the reversals at court. These are interesting hypotheses, but it seems more obvious that Coke married Marie for the simple reason that he had fallen in love with her. About Marie we know intriguingly little. She was certainly younger than Coke, probably somewhere in her twenties, when she married him. In this she would have been typical,

[74]Coke MSS., reordered packet 14, Coke to Gilbert Ward drafted on the back of Ward's letter to Coke dated 28 Jan. 1624.

[75]Coke MSS., packet 80, Coke to Marie, 23 Jan. 1624.

[76]Briggs, *History of Melbourne*, pp. 88-9.

[77]*Cowper MSS.*, I, 162.

[78]Lawrence Stone, *The Family, Sex and Marriage in England 1500-1800* (New York, 1977), pp. 4-9, 46, 48, 55-7, 202-6, 651-8.

but in her familiarity with Latin and Greek she surely was not typical of the woman of her day. In the selection of a mate, her range of choice had been more limited than Coke's, probably encompassing no more than the men who lived near her family home in Herefordshire and the few men, like Coke, who could have become acquainted with her through her father's work. Since her father was employed by Greville and did not always do his work well, he would have had reason to promote his daughter's marriage to Greville's closest friend and deputy.[79] Still, 'promoting' a marriage is not the same as 'arranging' it, and there is no hint in the surviving evidence that Marie married Coke for any reason other than the fact that she loved him. In their love for each other, Coke and Marie are a striking contradiction to the stereotypical view of early Stuart marriage.[80]

Yet Coke's love for Marie was not boundless; he was a man torn between the competing interests of his marriage and his work. It is to Coke's credit that he agonized over these competing interests and deliberated with Marie about them. Back in 1606, for example, he had asked Marie to 'communicate with me freely how you find your own resolutions sway . . . open yourself that I may indeed understand the true bent of your desires and the constant estate of your mind'. If Marie did this, Coke promised, 'you shall see that you have indeed very great power in me, and the cares and travails of my life shall be directed to your ends as well as mine own'.[81] Coke was not oblivious to what he called 'those real duties' owed to his wife and family, and he made an earnest effort to reconcile those duties with his smouldering ambition. The fact that Coke agonized over this dilemma, however, does not change the brute fact that Marie was forced to bear a greater burden, both physically and emotionally, because of his repeated absences. Nor could the gifts and reaffirmations of his love that Coke sent her on these occasions substitute for his presence. Much as Coke loved Marie, he did not give himself wholly to their relationship. Coke of course did not see it this way. He hoped through his success at court to give Marie a more comfortable life.[82] He looked upon the rewards of office as blessings they would share together.[83] The move to London was his feeble attempt to reconcile competing interests, to continue his work with less neglect of his family. From all that we can tell,

[79]Rebholz, *Fulke Greville*, p. 177.

[80]Stone, *The Family*, p. 117. The Coke marriage confirms the earlier view of Edmund S. Morgan, *The Puritan Family* (New York, 1966), pp. 47-54, 59-62.

[81]Coke MSS., packet 80, Coke to Marie, 5 June 1606.

[82]Coke MSS., packet 45, Coke to Marie, 16 Oct. 1622.

[83]Coke MSS., packet 80, Coke to Marie, 18 Nov. 1622.

however, Marie never evinced any enthusiasm for the move to London. She seems to have understood that the court was, more than anything, her real rival. It was Coke's first love; it had a prior claim to his attention and devotion. And in the end, after twenty years of marriage punctuated by hard work, child-bearing, and loneliness, it triumphed over her.

Sometime during the autumn of 1624, perhaps five or six months after the death of Marie, Coke remarried.[84] His second wife was Joan Gore, daughter of a former Lord Mayor of London and widow of a recent alderman.[85] The Gore household was located in Tottenham in a mansion where Henry VIII was reputed to have slept often, though under what circumstances is not clear. Coke stayed there periodically, but to be nearer the court in London he established a base of operations at Garlick Hill near St Paul's.[86] As far as can be determined, Coke and his second wife maintained a cordial relationship, but for both it was a marriage of convenience.[87] Coke's chief motive was presumably concern for the welfare of his five remaining children. Coke's care for his children is evident throughout the rest of his life, and he developed a special closeness to his eldest son, John, but there is an inescapable impression that after the death of Marie nothing ever again seriously challenged his obsessive love for the court.

[84]The exact date of Coke's second marriage is unknown, but the first references to it appear in November of 1624. *Cowper MSS.,* I, 176.

[85]It has been asserted elsewhere that Joan's first husband was Sir John Gore (*DNB*, IV, 701). In fact, however, she was married to his younger brother, William Gore. Her father was Sir Robert Lee, Lord Mayor of London from 1602 to 1603. Alfred B. Beaven, *The Aldermen of the City of London* (2 vols., London, 1908-13), II, 53, 177.

[86]Fred Fisk, *The History of Tottenham* (Tottenham, 1913), pp. 56-7. The first letters addressed to Coke at Garlick Hill occur in December of 1624. *Cowper MSS.,* I, 177-8.

[87]One measure of Joan's enduring ties with the home and family of her first husband is her will (Prerogative Court of Canterbury, 2 Pell). Letters from Joan to Coke are in packet 87 of the Coke MSS., one of the few packets not printed On the subject of Coke's marriage and the social psychology of a courtier's life, I have profited from conversations with James Sikora.

9

BUCKINGHAM'S AGENT: 1624-1625

The war that Parliament had been led to expect in 1624 did not materialize immediately for several reasons: Spain launched no attack, King James continued to resist war until his death, money was in short supply, and negotiations were under way to enlist allies on the Continent, particularly France. Through 1624 and 1625, as Buckingham tried to mobilize the English war effort and raise the necessary money, his dependence on Coke became ever greater and ever more visible.

Buckingham's reliance on Coke was evident in the extortion of £10,000 from the East India Company; Coke may even have been the architect of the scheme. According to his calculations, certain goods that the Company had recently seized by force, mainly from the Portuguese in the area of the Persian Gulf, were worth at least £100,000. As Coke saw it, there were only two ways by which the Company could have come into possession of this merchandise. Either they took it by lawful reprisal, in which case the Lord Admiral was traditionally entitled to a tenth of the spoils, which in this instance amounted to £10,000. Or they took it unlawfully by an act of piracy, in which case they could be forced to forfeit all their gains and more. As Coke explained to Buckingham: 'If. . . the goods were piratically taken, then both the goods and the ships that take them are forfeited [to] your Grace, and the takers and their estates are at his Majesty's mercy.' The intent, of course, was not to prosecute the Company for piracy. Actual prosecution, Coke thought, would harm both the Company and the Crown, but the threat of such prosecution could serve very well as a club over the Company's head. Faced with losing everything, they might agree to part with £10,000.[1]

The idea understandably appealed to Buckingham, and 'John Coke was willed to treat with some of the principals of the Company about it, which he did accordingly and at sundry times.'[2] The Company, for their part, were less enamoured of the idea. Their first response was to seek the advice of a lawyer, Doctor Steward. At first they put the question to Steward in a purely hypothetical manner, and

[1] PRO, CO 77/3/2. The plan is outlined in this paper by Coke dated 20 Jan. 1624. Another copy is in the Coke MSS., muniments room, miscellaneous papers.

[2] CO 77/3/17. This paper is a brief account of the full proceedings written by a contemporary who was obviously sympathetic to the Lord Admiral.

he replied that there would be two serious weaknesses in the claims of their hypothetical admiral. In the first place, his right to one-tenth of all prize goods was not a written law but only a matter of custom. In the second place, his claim was limited to cases where the merchants operated under letters of marque. These were essentially licences issued out of the High Court of Admiralty for committing acts of reprisal, usually against the enemy in times of war. This consultation revealed both the strengths and weaknesses of the Company's position. Hypothetically, they had a very defensible case. The people who spoke to Steward reported, however, that 'upon further conferences Doctor Steward declared himself, *when he understood the business had relation to the Lord Admiral of England,* that he would neither be of the Company's counsel in this cause, nor deliver his opinions against the Lord Admiral'. No matter how weak his legal position, Buckingham was a formidable adversary. Nevertheless, the Company leaders were convinced they owed the Lord Admiral nothing and still hoped to persuade him that he was entitled to nothing. They communicated this answer to Coke, whom they referred to as 'the party employed by my Lord Admiral'.[3] Despite their initial resistance, the Company was finally forced to capitulate. Buckingham broke their resistance by taking a step that Coke had considered too drastic — charging them with piracy in the High Court of Admiralty.[4] It was probably also more than a coincidence that the Company's East Indies fleet was prevented from sailing until they had satisfied Buckingham's demands.[5] By the time the Company capitulated, it had cost them not just the £10,000 originally demanded by Buckingham but also an additional £10,000 demanded by James.[6] In 1626 this act of extortion came back to haunt Buckingham as one of the eleven articles of impeachment against him.[7] In the meantime, however, it alerted him to a new source of revenue. He sought a formal commission from the High Court of Admiralty to issue letters of marque or reprisal in the future. Not surprisingly, it was Coke who gave the instructions for framing these letters, for keeping accounts

[3]Orbit House, London, East India Company court minute books, VI, 412-14. Italics mine.

[4]CO 77/3/17. See also *Calendar of State Papers, Colonial Series: East Indies, China and Japan,* ed. William Noel Sainsbury (5 vols., London, 1862-92), III, 236-7, 247-8, 252-3, 271-2, 290-2, 294-6, 301, 329.

[5]Gardiner, *History of England,* V, 237-41.

[6]Buckingham loaned nearly all this to the navy. On 19 May 1624 Coke wrote 'That our 12 ships are as forward as may be, if the victualler had his monies, which are daily expected from the East India Company.' Coke MSS., packet 45. Buckingham was evidently repaid the next summer. *CSPD*, 1625-1626, p. 3.

[7]Rushworth, *Historical Collections*, I, 314-22, 384-5.

of all reprisal goods brought into the country, and for collecting the Lord Admiral's one-tenth share.[8]

Coke's relations with the East India Company did not end with this incident. A few months afterwards, he was again the principal agent in what appears to have been another case of coercion. One of the boldest projectors of the period was Robert Sherley, a roving adventurer who returned to England about the beginning of 1624 with a grand scheme to establish a lucrative trade in silks with Persia.[9] Buckingham and James, always anxious to embrace any project that promised profits, were immediately enthralled by Sherley's proposals. Another vigorous supporter at court was Secretary Conway, whom Sherley referred to as his 'greatest Patron' and 'Archangel'.[10] But the East India and Levant Companies, who were more experienced in such matters, were far from enthusiastic. They cared little for Sherley or his proposition. As Coke observed, 'our merchants esteem no better of him than a juggler, and are not willing to harken unto him'.[11] Sherley painted a very appealing picture, estimating the annual value of the Persian silk trade at £5,000,000 and the resulting customs revenues at £500,000.[12] The East India Company scoffed at these predictions. In the first place, there were very serious obstacles to any trade with Persia. Besides, they declared, 'we find a wonderful mistake both in the quantity and value of the silk. . . it is most certain that the profit propounded to his Majesty's customs will not be an eleventh part of that which is projected'.[13] Since the English merchants could not be persuaded to join in the venture, the Crown decided to undertake it without them. Having decided to attempt the project alone, Buckingham and James then turned to Coke to find out how it could be done.

Coke received his instructions from Conway in November of 1624. According to Conway: 'His Majesty hath long since taken to heart the proposition of the Persian ambassador for drawing the trade of Persia[n] silks into this kingdom.' As if to preclude any criticism from Coke, Conway specifically told him that 'the points you may be

[8]SP 14/183/47. See also SP 16/1/112 and Coke MSS., packet 25, Sir Thomas Coventry to Coke, 7 Sept. 1625.

[9]David W. Davies, *Elizabethans Errant: The Strange Fortunes of Sir Thomas Sherley and His Three Sons* (Ithaca, New York, 1967), pp. 259-68; Boies Penrose, *The Sherleian Odyssey* (London, 1938), pp. 206-27.

[10]CO 77/3/68, 77. See also CO 77/3/32, 38, 49.

[11]Coke MSS., packet 45, Coke to Greville, 1 Oct. 1624.

[12]CO 77/3/33.

[13]CO 77/3/35. Compare court minute books, VII, 271.

pleased to inquire of and endeavour in are, not whether the undertaking be fit or no, but how it is to be done'.[14] Though rarely expressed so explicitly, Coke's instructions were often of this nature. The following day, Sherley wrote to Coke, asking for his cooperation and pointedly indicating that the king of Persia would generously reward him for his help.[15] It has always been assumed that Buckingham and James were entirely earnest about pursuing the venture alone. An equally plausible explanation, however, is that they hoped to force the East India Company into the project with the threat of this independent, Crown-sponsored competition. If not the intent, this at least was the effect.

Early in December, Conway informed the Company that James planned to send a fleet to Persia without their assistance. When the Company manfully protested that nothing could force them to participate in the scheme, it was noted that: 'Mr. Secretary seemed unwilling to argue the business.' He simply added as a matter of interest 'that if the Company would have any conference with Sir John Coke (who had commission from the king for that business) they might; or that [if] they had anything to propound concerning the same, they might repair to Sir John, otherwise they should not be sent for'. On several subsequent occasions, delegates of the Company reaffirmed their opposition in conversations with Coke, whom they referred to as 'the man principally used in the business'. Despite these protests, the Company eventually agreed to cooperate in the venture.[16] Then, just when Sherley seemed to be getting his way, King James died and the project collapsed.

Coke did not always act as an agent of extortion or coercion. Through these early transactions, he became an established intermediary between the East India Company and Buckingham. On rare occasions when the Company was able to speak directly with the Lord Admiral, he often referred them back to Coke. By the same token, the Company learned that they could use Coke to discover the Lord Admiral's intentions and influence his decisions. For example, on one occasion when the Company wanted to change Buckingham's mind, they acknowledged that they had 'no hope to do it, but by his Honour's [Coke's] means'.[17] In later years Coke continued to function as an intermediary between the Company and the Crown in his

[14]SP 14/174/84.

[15]CO 77/3/52.

[16]Court minute books, VII, 236-7, 241, 246, 271, 402.

[17]Court minute books, VIII, 197. See also VII, 371, 374-5, 388, 413, 416, 419; VIII, 44, 61, 65, 104, 143.

capacity as Secretary of State, indeed until 1640, but his influence was never so great as during these early years when he acted as Buckingham's personal representative.[18] What underlay Coke's special relationship with Buckingham was his vigilant defence of the Lord Admiral's authority. Coke was known as 'a man who doth much regard the privileges belonging to the Lord Admiral'.[19] This was illustrated in March of 1624 when English naval captains failed to carry out Buckingham's orders to capture Dutch merchant ships. The East India Company urged Coke to do something about this, and the governor of the Company expressed the opinion that Coke would act on their complaint 'not only for their sakes, but principally for my lord's sake whose commission hath been in this manner slighted'.[20]

Coke's vigilance on behalf of the Lord Admiral's authority was illustrated best of all at this time in his attitude toward the recently appointed Council of War. In June of 1624, Coke told Buckingham, 'out of my zeal and faith toward you, I must first inform you how they usurp your office'. To begin with, Coke related: 'I have received a letter written to your Grace by some of the Council of War and therewith certain articles for an exact account to be given them of all particulars concerning the navy.' The Council, in Coke's opinion, had no right to demand such an account. Their function was only to formulate or recommend policy. If they went beyond that limited role, they interfered with the administrative authority of the Lord Admiral and, incidentally, the commissioners of the navy. As Coke explained to Buckingham, 'their proper duty is only proposition. As for examination, provision, and execution, they are peculiarly yours. . . . And to this you must reduce them if you will not endure to come under their lee'. Through their request for an account of the navy, Coke argued, 'those who have had their titles and employments from you. . . seek to derive your authority to themselves and to grow greater by making you less'. If Coke used unusually strong language in condemning the Council of War, it was because he spoke from personal as well as professional motives. It need hardly be stated that few men more thoroughly detested one another than did Coke and Sir Robert Mansell, and it was Mansell's inclusion on the Council of War that particularly irritated Coke. As he emphasized at the end of his complaint to Buckingham, 'we must refer to your consideration

[18]This was a customary role for the Secretary. There are innumerable references to Coke's relations with the Company while he was Secretary, appearing throughout volumes VIII-XVI of the court minute books.

[19]*Cowper MSS.*, I, 176.

[20]Court minute books, VII, 375.

whether they are fit judges over us, whom we have discovered to be the authors of the corruptions of former times, and who by that means will climb up to be judges over you'.[21] The extent to which Coke and Mansell sparred over the workings of the Council of War would not be fully revealed until the summer of 1625 when it surfaced as an issue in Parliament.

By the autumn of 1624, Coke was recognized at court as a favourite follower of Buckingham and a likely prospect for further advancement. Early in September he was knighted, and soon afterward it was rumoured that he would succeed Calvert as Secretary of State.[22] John Chamberlain, the familiar court gossip, remarked that: 'Secretary Calvert is still upon resigning, and one Coke, Master of Requests. . . is in speech to succeed him.'[23] Chamberlain even speculated that Coke's recent marriage to Joan Gore had given him the means to buy the Secretaryship.[24] Another court observer reported that: 'Sir John Coke had a promise to be Secretary.'[25] Sir Dudley Carleton's nephew, a Clerk of the Council, also reported in regard to the Secretaryship that: 'The man for whom my lord of Buckingham told me formerly he was engaged, I hear now to be Sir John Coke, lately knighted, and a Master of Requests.'[26] Even Sir Guilford Slingsby, the ousted officer of the navy who had once threatened to shoot Coke, now asked for the privilege of buying the Mastership of Requests from him when he succeeded to the Secretaryship. Slingsby said he understood 'that the king is so well persuaded of you that he purposeth to advance you to the place of Secretary of State'.[27] Despite all of these confident predictions, Calvert was replaced in March of 1625 by a comparatively minor courtier named Sir Albertus Morton.[28] For the time being, Coke's only

[21] Coke MSS., packet 45, Coke to Buckingham, 14 June 1624.

[22] SP 14/172/19.

[23] SP 14/173/82.

[24] SP 14/181/29. William Gore left assets of about £20,000. Joan's share in this legacy came to about £13,000. Allowing for debts that could not be collected, she must still have had about £10,000. *Cowper MSS.*, I, 270; Coke MSS., reordered packet 15, an account endorsed by Coke: '1624. July 22. The catalogue of the debts due to alderman Gore.'

[25] SP 14/173/12.

[26] SP 14/172/57.

[27] Coke MSS., packet 45, Slingsby to Coke, 4 Oct. 1624. Slingsby had long since changed his tune, telling Coke in 1623, 'I find passion hath overruled me more than piety in wishing God's justice upon my oppressors and their children, forgetting Our Saviour's admonition – Love them that hate you and pray for them that persecute you.' *Cowper MSS.*, I, 138.

[28] *CSPD*, 1625-1626, p. 2.

tangible sign of advancement was his knighthood, but he was closer to the Secretaryship than he could possibly have known.

In the spring and summer of 1625, Coke's major employment concerned the navy, but he did other things as well. His work as Master of Requests, for example, was greatly increased when at the death of James all the king's servants anxiously sought to maintain their places under Charles. During this period Coke was also appointed to a new committee for the advancement of trade, he continued watching for ships that might be supplying weapons to Spain, and he facilitated the pardoning of a pirate.[29] He also drew up a proposal for the creation of a fleet to 'abate the pride and terror of the Spanish pretended empire' or more specifically 'to intercept his plate fleets, to invade his countries, to fortify and plant there, and to establish government, confederacy, and trade'. The most interesting feature of Coke's scheme was the way he proposed to finance it. He proposed that the enterprise 'be undertaken by a common charge of the kingdom by a company incorporated for the West, as there is already for the East'. Coke estimated that the £361,200 required for the first two years of operation could be raised through subscriptions from various individuals, classes, companies, and organizations in English society. There are at least two ways of interpreting this proposal. On the one hand, it was backward-looking. One can see reflected in it a romanticized memory of the days of Hawkins, Drake, and the Elizabethan war against Spain. Like many a military planner before and after him, Coke was entering a new war under the illusion that he was simply resuming an old one. On the other hand, Coke's proposal for a West India Company can be interpreted as forward-looking. It was modelled on the recently established Dutch West India Company, it anticipated the later Providence Island Company under the direction of men like John Pym, and it presaged two centuries of British imperial expansion.[30]

Coke's work in the navy at this time involved two specific tasks. One was the preparation of a fleet for the war that was now daily expected. Although precise plans for this fleet varied from day to day, the most probable strategy remained a direct assault against the coast of Spain. An army of 10,000 men would accompany the fleet in order

[29] SP 16/1/61; 16/2/53, 113; 16/3/51.

[30] The proposal written in Coke's hand is SP 16/1/59. It is endorsed by him: 'West Indies. This proposition was sponsored by me to the Lord Admiral 14 April 1625.' See also Arthur Percival Newton, *The Colonising Activities of the English Puritans* (New Haven, 1914), pp. 28-9, 204-6; Christopher Thompson, 'The Origins of the Politics of the Parliamentary Middle Group', *Transactions of the Royal Historical Society*, 5th series, 22 (1972), 80, 86; Russell, *Parliaments*, pp. 262, 299-300.

to capture a fortified Spanish harbour, where the English hoped to wait in ambush for a returning Spanish treasure fleet.[31] (This is the fleet that eventually attacked Cadiz; its dismal performance is analyzed below in chapter twelve together with the other war fleets.) The preparation of this fleet demonstrates both the continuing partnership between Coke and Secretary Conway and also the cumbersomeness of the administrative machinery through which they worked. Conway's new fellow Secretary, Sir Albertus Morton, was even less active in this sphere than Calvert had been earlier. Morton himself set the tone for the proceedings very shortly after his appointment, when, unable to answer an inquiry from Conway, he referred it to 'Sir John Coke, who best understands the importance of that business which concerns the navy'.[32] Even if Morton had been inclined to assume a larger role in these transactions, Buckingham had other plans for him. The Lord Admiral engaged Morton in his diplomatic efforts, taking him along to France in May and sending him to negotiate an offensive alliance with the Netherlands in June. Morton was consequently absent from England when the naval preparations were at their height. Coke and Conway were also forced into their close cooperation because nearly every action required a letter, warrant, order of Council, or privy seal to authorize and finance it. Coke continually needed these, and Conway was in a position to procure them, but not without constant prodding. For one service Coke drafted a warrant and sent copies to Conway on three separate occasions asking the Secretary to obtain the privy seal. With the third request, Coke added: 'I have sent this letter by Mr Nicholas and entreated him to put your Honour in mind from time to time till these main instruments for the furtherance of these services be procured.' At this same time Charles granted Buckingham a ship to search for the northwest passage. Where the Lord Admiral's interest was involved, Coke preferred not to rely entirely on Conway, telling him: 'If your Honour will but send me such a warrant, I will take order for the privy seal to be accordingly made ready.'[33] Fitting out the fleet depended on several men in various departments, a delay in any one of which could check the progress of the others. As Coke complained at one point: 'Having used my best care to set forward the king's service in every part, yet still I find interruption in matters appertaining to other men's charges.'[34] In one of his reports to Conway, Coke recounted his efforts to cut through the entangling red tape:

[31] Gardiner, *History of England*, V, 323-5.

[32] SP 14/185/85.

[33] SP 14/185/82. See also Coke's notes in the margin of SP 16/1/115.

[34] SP 16/3/46.

> I have also caused the several estimates to be drawn, upon which by your lordship's order to the Office of the Signet the privy seals must be made ready for his Majesty's signature. I have also given direction to Mr Johnson to attend your Honour and to follow both the privy seal and receipt of monies for all that concerneth the office of the ordnance. I will also send to the Treasurer of the Navy to attend you in like manner for the privy seal and receipts of his office.[35]

While Coke tried to expedite matters at home, Buckingham was occupied with his foreign negotiations. At Amiens in June, he took time to write to Coke: 'I have understood what care you have employed about the provisions of the navy and that your diligence hath therein supplied the defects of the victualler.' Buckingham expressed his 'hearty thanks' and told Coke that 'herein you have done no more than I ever expected from you'.[36]

Coke's second naval employment in this period concerned the famous agreement James and Buckingham had made near the beginning of 1625 to lend the French government eight ships, one from the English navy and seven merchant ships pressed into service. Originally the French had said these ships would be used to attack Genoa, an ally of Spain. While arrangements for the loan were being made, however, the French government faced a spreading Huguenot rebellion, and it looked increasingly as if the ships would be used against these Protestant insurgents.[37] Since nearly every English vessel was already being prepared for the attack against Spain, there was little left for the French to choose from. Coke was designated to speak to the French ambassador and agree on which ships to make available. He clearly did not relish this task and insinuated that the French demands were unreasonable.[38] By the end of March he grudgingly made a contract between the naval commissioners and the French ambassador, but he complained that the French were slow to honour their part of the bargain, and he cautiously warned that 'for the Lord Admiral's warrant and any under him [including Coke] a privy seal must be drawn for his Majesty to give allowance to the lending of these ships'.[39]

[35] SP 16/4/36. Other particularly interesting examples of Coke's working relationship with Conway are SP 16/3/23; 16/5/85; 16/6/25.

[36] Coke MSS., packet 25, Buckingham to Coke, 2 June 1625.

[37] Gardiner, *History of England,* V, 301-6, 328-9, 378-95; Donald Nicholas, *Mr. Secretary Nicholas (1593-1669): His Life and Letters* (London, 1955), pp. 42-6; Lockyer, *Buckingham,* pp. 229-31, 237, 252-4.

[38] SP 14/183/48.

[39] Coke MSS., reordered packet 17, Buckingham to the commissioners of the navy, 16

The contract with the French authorized them to use the English ships against whomsoever they wished except, of course, England. Within the terms of the contract, therefore, the ships could be used against the French Protestants. At the outset, Buckingham may have been willing to permit them to be used thus if it helped to obtain a French wife for Charles and a military alliance with France, but matters had significantly changed by the time the ships were ready to sail. By then, Henrietta Maria was already safely married to Charles, hopes of a broader French alliance were fading, the popular Protestant stronghold of La Rochelle had joined the rebellion, the French government definitely planned to use the ships against La Rochelle, and Buckingham realized that this had to be prevented from happening. Consequently, on 18 May, before the ships left for France, Coke sent the following message to the commander, Captain Pennington:

> For your better understanding of the instructions given by the Lord Admiral, and especially of the articles of contract betwixt the French ambassador and the commissioners of the navy, I am by direction to inform you: First, that no clauses therein may be strained to engage or embroil you, and the ships and companies under your command, in the civil wars of the French if any happen, or against them of our religion in that kingdom or elsewhere. And secondly that the true intention of your employment is to serve the French king against the foreign enemies and opposers of his honour and estate.[40]

These instructions left Pennington in an extremely awkward position. He was required to resist a perfectly obvious interpretation of the contract on the part of the French and to insist instead upon this contrived and strained interpretation. Pennington was given a brief reprieve when Coke ordered him to delay his departure on the pretext that he might be required to transport the new queen to England.[41] On 9 June, perhaps because of false indications that Louis was about to make peace with the Huguenots, Pennington was allowed to sail for France where he discovered that the French did indeed plan to use his ships against La Rochelle. In order to obey the private instructions he had

March 1625; notes on the back of a letter to Coke from Thomas Alured, Coke MSS., packet 25, dated the last of March.

[40] SP 16/2/74. The draft of this letter is in Coke MSS., packet 25. Pennington also referred to the 'special' and 'absolute' command from Coke not to use his ships against La Rochelle or other Protestants in SP 16/3/71 and Coke MSS., packet 46, Pennington to Buckingham, 28 June 1625.

[41] SP 16/2/83. In this letter to Secretary Conway, Pennington referred to 'a command from his Majesty by Sir John Coke to detract the time as much as I could for the wafting over of the queen'. Five days later Pennington again referred to 'the wafting over of the queen according to order given me by word of mouth from Sir John Coke'. SP 16/2/98.

received from Coke, Pennington refused to relinquish control of his ships to the French, who naturally believed this refusal violated the contract. On 15 June Pennington voiced his concern to Coke that the French would press their demands 'with the words of the contract which lie open for them'. The rumour had begun to circulate among the ships' crews that they were to be used against their fellow Protestants at La Rochelle. 'But for this', Pennington said, 'I have a special command by a letter from yourself in his Majesty's name, not to engage myself nor the rest of my ships in any of the civil wars of France, or against any of our religion in that kingdom or elsewhere, by which you may see in how difficult a business I am embarked.'[42]

Coke's attitude toward these proceedings and his major contribution both appear in a letter he wrote to Conway on 11 July.[43] Coke obviously sympathized with the captains, masters, and owners of the ships who had complained to him about the treatment they and their ships received from the French. As for the seamen, Coke said, 'they will rather be killed or thrown overboard than be forced to shed the innocent blood of any Protestants in the quarrels of papists, so as they will account any commandment to that end to be, in a kind, an imposition of martyrdom'. Speaking for himself, Coke saw little reason to satisfy the French. It would alienate the English from the French Huguenots, and, said Coke, 'if we add the discouragement of our party at home and abroad, the late murmuring against it in Parliament, and the open exclaiming made in the pulpits. . . we can hardly balance these consequences with any interest or assistance we can have from the French'. Coke honestly believed that using the ships against La Rochelle violated the original intention of the contract, but he also understood that the literal language of the contract permitted it to happen. The problem was still how to prevent it without appearing to be guilty of wilfully breaking the contract. Coke offered a reasonable solution to this dilemma. He suggested that Pennington be given stern, public commands to surrender his ships to the French while privately he should be instructed to find inconveniences which made it impossible to comply. The English government, of course, would make a great show of trying to eliminate these inconveniences in order to proceed with their bargain. It would be even better, Coke said, if these inconveniences could be attributed to the French, so that the blame might be transferred to them. Of course, Pennington would have to be instructed to ignore the strong, public demands sent to him to satisfy the French. Coke suggested that

[42] Coke MSS., packet 46, Pennington to Coke, 15 June 1625.

[43] SP 16/4/40.

someone be sent to speak privately with him so that, 'Captain Pennington by the unexpected style of his Majesty's letters may not be surprised.'

The balance of the proceedings followed the course proposed by Coke. The task of giving Pennington his secret instructions was delegated to Edward Nicholas, Buckingham's personal secretary, whom the French made every effort to prevent from seeing Pennington in private. The subsequent manoeuvring reached nearly comic proportions, while the English seamen mutinied and Pennington was driven to utter despair, at one point pleading with Coke to be relieved of his command.[44] Valuable time was gained, however. Near the beginning of August the French seemed on the verge of concluding a peace with the Huguenots, and Buckingham judged it would be safe to surrender the ships. One captain defiantly took his ship back to England, and all the seamen but one refused to stay with their ships, but the remaining vessels were at last turned over to the French. Only then, too late for Buckingham, did it become apparent that the French government had not reached accord with the Rochellois. Coke was able to report to Fulke Greville in good conscience: 'For the French I will excuse no error, nor can give you any good account how the instructions for the ships not to be employed against them of the religion was changed. Only this I can assure your Honour that I had neither hand [in it] nor foreknowledge of it.' Coke, who had disliked this business from the start, was anxious now to retrieve the ships from France and to aid La Rochelle because, he said, 'if once they extinguish the [Protestant] religion in France, they will. . . be to us worse neighbours than Spain'.[45]

The machinations to keep Pennington's ships out of the hands of the French were especially important because they coincided with the first Parliament of Charles I's reign. Parliament convened on 18 June, just one week after Coke proposed means to evade the French demands, and it was dissolved on 12 August, just one week after the ships were finally turned over to the French. Charles and Buckingham were loath to offend Parliament because they needed hundreds of thousands of pounds from it in order to meet their obligations toward the armies of their Continental allies and their own fleet now preparing to sail for Spain. Coke, who again sat as a member for St Germans, occupied a unique position in this Parliament. By virtue of the confidence the Lord Admiral placed in him and the unequalled

[44]Coke MSS., packet 46, Pennington to Coke, 18 July 1625.

[45]Coke MSS., packet 46, Coke to Greville, 5 Nov. 1625. Bodleian Library, Tanner MSS., vol. 72, fol. 26.

knowledge he had of the naval requirements, he became the Crown's chief spokesman.[46]

The Parliament of 1625 began not so much ill-managed as unmanaged. For two weeks Charles and Buckingham neglected to outline their war plans or to specify their monetary requirements. The result was a grossly inadequate grant of only two subsidies worth about £140,000.[47] The opportunity to provide for the government's wants would seem to have been lost, but Buckingham determined to press the Commons for more, and for his spokesman he chose Coke. Either of the two Secretaries of State would have been a more likely choice, but Conway was in the Lords and Morton was still attending the negotiations at the Hague. It has been alleged that three other Councillors (Weston, May, and Edmondes) were passed over because they were less willing than Coke to follow Buckingham's policy.[48] There may be some truth in this, but the more obvious explanation is that Coke was simply best qualified for the task because he knew more than anyone else about the requirements of the navy.[49]

On 8 July, Coke rose to 'give the House trew informacion of his Majestie's estate'.[50] This, of course, is what should have been done two weeks earlier. Coke began by noting that the two subsidies had been hastily passed 'without attending the ministers of state whose voices were scarce heard'. To take the sting out of this criticism, Coke attributed this action to the 'forwardness' of the Commons. He then proceeded to explain how the funds granted by the last Parliament had been spent and to outline the way in which future grants would be employed. According to his calculations, £280,000 had already been spent (£32,000 for Ireland, £37,000 for the navy, £47,000 for munitions and forts, £99,800 for the English regiments in the Low Countries, and £61,000 for Mansfeld's mercenary army). Coke's calculations for the future were equally awesome. He estimated that the expedition against Spain would cost at least £293,000 (£200,000 for the fleet, £48,000 for ordnance, £45,000 for soldiers, plus other

[46] *Returns of Members of Parliament*, I, 463; Willson, *Privy Councillors*, p. 66.

[47] Gardiner, *History of England*, V, 336-47; Russell, *Parliaments*, pp. 219-26. I disagree with Russell's assessment that the 'stage was well set for a grant of supply'.

[48] Willson, *Privy Councillors*, pp. 66, 177.

[49] This event was the occasion of Sir John Eliot's often quoted, derogatory description of Coke which we have already considered and will further examine in chapter eleven. Eliot, *Negotium Posterorum*, I, 113-14.

[50] S.R. Gardiner, ed., *Debates in the House of Commons in 1625* (Westminster, 1873), p. 56. I am not at all certain, as others have been, that a set of preliminary instructions in the state papers were intended for Coke or properly belong to this date: SP 16/4/26.

wages and allowances). Worse yet, this £293,000 did not include the additional expenses of £40,000 promised to Denmark and £20,000 monthly for Mansfeld's army. These costs greatly exceeded Parliament's grant of two subsidies, even if those subsidies brought in £160,000 as Coke generously allowed. It was imperative to give Charles further provision, Coke argued, because 'the establishing of his throne, the support of true religion, the welfare of our country, and the peace of Christendom do in a good degree depend upon the proceeding and success of this fleet'. In conclusion, Coke repeated: 'This fleet must then proceed whatsoever it shall cost. And the king must be enabled *with monies or with credit* to prosecute his designs.' Coke even intimated that if Parliament failed to provide further funds, Charles, rather than abandon the fleet and the cause, would resort to extraordinary measures for raising money.[51]

What exactly was Coke asking for in his speech on 8 July? One historian has contended that Coke flatly requested an immediate vote of additional subsidies, and this 'was regarded as a shabby trick to obtain a vote on supply in a thin house'.[52] However, this interpretation does not take into account other evidence indicating that what Coke asked the Commons for was actually a declaration announcing their mere intention to increase supply in the future. According to one observer, Coke explicitly stated that: 'A present resolucion for mony is not expected. . . [instead] it is requisit we should expresse our owne affection to the busines now in hande, and that when we retorne againe wee are willinge to releeve his Majestie in some farther proportion.'[53] Further analysis suggests the truth of the matter is a combination of both these interpretations. Certainly Coke would have been happy to elicit an immediate vote of additional subsidies. He broached this as a possibility, however remote. On the other hand, he also gave the Commons the more palatable option of declaring their intention to make some further provision in the future. This would at least improve the king's credit and give him, as Coke said in one draft of his speech, 'a gauge for his proceedings'.[54] Sir John Eliot understood that this was the choice Coke laid before the Commons.

[51] Quotations are taken from Coke's own copy of his speech: SP 16/4/23. Italics mine. This final version varies only slightly from his two rough drafts: SP 16/4/24, 25. For firsthand accounts of Coke's speech see BL, Add. MS. 48,091, fols. 21-2 and Gardiner, *1625 Debates,* pp. 56-9. Both these sources erroneously record the figure for the fleet as £20,000 instead of the correct £200,000.

[52] Willson, *Privy Councillors,* pp. 170-1, 212. Compare Lockyer, *Buckingham,* p. 247.

[53] Gardiner, *1625 Debates*, pp. 58-9.

[54] SP 16/4/24. See also SP 16/4/23.

According to Eliot, Coke 'concluded with this motion, that either they would presentlie make an addition of supplie, or pass some ingagement to the K[ing], that at the next meeting they would doe it; wch might give him credit in the interim, & soe the expedition to goe on'.[55] This clarifies what Coke intended to communicate on 8 July. The fact remains, however, that his speech was sufficiently ambiguous to allow at least some of his listeners to construe it as a sinister motion 'in a thin House for more supply'.[56]

There was nothing ambiguous about the response to Coke's motion: it went down like the proverbial lead balloon. Only a handful of members was present, the plague was raging in London, and adjournment was expected any moment. It had been generally assumed that Charles would settle for the two subsidies he had been given. Under these circumstances, only one person spoke in favour of Coke's motion. Indeed, it might have provoked an angry response if it had not been 'that MR SOLLICITOR (desperate of bringinge it to effect) took care only to lay it aside quietly'. Without further consideration of supply, Coke announced on 11 July that Charles had decided to allow Parliament a brief recess.[57]

Parliament reconvened on 1 August at Oxford, the new location having been chosen to avoid the plague. Three days later Coke was again employed to convince the Commons to increase their supply, and again he was handicapped by both the unpopular content of his speech and the unfavourable circumstances under which he was required to speak. Both Houses were assembled before the king in Christ Church Hall. Charles gave a brief speech followed by a larger account by Conway. Then to everyone's surprise, including Coke's 'SIR JO. COOKE was called up to the Kinge, and privatly received from him some short instructions, and then returninge to the middle of the hall entred into a large discourse'.[58] No one understood the unfortunate planning of this event better than Coke himself. In a letter written later that same day, Coke described the confusion leading up to his speech:

> I came but on Tuesday, and that night had my instructions to deliver the present state of affairs to the nether House, which on

[55] Eliot, *Negotium Posterorum,* I, 116-17.

[56] These words were used by Lord Cavendish in the 1626 Parliament to describe what had occurred in 1625. Whitelocke diary, fol. 66v. In a personal letter Thomas Locke described Coke's speech as 'tacitly inferring' that additional subsidies should be supplied. SP 16/4/29. See also Russell, *Parliaments,* p. 236.

[57] Gardiner, *1625 Debates*, pp. 59, 67. Compare SP 16/4/29; *CJ*, I, 808.

[58] Gardiner, *1625 Debates*, p. 74.

> Wednesday night was changed and left doubtful whether the Lord Conway or I should relate it to both Houses in the presence of the king, and this morning even in the Hall where we met the counsel varied again, and the Lord Conway was required to say something and I to present the rest.

Summing up the situation, Coke lamented that 'a greater charge with so little warning and many changes could hardly have been laid upon so weak shoulders'. These clumsy changes show that Charles was unsure whether or not to present his case to both Houses at the same time and unsure how to divide the chore between Conway and Coke, but his indecisiveness went much deeper. Even the purpose of Coke's speech was changed at the last minute. According to Coke, the original intention had been to let Parliament judge 'whether they would now proceed to a resolution or adjourn till winter in regard of the sickness'. This would not necessarily have required a reconsideration of supply. But the king's altered instructions 'which the king himself delivered to me in his chair was to show the importance of the fleet, and that it could not proceed without a present supply by money or credit'.[59] This did require Coke to press the issue of supply again.

The line of argument Coke employed on 4 August was different in emphasis from that which he had employed on 8 July. This time much of Coke's speech was a recapitulation of the diplomatic manoeuvres that had occurred between the Parliaments of 1624 and 1625. Obviously Coke hoped to persuade his listeners that war was not being entered into precipitately. On the other hand, some members of Parliament were beginning to doubt whether Charles and Buckingham really intended to wage war at all. Coke's speech can be interpreted as an effort to convince these doubters that, although outright war had not immediately resulted from breaking off the treaties with Spain, still the long-promised war would materialize.[60] Coke explained that the person responsible for the delay was King James who before his death had tried to engage the assistance of as many Continental allies as possible before openly embarking on war. Another argument used by Coke in his 4 August speech was the familiar one that the Commons had authorized the war in 1624, and consequently they were now obliged to finance it. At Parliament's behest, Charles had made expensive commitments to his Continental allies and had prepared his own fleet for action. Now, said Coke, 'of necessity this expense must be supported by your assistance with money or credit,

[59]Coke MSS., packet 69, Coke to Greville, 4 Aug. 1625.

[60]Russell, *Parliaments,* pp. 241-2.

according to your former engagement, whereby he was drawn to cast himself into this condition'.[61]

Coke's plea for 'money or credit' on 4 August was as unsuccessful as his plea on 8 July had been. Some persons even protested the fact that he had been allowed to speak at all. 'The envy that I bear', Coke wrote, 'is that it hath not been known nor is agreeable to the orders of the House (as some think) that a nether House man was ever employed to deliver the king's pleasure to both Houses of Parliament.' Coke was sincere in claiming that he did not covet this dubious honour. As he said, it devolved upon him 'only by reason of the sudden change of counsel which gave not time to any other to be instructed for a speech of near an hour long. For my part I neither had ambition nor thought of speaking in that place'.[62] A more unfavourable and cynical interpretation of the event came from Sir John Eliot. His description of Coke's performance may be taken as representative of those who most strongly objected to it:

> Sr John Coke. . . though yet noe publicke minister of the State, & a member of the Commons, was without leave from them, & that never done by anie man before, in their presenc made a dictator for the K[ing]. & after some formalitie of seeming to take instructions at the present, in that which he had studied long before, having the honour in the face of that assemblie to be cal'd up privatlie to the State, & from thenc returning, as from an Oracle inspir'd with a new spirit & wisdome, thus he propounds those sacred reasons he had gather'd for the occasion of that time.[63]

The third highlight of Coke's participation in the Parliament of 1625 occurred on 8 August, when he assisted Buckingham in addressing both Houses. This time permission was asked from the Commons in advance, and they granted Coke leave 'but to speak as the King's Servant, and not as a member of the House of Commons'.[64] Buckingham paused at one point in his speech on 8 August to allow Coke to present the financial accounts of the naval preparations. At

[61] SP 16/5/14. Coke endorsed his speech, 'Instructions for a message first appointed to be delivered in the nether House, but afterwards, by commandment, delivered in the upper House before the King, Lords, and Commons at Christ Church Hall at Oxford.' A diarist's summary of this speech is printed in Gardiner, *1625 Debates*, pp. 74-7. See also SP 16/5/30.

[62] Coke MSS., packet 69, Coke to Greville, 4 Aug. 1625.

[63] Eliot, *Negotium Posterorum,* II, 18. Another account of Coke's speech, the parliamentary reaction to it, and the subsequent dismay of Charles can be found in a journal kept by Lord Montagu. HMC, *Buccleuch and Queensbury MSS.,* III, 248. See also HMC, *Rutland MSS.,* I, 473-4.

[64] *CJ,* I, 812. Compare Gardiner, *1625 Debates,* p.92.

another point Coke interjected that Buckingham had personally contributed £44,000 to those preparations. Buckingham's conspicuous reliance on Coke in this 8 August report to Parliament faithfully reflected his daily reliance on Coke where the navy was concerned. The substance of Buckingham's speech likewise attested to this fact. Buckingham tried to persuade Parliament that he had made all his war plans in close consultation with other people, particularly the Council of War. His summary of what had taken place, however, showed that no one was more prominent in those consultations than Coke, who was not an official member of the Council.[65]

How far the Council of War had participated in Buckingham's military plans was an issue earlier in this Parliament, but it was apparently Buckingham's speech on 8 August that brought the issue to a head just two days later. On 10 August, Sir Robert Mansell complained in the Commons that 'whereas ther had bene speech of consultation with the Counsel of Warr, he was not at any debate since February last'. Furthermore, said Mansell: 'When he heard the direction given for 10,000 men, he refused to deliver his opinion in the presence of Sir Jo[hn] Cooke, beinge no Counsellor of Warr, nor of State.'[66] Mansell thus raised three points of contention: first that the Council of War had not been adequately consulted, secondly that he himself had not been adequately consulted, and thirdly that Coke had been consulted though he should not have been because he did not officially belong to the Council. These charges were answered by the Solicitor General, Sir Robert Heath. Heath explained that in December of 1624 King James had commanded Coke, Mansell, and Mansell's partner from the Algiers voyage, captain Love, 'to meet often with my Lord of Buckingham... when by examination of mapps and plotts, it was debated how they might best annoy the Kinge of Spayne'. Presumably this small, specialized committee was to provide the Council of War with expert opinion. Heath affirmed that 'The Lordes of the Counsell of Warr were often call'd'. He expressed confidence that the Council members would be willing to testify that they were satisfactorily involved in the deliberations. Thus Heath disputed Mansell's contention that the Council of War was not adequately consulted, but his testimony did serve to confirm the charge that Coke was able to influence the Council's decisions despite the fact that he was not officially one of its members. As for Mansell's contention that he himself had been excluded from the Council's

[65] Bodleian Library, Tanner MS. 276, fols. 154-8; Rushworth, *Historical Collections*, I, 186-91.

[66] Gardiner, *1625 Debates*, p. 115.

deliberations, Heath said this was Mansell's own fault: 'It is trew Sir R[obert] M[ansell] was full of meditation upon his owne divises, which, though they seem'd probable to himselfe, did not give others such satisfaction. In Febru[ary] he gave over upon discontent; and ther be those that can witness that he sayd, if he might not have his owne desyer, he would meddle no more with the business. Afterwarde he never came to the Counsell.'[67] According to Heath, then, Mansell withdrew voluntarily from the Council's deliberations out of pique.

Other, fragmentary, evidence supports Heath's testimony. It appears that Mansell's pique arose from a quarrel he and Coke had regarding the best war strategy for England. Poring over the maps and plots together, these two old rivals could not agree on the best way to annoy the king of Spain, but they certainly annoyed each other. Mansell had apparently presented his own plan to the Council of War back in January when Coke was absent. In February, Coke discovered what had happened and complained to Buckingham: 'I attended the Lords of the Council of War and understanding by them the propositions made in my absence for increasing the proportion of victuals from 6 to 8 months and for dividing the fleet [in]to two remote services, I showed how thereby the service was made impossible both for the charge and for the time.' Coke implored the Lord Admiral not 'to be diverted by new propositions', arguing from experience that 'that which the propounders of exorbitant attempts do least consider is the provision of monies'.[68] Mansell was indignant at having to defend his opinion against Coke, whom we have seen him describe as 'no Counsellor of Warr, nor of State'. Failing to get his own way in the Council of War, Mansell refused to attend any more of their meetings. We know too little about Mansell's proposal to judge conclusively whether he should have got his way. However, it seems from Coke's description to have been a more adventuresome and costly strategy than the one eventually adopted. Mansell himself confirmed this impression when he complained that the strategy approved by the Council of War was 'to no purpose, beinge such as would galle the enemy [rather] than hurte him; and [he] doubted not but to offer a proposition which shall produce such effects as will procure the restitution of the Palatinat'.[69] Considering the inadequacy of the government's resources and how badly it executed the strategy that was adopted, it is likely that a grander strategy would only have resulted in grander losses.

[67] *Ibid.,* pp. 122-3, 147-8, 162.

[68] SP 14/183/48.

[69] Gardiner, *1625 Debates*, p. 116. Compare BL, Harleian MS. 161, no. 24, fol. 68.

Mansell was one of Coke's personal enemies; another was Sir John Eliot. Appropriately enough, the Parliament of 1625 witnessed the first documented clash on the floor of the House of Commons between Coke and Eliot: Eliot attacked the commissioners of the navy, and Coke promptly rose to their defence. It was a minor incident about which we have only a brief notice. As it turned out, however, this was the first of many such confrontations between Coke and Eliot in Parliament. Eliot's contemptuous descriptions of Coke, which have already been cited, clearly betray their author's personal animus. Eliot disliked Coke for many reasons. Coke worked closely with Eliot's major competitor in the local admiralty affairs of Devon, Sir James Bagg. In fact, shortly before the opening of Parliament, Eliot and Bagg had been involved in a bitter feud over the pressing of mariners in the Exeter district. Coke also questioned Eliot's honesty. More fundamentally, Eliot's animosity toward Coke stemmed from a conviction that Coke contributed to his loss of favour with Buckingham. Eliot's famous opposition to Buckingham should not induce us to forget the extent to which he originally curried the Lord Admiral's favour. A critical point in the relationship between these men had been reached early in this Parliament, on 8 July, when Eliot unsuccessfully urged Buckingham not to ask for further supply. As we saw, Buckingham persisted in asking for greater supply and chose Coke for his spokesman. Years later, when Eliot recorded this incident in his *Negotium Posterorum,* he interpreted Coke's selection for this task as 'an indication of his preferment then at hand'. The preferment Eliot alluded to came shortly after the Parliament of 1625 and no doubt drove Eliot further away from Buckingham. It was Coke's appointment as Secretary of State.[70]

[70]Gardiner, *1625 Debates*, p. 90; Gardiner, *History of England,* V, 366-71, 414. Coke MSS., packet 25, Thomas Bridgman to Bagg, 1 April 1625; George Chudleigh to Bagg, 2 April 1625; Bagg to Coke, 2 April 1625; Bagg to Coke, 18 April 1625. SP 16/1/25; *Cowper MSS.,* I, 177, 179; Hulme, *Life of Eliot,* pp. 66, 69-71, 85; Harold Hulme, 'Sir John Eliot and the Vice-Admiralty of Devon', *Camden Miscellany*, vol. 17 (London, 1940), pp. v-xiv. The most objective studies of Eliot have come from J.N. Ball. See his 'Sir John Eliot at the Oxford Parliament, 1625', *Bulletin of the Institute of Historical Research,* 28 (Nov. 1955), 113-27 and 'Sir John Eliot and Parliament, 1624-1629', in Sharpe, *Faction and Parliament*, pp. 173-207. Eliot, *Negotium Posterorum,* I, 113.

10

SECRETARY OF STATE

The failure of the 1625 Parliament to grant adequate supplies and the nearly complete loss of confidence in Buckingham's leadership made it all the more imperative that the fleet destined for Cadiz succeed. Charles and Buckingham pinned their hopes on an impressive naval victory. Near the beginning of September, therefore, Coke was sent to Plymouth in order to supervise the fleet's dispatch in person. About the same time that Coke went to Plymouth, Secretary Morton returned from his mission to the Netherlands. Morton came back to England a very sick man, and on 6 September he died after serving only seven months as Secretary of State. Less than two days later his successor was publicly known to be Sir John Coke.[1]

Coke's appointment as Secretary was swift and decisive; it lacked all the elements of scrambling competition that usually surrounded the filling of a vacant court office. As one observer remarked, Coke was Secretary before Morton was buried.[2] The chief reason for this alacrity was the fact that Morton's death conveniently allowed Buckingham to discharge several obligations at one time. As noted earlier, it had been rumoured for over a year that Coke had been promised the Secretaryship. Indeed, it had come as a surprise when not he but Morton succeeded Calvert. This was probably due to the special requirements of the time: Buckingham had needed a man he could send on foreign assignments, and Morton could easily be spared for such work. Coke, on the other hand, had to stay in England where his work in the navy was indispensable. In this sense, Morton's appointment had been only an interim measure, though of course no one could have known how short the interim would be. In addition to Coke, Buckingham had made promises to two of his other faithful servants, Sir Thomas Aylesbury and Sir Edward Nicholas. Thus when Coke was elevated to the Secretaryship, Aylesbury succeeded to the vacated Mastership of Requests, and Nicholas moved up to replace Aylesbury as Buckingham's naval secretary. This was largely

[1]SP 16/6/34, 35, 97. Coke was sworn into his new office about the middle of September when the king and Buckingham joined him at Plymouth to attend the sailing of the fleet. Coke MSS., packet 15, Coke to Greville, 18 Oct. 1625. The sign manual warrant for Coke's appointment was dated 2 November. SP 39/18/85. His letters patent were finally issued on 9 November. PRO, Index 16,787, fol. 16a, no. 88; Index 6,807 (Nov. 1625); PRO, C 66/2,371. A copy of his grant is printed in Thomas Rymer, *Foedera,* ed. Robert Sanderson (20 vols., London, 1704-35), XVIII, 226.

[2]SP 16/6/97.

a foregone conclusion, which left little opportunity for other competitors. As Sir Dudley Carleton, the perpetual suitor, was told by a colleague, 'a double former engagement for the persons above named, whensoever any such occasion should happen (though not suspected this way) prevented us all'.[3]

The Secretaryship usually commanded a high price. Morton, for example, had paid £6,000 to Calvert for the office; and earlier in the century, Sir Ralph Winwood had paid the earl of Somerset £7,000 for it.[4] It has been erroneously claimed that Coke paid Morton's widow £3,000.[5] The letter upon which this claim is based, however, shows that Coke did no such thing. What actually happened was that King Charles promised Morton's widow £3,000, and Buckingham instructed Sir Robert Pye 'to find out where it might be raised'. Pye requested Coke's help in recovering a particular sum owed to the Crown which could be put to this use, but he assumed that Coke had no prior knowledge of the business, and he certainly did not ask Coke to pay anything out of his own pocket.[6] It appears, then, that Coke paid nothing for the Secretaryship. Perhaps no money changed hands this time because the three offices involved were all kept within Buckingham's family of clients. Besides, Coke had already paid abundantly for the Secretaryship in other ways, specifically through his unwavering loyalty and his hard work. These very same assets, however, which helped to win Coke higher office could turn to liabilities. People like Sir John Eliot resented Coke's success and were prejudiced against him precisely because he worked so hard and dutifully on Buckingham's behalf.[7]

[3]SP 16/6/35. Nicholas left his own interesting memorial of the event: 'In the year about July [*sic*, Sept.] 1625 (Sr Albertus Morton, one of His Majestys principal Secretaries of State, dying at Southampton), K. Charles I. being then in the New Forest, my Lord Duke procured Sr John Coke, Mr of Requests, to be Principal Secretary in his place and Mr Aylesbury to be Master of Requests in his place. And at Plimouth in September following, Sr John Coke having the signet given him and being then sworn Principal Secretary, Sr Tho. Aylesbury was then sworn Master of Requests. And then his Grace of his own motion made me his Secretary for the Admiralty in Sr Tho. Aylesburys place.' George F. Warner, ed., *The Nicholas Papers: Correspondence of Sir Edward Nicholas* (4 vols., London, 1886-1920), I, xiv-xv. The Venetian ambassador similarly reported to his superiors: 'The post of Secretary of State has been conferred upon John Cuck, Master of Requests, a man of erudition in languages and affairs and above all in naval matters. He is a dependent of the duke who has established his secretary of the sea in the post of the Requests, a very high office. The duke disposes of everything, as the king only desires his pleasure.' *CSPV*, 1625-1626, p. 168.

[4]Evans, *The Principal Secretary*, p. 85; Birch, *The Court and Times of James the First*, I, 375.

[5]Coke, *The Last Elizabethan*, p. 137.

[6]Coke MSS., packet 25, Pye to Coke, 27 Sept. 1625.

[7]Gardiner, *History of England*, VI, 9.

Coke's appointment to the Secretaryship did not mark the beginning of a dramatically new stage in his career. His rejection from the court in 1604, his return in 1618, and his appointment as Master of Requests in 1622 had all been more important crossroads. After his appointment to the Secretaryship, much of his work still revolved around the navy. Furthermore, he and the other Secretary of State, Conway, had already been working together as colleagues for over two years. Fulke Greville saw these two old disciples of his labouring smoothly beside one another when he told Conway that Coke would be 'a passing safe and easy yoke fellow for yourself'.[8] Greville had been through much with Coke since those distant days when they first worked together under Queen Elizabeth. Now, as Greville's own career drew to a close, he wrote the following words to Coke:

> From my lord of Buckingham I received a letter . . . to let me know you were advanced to this place. . . . The expectation of your preferment in the world is great, your powers by nature and education I think as equal as any man's living for that place. Counsel I cannot give you other than not to change the many years' acquaintance with yourself for any sudden or tempting liberties of a brave undertaking court. This motion (if I know you) is freely granted me, and then am I confident the world shall be beholding to the duke for this seasonable advancement of yours. . . . Farewell honest and honourable Sir John Coke. Prosper as I wish you, not for my sake, but the world's, and believe that I am and ever will be your old, loving, and true friend.[9]

Coke's work in the navy during his early years as Secretary will be dealt with specifically in chapter twelve. By analyzing that sad succession of fleets together in one chapter, a better understanding of why they failed so miserably may be reached. To understand Coke's other work during his early years as Secretary, it will help to begin with a brief survey of the duties and powers attached to his new office.

First of all, the Secretary was the chief avenue of communication with the king. Like the less important Master of Requests, the Secretary functioned daily as an intermediary between the Crown and all kinds of petitioners. As the guardian of the signet, he was also responsible for initiating documents through the seals and for personally drafting many of the king's official letters. As one of the chief Privy Councillors, he was responsible, along with the Lord President, for calling Council meetings and conducting Council business. As the

[8]SP 16/521/173.

[9]Coke MSS., packet 46, Greville to Coke, 12 Oct. 1625.

acknowledged public agent of the Crown, he represented its interests in Parliament and came to preside over the developing diplomatic corps. Beyond these specific functions, the more general question of how much independent authority the Secretary enjoyed or how much personal influence he could exert varied greatly with the character of the man and the disposition of his sovereign. It has been said that the Tudors allowed great latitude to their Secretaries. One need only recall the famous examples of Thomas Cromwell, Walsingham, and the two Cecils. But after the death of the earl of Salisbury, the Stuarts denigrated the office, using their Secretaries as mere administrative bureaucrats. This comparison is largely true, and no one better proves the case than Coke.[10]

The role of the Secretary depended on another important factor. From 1540 onwards the office was frequently divided between two men; it was a partnership. Coke, though he came to office at the age of sixty-two, managed to outlive two of his fellow Secretaries and nearly survive a third. In each case, the character of Coke's colleague and the use the king chose to make of him had a great deal to do with how the two men divided the duties of the office. In these early years, Conway practically monopolized one area of the Secretary's work: foreign affairs. This is not to say that Coke was completely excluded from foreign affairs. There are some instances of his writing to English ambassadors abroad, dealing with foreign ambassadors in London, and even participating in negotiations, but each of these instances arose from special circumstances. He was assigned to treat with the Danish ambassador on the subject of sending English troops to Denmark probably because he was best informed on the recruiting and dispatching of the English forces. The issue of prize goods brought him into contact with the Dutch ambassadors with whom he had long since been employed in the East India Company's behalf regarding the atrocity at Amboyna.[11] And, of course, when Conway was sick, Coke could fill in for him.[12] Apart from these exceptions,

[10]Evans, *The Principal Secretary*, pp. 1-9. One of Coke's own servants drew up a useful description of the Secretary's office: Coke MSS., packet 31, Richard Poole to Coke, Oct. 1628; *Cowper MSS.,* I, 368-9. See also the orders to be observed in Council meetings printed in HMC, *Third Report*, p. 69 and Evans, *The Principal Secretary*, pp. 228-9. There are several discourses on the Privy Council among the state papers for 1625, some of which the published calendar attributed to Coke (SP 16/8/77-82), but in fact they are not in Coke's hand.

[11]Coke MSS., packet 29, Conway to Coke, 7 Sept. 1627; Coke to King Charles, 8 Sept. 1627; Conway to Coke, 23 Feb. 1628; packet 47, Conway to Coke, 27 Feb. 1627; SP 16/56/1, 30, 35; 16/61/72; 16/67/76; 16/94/15, 26. Conway's monopoly of foreign affairs is most apparent in the foreign state papers in the PRO. During the period 1625-9, for example, there are less than two dozen letters between Coke and foreign agents in France.

[12]SP 78/77/fol. 211.

foreign affairs remained Conway's domain. Looking back from our modern vantage point, therefore, the partnership of Conway and Coke seems to have foreshadowed the modern development of the foreign and home offices. If Coke had monopolized domestic affairs the same way Conway monopolized foreign affairs, the foreshadowing would have been more complete, but this did not happen because Coke was often preoccupied with naval affairs and Conway conducted a great deal of the domestic business. Nevertheless, the evolution had begun and the basis was laid for an even clearer differentiation to develop in the future when Dudley Carleton would replace Conway.[13]

With the notable exception of foreign affairs, Coke participated in all the other facets of the Secretary's office. He drafted numerous royal letters – to Captain Pennington, Buckingham, the French ministers, the Duke of Savoy, the Doge of Venice, and others.[14] He also frequently summoned meetings of the Privy Council and introduced matters on behalf of the king. For example, on one occasion Conway followed the king on progress, leaving Coke and the Council behind at Whitehall. During that period Conway frequently sent the king's instructions to Coke regarding when to call a Council meeting and what business to lay before it. At one time he gave Coke the king's directions 'that you forthwith call a Council, acquaint the board with the letter, and cause a present course to be taken'.[15] At another time he wrote: 'I have acquainted his Majesty with the contents of the Hamburg letters.... His Majesty's pleasure is that you assemble such of the Council as are now about London . . . and enter into consideration of the contents thereof.'[16] Conway was advantageously close to the king at such times, but he was often out of touch with the actual progress of affairs being conducted back in London by Coke and the Council.[17] This divided Secretariat worked best when the peripatetic court moved closer to London. Then, as Conway told Coke, they were 'able to play our balls with quicker returns'.[18]

[13]Evans, *The Principal Secretary*, pp. 87, 274; *CSPV,* 1626-1628, p. 312.

[14]SP 16/56/18; 16/25/104; 78/80/fols. 229-39, 248; 78/82/fol. 59; *Cowper MSS.,* I, 330. It was probably due to Coke's command of naval affairs that he wrote the royal instructions for Cecil's expedition to Cadiz a few weeks before his actual appointment to the Secretaryship. SP 16/5/87.

[15]Coke MSS., packet 28, Conway to Coke, 5 Aug. 1627.

[16]Coke MSS., packet 28, Conway to Coke, 22 Aug. 1627. See also packet 28, Conway to Coke, 24 Aug. 1627 and packet 29, Conway to Coke, 27 Aug. 1627.

[17]Coke MSS., packet 29, Conway to Coke, 13 June 1627.

[18]Coke MSS., packet 47, Conway to Coke, 5 March 1627; SP 16/56/35; *Cowper MSS.,* I, 298, 308, 313, 317.

Drafting royal letters and conducting Council business when necessary were two of the more formal duties associated with Coke's new office. A less formal development during these early Secretarial years was the role he played as an intermediary between commercial interests and the Crown. For example, he continued to work with the East India Company.[19] Among other things, he procured licences for the Company to transport gold bullion, he supported their demand that Dutch East India Company ships be captured in retaliation for the murders at Amboyna, and he assisted the Company in trying to establish their own mills for manufacturing gunpowder.[20] Examples of Coke's efforts with regard to other trading interests include the Muscovy Company, the Eastland Company, and various other merchants trading with France and Africa.[21] Coke had already worked with several commercial figures on the naval commission (Sir John Wolstenholme, Sir Thomas Smythe, and Sir William Russell), and two of these were associated with a fishing company that Coke helped to found in the 1630s.[22] Even Coke's marriage to the widow Gore may have reflected and strengthened ties he had with London trading interests.

During Coke's early years as Secretary, much of his time was still spent supervising the preparation of fleets and frantically searching for the money to finance them. Of all the means employed by the Crown to raise money, one was particularly associated with Coke. He had been instrumental in resurrecting the law of reprisal or prize goods in order to prosecute Mansell in 1622 and to extort £10,000 from the East India Company in 1624. When war broke out, he likewise took the lead in pressing the High Court of Admiralty to issue a commission that would authorize the seizure of Spanish goods.[23] This captured merchandise or contraband, it was hoped, could be sold by the Crown to finance the war. The English quickly captured several

[19]Coke's relations with the East India Company appear throughout volumes VIII-XVI of their court minute books. There is a possibility that Coke was a member of the Company. See Theodore K. Rabb, *Enterprise and Empire: Merchant and Gentry Investment in the Expansion of England, 1575-1630* (Cambridge, Mass., 1967), p. 269.

[20]For Coke's acquisition of the bullion licenses see *APC,* 1625-1626, p. 338 and 1627, p. 38. For the reprisal against the Dutch see Coke MSS., packet 29, Sir Sackville Trevor to Coke, 17 Sept. 1627; Conway to Coke, 28 Sept. 1627; SP 16/79/14, 48. For the gunpowder question see SP 16/5/85, 92; 16/6/25, 110. But also compare SP 16/11/24.

[21]*APC*, 1626, pp. 367-8, 374; 1627, p. 436; SP 16/56/36; 16/118/90.

[22]SP 16/152/57. For the fishing company, see below, p. 210.

[23]SP 14/183/47; 16/1/112; Coke MSS., packet 25, Sir Thomas Coventry to Coke, 7 Sept. 1625.

French and Dutch ships suspected of carrying goods between Spain and the Spanish Netherlands. Unfortunately, the Admiralty Court had not yet actually issued the commission for prize goods. Coke was too desperate for money to allow this technicality to delay the operation. He promptly drafted a personal warrant for Buckingham to sign which named the men to be put in charge of unloading, inventorying, and selling the prize goods and authorized them to proceed until the formal commission was issued.[24] The sale of part of the merchandise from the captured ships led to international complications. The French and Dutch Ambassadors justly complained that it was unfair to sell the cargoes in question before a court of law had determined that they were in fact contraband. Coke insisted that the government had to sell the goods for immediate cash. As he told Greville, the English war plans were dependent on 'the sale of prize goods to raise monies without which our intentions will fall to [the] ground'.[25] He had no doubt that afterwards, he could prove the goods had been genuine contraband to the satisfaction of any court. Desperate for money, Coke rationalized that he was not circumventing the law. Rather, he viewed the demands of the French and Dutch for the immediate restitution of their ships as an effort on their part to circumvent the law. He, too, insisted that the case be submitted to the Admiralty Court, albeit after some of the goods in question had already been sold.[26] Meanwhile, the laborious task of proving that the seized goods were really contraband fell to Coke.[27] In his own words, this was: 'Tedious and difficult work which I have still in hand. Namely to peruse all the letters written in Spanish, Italian, French, Dutch, and English, and some in Arabic; and to gather out of them what may discover the propriety of every piece of goods. Besides to survey all the bills of lading and to compare all the merchants' marks.'[28] The papers that had to be examined, Coke said, were 'more than a strong man can carry upon his back'.[29] It is not surprising that on one occasion, when Conway wrote to Buckingham, he gave full acknowledgement to 'Sir John Cooke, whose discreet diligence and

[24] SP 16/8/41, 47.

[25] Coke MSS., packet 46, Coke to Greville, 6 Dec. 1625.

[26] SP 16/12/1.

[27] This was more properly the work of the commissioners appointed for prize goods, but as Coke explained to Buckingham, 'your Grace's servants whom you made commissioners are either by sickness or other employments drawn away'. Bodleian Library, Tanner MS. 72, fol. 26.

[28] SP 16/11/64.

[29] SP 16/11/24.

care make him best understand all that concerns the shipping and the prizes'.[30]

To summarize, then, Coke originally promoted the idea of using prize goods to finance the war, he pressed for a commission to carry this out, seized the initiative when the commission was delayed, directed the handling and sale of the goods, defended these actions before the Council and foreign ambassadors, and laboriously prepared the government's case to prove that the goods were contraband. The results of these efforts were mixed at best. On the positive side, Coke did get some of the money he needed, and this source of revenue continued to contribute substantially to the war effort.[31] Moreover, the case in the Admiralty Court was at least not lost: it was protracted and seems to have ended without a judgement. On the negative side, however, the issue of prize goods exacerbated relations with France and may even have brought the two nations closer to war. Furthermore, as Coke was about to discover, one of the French ships seized, the *St Peter*, became the focus of an attack on Buckingham in the Parliament of 1626.[32]

All the Privy Councillors were to some degree representatives of the Crown in Parliament, but this had come to be particularly true of the Secretaries of State. After Conway was elevated to the Lords, this responsibility devolved solely upon Coke. Along with the special reliance upon the Secretary, the practice had developed of assuring his election through a 'safe' university seat. Thus Cambridge elected Naunton in 1621 and 1624, Sir Albertus Morton in 1625, and Morton's successor, Coke, in 1626 and 1628.[33] In Coke's case, however, the university seat was not as safe as it first appeared to be. There is evidence that he had difficulty procuring his election at Cambridge in both 1626 and 1628. In 1626 Coke evidently tried to

[30] Philip Yorke, second earl of Hardwicke, ed., *Miscellaneous State Papers from 1501 to 1726* (2 vols., London, 1778), II, 9.

[31] Lockyer, *Buckingham,* pp. 294-5, 303.

[32] In addition to the sources already cited, Coke's role can best be seen through the following: SP 16/6/126; 16/7/41; 16/9/5; 16/10/29; 16/11/19; 16/12/25, 102; 16/18/81; 16/21/47; 16/56/1, 30, 35; 16/94/14; 16/106/82; 16/525/92; *APC,* 1625-1626, pp. 290, 350, 384; 1626, pp. 220, 428-9; 1627, pp. 83, 458; *Cowper MSS.,* I, 210-36 *passim*. See also Gardiner, *History of England*, VI, 39-47, 142-53.

[33] Joseph R. Tanner, ed., *The Historical Register of the University of Cambridge* (Cambridge, 1917), p. 30. As we already know, Naunton and Coke were former fellows of Trinity College; Morton was a former fellow of King's College. In 1625 Morton chose to represent Kent County, a second constituency which had elected him, thereby freeing the Cambridge seat for Naunton again. Willson, *Privy Councillors,* pp. 75, 99-100. See also Millicent B. Rex, *University Representation in England, 1604-1690* (Norwich, 1954), pp. 106-19, 127-35, 214.

hedge his bets by standing for election at both Cambridge and the borough of St Germans. As we have seen, he had already been elected to the two preceding Parliaments as a burgess for St Germans through the influence of his brother-in-law, Valentine Carey, the bishop of Exeter. Coke wrote to Carey in January of 1626 and received the following reply: 'Before you wrote unto me or I received your letter, I was mindful of you for your place of burgess from St Germans; and to that purpose I wrote unto the corporation. . . as soon as I heard word of a Parliament called. I make no doubt of their willingness to satisfy my desire.'[34] A week later, however, Carey reported that the borough was not responding with the sort of prompt compliance he had expected. Sir John Eliot was obstructing Coke's election. Carey observed that Eliot 'bears (as it seems) a great sway amongst' the voters, but the bishop was confident that Eliot 'could not divert them from their due respect to me'.[35] Carey, however, was blithely underestimating the extent of Eliot's influence. By this time too, serious difficulties had arisen at Cambridge, although the details of the incident are not clear. Thus Coke stood a very real chance of losing in both elections. An old friend, Sir George Chudleigh, offered to insert Coke's name in his own blank burgess-ship for East Looe if necessary.[36] In the final event, Coke was not forced to accept this offer. Whatever the nature of the opposition at Cambridge, Coke ultimately prevailed in the contest there and went to Parliament as the university's representative. Meanwhile, the borough of St Germans boldly defied the bishop of Exeter and elected a new burgess to Coke's old seat: Sir John Eliot.[37] It was an ominous portent of things to come.

The Parliament of 1626 met in exceedingly hostile circumstances. Members of Parliament were incensed over a number of issues, most of which intimately involved Coke. The ships loaned to France had been used against La Rochelle and were still in the possession of the French government when Parliament met. The detention of the

[34] Coke MSS., packet 46, Valentine Carey to Coke, 13 Jan. 1626.

[35] Coke MSS., packet 77, Valentine Carey to Coke, 22 Jan. 1626.

[36] Coke MSS., packet 46, Sir George Chudleigh to Coke, 1 Feb. 1626. Chudleigh wrote, 'Finding by my lord bishop that he is not certain of your being chosen a burgess for St. Germans, and that Cambridge is in some competition, I thought good to make your Honour the tender of my fortune if your own should chance to fail in other places.'

[37] Eliot was returning to his home borough which he had previously represented in 1614. The elections of Coke and Eliot are both recorded in *Returns of Members of Parliament*, I, 468. According to the Venetian ambassador, an attempt was made afterward to disqualify Coke's election. See *CSPV*, 1625-1626, pp. 380-1. The evidence of difficulty in 1628 comes from a letter written by the Vice-Chancellor of Cambridge to Coke. Coke MSS., packet 29, Thomas Bainbrigge to Coke, 13 March 1628. Bainbrigge apologetically wrote: 'We humbly crave our late choice of you to be a burgess of our university may not prejudice her in your better thoughts.'

French ship, the *St Peter*, for prize goods had apparently provoked the French into retaliating by seizing English goods and ships. This was a matter that concerned English merchants, as well as others who saw it as a sign of deteriorating relations with France. A storm had disrupted a Dutch blockade at Dunkirk, allowing numerous privateers to escape. These endangered the English coasts and shipping at a time when the English government was least able to provide naval protection. Even the extortion of £10,000 from the East India Company surfaced as an issue in Parliament. Above all, there was the totally unsuccessful and humiliating voyage to Cadiz. Eventually the Commons transformed these and other grievances into impeachment charges against the duke of Buckingham. At the outset of the session, however, one might just as logically have predicted that the person impeached would be Coke. He bore a great deal of responsibility for the grievances complained of, and he had good reason to heed the warning of a friend: 'To the end you might the better be prepared to answer such unjust reports if they should be questioned in Parliament as it is said by some they will be. For the general it was said that the affairs of his Majesty's navy hath been ill carried and the chief cause thereof is imputed to your Honour.'[38]

Much of the criticism against Coke and Buckingham in this Parliament was motivated by righteous indignation and high-minded principle. Much of it, too, was motivated by court factionalism and petty, personal rivalries. Coke's two chief critics were men he had worked against in the navy's administration: Sir John Eliot and Sir Robert Mansell. There is no proof that these two men were conscious allies, and Eliot attacked Coke more directly and more frequently. But both men were of one mind on the subject of Coke. Mansell's long-standing hostility toward Coke was exacerbated at this time because Mansell, who was still Vice-Admiral of England and aspired to be a naval hero, was deprived of any real voice in the Council of War and the war effort in general. The death of King James had robbed him of his only remaining source of support at court, and he had already turned to Parliament in 1625 as a way of retaliating, particularly against Coke. For Mansell the Parliament of 1626 was a new arena in which to battle against an old rival. As for Eliot, we have seen that his growing enmity toward Coke, though not as long-standing as Mansell's, had also found expression in the Parliament of 1625. In the words of J. N. Ball, 'something of a personal feud was developing between the two men as early as August 1625', and 'it was possible for some to see Sir John Coke, and not the duke himself as the object of Eliot's early

[38] Coke MSS., packet 26, Hild. Sprusen to Coke, 7 March 1626.

attacks in the parliament of 1626'.[39] For both Mansell and Eliot, then, the Parliament of 1626 provided an opportunity to renew the attack on Coke.

The first issue that brought Coke and Eliot into conflict was the stay of the *St Peter*, an action that appeared to have provoked the retaliatory arrest of English merchant ships in France. The *St Peter* had actually been released briefly but was arrested again before it could sail. Technically it was this second arrest upon which discussion focussed. The Commons referred the subject to a select committee. Three of the ten men on that committee were Eliot, Mansell, and Sir Henry Marten, judge of the Admiralty Court. Eliot reported for this select committee on 22 February and 1 March, and on both occasions there was heated debate involving Coke. Coke defended the *St Peter's* second arrest and implied that it had been sanctioned by Marten. This imputation offended Marten, who was not only a member of the select committee but also Eliot's fellow-member for St Germans. Marten denied advising the stay of the *St Peter* and implied that Coke had done more than he to persuade the Council to support this action. On 1 March Eliot reported: 'Sir H. Marten said that there was an eloquent and elaborate oration made by Sir Jo. Coke at the Table.' In view of the discrepancy between the accounts of Coke and Marten, Eliot concluded his report by formally demanding an explanation from Coke. When Coke tried to explain his way out of this disagreement, the debate only intensified. Dr Turner, the man who later opened the direct attack against Buckingham, moved 'that Sir Jo. Coke may prove that Sir H. Marten did give this advice'. Another member, seeing that personal antagonisms were obscuring the issue, moved 'that some speedy course may be taken for the relief of the poor men and not to make a quarrel amongst ourselves'.[40] For the time being, the issue of the *St Peter* was dropped. This is what Coke had wanted from the start, arguing that the matter was best left to the king's ambassadors who were already negotiating with the French about it. Eliot achieved a belated victory, however, when later in the session the cause of the *St Peter* was resurrected and added to the impeachment charges against Buckingham.

The debate over the *St Peter* coincided with a barrage of criticism regarding the failures of the English navy, particularly the failure to guard the Narrow Seas and of course the strikingly unsuccessful

[39] Ball, 'Eliot at the Oxford Parliament', pp. 126-7.

[40] Quotations are from Rich diary, fols. 52v, 54. See also fols. 23v-30, 32, 53-4; Whitelock diary, fols. 12-14, 53v, 54v, 68-75; *APC*, 1625-1626, p. 290; *DNB*, XII, 1,147; *CJ*, I, 821, 823; *CSPV*, 1625-1626, pp. 339-41.

expedition to Cadiz. On 25 February Coke, though significantly silent on the subject of Cadiz, defended the guard of the Narrow Seas and tried to direct the attention of the Commons to the subject of supply for future naval requirements. But Eliot repulsed this effort and succeeded in persuading the House to seek the cause of past evils before providing for the future. This triumph by Eliot was followed immediately by a speech from Mansell, who disapproved 'that which is mentioned by Sir John Coke' and then proceeded to open a new topic and a new line of attack on the government's conduct of the war.[41] He complained that he was being kept in the dark, that he knew 'nothing as Admiral nor as Counsellor of War'. On the other hand, he claimed to have important knowledge about the deliberations of the Council of War, to which he still ostensibly belonged. He aroused the curiosity of the Commons by promising to tell all he knew if it could be arranged through their intercession. According to one account of his speech, Mansell moved 'that by the means of this House he may open what he knows to some of the [Privy?] Council'.[42] According to another account, he moved: 'That if it may be that before some few Lords he may speak his knowledge, he will discharge his duty.'[43] Mansell obviously wanted to undermine confidence in the Council of War, as he had done in the previous Parliament, but he was contriving to protect himself. The information had to be elicited from him in such a way as to make it appear that he was not irresponsibly betraying the king's secrets. Mansell may have belonged to the earl of Pembroke's faction.[44] Raising the issue of the Council of War at this juncture on 25 February may have been part of a calculated assault on Buckingham. Eliot was either in collusion with Mansell or quick to recognize and seize an opportunity when it presented itself. Eliot moved 'that Sir Ro. Mansell may open thereto first to some select committee and then, if they think it fit, that the House might recommend him to the Lords'. The Chancellor of the Exchequer, Richard Weston, skilfully intervened at this point and promised to take the matter up with the king, who he was sure would appoint 'fit hearers'.[45] This diversion was only temporarily successful, however. Three days later the Commons returned, as one member expressed it, to the question whether 'Sir Robert Mansell may be enjoined to speak his knowledge'.[46] It was

[41] Whitelock diary, fol. 61v.

[42] Rich diary, fol. 42.

[43] Whitelocke diary, fol. 61v.

[44] Russell, *Parliaments*, pp. 255, 281.

[45] Rich diary, fol. 42v.

[46] Whitelocke diary, fol. 56v.

decided that not just Mansell but the whole Council of War should be required to testify directly to the House. Later, between 3 March and 11 March, the Commons inquired four times of Mansell and other members of the Council of War what advice they had given and whether it was followed, but all, including Mansell, refused to answer. They had been ordered by Charles to account only for their disbursements of money. The king acknowledged that this much was required by the subsidy act of 1624, but he adamantly refused to open the policy deliberations of the Council to public view. Having reached this impasse, the House dropped the matter. Charles meanwhile appointed a new Council of War, significantly dropping Mansell and adding Coke.[47]

Throughout these proceedings, Mansell had been distinctly more eager than the other tight-lipped Councillors of War to testify to the Commons.[48] He only reluctantly bowed to power. Indeed, near the beginning of this affair the Privy Council had made a special point of trying to intimidate him. On 1 March Mansell reported to the House that he had been ordered the previous day to attend the Privy Council. There 'Sir John Coke spake that they were commanded to hear and receive such propositions as he had to make concerning the king's service'. Mansell explained to the Commons that he had refused to say anything to the Council 'because he conceived this proceeding was upon the motion in this House'. As if to show that he had not been cowed by this incident, Mansell ended his relation of it by announcing to the Commons the naval strategy he wanted the government to adopt. Unfortunately, accounts of this speech are too brief to reveal the nature of that strategy, but they do reveal Mansell's continuing rivalry with Coke. Mansell told the house: 'He did disallow Sir John Coke's advice and would have read what Sir John Coke said.' Coke promptly responded, perhaps even interrupting Mansell's speech, saying: 'He did not propose any advice but only made a narration of the propositions made by others for defence of the coast.' At this point, the diarist tells us, the argument was terminated by the House 'because it begat some heat'.[49]

As can be seen from the confrontations which occurred on 25 February and 1 March, the subject of guarding the Narrow Seas and English coasts against pirates was a particular bone of contention between Coke and Eliot. As Vice-Admiral of Devon, Eliot had a

[47] *Ibid.,* fols. 31, 32, 33v, 34v, 35v, 36v, 40v, 45v, 48v; *CSPD*, 1625-1626, p. 328.

[48] Mansell seemed particularly pained at having to withhold his information from the Commons on 3 and 10 March. Whitelocke diary, fol. 34v; Rich diary, fol. 58.

[49] Rich diary, fol. 51v. Compare Whitelocke diary, fol. 54v.

professional as well as personal interest in this problem which was compounded by the addition of the Dunkirk privateers in the autumn of 1625 when the naval resources of the Crown were already strained to the limit. The evidence shows that although Coke was handicapped by a shortage of ships and money, he worked hard to provide adequate guard for the Narrow Seas and responded promptly to the Dunkirker menace. Eliot, however, typically ignored the administrative difficulties and charged Coke with personally failing to protect the coasts through the summer and autumn of 1625. As Eliot told the story in his *Negotium Posterorum,* he had gone to the king in the summer of 1625 in his capacity as Vice-Admiral of Devon. He had told the king of the threat posed by the pirates, whereupon the king and Privy Council had ordered eight ships to be deployed against the pirates. This order was handed to Coke who refused to carry it out. According to Eliot, Coke ignored the order for two reasons. First it interfered with his preparation of the Cadiz fleet, and secondly (at least this seems to be Eliot's implication) Coke was annoyed because the order had been procured by Eliot. According to Eliot, 'this bred both wonder and distast. that a privat Commissioner of the Navie should presume to oppose an order of the Councell, that that order being fortified by a speciall direction from the/K[ing] should haue noe more observanc in a matter somuch concerning the publicke good & securitie of the kingdome, it was thought strange & fearfull'.[50] Eliot presented the case in Parliament in much these same terms. The issue was principally debated on 6 March, and the House resolved in Eliot's favour that the Narrow Seas and coasts had not been adequately guarded. On that day, according to Whitelocke's diary, Eliot spoke twice and Coke six times in a noteworthy display of their personal antagonism.[51] Eliot told the Commons that Coke had ignored an order of the Council. Coke answered that this was 'a heavy charge that any private man should contradict an order of the Council'. Admitting that he had received such an order, Coke explained that 'he gave account to the Lords and answered that if the Lords would find money, they would find ships. There being no money, this direction ceased'.[52] Coke argued that the government had not been entirely negligent, that it had done the best it could with the limited means at hand, an

[50]SP 16/5/91, 92; 16/8/2, 22, 23, 29, 33, 47; 16/11/19; Coke MSS., packet 26, Sir Allen Apsley to Coke, 2 Dec. 1625; packet 46, Coke to Greville, 6 Dec. 1625; *Cowper MSS.,* I, 236; S.R. Gardiner, ed., *Documents Illustrating the Impeachment of the Duke of Buckingham in 1626* (London, 1889), pp. 9-17; *APC,* 1625-1626, pp. 213-14; Lockyer, *Buckingham*, pp. 270, 277, 301-2, 318; McGowan, 'Royal Navy', pp. 286-7; Eliot, *Negotium Posterorum,* II, 7.

[51]Whitelocke diary, fols. 18a, 18b; Rich diary, fols. 59-60.

[52]Rich diary, fol. 59. Compare Whitelocke diary, fol. 18a.

argument that did not in the least impress the Commons. Another clash over this same issue occurred on 24 March, when Eliot reported from the subcommittee on 'the cause of causes' (that is, Buckingham). This was another subcommittee, incidentally, which included Mansell.[53] In Eliot's 24 March report, the blame for not adequately guarding the Narrow Seas was placed on Buckingham. According to Whitelocke's diary, the initial speakers on this occasion and the order in which they spoke were: Eliot, Coke, Eliot, Coke, Mansell. Coke again argued that the government had taken action but was hampered by a lack of funds. He also asked the Commons 'to consider how unjustly these things are laid upon the Lord Admiral'. Eliot wanted the House to censure Coke for these words, but Coke promptly apologized.[54] Failure to guard the Narrow Seas went on to become an article of impeachment against the duke of Buckingham.

Coke is known to have entered into debate on two other issues that culminated in impeachment charges against Buckingham. Regarding the extortion of £10,000 from the East India Company, he conceded that he had spoken with the Company at the king's behest, but he made his role appear nothing more than that of a messenger.[55] Regarding the loan of the ships to France, Coke made a much more forceful defence, but he was handicapped because he could not reveal the secret instructions to Pennington. Instead, he accused the French of breaking the contract, but this argument was undercut when the French ambassador gladly showed the contract to interested members of Parliament. Meanwhile, Eliot rejected the claim that secrets of state were involved, and Mansell said that if he had been advising Buckingham, he would 'rather have died in prison than have given way to the sending of these ships'. Perhaps with Coke in mind, Mansell added, 'those that had a hand in it should have an exemplary punishment'. Yet Coke made no effort to conceal his role. He had never liked this transaction. He freely confessed: 'I had a great hand in that which was done by the commissioners of the navy and some particular employment besides. I drew the instructions, wherein if there was not a command to the merchants not to suffer the ships to be employed against Rochelle, let me suffer for it.' Coke truthfully stated his understanding of the transaction when he said: 'I never heard from the king nor the Admiral that the ships should be employed against Rochelle, but for the procuring of a peace for it and to go for Genoa.'[56]

[53] Hulme, *Life of Eliot*, p. 115 n. 2.

[54] Whitelocke diary, fols. 17v, 18av, 18bv.

[55] *Ibid.*, fol. 141,

[56] *Ibid.*, fols. 58-9, 147v-148v; *CSPV,* 1625-1626, pp. 381, 391.

The major remaining issue that engaged Coke was the paramount one of supply. On 23 March, Coke was delegated, as in the previous Parliament, to explain the financial needs of the Crown. He began by representing the danger posed by Spain in as alarming terms as possible. 'The condition of our enemy', said Coke, 'is in extent of his power; they boast that the sun shines continually on his dominions.' The power of Spain, however, was not nearly so alarming as the costs of war outlined by Coke. Over £313,000 was still owed for the fleet that had been sent to Cadiz. Another £107,000 was required for the fleet presently being assembled. Continental allies had been promised considerable support: Denmark £30,000 per month, Count Mansfeld £20,000 per month, and the Low Countries £8,900 per month. Guarding the coasts, which was so great a concern to the Commons, cost £10,000 per month. Altogether to continue the war effort through the next eight months, Coke estimated the government required £1,067,221.[57] Of course the House was in no mood to provide anywhere near this amount. As the Venetian Ambassador described it: 'The Secretary Cuch, as a further inducement, represents the enemies' forces as rather increased, and the expenses required by the king, to a penny. The demands are considered exorbitant, and they consider that the king has received more money than all the expenses amount to.'[58] On 27 March the Commons agreed to a sum of three subsidies and three fifteenths. But this was a conditional grant to be actually provided only after the king had satisfactorily responded to their grievances, a condition which was never met. Coke experienced two small successes on 27 March when he helped block Eliot's proposal to refer the question of supply to a subcommittee and when he persuaded the House to accept a more accelerated schedule of payments than Eliot proposed.[59] But as Parliament was dissolved before any real bill for supply was considered, these were quite empty successes.

Parliament's refusal to finance the war was based upon a fundamental difference of opinion that vitally affected Coke. Parliamentary critics did not believe that they had committed themselves to war, at least not the kind of war being waged by Charles and Buckingham. More particularly, many members of Parliament did not see the military expenses outlined by Coke as legitimate consequences of the four points embodied in the subsidy act of 1624.

[57] Whitelocke diary, fols. 77-80. Coke's notes for this speech are SP 16/521/181. It is also represented in BL, Add. MS. 22,474, pp. 27-9.

[58] *CSPV*, 1625-1626, p. 380.

[59] Whitelocke diary, fols. 4v, 5v.

Buckingham and Charles believed just as firmly that they had been drawn into war by the advice of a Parliament that was now leaving them in the lurch. Sir Benjamin Rudyerd expressed the government's point of view on 23 March when he told the Commons: 'We are bound to make good our former protestations. . . . Other Parliaments led the king, invited him, besought him to these actions.' Rudyerd dismissed what he called 'sly objections that we are not bound by a former Parliament's engagement'.[60] The sense of betrayal was expressed more colourfully by Charles when he told both Houses of Parliament: 'You did with your counsel and perswasion perswade both my Father and me to break off the Treaties. . . . Now that you have all things according to your wishes, and that I am so far ingaged, that you think there is no retreat; now you begin to set the Dice, and make your own game.'[61] Buckingham similarly grumbled to Parliament that he wished 'you that were the persuaders of this war would take some more of the burden upon you.'[62] There was at least theoretically a middle ground where Charles and Buckingham could have met Parliament. If both parties could have agreed upon a more economical war, a more narrowly defensive war, a war that did not involve costly subsidies for mercenary forces on the Continent, an accommodation might have been reached. That is why the Council of War's deliberations were so crucial. It was a forum where ideally these competing views could have been expressed and reconciled. But the Council of War failed. The fact that the Council members were prevented from testifying in the Commons prevents us from knowing exactly why it failed. Its members were military men who, as in the case of Mansell, may have been just as likely to endorse as to oppose inordinately expensive and adventurous undertakings. On the other hand, the Council did baulk at subsidising Mansfeld's army, and their opinion was simply ignored.[63] Perhaps the Council was too uninformed, too obedient, or too fearful to moderate the grandiose plans of Charles and Buckingham. In this respect, Coke must bear a major responsibility. As we have seen, his expert opinion was given great weight, and, if less subservient and more sceptical, it could conceivably have made a difference. There is also another possibility, however remote, that Coke and the Council of War did in fact act as a moderating influence, in which case we can only marvel that things could have been even worse than they were. Assuming that the Council of War failed,

[60] *Ibid.*, fol. 80.

[61] Rushworth, *Historical Collections,* I, 225.

[62] Whitelocke diary, fol. 109v.

[63] Gardiner, *History of England,* pp. 223, 265.

Parliament was a final forum where communication and accommodation should have occurred. It can be argued that a compromise was pursued behind the scenes in 1626, but the evidence for this novel thesis is circumstantial at best.[64] A more traditional view is that Charles and Buckingham were disinclined either to understand or to accept compromise. They went into Parliament seeking support for their entrenched position and left exasperated and unchastened when they failed to obtain it. Whichever of these two explanations one chooses to accept, the result remains the same: after the Parliament of 1626 the government was still engaged in a war which it did not have the financial means to support.

Although Coke was obviously on the side of Charles and Buckingham in this monumental disagreement, there is another sense in which he was caught in the middle. While Charles and Buckingham persisted in their military enterprises and Parliament just as tenaciously resisted committing themselves and their purses to those enterprises, the navy was strained to its limits. Coke was chief administrator of the navy at a time when the financial resources available to it were not at all commensurate with the enormous demands being made upon it. This circumstance and other liabilities which will be examined in chapter twelve made Coke's work in the navy impossibly difficult. And this in turn adversely affected his work in Parliament. Coke's effectiveness as a spokesman for the Crown was undermined by his close association with the inglorious navy, particularly when Eliot and Mansell kept drawing attention to the fact. As David H. Willson observed: 'Coke's close connection with the navy exposed him to attack, and there were frequent demands that he explain events and policies, demands so hostile in tone as to indicate in advance the reception his explanations would receive.' We have seen ample evidence to confirm both this observation and Willson's further comment that: 'Attacks and interruptions of this kind came most frequently from Eliot and show that his noble rage could easily betray him into unfair and unreasonable conduct.'[65]

Illness apparently forced Coke to be absent from Parliament between 21 April and 9 June.[66] At the end of May, Conway wrote to Coke: 'I am thankful to God that your health is in so good a way of recovery, as to be able to seek and make benefit of good air and

[64] Russell, *Parliaments*, pp. 294-322.

[65] Willson, *Privy Councillors,* pp. 260-1.

[66] Coke's last appearance before this illness is in Whitelocke's diary on 21 April (fol. 148v), and he first reappears on 9 June (fol. 227v).

exercise.'[67] This illness forced Coke to be absent from Parliament when the impeachment movement against Buckingham reached its height. It can only be imagined what Coke would have said in the Commons regarding Eliot's controversial presentation of the charges to the Lords and his consequent imprisonment. There are some rough notes among Coke's papers in answer to a few of the charges against Buckingham, although there is no evidence that these were ever put to any use. Coke mainly emphasized how beneficial the duke's direction of the navy had been since the reform of 1618.[68] Buckingham used this same argument when making his own defence, also stressing that he had continually shared administration of the navy with the commissioners.[69]

Coke's last known speech in this Parliament occurred on 12 June, when he warned the House that the Spaniards were preparing an invasion force greater than the Armada of 1588. Mansell for once agreed, but he added threateningly: 'If anything do happen in Ireland or here, I can charge the duke of Buckingham and those that had the charge of the sea businesses to be the cause of it.'[70] These final words were no doubt aimed at Coke, and thus our survey of Coke's role in the Parliament of 1626 ends as it began – with a warning that he would be held responsible for the failures of the navy.

If Parliament would not finance the war, where would the money come from? Coke had been engaged in efforts to pawn the Crown jewels, and of course some money would continue to flow from prize goods, but far greater sums were required.[71] After the dissolution of Parliament, one of the first avenues explored by Charles was a loan from the City of London. As Coke reported, however, 'we found in the City the same spirit of interruption which misled us in Parliament'. Twenty aldermen were at last intimidated into lending £1,000 apiece, and this encouraged Coke to hope for 'more from the rest by treating with them not in troops but apart'. At this point, said Coke, the king was still resolved 'to take no violent or extraordinary way to levy monies'. The king also showed new resolve to put his own house in

[67] Coke MSS., packet 47, Conway to Coke, 30 May 1626. Apparently Coke did not return to full attendance on 9 June because he received a report of occurrences in Parliament dated 17 June. Coke MSS., packet 47, Sir Edwin Sandys to Coke.

[68] Coke MSS., packet 113. I do not know why these are dated Sept. 1626 in *Cowper MSS.,* I, 285.

[69] Rushworth, *Historical Collections* I, 379. Buckingham had touted the reform of 1618 when defending himself earlier in the session on 30 March. Whitelocke diary, fol. 112.

[70] Whitelocke diary, fol. 233.

[71] SP 16/12/12; 16/21/13; 16/22/11.

order. Coke was one of the men appointed in July of 1626 to a commission charged with augmenting the Crown's revenue and reducing its expenses through 'retrenchment and reformacion'. Coke greeted this new opportunity to reform the royal finances, declaring that: 'His Majesty closeth his own hands and stoppeth all the doors of largess and resolveth to husband his crown after the precedent of the best and most approved times and so redeem himself.'[72] Charles, however, was far from redemption. The commission produced a full report predicting a deficit of £157,456 for the current year.[73] They also made numerous proposals for reform, but as in so many of the projects Coke participated in, no real reform was forthcoming.[74]

The need for money grew even more urgent in 1627 as Buckingham prepared to lead a fleet to the aid of the French Protestants. Coke made a personal donation to the cause by providing two horses, saddles, and pistols, whereupon Buckingham was said to comment that 'those two sent so freely were better than four asked'.[75] Coke also formulated a curious plan for an association of 'good patriots, faithful Christians and loyal subjects to maintain the common cause'. Members of this association would have been entitled to wear a special badge or ribbon and to enjoy certain privileges such as precedence at public meetings. Official entrance fees would have ranged from £10 for a duke to a mere half crown for the 'poorer sort', though of course larger contributions would have been encouraged.[76] The whole idea may seem a bit ridiculous to the modern reader, but it was not altogether preposterous. Coke had in mind a similar plan which had actually been implemented under Elizabeth I. What he failed to appreciate was the huge gulf that separated 1588 from 1627. Public sentiment was not mobilized behind the war effort as it had been forty years before. Many Englishmen doubted that England was in any real jeopardy this time, or that Charles and Buckingham were comparable to Elizabeth I and Sir Francis Drake.

Of course the government found more practical expedients to raise revenue, most famous of which was the forced loan. Coke may not

[72] Coke MSS., packet 47, Coke to Greville, 2 July 1626; *APC*, 1626, p. 51.

[73] This sum is taken from Coke's sixteen-page report preserved in packet 113 of the Coke MSS. and entitled by Coke, 'The account of our proceedings in the commission for retrenchment of his Majesty's charges and increase of his revenue.' A fair but not exactly verbatim representation of the report is printed in *Cowper MSS.*, I, 291-5.

[74] Compare Aylmer, 'Administrative Reform', p. 248.

[75] Coke MSS., packet 29, Richard Graham to Coke, 15 May 1627.

[76] SP 16/88/78. The plan, written sometime in 1627, is entitled by Coke, 'A proposition for the settling of his Majesty's affairs.'

have favoured the forced loan. There is reason to think that he was one of the traditionalists on the Council who resisted so drastic a solution.[77] This would square with the fact that he made no effort to defend the forced loan when it came under fire in the Parliament of 1628. Indeed, as we shall soon see, he actually encouraged the Commons to petition against it. On the other hand, in March of 1627 when the collection of the loan was under way, Coke worried that laxity on the government's part might encourage subjects to be neglectful of their duty. 'I could therefore wish', he said, 'that some commandment were sent from his Majesty to require the board to press for these payments in a more earnest manner.'[78] Coke assured those who objected to the loan that it was not the king's intention 'to take away Parliaments'. Previous kings, said Coke, had raised money without the approval of Parliament. 'Some have done it', he went on to explain, 'by ways and upon occasions which are worthy to be forgotten, but the best kings have done it in cases of necessity, and by such ways as came nearest to consent.' In both these respects, Coke argued that Charles had proceeded 'with royal care and moderation'.[79]

When Buckingham's expedition bogged down on the Isle of Rhé, the Crown was driven into even more desperate financial straits. Coke entered into negotiations with the farmers of the petty customs, though he still hoped that income from prize goods would allow the king to escape 'such desperate bargains'.[80] The deal concluded between the Crown and the customs farmers did not prevent the situation from worsening. The most well-known description of the government's plight at this point came from one of Coke's friends, Sir Robert Pye. Writing to Buckingham in the autumn of 1627, Pye declared, 'his Majesty's revenue of all kinds is now exhausted, we are upon the third year's anticipation beforehand, land much sold of the principal, credit lost, and at the utmost shift with the Commonwealth'. Another line taken from Pye's letter is less well known: 'Secretary Coke . . . I assure your lordship [is] very desirous to do anything.'[81]

As 1627 came to a close, the Council temporarily entertained the possibility of an excise tax on ale, beer, and cider. It was decided that

[77] I am grateful to Richard Cust of the University of Birmingham for sharing this conclusion with me.

[78] SP 16/56/1. See also 16/49/8.

[79] SP 16/527/55.

[80] SP 16/75/9.

[81] SP 16/79/2.

a royal proclamation should be used to implement the new tax so that offenders could be prosecuted in the Star Chamber.[82] Coke wrote this proclamation, including the argument that the king was forced 'to have recourse to those ways of levies or contributions which in times of such necessity are warranted by divine and human laws and which our ancestors have used sometimes in less extremities and for their own interests, which we never intend to do'.[83] Necessity was the best justification Coke could muster for a new tax imposed by royal fiat. When Charles set aside this and other radical proposals in early 1628, reluctantly agreeing instead to the summoning of a new Parliament, Coke was left to face an outraged House of Commons that would not be much impressed by the argument from necessity.

[82] Gardiner, *History of England,* VI, pp. 222-8.

[83] SP 16/527/42.

11

THE PARLIAMENT OF 1628

Revisionists have argued that the so-called constitutional conflicts of the 1620s between the Crown and its opponents were often in fact personal rivalries within the court that happened to spill over into the arena of Parliament. There is certainly some truth in this view. It is consistent with Coke's experience in 1626, beleaguered as he was by two old adversaries, Mansell and Eliot. In the Parliament of 1628, Eliot's personal feud with Coke continued on an even more venomous level. On the other hand, it is difficult to deny that Eliot and other members of Parliament in 1628 were also genuinely and profoundly concerned about such constitutional issues as billeting of soldiers, martial law, the forced loan, imprisonment without showing cause, and the case of the five knights. There were only three Privy Councillors in the Commons in 1628: Sir Thomas Edmondes, Sir Humphrey May, and Coke. By far the most active of the three was Coke. It was his task not only to mollify the angry members of the Commons but also to extract further supply from them. Given the hostile climate of the Commons, this was a next-to-impossible task that repeatedly drew Coke into unpleasant debate. Historians have shown varying degrees of sympathy for Coke's predicament, but their verdict on his performance has been generally negative.[1] The following reexamination of Coke's work in the 1628 Parliament (including, where appropriate, the 1629 session) will show that even this time-honoured verdict is subject to revision.

The strategy Coke used in 1628 is evident in his first recorded speech of the session. The most striking feature of this speech on 22 March is the fact that Coke did not deny the illegality of the government's actions. 'Illegal courses have been taken', said Coke, 'it must be confessed.' Although Coke made no pretence that the government had acted legally, he did try to justify its actions on grounds of necessity. Financial desperation in the face of war forced the Crown into illegal measures. The conclusion of this simple syllogism was obvious: provide the king with adequate supply and he will no longer be forced by necessity to follow illegal paths.[2] Coke

[1] The old standard account of the 1628-9 Parliament is Gardiner, *History of England,* chapters 62-4, 67. A newer, revisionist account is Russell, *Parliaments,* chapters 6 and 7. Both frequently refer to Coke in passing. More specific evaluations of Coke by D.H. Willson, F.M.G. Evans, and Millicent Rex will be cited below.

[2] Robert C. Johnson *et al,* eds., *Commons Debates 1628* (4 vols., New Haven, 1977), II, 65.

persisted in this line of argument throughout the session. On 2 April he told the Commons: 'As for the disorders that have happened, the King joins with us in this sense; for things past, necessity forced us. Necessity followed our counsels. The King and we join to come into a regular way.' This strategy was intended to forestall arguments over the Crown's past conduct by admitting straight out that the conduct in question was illegal. 'Look not back', said Coke. For the future, adequate supply would insure that 'we shall never come to necessity again', and this in turn would insure a return to the legal, 'regular way'.[3] Coke gave his most elaborate exposition of this argument on 1 May:

> Has there been any defense made of that which has formerly been done, when means are denied? His Majesty being a young king and newly come to his crown, which he found engaged in a war, what could we expect in such necessities? His Majesty called this parliament to make up the breach. His Majesty assures us we shall never have the like cause to complain. He assures us the laws shall be established. What can we desire more?[4]

Coke has been criticized for confessing the illegality of the government's actions. These confessions have been called 'very damaging admissions' that 'were dangerous and rendered the defense of the crown more difficult'.[5] But would the Crown's defence have been more effective, and would its spokesmen seem more admirable to us, if they had argued on any grounds other than necessity? The Crown's strategy had several strengths. First, it was honest. Charles and his Councillors truly believed they had been driven to desperate measures by regrettable necessity. Secondly, this line of argument respected the distinction between legality and illegality. A despot would not have bothered with this inconvenient distinction. Thus Charles and his advisers portrayed themselves as men who at least wished to be law-abiding. Finally, the merit of this strategy becomes apparent the instant one considers the alternative. Admissions of guilt were unheroic and self-incriminating, but they might also be disarming. To choose the other course, pretending to be guiltless and tenaciously defending actions which were indefensible on any ground other than necessity, would only have made the government appear more villainous and pugnacious. The old adage says that it takes two to make a fight, and the Crown's strategy was calculated to deny its

[3] Johnson, *1628 Debates,* II, 246, 261.

[4] *Ibid.,* III, 189.

[5] Willson, *Privy Councillors,* p. 263.

critics an opponent. In other words, Coke's 'damaging admissions' were preferable to what could only have been more damaging, inflammatory denials.

Nevertheless, there were numerous disadvantages in the Crown's defence. To begin with, the Commons, far from forgiving past offences, were obsessed with them, and Coke, having already admitted the illegalities, had no leg left to stand on. This was most evident on 2 May when Thomas Wentworth proposed to inform Charles that the Commons were preparing a bill to insure the observance of the law in the future because 'after a public violation has been made by his ministers, less will not satisfy his subjects than a bill'. Coke accepted the proposal in general, but he objected to these particular words about a public violation by the king's ministers. He thought these words were too harsh and would irritate the king. Wentworth quickly pointed out that he alleged no violation by the king, 'but this I say, and will say it again, there has been violation in his ministers'. Sir Francis Seymour, directing his remarks squarely at Coke, trenchantly observed that there was nothing in Wentworth's proposal 'but what has formerly been confessed by some honorable persons near the chair'.[6] Another problem with the argument from necessity was that it raised the question of whether or not a necessity had really existed and, if so, why it had existed. Again it was Sir Francis Seymour who went to the heart of the matter and turned Coke's words around on him: 'Sir John Coke said the greatest grievance was want of supply. I think the greatest grievance is the necessity.' Seymour recited the various means used by the Crown to raise money, and he marvelled that despite these sums the king had been reduced to a state of necessity. Seymour charged that necessity had resulted from the profligacy of the Crown's servants. He stopped short of arguing on a higher level that Charles and Buckingham had brought necessity upon themselves by stubbornly perpetuating an unpopular war and by waging it in an exorbitant fashion, but these thoughts could not have been far from his mind. Furthermore, the necessity of the past was only part of the problem. What about the necessities that would arise in the future? As Seymour pointed out, 'if men of judgment and ability be not employed, we shall but throw our money into a bottomless pit'.[7] Coke only heightened fear of future necessities when he insisted that the nation must continue the war in an offensive manner. Another English fleet failed to relieve La Rochelle even while Parliament deliberated, and Coke, no doubt

[6]Johnson, *1628 Debates,* III, 212, 226.

[7]*Ibid.,* II, 261, 265.

echoing the opinions of Charles and Buckingham, succeeded only in alarming the Commons by declaring that: 'The reason of the demand of the army is to make an offensive war, for a defensive war is a miserable and wasting charge for no purpose.' Sir Edward Coke retorted that, to the contrary, a defensive war was more appropriate for an island-nation. Moreover, Coke's assertion simply called attention to the fact that it was precisely the government's own offensive exploits that had turned out to be miserable and wasting charges to no good purpose. Sir John Eliot was quick to seize on this point. In a manner similar to Seymour, Eliot recited the disastrous naval efforts of the previous few years and then asked the Commons to consider what would be the consequence 'if on the like occasion or with the like instruments we shall again adventure another expedition'.[8] Seymour and Eliot both implied that the conditions which caused past necessity, if unremedied, would lead to future necessity. And following Coke's own logic, though turning it on its head, future necessity could be expected to be accompanied by future illegalities. Coke had a valid point when he argued that actions which the Commons themselves desired — for example, better guarding the Narrow Seas and an end to billeting — could only be achieved when the Crown was provided with sufficient funds to execute these wishes. As Coke explained: 'You must habilitate [enable] the state to do what you require.'[9] But Seymour and Eliot had a better point when they persuasively argued from past experience that, unless precautions were taken, all that could be expected in the future was more of the same.

On a more philosophical level, the 1628 Parliament was exploring the outer limits where the king's prerogative and his subjects' rights came into conflict. Coke understood what was at issue here, but, for reasons both philosophical and pragmatic, he shrank back from exploring this frontier while men like Sir Edward Coke, Seymour, and Eliot ventured on. On 22 April, Coke acknowledged both sides of the argument. On the one hand, he said: 'There is no man but desires to live under the law, and we all hold the common law our inheritance that does preserve us.' On the other hand, kings are 'God's captains and leaders of His people. The name of kings is sacred, and the foundation of the commonwealth depends on them.' Much as Coke revered the law, he worried that anarchy might result if men pushed its

[8] *Ibid.*, II, 247-50, 257, 262, 266, 269-71.

[9] *Ibid.*, II, 65, 121, 487, 489; III, 269, 292. Inadequate guarding of the Narrow Seas had been a perennial complaint of the Commons. Perhaps that is why it headed the list of fourteen things Charles proposed to do with supply when it was voted. But the Commons showed little interest in the list.

claims too far against the authority of the Crown, the source from which all else sprang and upon which all else depended. This line of argument was most tenable on 22 April because the specific grievance being debated was martial law. Coke observed that martial law partook of monarchy more than any other form of law. Military discipline had to be autocratic. Members of Parliament and their constituents would only suffer more grievously if they checked martial law and thereby loosed mutiny and disorder among the soldiers and seamen.[10] Another 350 years of experience since Coke's day has shown that the tension between civil law and the authoritarian, illiberal modes of martial law cannot be entirely eradicated.

Of course Coke's position on martial law was far from unassailable, and his conservative defence of the royal prerogative was even shakier when debate turned to other specific grievances. On the topic of the forced loan, for example, Coke was so sympathetic to the rights of the subject that he actually encouraged the Commons to petition for redress. Interestingly, only moments after Coke proposed this 'petition', Sir Edward Coke, who was looking for some way out of the impasse that had been reached, proposed a more inclusive petition that became the Petition of Right. Perhaps this is only a curious coincidence, but it would be a wonderful stroke of irony if Sir John inadvertently planted the seed for the Petition of Right in Sir Edward's head.[11] On another topic, imprisonment without showing cause, Coke inclined toward the king's prerogative. 'We are come to the liberty of the subject, and the prerogative of the King', said Coke. 'I hope we shall not add anything to ourselves to depress him.' Coke charged that the Commons was upsetting the ancient, delicate balance between the royal prerogative and the subject's rights. He urged them not 'to bring ourselves into a better condition and greater liberty than our fathers had, and the crown into a worse than ever'. What Coke failed to appreciate was the fact that Charles had already upset the delicate balance. Coke was arguing for a return to the status quo prior to the outrages of 1626-7. He told the Commons that Charles desired them to stay 'within the bounds and laws of our forefathers without straining them or enlarging them by new explanations, interpretations, expositions, or additions in any sort'. But it was Charles who had already exceeded those bounds. Now, as a consequence of his own actions, he was in no position to ask the Commons to respect a status quo which from their point of view no longer seemed to exist. The Commons were as

[10]*Ibid.,* III, 23-4, 27-8. On 24 March, Coke had said, 'Our liberties are our birthrights'. *Ibid.,* II, 88.

[11]*Ibid.,* III, 271-2, 277, 282-3.

anxious as Coke and Charles to restore equilibrium, but it would have to be restored on a new, firmer basis. Charles hoped to get by with an insubstantial promise not to do in the future what he had done in the past. He instructed Coke to ask the Commons whether they would 'rest on his royal word or no'. The Commons answered this question at first with a stunned 'silence a good space' and in due course with the Petition of Right.[12]

There is a more utilitarian and pedestrian explanation for the views Coke expressed in Parliament: he was doing his job. This means something more than that Coke simply did what Charles and Buckingham told him to do. Coke repeatedly pleaded with the Commons for support and supply not only because these were his instructions but also because these were his convictions. Day after day, month after month, year after year since 1625, Coke had been absorbed in efforts to manage the war, feed and clothe troops, rig and arm ships. Nothing handicapped him more in these efforts than the shortage of money. What a remarkable change in mental environment it must have been for Coke to go from these labours into the House of Commons, where men debated for weeks on end about the finest points of law while provisions rotted, soldiers mutinied, and ships sprang leaks. Coke's pleas for supply are too numerous to cite. So also are his expressions of impatience and amazement over the Commons' ability to spin out time discussing abstractions to the exclusion of concrete action. On 22 March, Coke compared the state to a house on fire: 'We are all inhabitants in one house. . . Somewhat is amiss, but if all the house be on fire, will you then think of amending what is amiss? Will you not rather quench the fire?' Coke did not get the answer that he expected to this question. To many of his fellow members, it was a false analogy. The state was imperilled more by the cracks in its foundation than by the fire that Coke alleged to exist. As Sir Robert Phelips put it: 'I more fear the violation of public rights at home than a foreign enemy.' Both points of view were sincere, but what seemed to Coke to be a matter of the utmost urgency, seemed to the Commons to be an exaggerated or false alarm. On 25 March, Coke declared: 'If we think we can spend many days in debates, we are deceived.' But if Coke thought he could curtail such debate and move the Commons to action, then he was the one who was deceived. Coke reminded the Commons of the familiar expression Charles had used in addressing them — 'time is precious'. Coke said he still had the sound of these words ringing in his ears, but the Commons did not. At the beginning of April, Coke lamented: 'We all know February and March are the

[12] *Ibid.*, III, 189, 213.

times for provision, and they are already spent. . . Let us not suffer ourselves to be diverted, but do our work.'[13] The Commons, however, were not absorbed in the same 'work' that Coke was. Try as he might, he could not convince them that the heavy responsibility he had been desperately struggling to discharge for years was also their responsibility.

Too few members of Parliament evinced that 'team spirit' beloved of modern corporate managers. Viewed this way, Coke and his parliamentary opponents were not so much high-minded advocates of different philosophical positions as biased captives of their peculiar vantage points. Take the case of Sir Thomas Wentworth, for example. It has recently been emphasized that Wentworth should not be portrayed as a man who changed sides, who switched his allegiance from one entity, the country, to another separate and contrary entity, the court.[14] There is real merit in this caution: Wentworth's behaviour in the Parliament of 1628 can be interpreted as consistent with his behaviour afterwards when he was appointed Lord President of the Council of the North. Admitting this continuity, however, should not require us to deny all discontinuity. Even if high office was what Wentworth wished for all along, this does not mean that his perspective was entirely unaffected when he obtained his wish. The fact that Charles bestowed a peerage and high office on Wentworth after the 1628 session almost suggests that Charles possessed some political *savoir faire* after all. Even if he did not exactly coopt a critic or induce Wentworth to defect from one side to another, neither did he fail altogether to alter Wentworth's view of things.

Possession of high office in a government is likely to affect one's view of that government. Coke admitted to the Commons that if they approved a bill limiting the king's power of imprisonment, then 'he as a councillor would not persuade him to accept or do it'. One must wonder how many members of the Commons, if they had been seated 'as a councillor' at the Privy Council, would have begun to see things Coke's way. Coke went even further in admitting: 'Make what law you will. If I discharge the place I bear, I must commit men and must not discover the cause to any jailer or judge.' In fairness, it should be pointed out that Coke went on to explain that if he imprisoned a person without a truly just cause, then he expected to be punished by

[13]Ibid., II, 61, 65, 97, 170, 228. This point was fully appreciated by Millicent Rex, who called Coke 'the busiest and most badgered' of the king's administrators. *University Representation,* p. 116.

[14]Conrad Russell, 'Parliamentary History in Perspective, 1604-1629', *History,* 61 (1976), pp. 3-4.

the king. How Coke thought this assumption fitted the case of the five knights is a mystery, but it does remind us that Coke was as interested in justice as his fellow members in the Commons, and he still clung to the idealistic belief that the king was a guarantor of justice. What is most interesting, however, is the punishment Coke expected from the king: 'I shall have a greater punishment than the law can inflict, the loss of the King's favor and my place.'[15]

Up to this point, we have chiefly explored Coke's state of mind. Let us now turn to a more finite evaluation of how he actually performed on the floor of the House of Commons. First one must understand what has been called the 'very unfriendly atmosphere in which Coke struggled'.[16] Coke was a messenger travelling between Charles and the Commons, and the messages he delivered were rarely pleasing to either recipient. Coke's messages from Charles to the Commons had two principal objectives: one was to dissuade them from encroaching on the royal prerogative, the other was to cajole and intimidate them into granting supply. Because the Commons deluded themselves into thinking that the king had no cause to be dissatisfied with their conduct, they were baffled when the king sent messages expressing dissatisfaction. Under these circumstances, it is not surprising that the messenger was sometimes blamed for the message. Besides, it was safer and more convenient for the Commons to direct their displeasure at Coke than at the king himself. Twice the Commons simply sat in silence when Coke delivered a royal message, and it was Coke's unenviable chore to break this silence and elicit a favourable response from his unhappy listeners.[17] Neutral silence, however, was preferable to the open hostility he sometimes encountered. On 12 April, for example, Coke warned the Commons that their 'tedious or needless delays' could lead to 'an unpleasing end'. Coke begged the House 'not to undervalue or overstrain this message'. What he could not tell them was that these threatening, inflammatory words had been expressly added to his speech by King Charles. The Commons objected to Coke's speech and required him to repeat the message. Not trusting Coke to deliver their answer, the Commons appointed a select committee to draft an answer which was then approved by the whole House to 'be *verbatim* presented to the King by the Speaker only'.[18] Several weeks later, Sir Walter Erle charged

[15] Johnson, *1628 Debates,* III, 189, 198, 203.

[16] Evans, *The Principal Secretary,* p. 246.

[17] Johnson, *1628 Debates,* III, 189, 268 n. 2.

[18] *Ibid.,* II, 430-3; SP 16/100/70.

that the king was still 'misinformed' despite the fact that they had asked him 'to receive no information but from ourselves'.[19]

Nevertheless, it is surprising how often the charge of misrepresentation was fomented by one man, Coke's old nemesis, Sir John Eliot. On 1 May, Eliot called Coke's remarks 'a scandal' and 'an unfit speech'. Eliot also insinuated that Coke should have delivered the king's message sooner. Coke declined to argue about the substance of his remarks, but as for the timing of the message, Coke explained, 'he that gave me the command commanded me the time when to speak'.[20] On 2 May, Charles again made Coke the bearer of a distasteful message. Coke warned the Commons not to intrude on the royal prerogative, and he announced that 'this session of parliament must endure no longer than Tuesday come sevennight at the furthest'. As if to check the authenticity of this message, the House required Coke to present it the following afternoon in writing, a tactic they had already used at least once earlier in the session. Accordingly, Coke wrote out the message and 'showed it to the King, who perused and allowed it'. The next day, when Coke presented the written message and it was read to the House, Eliot responded predictably. 'This makes me fear his Majesty is misinformed in what we go about', said Eliot. 'And look how many messages we have, so many interruptions, and those misreports and misinterpretations to his Majesty produce those messages.'[21]

The best example of Coke's vulnerable position and Eliot's attempted exploitation of it comes from the 1629 session. Coke entered the session with high hopes, believing that Charles had regained public confidence to the point of eliminating 'all distempers which have transported men's minds', but of course these hopes were not fulfilled.[22] It was originally planned that Sir Humphrey May would present the bill for tonnage and poundage in the 1629 session, but May was confined to bed by illness and passed the chore on to Coke. When Coke presented the bill on 26 January, the House protested that he had acted improperly by introducing the bill in the king's name and by making it appear as if the king was commanding the Commons to pass the bill. On 3 February Coke again urged consideration of the bill and answered the unwarranted complaints of the previous week, declaring: 'I have used all diligence to do all the

[19]*Ibid.,* III, 209.

[20]*Ibid.,* III, 190, 199.

[21]*Ibid.,* II, 296-7, 323-4; III, 209, 213, 233-5.

[22]SP 92/14/fols. 145-6.

commands of my Master and of this House, and yet I find some exceptions have been taken at some words by me used when I delivered the Bill of Tonnage and Poundage.' Coke explained the words he had used, apologized, and read a conciliatory statement from Charles on the subject. Coke observed that he travelled 'a slipery [sic] way betweene his Majestie and his people'. Eliot would not let the issue die, however. He claimed that there was a significant difference between Coke's language and the king's language; he characterized this as a wrong done to both the king and the Commons; and he concluded by charging that Coke was 'not worthy to sit in this House'. Eliot wanted to expel Coke from the Commons, but the suggestion fell flat. Sir Humphrey May, now recovered from his illness, gave the most persuasive argument against Eliot: 'If you be too quick to except against the Ministers of his Majesty that serve his Majesty and this House, it will discourage and stop our mouths, whose service you daily command.'[23]

Eliot's attempt to expel Coke has been described as 'a complex piece of wilful misunderstanding'.[24] As this description indicates, historians have finally revised the traditional, idolatrous view of Eliot.[25] It is now acknowledged that Eliot had human foibles; and one of his foibles was a tendency to ignore complex administrative difficulties and simply blame the problems of his day on persons he disliked.[26] With the possible exception of Buckingham, the person Eliot disliked most of all was Coke. Eliot's running feud with Coke made it practically impossible for Coke to obtain the sympathy and goodwill he needed in Parliament. In the 1628 session, Coke told the Commons: 'My desire is not to stir but to quiet, not to provoke but to appease.' A few weeks later, he said: 'I now speak with more fear and care than ever I spake. I hear that jealousies possess some of us. I fear jealousies may be elsewhere. Let us all here speak freely and take no exceptions at that that escapes out of men's mouths.'[27] But Eliot repeatedly assailed Coke and undermined the chances for mutual understanding. Of course it would be a mistake to reverse the traditional view completely. Eliot should not be vilified and Coke can

[23]Wallace Notestein and Frances Relf, eds., *Commons Debates for 1629* (Minneapolis, 1921), pp. 12, 31-3, 108, 121, 246. See also pp. 112-13. Coke MSS., packet 31, May to Coke, Jan. 1629.

[24]Russell, *Parliaments,* p. 413 n.2.

[25]For the old idolatry see Gardiner, *History of England,* VI, 60, 272.

[26]J.N. Ball has contributed most to the reevaluation of Eliot. For this point, see Ball's 'Sir John Eliot and Parliament, 1624-1629' in Sharpe, *Faction and Parliament,* pp. 204-5.

[27]Johnson, *1628 Debates,* II, 65, 413.

hardly be idolized. But it certainly did not make Coke's job any easier and may not have been wholly in the nation's interest that he laboured in Parliament with Eliot like an albatross round his neck.

Against this general background, several particular incidents can be examined which have a bearing on Coke's performance. Twice Coke made an outright mistake. On 10 April he announced that Charles did not wish the Commons to take an Easter recess. He knew this the preceding day and should have told the Commons then, but he failed to do so. Both Coke and Sir Humphrey May accepted responsibility for this oversight, apologized, and apparently succeeded in deflating Eliot's insinuation that this was a 'plot'.[28] In the 1629 session, Coke tried to blunt the attack on the customs farmers by claiming that their commission empowered them to seize goods, but their commission was read and found to contain no such clause.[29] Apart from these two errors, which are hardly of an egregious magnitude, aspects of Coke's performance become more a matter of judgement than of fact. For example, it does appear that Coke was praised near the beginning of the 1628 session for openly questioning a speech by Sir Robert Phelips rather than carrying tales to court. It is true that Phelips thanked Coke for calling 'upon me openly in this House, not privately traducing me', but it is also true that Phelips denied the charge, and another courtier agreed that Coke had mistaken Phelips 's meaning. From what remains of Phelips's speech, it seems that Coke may have misconstrued his words, but the speech was also decidedly inflammatory, and Coke's challenge may have put the Commons on guard to use more temperate language. Four days later, Phelips compared the collection of the forced loan to the Spanish Inquisition, and Coke, 'to forbear phrases of suspicion and asperity', again admonished Phelips 'to be more careful of his words'. In these exchanges with Phelips, it is not clear whether Coke deserves praise or blame. He does, however, appear to have contributed to moderating the level of rhetoric in the Commons. After the second exchange between Coke and Phelips, another member voiced his 'joy to hear that sweet moderation, and that we avoid all shows of exception'. Furthermore, on this same day, 26 March, Coke asked the Commons to disregard the objectionable remarks of another speaker. Coke's pacific intervention caused Sir Thomas Wentworth to draw the following conclusion: 'We are all beholding to Mr. Secretary Coke, and I beseech you observe the temper of this House, never such in the world. I have sat in the House when, upon such a motion, they

[28] *Ibid.,* II, 398-400, 403.

[29] Notestein, *1629 Debates,* p. 91.

have all been in an uproar.'[30] Coke also tried to avert misunderstanding by carefully drafting his speeches.[31] Another specific incident for which Coke has been criticized was his attempt, on 24 March, to frighten the Commons into action by announcing the discovery of a Jesuit college at Clerkenwell. Although Coke was probably alarmed by the Jesuits, this announcement could hardly have been more completely ignored by the House. It appears to have been a crude tactic that failed entirely, but two qualifications need to be made. First, although this ploy was consonant with Coke's own prejudices, we cannot rule out the possibility that he was merely following instructions. Secondly, although the topic failed to excite interest in the 1628 session, it was a matter of passionate interest in the 1629 session. By then, however, the government had allowed the ten alleged priests to escape without punishment, and so the topic backfired against the Crown, and Coke was hard-pressed to defend the Crown's leniency.[32]

Finally, Coke has been criticized for tactlessly referring to Buckingham in his speeches. According to D.H. Willson, Coke's 'rapturous praise of Buckingham at the most inopportune moments grated on the nerves of members'. There were two prominent occasions when Coke did refer to Buckingham. On 3 April, Coke assured the Commons that, despite a false rumour to the contrary, Buckingham had spoken no 'malicious words' about them in a recent meeting of the Privy Council. Indeed, said Coke, Buckingham had been 'the first mover and persuader of this assembly of parliament to the King'. There is no evidence that this speech 'grated on the nerves of members'. Eliot denied that there had been such a rumour circulating in the House, but he significantly refrained from protesting at Coke's reference to Buckingham, and he joined other members in graciously accepting Coke's speech. If the alleged rumour really existed, Coke successfully squashed it. And even if Coke's remarks had caused an uproar, he could not be blamed for delivering a message that was expressly commanded by Charles.[33] Coke's second major reference to Buckingham occurred on 7 April, when he delivered the

[30]Willson, *Privy Councillors,* pp. 206 n. 4, 264, 300 n. 18; Johnson, *1628 Debates,* II, 61-6, 68-70, 72-5, 123, 125, 130, 131, 134, 142.

[31]Willson, *Privy Councillors,* p. 197. SP 16/527/55, 59. A draft of his 3 April speech is in Coke MSS., packet 69.

[32]Gardiner, *History of England,* VI, 239; VII, 57; Johnson, *1628 Debates,* II, 82; Notestein, *1629 Debates,* 70-1, 75-8, 145-6, 148, 205, 208-10, 249-50; John Gough Nichols, 'The Discovery of the Jesuits' College at Clerkenwell in March 1627-8', *Camden Miscellany,* vol. II, no. 4 (London, 1852), pp. 5-15.

[33]Willson, *Privy Councillor,* p. 96; Johnson, *1628 Debates,* II, 275-8, 282-3.

king's thanks for the Commons' intention to vote five subsidies. Coke did not stop with the king's thanks. Instead, he proceeded to relay Buckingham's thanks, too, by describing a magnanimous speech of gratitude made by Buckingham at the Privy Council. This time Eliot promptly protested against the reference to Buckingham, although it is not clear how solitary his protest was. One correspondent of the period reported that many members of the House said: 'Well spoken, Sir John Eliot.' But this correspondent was writing at least third-hand, and the source he was relying on attributed these events to the wrong day. Furthermore, there is no evidence at all in the published parliamentary diaries that anyone joined in Eliot's complaints. The really adverse reaction to Coke's remarks occurred in the days immediately following, when what Coke had reported to Parliament was circulated in London in printed form. On 11 April the Commons appointed a committee to investigate this pamphlet. Coke's unnecessary report of Buckingham's speech to the Council, followed by the publication of the duke's offensive speech, was indeed an act of monumental stupidity. But it was Buckingham's stupidity, not Coke's. As Willson himself observed, it was Buckingham who made this decision, and Coke was only 'carrying out instructions'.[34] The most that can be said against Coke is that he was perhaps naive and insensitive enough to believe that this clumsy strategy would work.

Where are we left, then, regarding an overall evaluation of Coke's performance in Parliament? The standard, harshest evaluation of Coke comes from Willson and runs as follows:

> He made no allowance for the temper of the house and could not shift his ground or alter his tactics on the spur of the moment, as a skillful debater must do. He prepared his speeches with such care that they lacked spontaneity. He made damaging admissions which on several occasions increased the difficulties of the government. He was, in short, a clumsy parliamentarian.

Willson was appreciative of the adverse circumstances Coke faced, but he still saw Coke as 'constantly blundering' and judged him to be a 'liability' to the Crown in Parliament.[35] On what facts did Willson base this judgement? Concerning damaging admissions, it is true that Coke on several occasions confessed that illegal courses had been taken, but, as we saw, this was not entirely contemptible and may even

[34] *Ibid*., II, 324-31, 411-12, 416, 423; Willson, *Privy Councillors,* p. 175; Thomas Birch, *The Court and Times of Charles I* (2 vols., London, 1849), I, 338-40. SP 16/100/44, 16/101/3.

[35] *Privy Councillors*, pp. 96-7, 211-12, 294-5, 306. See also Evans, *The Principal Secretary,* p. 246.

have been the wisest path to follow in the Commons. On the other hand, it was impolitic for Coke to admit that he would continue to imprison without always showing cause. This was certainly a foolish admission, though not necessarily a damaging one. As for blunders, Coke made some minor mistakes, but the true blunders were made by Charles and Buckingham who unfortunately set the boundaries within which Coke had to operate. What we are left with in Willson's criticism of Coke is more a matter of style than of substance. Coke is especially blamed for lacking agility and spontaneity. This view of Coke can be traced back to the hostile testimony of Sir John Eliot. Willson, like many other historians, quoted Eliot and uncritically echoed his appraisal of Coke. But Eliot was Coke's enemy, and he was a prisoner in the Tower trying to vindicate his own actions in retrospect when he wrote his caustic comments about Coke in the *Negotium Posterorum.* Both the author and the circumstances should caution against taking the words at face value. We have already examined Eliot's animadversions, including the particularly relevant claim that Coke's 'expressions were more proper for a schoole, then for a State & councell'.[36] In the Parliament of 1628, Eliot similarly implied that a speech by Coke on 28 April was long-winded, inaccurate, and imprudent, which he attributed to 'the weakness of the speaker'.[37] Judging from surviving accounts, Coke's speech on 28 April was inordinately long, but his others were not, especially when one considers how much of the responsibility he bore for representing the king's position. Coke did tend to develop his line of argument tediously and to use florid language, but this criticism could be made of many other speakers in the Commons. Sometimes, apparently when Coke was following instructions, his speeches to the Commons were threatening. Just as often, however, his speeches displayed a marked willingness to acknowledge the other side of the argument, a prudent approach that made it harder to vilify Coke and to polarize opinion against the Crown. It is true that Coke's style was very different from Eliot's. This bothered Eliot, and it has bothered historians like Willson ever since. Coke was cautions and deliberate. His speeches never quite achieved the inspirational effect he was aiming for. By contrast, Eliot was melodramatic and impetuous, and his speeches were sometimes eloquent. He had all the potential for charismatic leadership that Coke lacked. In Willson's criticism of Coke there is an implied assumption that he would have been a better parliamentarian if he had been more like Eliot. The truth may be, however, that both men were well suited for the different roles they

[36]*Negotium Posterorum,* I, 114.

[37]Johnson, *1628 Debates,* III, 129, 134, 141.

played. Eliot, especially when complemented by cooler heads like Sir Edward Coke and Sir Thomas Wentworth, could afford to wax eloquent about the sufferings of the nation. Coke, by contrast, was defending a very weak position. No attributes were more important to his success than caution and moderation. He was dealing with an extremely volatile situation, and the most he could realistically hope for was not to control or even to manage the Commons but simply to minimize the damage. At the same time, especially in the light of his notorious subservience toward Buckingham, Coke had to maintain as much personal confidence and goodwill in the Commons as he could. And he had to do this in the face of Eliot's constant personal attacks.

Fortunately, the rest of the Commons did not find Coke as easy to hate as Eliot did. If Coke was not a positive asset to the Crown in Parliament, neither was he a liability. At the worst, he was innocuous. Perhaps his unexceptionable religious views, his sincerity, his ingenuousness, even his simplicity, helped him in the Commons. A stronger, more formidable man in Coke's place, matching wits with people like Sir Edward Coke, Wentworth, and Eliot, when the justice of the argument was overwhelmingly on their side, might easily have drawn more fire on both himself and the Crown. As it was, Coke continued on his 'slippery way' between the Crown and the Commons, and he did not do all that badly. This is not to say that a more talented man could not have done better, but others could also have done far worse. One need only ponder for a moment what might have been the outcome if, instead of Coke, the Crown's chief spokesman had been another glory-seeker as 'unbalanced' (the word is J.P. Kenyon's) as Eliot.[38]

[38] *Stuart England* (Harmondsworth, 1978), p. 97.

12

SHAMEFUL WAR FLEETS

Coke's last speech in the Parliament of 1628 occurred on 17 May.[1] At about this time Charles learned that a fleet he had sent under the earl of Denbigh to relieve La Rochelle was instead returning to England after abandoning its mission. In view of the awesome French blockade of La Rochelle, Denbigh had not even tried to relieve the city. Following the advice of Sir Richard Weston, Charles decided to send Coke to Portsmouth to meet Denbigh's fleet, stop it from disbanding, refit it, and send it back to La Rochelle.[2] Coke arrived in Portsmouth on 19 May, thinking his work could be accomplished in a week, but instead it dragged on for more than three months.[3]

Charles was very earnest about the fleet returning to La Rochelle, and there is no solid reason to doubt that this is why he sent Coke to Portsmouth. There is a remote possibility that he was also dissatisfied with Coke's work in Parliament and found this a convenient way of removing him from the Commons. The fact is, however, that things actually went worse rather than better in Coke's absence. Instead of stopping with the Petition of Right, the Commons, under Eliot's renewed leadership, attacked the Crown's religious policy, the collection of tonnage and poundage, and the duke of Buckingham. Although we have no evidence on Charles's feelings, Buckingham's opinion of Coke was said to have risen during this period. A friend of Coke's told him that Buckingham 'both thought and now found (perhaps the more in your absence and upon the trial of others) that you were both honest and wise'.[4]

The fact remains that Coke was forced to trade the headaches of Parliament for the headaches of the navy, and this is fortunate for us because no other episode from the entire period better illustrates why the navy performed so badly. Naturally the navy's inadequacy has always been a topic of considerable interest to historians, but recent work has made it even more so. On one front, new studies of Buckingham have made him seem less personally culpable for the

[1] Johnson, *1628 Debates,* III, 449-50.

[2] Gardiner, *History of England,* VI, 292-3; SP 16/104/21, 22; 16/528/75; Coke MSS., packet 30, Weston to Coke, 17 May 1628; packet 31, Weston to Coke, 5 September 1628.

[3] SP 16/104/60, 62.

[4] Coke MSS., packet 48, Thomas Alured to Coke, 21 June 1628.

navy's failures. On another front, the Crown's inability to wage war has received increasing blame for the 'functional breakdown' of English administration and the souring of relations between king and Parliament.[5] Consequently, more importance has been attached to the failures of the English navy at precisely the time they can no longer be simplistically blamed on Buckingham. We therefore need to know more about what was wrong with the navy, and no one can shed more light on this subject than Coke. As chief commissioner, he was the one man in England most responsible for the actual preparation of the war fleets. He was on the scene where the 'functional breakdown' of naval administration occurred, and he left a copious record of what he saw, particularly at Portsmouth in the summer of 1628.

Of course much about the navy's inadequacies had already come to light through the two previous major fleets: the Cadiz fleet in 1625 and the Isle of Rhé fleet in 1627. A brief, backward glance at these — with special emphasis on Coke's viewpoint — will help us to understand his struggles at Portsmouth in 1628. The Cadiz fleet suffered from innumerable handicaps. Chief among these, of course, was lack of money. Coke's pleas in Parliament for additional supply had gone unheeded. Now, 'As Buckingham and Sir John Coke had predicted, the failure to gain additional supply led to military defeat and disgrace.'[6] By itself, however, more money could not have made the Cadiz expedition a success. Its personnel, from the illustrious, noble commanders at the top to the wretched, unwilling sailors pressed into service at the bottom, were incompetent. Troops were debilitated by disease and desertion. The fleet set sail into a destructive storm. The commanders sailed without having decided on their objective, and planning remained confused throughout the mission. The king's ships, as was usual, had to be augmented by merchant ships whose captains were reluctant to expose them to danger. Rampant corruption combined with the lack of funds to insure that supplies were unreliable and insufficient.[7] Coke implored the victualler to go in person to the fleet and to send a 'sufficient deputy along with the fleet, for without a victualler the army cannot march'. As we saw, however, it was not the victualler but Coke who was dispatched to Plymouth to oversee the preparations. Coke drafted the letter of appointment and the formal instructions for Sir Edward Cecil, Lord General of the fleet, whom he was surprisingly bold in

[5] McGowan, 'Royal Navy', *passim;* Lockyer, *Buckingham,* especially pp. 366-7; Russell, *Parliaments,* pp. 64, 70-84, 323-7, 423, 431.

[6] Russell, *Parliaments,* pp. 238, 262.

[7] Gardiner, *History of England,* VI, 10-23; Oppenheim, *Royal Navy,* pp. 219-25.

berating for his bumbling leadership. Coke exhorted the reluctant captains to set sail, ordering the last fourteen ships 'upon pain of death to weigh anchor'.[8] Coke was sensitive to the complaints about billeting, particularly of sick soldiers. He advised that soldiers left behind should be discharged 'out of commiseration of the poor distressed creatures which ought not be neglected' and so as not to 'pester this country which hath already been overcharged'. Coke advised local officials to gather financial accounts of their costs for pressing and billeting, and he assured them that he would facilitate their reimbursement. In fact, however, as we now know, the inability to reimburse local officials strained the relationship between the Crown and the counties.[9]

When the fleet straggled home, Coke participated in the post mortem.[10] Lord General Cecil blamed everybody but himself. He told Coke that 'more ignorant captains and officers can hardly be found', and he described the sailors as 'so stupefied that punish them or beat them they will scarce stir'. Perhaps to avert criticism, Cecil also flattered Coke by referring to the accomplishments, of the naval commission 'wherein everyone knows you to be the soul of the commission and the sole doer'.[11]

Cecil had begun to make excuses for his failure while the fleet was still at sea, and some of his explanations were admittedly valid, but it is difficult to feel sympathy for a commander who in the midst of such a disaster struggled over the decision whether to style himself Viscount of Wimbledon or Viscount of Latymer.[12] His troops, alluding to his tactics, called him Viscount Sit-Still.[13] One valid point made by Cecil was that twenty years of peace had left England without an experienced fighting force. Coke appreciated the difficulty of waging war when unskilled, undisciplined men had to be forced into service for each new campaign. He proposed that the returning land soldiers, instead of being discharged, should be garrisoned, 'to have them exercised there and kept in readiness as in Queen Elizabeth's

[8]SP 16/5/77, 87; 16/7/39-41, 56; BL, Egerton MS. 2,541, fols. 49-50.

[9]SP 16/522/15; Coke MSS., packet 25, Coke to Sir Edward Giles, [6] Oct. 1625; Coke to 'my honourable friends the Deputy Lieutenants and Justices of Peace of the county of Devon', 6 Oct. 1625; packet 46, Coke to Buckingham, 8 Oct. 1625. Anthony Fletcher, *A County Community in Peace and War: Sussex 1600-1660* (London, 1975), pp. 193-201.

[10]*Cowper MSS.,* I, 241-4.

[11]Coke MSS., packet 46, Sir Edward Cecil to Coke, 27 Feb. 1626.

[12]*Cowper MSS.,* I, 224-5.

[13]Russell, *Parliaments,* p. 262.

time'. Coke said these men 'trained and hardened to the wars' would give England a 'ready army'.[14] On the whole, however, Coke's enthusiasm for war was profoundly dampened by the Cadiz fleet. On 14 December, he cried out to Conway: 'For God's sake (my good lord) let us first see how possibly we can raise money to discharge this unfortunate army and fleet that cometh home before there be any debate or mention of increasing more charge.' Three days later, Coke prophesied, 'if we proceed to work without means, and do not at this very time consider and prepare for that which is to be done against the spring, we shall but expose all our actions to the scorn of the world and shall draw upon us more danger than is yet taken to heart'. Coke promised to 'do my best to make my Lord Admiral sensible thereof', but apparently Coke's best was not good enough.[15]

Buckingham's expedition to the Isle of Rhé in 1627 reveals many of the same underlying problems that plagued the Cadiz fleet. Again there was difficulty pressing enough men into service, preventing them from deserting, and getting them to fight at all effectively. One historian has found that throughout the war years the system of pressing was 'irremediably corrupt and inefficient', and the army became 'a convenient dumping ground for its human trash'. Royal officials knew how the system could be improved — principally by employing a more professional and efficient staff under direct royal supervision — but lack of money forced the Crown to continue relying instead on the voluntary and less efficient cooperation of county officials.[16] Coke struggled with the familiar lack of money throughout this fleet's history. Shortly before it sailed, he explained to Conway: 'I solicit the Treasurer for the monies who still telleth me in his usual phrase that tomorrow they will take it into consideration, but this serveth not my turn who harken to no time but to this day.' 'Money', said Coke, 'is the mercury which till it be fixed will never produce the philosopher's stone, nor bring our motions and resolutions to a wished and happy end.' One way of raising money was through the sale of prize goods. Coke, who had done so much to establish this source of revenue, continued to exploit it for 'the monies which are the sinews without which we cannot move'.[17] It has been estimated that without these sales, the English war fleets, particularly the expedition

[14] SP 16/11/34.

[15] SP 16/11/64; 16/12/1.

[16] Stephen J. Stearns, 'Conscription and English Society in the 1620s', *Journal of British Studies,* vol. 11, no. 2 (1972), 16-23.

[17] SP 16/67/76, 16/56/1.

to Rhé, might not have been possible.[18] When Buckingham reached Rhé, he laid siege to the fortress of St Martin's, but the French were more successful in supplying the besieged fortress than the English were in supplying Buckingham. It did not help that Buckingham had come to Rhé with unprocessed grain that had to be ground into flour before it could be used to feed his troops. More important, as others have pointed out, siege warfare favoured the nation whose money and provisions would hold out the longest. England was in no position to fight such a war of attrition. When additional supplies and men were finally ready for Buckingham, adverse winds prevented their delivery. Of course the weather was not so much to blame as the fact that the Crown did not have enough money to marshal these reinforcements while the wind was still favourable.[19] Numerous other problems contributed to Buckingham's failure at Rhé, but his own quality of leadership was at least passable. As S.R. Gardiner long ago said, 'the charge which history has to bring against Buckingham is not so much that he failed in the expedition to Rhé, as that there was an expedition to Rhé at all'.[20]

On his return, Buckingham lashed out at Coke for failing to resupply him, and he determined to do away with the whole naval commission. On 20 February 1628, the naval commission was officially revoked and the principal officers were restored to power, thereby undoing the administrative reform of 1618. After nine years as chief commissioner, this must have been a slap in the face for Coke. Now all he was left with was the official notice of the commission's revocation, which Conway gave him, thinking it 'fittest to be kept by you or such as you shall think good'.[21] Buckingham is known to have regretted this precipitate action later, but it does raise an important question: how far were Coke and the other naval commissioners themselves responsible for the navy's poor performance? Unfortunately, this question cannot be answered definitively. We have already seen how the commission lost its momentum and Coke began to suspect some of his fellow commissioners during the Algiers voyage of 1621. The one commissioner specifically charged with wrong-doing was the shipwright, William Burrell. Coke harried Burrell mercilessly for

[18] Gardiner, *History of England,* VI, 178; Lockyer, *Buckingham,* p. 367.

[19] Gardiner, *History of England,* VI, 183, 192; Russell, *Parliaments,* pp. 329-31; SP 16/72/48, 16/75/9; Frederick C. Dietz, *English Public Finance, 1558-1641,* 2nd ed. (2 vols., New York, 1964), II, 240-3.

[20] *History of England,* VI, 200. For the whole expedition see pp. 168-200.

[21] Willson, *Privy Councillors,* p. 176 n. 26. SP 16/94/26. The revocation survived among Coke's papers (Coke MSS., packet 29) and is printed verbatim in *Cowper MSS.,* I, 339. *CSPV,* 1626-1628, p. 499.

years, but the surviving evidence does not fully justify his crusade against Burrell. It has also been observed that the composition of the commission changed over time. In 1625 the most active commissioners, apart from Coke, had a financial interest at stake, but even if this provides motive, it does not constitute proof of any misconduct. Another criticism of the commission was that Charles and Buckingham thought it was too slow and cumbersome for wartime. In 1625 a special commission of inquiry had been appointed to investigate the situation. The fact that Coke was included on this commission meant that he was, in effect, investigating himself, but presumably his expertise was necessary and he was considered above reproach. Unfortunately, under the press of war, the investigatory commission disbanded without producing a formal report, thereby leaving the question of the commission's culpability unanswered. The very lack of evidence is a point in its favour, however. Furthermore, the commissioners surely did a better job than the principal officers they replaced in 1619 would have done, and it soon became apparent that reinstating the officers in 1628 was a truly retrogressive step. On balance, then, there is no reason to dispute the longstanding opinion confirmed by more recent study that the commissioners worked competently enough until they were asked to 'perform impossibilities'.[22]

The Cadiz and Rhé fleets had brought to light five further points of a more general nature that need to be understood before proceeding to examine Coke's work at Portsmouth in 1628. First there is the minor point of wages. The low wages paid by the English government encouraged desertion and failed to attract the better sailors. After his failure at Cadiz, Sir Edward Cecil said that the chief remedy for the future would be to raise wages so that the king would not lose the services of the better sailors.[23] On these practical as well as humanitarian grounds, Buckingham has been praised for raising the monthly seaman's wage from 10 to 15 shillings. Coke, by contrast, seems stingy to a fault for opposing this increase. By his own account, he 'often protested both at the Council board and to my lord duke and otherwise: that the late increase of payments both to our landmen and seamen will make the wars unsupportable and be a greater enemy to our designs than their forces [which] we go against'. Coke's concern was economy, which was not an entirely unjustified concern. The wage increase was approved in the wake of the Cadiz fiasco which cost the Crown half a million pounds which it did not have. How, then,

[22]Manwaring, *Sir Henry Mainwaring,* I, 154-5; McGowan, 'Royal Navy', pp. 2, 122, 265-6, 273-5; Aylmer, 'Administrative Reform', pp. 234-6; Lockyer, *Buckingham,* pp. 273, 341, 344-5, 360, 367, 399, 423; Oppenheim, *Royal Navy,* pp. 196, 228-9.

[23]*Cowper MSS.,* I, 258.

could it afford to increase wages by 50 per cent? Of course it could not. As Buckingham's biographer acknowledged, 'seamen could not even be paid the old rates, let alone the new'. By the most generous estimate, only 32 per cent of what was owed to seamen was actually paid during the war years. Interestingly, if the same amount of money had been disbursed but according to the old rate, then seamen would have received 48 per cent of what was owed them. It is at least debatable whether it would have caused less discontent to pay seamen almost half of what was owed them under the old rate instead of paying them only one-third of what was promised them under the new rate.[24] In reality, all that Buckingham raised was expectations that he could only fail to meet.

The second point to be made before examining Coke's work at Portsmouth is a simple, strategic one: England was fighting the wrong kind of war. Coke was quite wrong in the Parliament of 1628 when he said that a defensive war was 'miserable and wasting'. Eliot and Sir Edward Coke were absolutely right to reply that a defensive war was best, especially for an island-nation. Perhaps Coke was more on the right track in encouraging what amounted to guerilla warfare on the high seas through letters of marque, a limited offensive strategy that harkened back to the Elizabethan war against Spain. Of course the large-scale attack on Cadiz was also intended to echo Drake's famous raid under Elizabeth, but given the inferior leadership and seamanship of the 1620s, what it produced was the disgrace of the English armada, a grotesque reversal of Elizabethan history. The assault on Rhé is even clearer proof of the difficulty of maintaining supply lines to a distant army on foreign soil. Of course there is an obvious rebuttal to this line of argument: unless Spain or France could somehow be provoked into attacking England, Charles was forced to take the battle to them. In other words, if Charles positively insisted on engaging in battle, then he had to go looking for a fight. But this was a big 'if', and when Charles did go looking for a fight, the advantage lay with his enemies.[25]

The third point is the matter of money: Charles had a 'cash-flow' problem. He did find extraordinary ways of raising revenue, but these ways did not bring in the amount needed when it was needed. As we saw, for example, the Crown did manage to raise money to supply Buckingham at Rhé, but the money and the reinforcements materialized

[24]McGowan, 'Royal Navy', pp. 111-12, 116; Oppenheim, *Royal Navy*, pp. 225-6; SP 16/11/64, 16/71/69; Lockyer, *Buckingham*, p. 298; *APC*, 1626, p. 206.

[25] Johnson, *1628 Debates*, II, 247-50, 257, 269-71. Russell, *Parliaments*, pp.80-1, 325-6, 329.

too late. Lack of money also cost Charles more money in the long run. Because he could not afford to pay off soldiers, he continued to keep them in service, and this in turn increased what he owed them. At one point Charles was incurring an additional debt of £4,000 each month because he did not have £14,000 to pay overdue wages. What was true of men was also true of ships. When some ships were ready, it was expensive to keep them in harbour consuming their provisions while awaiting the preparation of others. The economic fact was that it cost nearly as much to keep a ship at anchor as at sea. In 1625, for example, Coke complained that because he could not get money to victual a particular ship, it 'putteth his Majesty to as much charge as if she were in service at sea'. Because Charles was forced to live on credit, he fell more deeply into debt. The simple fact is that the war would not have cost as much as it did if the Crown had been able to pay for it in the first place.[26]

The fourth point concerns corruption. One must wonder what happened to the reforms of the naval commissioners.[27] Either they were superficial to begin with or they were swept away by the tides of war. Corruption was a chronic problem in the navy, and the reforms of 1618-23 had managed at best to hold it in check for a while. As we saw earlier, symptoms of corruption resurfaced with Mansell's Algiers fleet, but these were nothing when compared to the rampant thievery of the war years. Although corruption has not figured prominently in our analysis of the Cadiz and Rhé fleets, it was there, and it will be vividly demonstrated when we turn to Coke's work at Portsmouth.

Closely allied to corruption is the fifth and last point: appalling organization. The English bureaucracy was too primitive. The Crown relied on amateurs, and it did not have the money and the personnel necessary to reward and supervise these amateurs properly. The deputy lieutenants and other county officials are familiar examples. The navy provides other examples. We saw how exasperated Coke was that the victualler did not employ adequate, competent deputies. As for the naval commissioners, they were better than the former principal officers, but they were not all highly professional, full-time commissioners. Sir Edward Cecil meant to flatter Coke when he called him 'the soul of the commission and the sole doer', but this was also a criticism. Coke could not be, though during the war years he sometimes seemed to be, a one-man naval administration. There were too few other men who knew what they were doing, and Coke was

[26] Oppenheim, *Royal Navy,* p. 227; SP 16/12/25; Dietz, *English Public Finance,* II, 240-1.

[27] Aylmer, 'Administrative Reform', p. 235.

partly to blame for this state of affairs. He was not good at delegating authority or cultivating leadership and expertise in others. On the other hand, circumstances were also to blame. A highly competitive, jealous, and unregulated court encouraged Coke to hog the limelight, as Cranfield had done, to hold power and to prevent others from taking it away. Other circumstances prevented the Crown from exercising adequate control over old offices or creating new offices where they were needed.[28] Nor could the government keep good men where it needed them most. Coke, for example, was needed most in the navy, but he was not satisfied with his post there even when he was getting £300 a year. He wanted and got a higher office, but there were not enough such higher offices to support all the administrators who were needed, especially in wartime. And Charles hardly had the money necessary to lure them into less attractive, lower offices. Moreover, the government needed not just more bureaucrats but a more bureaucratic mentality. Regulations, job descriptions, systematized procedures, reports, and accountability – these things were second-nature to Coke but alien to many others upon whom the Crown depended for its administrators. For example, when an attempt was made to require impartial records of debts incurred by military officers, Coke was told that the officers considered this a 'great indignity', and they complained of being treated 'like children who must be taught to pay their debts'.[29] In general, then, the Crown possessed too few capable administrators. This was illustrated in 1625 when Coke had to be sent in person to oversee preparation of the Cadiz fleet at Plymouth and again in 1628 when he was dispatched to Portsmouth. The Crown's excessive dependence on Coke is particularly striking in 1628 because by this time the naval commission had been revoked. Officially Coke was no longer associated with the navy, but in fact Buckingham had no one else he could turn to.

Coke's sojourn at Portsmouth is exceptionally well documented. In addition to the many surviving letters between Coke and major court figures who remained back in London, there is also a seventy-eight-page diary by Coke entitled, 'Journal for Portsmouth to send back the fleet for Rochelle'.[30] No other documentation from the war years better illustrates how it was that Coke could work so hard yet achieve so little.

[28] Aylmer, *The King's Servants*, pp. 281-2, 460-1, 465-6.

[29] Coke MSS., packet 27, Sir George Chudleigh to Coke, 14 Sept. 1626.

[30] Coke's journal has been broken into two parts. The first thirty-two pages, 19 May to 4 June, are in packet 30 of the Coke MSS. The final forty-six pages, 4 June to 13 August, are in the PRO as SP 16/106/32. Coke's work at Portsmouth has been noted by several historians, particularly Manwaring, *Sir Henry Mainwaring*, I, 192-6.

Coke arrived at Portsmouth on 19 May to meet Denbigh's fleet which was coming back from La Rochelle without having done anything. The original intention was to keep all men aboard the ships, restore the provisions that had been depleted, strengthen the fleet, and send it directly back to La Rochelle to accomplish what it had shrunk from accomplishing the first time.[31] Coke estimated this work could be finished in little more than a week, but Denbigh's fleet straggled back in three separate parts, the last arriving on 1 June, and several of the vessels loaded with food for La Rochelle were lost to Dunkirk privateers along the way.[32] What crippled Coke's work even more, however, was the tactical decision to hold back all the ships and augment them with fire ships to break the French blockade. Holding back the entire fleet to depart in unison was not expected to cause a great delay. Buckingham first broached the possibility of detaining the fleet in a letter to Coke on 28 May, and he reported that Charles and the Council concurred on 1 June. This decision was therefore made between the time Charles received the Petition of Right and the time he delivered his first answer to it. Buckingham expected Parliament to end on 11 June with 'as happy agreement between the king and his people as ever was between a sovereign and his subjects'. He can be excused for not knowing in advance that the Commons would be dissatisfied with Charles's first answer and that Parliament would continue two weeks longer than expected. Nevertheless, as the Lord Admiral should have understood, this initial delay bred still further delay, and in the end it was fatal for both the fleet and Buckingham. Although Buckingham lavishly praised Coke for his 'extraordinary diligence', he had by his own orders practically doomed his work to failure.[33] Coke understood what Buckingham failed to understand – that delay would undermine any resolve on the part of the seamen to return to La Rochelle, that they would desert their ships, that provisions would be consumed and even sabotaged, that endless pretexts would be invented to free ships and men from service, and that generally the longer the fleet was detained the less it would be prepared to sail. Coke told Buckingham from the outset that 'the time which is allowed to send the fleet together will consume the provisions and disable it to proceed'. To Conway he explained, 'now you have changed the course, all men here make advantage of this prolongation of time to make their ships and men more unready'. Writing again to Buckingham, Coke declared, 'so soon as notice was taken here of the

[31] SP 16/104/21.

[32] SP 16/104/60, 61; 16/105/7, 44.

[33] Coke MSS., packet 48, Buckingham to Coke, 23 and 28 May and 4 June 1628; packet 30, Buckingham to Coke, 1, 10, and 14 June 1628.

change of counsel and the fleet should not presently be sent to sea, the very thought of further service seemed to be cast off'. Coke later apologized for the 'passion' he exhibited in this letter, but he was unrepentant in his criticism. More than a month later, he told Buckingham that he had signified 'almost in every letter, how by protraction of time, the victuals and provisions waste and. . . the men run away and new pressed men appear not'. Yet, 'as if these things were not read or not regarded', Coke broadly insinuated to Buckingham, the Lord Admiral's replies continued to be unjustifiably optimistic. Coke estimated that every day the fleet was delayed cost the Crown £300, which would make the total cost for the summer amount to over £25,000. Coke was unequivocal in claiming that this policy of delay undermined all his work. Near the end of June he asked to be relieved of his 'fruitless' abode at Portsmouth, lamenting: 'The longer I stay here I shall every day see the fleet and voyage go further backward and all my travails and endeavours spent in vain and worn out. The time consumes our victuals, our provisions, and our men, and will make that impossible [which] was in some degree of hope.' Coke acknowledged that it did no good to complain. 'All I desire', he said, 'is to be blameless if I have not deserved it.' As usual, then, Coke was expected to implement policy, not to make it. What is more unusual in this case, however, is the degree to which Coke was unreserved in his criticism of a policy with which he disagreed. Coke had just enough power to be charged with great responsibility for the execution of policy but not enough power to reverse bad policy. This prevented him from going to the real root of the problem and forced him to struggle instead against the manifold symptoms of that problem. As Coke himself described his predicament: 'The means to prevent ill effects is to discover the true causes, to which neither my commission nor my powers do extend.'[34]

The policy of delay adopted by Buckingham was doubly fatal because it ignored the attitude and morale of the men in the fleet. The morale in this fleet was especially low because on its first voyage to La Rochelle it had already observed the frightening strength of the enemy. Naturally the rumour spread through the fleet at Portsmouth that they were being sent on what amounted to a suicide mission, and, as Coke discovered, the 'rumour of impossibility to prosper there hath by degrees enforced almost an impossibility here'. Coke hoped the commanders would suppress the rumour, but he learned that they were its likely authors. After all, it was in the interest of the commanders to spread the impression that the French defences were

[34]SP 16/106/17, 25, 31, 35; 16/108/18, 22; 16/110/10.

impregnable, since otherwise they might be required to justify their inaction on their first trip to La Rochelle. Coke professed not to believe this aspersion on the commanders, but he advised the earl of Denbigh that 'now there is no way to redeem or make good your honor with his Majesty but by advancing the action, encouraging the mariners, and making way through all fears'. This is only the first several indications that Coke was not much impressed by Denbigh.[35] Meanwhile, seamen threw their victuals overboard, alleged defects in their ships, and broke up the barrels used to carry fresh water. 'So by degrees', Coke wrote in his diary, 'they discover their defects and disable themselves to proceed.' To Buckingham he reported: 'I now see there is no end of new defects.' The more obvious and direct course was for the men simply to run away, and many did so. Coke regretted that Portsmouth was overburdened with sick seamen, but he knew that lodging them farther from the fleet was tantamount to discharging them. The number of men still attached to the fleet dwindled so much that Coke became even more concerned about the lack of men than about the familiar lack of money. Skilled masters, surgeons, and gunners were in especially short supply. The system of pressing men into service had almost completely broken down. Coke issued orders for men to be pressed, but so ineffectual were they that he concluded 'to proceed further were to cast away money and draw contempt upon the government'. Coke understood, too, how the burden of billeting eroded the government's reputation in the countryside. The victualler was alloted eight pence per day for each billeted seaman, but he kept one penny for himself and paid only seven pence to the householders. Coke ordered that all eight pence be paid to the householders 'for the better contentment of the country and them that lodge and cherish the poor men'.[36]

For a usually stern disciplinarian, Coke demonstrated a surprising degree of sensitivity at Portsmouth. He argued against the exemplary punishment of a few offenders, explaining that 'punishment before comfort be given' would only cause more offences, discouragement, and desertion. He was more inclined to 'a patient and moderate way of proceeding with them here when they fall into disorder, as I find them apt to do'. This lenient approach was put to its severest test when mutiny broke out. The mutiny on 23 June involved not just one ship but the whole fleet. At least 150 men were said to be marching with a flag to draw other seamen from the ships. Denbigh had decided upon a

[35] SP 16/106/10, 10I; 16/106/32, fols. 68, 72v, 74-6.

[36] Coke MSS., packet 30, 'Journal', pp. 28-9; SP 16/106/10, 17, 35; 16/106/32, fols. 72v-74; 16/108/33; Coke MSS., packet 30, Coke to Buckingham, 3 June 1628.

'sharp course to fall upon some chief mutineers', but Coke countermanded that course, fearing that violence would 'more probably increase than lessen the evil'. Instead, Coke instructed the captains to take their better affected officers ashore and entreat as many seamen to return by mere persuasion as possible. This successfully reduced the mutineers to scattered bands of only a few men each, and 'the tumult was quieted'. Apparently Coke was felt to be a sympathetic man because the next day three of the mutinous seamen came to him with a petition. Coke gave them what assurances he could, and they went away satisfied. Coke's compassion is evident in the words he used to report this incident to Buckingham:

> These poor men have continued some of them divers years in the service without ever being discharged, and to most of them nine or ten months' pay is now due. They have no shift of clothes, some have no shirts, and others but one for the whole year. All I have promised them is that before they go to sea upon any voyage of service, they shall receive monies. And if this be not performed, or if his Majesty or your Grace shall come hither and not bring monies with you, all will fall in uproar, and you will not be able to set this fleet to sea with any hope of good success.

Several days later, Coke again told Buckingham that 'nothing but money will revive their spirits' and settle that 'humour which hath both disheartened and discontented them all'. Coke noted that there were 2,649 men to be paid, and their wages were ten months in arrears. He suggested that they be paid for nine months, leaving just one month in arrears. He calculated this would require £23,841.[37]

One problem nearly beyond Coke's control was victualling. Sometimes the victuals were unwholesome to begin with. On one occasion, for example, Coke inspected a charge that beef and pork were spoiled. He discovered that the animals had been slaughtered in remote parts and then hauled in carts through the hot summer weather to Portsmouth. He directed that in the future the animals be brought to Portsmouth alive and then slaughtered. On another occasion, Coke investigated a charge that the fish supplied to one ship were so small as to be 'a just cause of mutiny amongst the men'. He was informed that only one fish in six was sufficiently large. All the officers of another ship certified that their meat was adulterated because 'twigs were put [in] to fill up the barrels instead of beef and pork'. Not all such charges were valid, of course. When one ship refused to accept nine tuns of beer because it was 'stinking', Coke and his assistants looked into the matter, and 'we all found it very good and without any just exception'.

[37] SP 16/108/13, 18; 16/109/20; 16/106/32, fols. 74v-76.

Victuals which were sound when delivered were in constant danger of spoiling. Dampness on shipboard was a common cause of spoilage, and Coke gave instructions for damp grain and bread to be laid out in the sun to salvage as much as possible. The size of the problem is revealed in Coke's order to destroy the inedible victuals on *The Vanguard,* which amounted to: 471 pieces of beef, 494 pieces of pork, 4 hogsheads of peas, 140 pounds of cheese, 10 tuns of beer, and 1,034 fish.[38] It should be remembered, too, that this fleet needed to carry not only victuals for itself but enough additional food to relieve the starving Rochellois. Better victuals in adequate quantities might have been obtainable if the Crown had possessed the money to purchase them, but Coke's letters are full of the chronic complaint about lack of money. Near the end of May, he complained that: 'I have not yet received one penny to set out all these ships save only in letters.' A month later, he reported that 'our stock and credit, as I wrote before, is all expended'. Meanwhile merchants raised prices on goods they knew were desperately needed.[39] The chief victualler, Sir Allen Apsley, appealed to Coke that he needed £700 weekly to supply the fleet, but he had no money at all and his creditors would no longer provide goods unless they were paid in cash. It is tempting to blame Apsley personally for the poor victualling of the war fleets, but he would have needed a far more elaborate supporting bureaucracy to have done the job well, and he claimed to have drawn himself and his friends nearly £100,000 in debt for the king's service. Corruption and mismanagement certainly existed among the victuallers, but they had neither the money nor the administrative apparatus necessary for success, and the technical problem of supplying perishable commodities was not overcome for another century or more.[40]

Corruption was the endemic disease of the navy, and it flourished at Portsmouth. As Coke observed in his diary: 'The boatswains, masters, carpenters, gunners, and the mariners themselves, though they have had no money in ten months, yet they come ashore and want not money to spend in the alehouse; and this they get by no way but stealing of the king's stores of all sorts.' Here again, Buckingham's decision to delay the fleet aggravated the situation. The longer men sat idle without pay, the more they were tempted to steal, and this rule applied to the officers as well as the lower seamen. 'While the king's ships stay in harbour', Coke wrote, 'all the officers will be ashore and,

[38] SP 16/106/32, fols. 63, 70, 71v, 73v, 74v, 76v, 77; 16/106/35.

[39] SP 16/105/78, 16/108/33, 16/113/53, 16/528/74.

[40] Coke MSS., packet 30, Apsley to Coke, 29 May 1628; *CSPD,* 1628-1629, p. 139; Oppenheim, *Royal Navy,* pp. 233-4; McGowan, 'Royal Navy', pp. 245-56.

wanting other means to maintain their expenses, they will sell whatsoever belongeth to the provisions of their ships, as casks, cordage, nails'. Searching one ship for stolen cordage, Coke found not only the cordage but also other unauthorized materiel, and he arrested the ship's master. Pursers were in an ideal position to steal from the ships' stores. Coke knew of one purser who insisted on victuals for a full crew of eighty although the true size of the ship's crew had shrunk to less than thirty. How could so many people get away with so much thievery? Coke found the explanation in too little supervision and too few written records. For example, the ordnance officers who supplied munitions and the gunners who received them aboard ship were free to conspire because no one supervised their transactions. Coke knew one captain who 'hath served ever since the king came to the crown and never was asked nor gave allowance to a gunner's bill'. Coke thought that gunners should routinely submit their accounts to the captains for approval. Similarly, he thought that boatswains should be required to submit their accounts to the inspection of the masters. Coke also bemoaned the lack of supervision over pursers. He observed that only 'ancient pursers' knew what allowance they were supposed to receive while all the rest took 'whatsoever the victualler will give'.

The problem was as much a matter of mentality as morality. To a man of Coke's bookkeeping mentality, Portsmouth represented intolerable chaos. As his own written record – his diary – attests, throughout his stay there he repeatedly asked for accounts, surveys, or inventories, preferably certified under several hands. Bureaucratic as Coke was, however, he could not transform the motley assortment of men at Portsmouth into a smooth-running bureaucracy. In this respect, Coke was a lonely forerunner in the process of rationalization and bureaucratization made famous by Max Weber. Indeed, Coke struggled throughout his career to implement what the modern administrator would readily recognize as job descriptions, managerial objectives, routine record keeping, and the principle of accountability. Such concepts were alien to the men with whom Coke laboured in the summer of 1628, men who, as Coke complained, 'neither know nor love order'.[41]

We have suggested that Coke's work was part of a wider historical process of rationalization and bureaucratization taking place throughout Europe at this time. If this is true, then there should be comparable examples from other countries. Perhaps the best comes from Spain.

[41] SP 16/106/32, fols. 63v, 64v, 67v, 69v, 77v-78v, 80, 81v, 82v, 84; 16/106/31.

Here is how I. A. A. Thompson described the problems of naval administration in Spain at the beginning of the seventeenth century:

> There was nothing new about corrupt and greedy officials, but a hundred years of complaints had shown that their misdemeanours were ineradicable. The numerous proposals to clean up the administration concentrated primarily on stricter methods of accounting, requiring that disbursements be made only in the presence of the captain or *veedor* general, and only at fixed periods and not at will, demanding the personal attention of the finance officers to their duties, calling for the more frequent submission of accounts and estimates, and for the prompter and more certain punishment of offenders.

If one did not know that Thompson's subject was the Spanish navy, one might just as well think he was writing about the English navy. Improved accounting procedures, closer supervision of personnel, regulations to require men to do their duty, and prompt punishment of men who failed to do their duty – how often have we seen these themes recur in Coke's work? How often, too, have we seen the conclusion reached by Thompson: 'But it was one thing to issue instructions, another to have them obeyed.'[42] Coke often described the administrative problems he faced as 'disorders'. Looked at this way, his task was to cultivate habits of orderliness, to make unruly men work by the rules, often rules he himself wrote. But the bureaucratic mentality could not be fostered over night, least of all without professional training, promotion by merit, higher salaries, job security, and assured pensions.

The administrators who did exist in the summer of 1628 and should have sufficed were the principal officers of the navy whom Buckingham had put back in charge at the beginning of 1628, but the very fact that Coke was dispatched to Portsmouth indicated that the principal officers could not do the job. At the beginning of July, Buckingham's secretary, Edward Nicholas, explained that the 'remissness and ignorance of the officers of the navy have been principal hindrances that the fleet and provisions here preparing are not sooner ready'. Nicholas further told Coke that the Lord Admiral 'now finds that he was mistaken when he changed the commissioners for these officers of the navy, who are above their places in their imaginations, and for their want of understanding in such business not able to execute the same'. Coke deeply resented having to do the work of the officers for them. He considered it a particular 'indignity' and

[42] I.A.A. Thompson, *War and Government in Habsburg Spain 1560-1620* (London, 1976), p. 49.

'disparagement' when the officers sent £500 to Portsmouth and expected him to account to them for its disbursement. Of course Coke agreed that someone should keep account of this money, but he believed the Treasurer of the Navy should have provided a clerk for the task or a deputy should have been specially appointed. Coke was busy with other responsibilities, and it galled him to think that even though he was now a Secretary of State, he was being placed in a position relative to the officers of the navy which was inferior to the one he had occupied when he was a mere commissioner of the navy. As he expressed his dissatisfaction to Buckingham: 'I thought it not agreeable to the king's honour that his Secretary should become a clerk to the officers of the navy, who when I was employed in that proper service was no accountant unto them.'[43]

Tension with the officers of the navy was only part of what Coke objected to at Portsmouth. He asked several times to be released from his 'imprisonment' in the most expensive 'and most tedious place of this kingdom'. At the age of sixty-five, he was especially concerned about his health in the disease-ridden city. He likened the inn where he lodged to a 'hospital amongst multitudes of sick men'. There were other dangers, too; he recorded in his diary that one night he was shot at. But underlying all these complaints was a more pervasive awareness of the futility of his work. Back in London, Conway could not obtain release for Coke, but he could offer some consolation. While Parliament was still in session, he told Coke: 'You have escaped the delivering of many messages in which you would have had no delight nor for which you would have received thanks. And you have missed the lending of £200, too, for the setting out of those ships.'[44]

In summary, Coke's work at Portsmouth illustrates many of the reasons why the war fleets performed so shamefully: an inordinately long period of preparation in port, poor leadership, unskilled and disheartened men, disease, rampant corruption, and a crippling lack of money, men, and administrators. The Portsmouth episode also helps us to understand better what kind of man Coke was. He sedulously carried out his orders, as might be expected. But he was also surprisingly critical of the decision to delay the fleet, perceptive about the interrelated problems of the navy, and sympathetic to the grievances of the seamen. In other words, he carried out his orders, but he did not do so unthinkingly. Reflecting back more generally over

[43] SP 16/106/25, 26, 31. Coke MSS., packet 48, Conway to Coke, 18 and 25 June 1628; packets 48 and 30, Nicholas to Coke, 2 and 3 July.

[44] SP 16/106/71; 16/108/18, 22, 51.

all these fleets, one cannot help but recall Coke's advice in the wake of Cadiz – his warning 'for God's sake' to pay off the cost of the Cadiz expedition before attempting another enterprise and his prophecy that to proceed without means would 'expose all our actions to the scorn of the world' and incur 'more danger than is yet taken to heart'. Had Buckingham heeded such advice in December of 1625, he might have avoided what lay in wait for him at Portsmouth in the summer of 1628.

Buckingham arrived in Portsmouth on 17 August, having by then decided to lead the fleet back to La Rochelle in person. On 25 August, however, he was stabbed to death by John Felton. One of Coke's last services to the Lord Admiral was to interrogate his assassin.[45] The fleet that Coke had worked so long and hard to prepare did sail at last in September, but it achieved little more than it had on its first voyage, and the starving Rochellois surrendered even while the English ships sat helplessly off shore.

Buckingham's death was the most outstanding event among several that profoundly affected Coke at this time. By a tragic coincidence his first patron and beloved friend, Fulke Greville, was also stabbed to death only a few weeks after Buckingham.[46] Within a few months, another longtime colleague, Conway, who was struggling with age and illness, relinquished the other Secretaryship. Thus Coke acquired a new fellow Secretary, Sir Dudley Carleton, Viscount Dorchester.[47] Then, too, the Parliaments and the fleets that had dominated Coke's work for so long were at last coming to an end. In the first months of 1629 Coke represented the Crown in Parliament for the last time as the war period drew to an unlamented close.

All of this taken together, but especially the death of Buckingham, marked the end of an era for Coke. The most turbulent decade of his life had reached a sudden, unexpected conclusion. Ten years had passed since the summer of 1618, when Naunton and Greville had lured him back to the court, ten years during which he had risen from

[45] Henry Ellis, ed., *Original Letters Illustrative of English History,* first series (3 vols., London, 1824), III, 258. Dudley Carleton reported that Felton was seized and taken to the Governor's House in Portsmouth. 'My Lord High Chamberlaine and Mr. Secretary Cooke were then at the Governor's House, [and] did there take his examination of which as yet there is nothing knowne.' See also SP 16/118/54, 16/114/16, and Coke MSS., packet 30, Conway to Coke, 23 Aug. 1628.

[46] *DNB,* VII, 604. Coke was appointed one of Greville's executors and arranged for his body to be buried at Warwick. SP 16/118/24.

[47] Gardiner, *History of England,* VI, 372. Though Dorchester did not replace Conway until December, Coke received news of the rumoured change at least as early as July. Coke MSS., packet 69, Humphrey Fulwood to Coke, 17 July 1628. Coke actually began working with Dorchester as early as September. See SP 16/116/29, 30, 61-3; 16/118/90.

naval reformer to commissioner of the navy, to Master of Requests, to Secretary of State. Yet throughout those years, whatever office he held, Coke was basically Buckingham's servant. All that he gained and all that he sacrificed was due to Buckingham, to whom he had subordinated his life and his work. Coke's career did not end in 1628. He still had more than eleven years left in the Secretaryship, and his work in those years would not be insignificant, but it would seem pedestrian compared to what had preceded it. For Coke the 1630s were years of anticlimax, years during which he continued to occupy one of the highest offices of state but ceased to be included in the king's innermost thoughts and designs. Much as Buckingham had wasted Coke's talents and wrecked his reform of the navy, he had also given Coke a sense of importance and expectancy that could only come from being a trusted agent of the most powerful man in the kingdom. Buckingham's assassination therefore brought to an end not only the worst exploitation of Coke's ability but also his highest hope of achieving something more. For Coke, there was no successor to the Lord Admiral, no new patron who could make him something more than just another functionary at court. For Coke – as indeed for Charles – there would never be another Buckingham.

13

POLITICS AND BUSINESS IN THE 1630s

Coke's work as Secretary of State depended to some extent on the character and activities of the other Secretary. From December 1628 until February 1632, the second Secretary was Sir Dudley Carleton, Viscount Dorchester. The smooth-running partnership that had existed between Coke and Conway continued between Coke and Dorchester. The differentiation of duties continued also. In fact, Dorchester exercised an even more complete monopoly over the foreign correspondence than Conway had, and that left Coke absorbed more exclusively with domestic matters, so much so that his work in these years has been interpreted as the 'dim beginnings of the modern home office'.[1] The staggering amount of business Coke transacted during these years is difficult to convey to anyone who has not paged through the domestic state papers of the period. John Bruce, who edited those papers for 1631-3, observed that: 'Secretary Coke is to be found throughout the volume ever active and intelligent, having a share in many kinds of business, and in some cases applying to the matters before him an almost incredible amount of clerk-like pains.'[2] Of course a great deal of this business, although it absorbed Coke's time and energy, was trivial. His most important work probably occurred on the select committees of the Privy Council where the central government of England was concentrated in the 1630s; Coke was one of the few men who sat on all these committees.[3] Even here, though, it would be easy to exaggerate his importance. Despite the magnitude of work entrusted to him during these years, Coke did not have much voice, surely not a decisive voice, in the formulation of higher policy.[4]

Coke continued in the early 1630s to participate in reform projects that met with minimal success. He was a leading member of the commission that attempted reform of the Wardrobe in 1630. He drafted the orders intended to reform the Wardrobe by making the master and the clerk jointly responsible for the expenditures of the

[1]Evans, *The Principal Secretary*, p. 274.

[2]*CSPD*, 1631-1633, pp. xxvi-xxvii. Coke, *The Last Elizabethan*, p. 216. Bruce also noted Coke's appalling ignorance about the geography of Iceland and Newfoundland.

[3]Edward R. Turner, *The Privy Council of England in the Seventeenth and Eighteenth Centuries* (2 vols., Baltimore, 1927), II, 220-7; Michael Van Cleave Alexander, *Charles I's Lord Treasurer: Sir Richard Weston, Earl of Portland* (London, 1975), p. 151.

[4]Conrad Russell, *The Crisis of Parliaments* (London, 1971), p. 310.

department and requiring them to submit regular, annual accounts. By the end of 1633, however, it was apparent that the regulations of 1630 were not being observed and a new commission was appointed which again included Coke. As Coke's notes show, the master of the Wardrobe, the earl of Denbigh, had refused to cooperate with the clerk because he considered this 'a disparagement to his place'. In 1634, the commissioners simply reaffirmed the regulations of 1630. Some saving was achieved by these investigations, but the effectiveness of the commissioners was necessarily limited as long as the master of the Wardrobe continued to be a nobleman who was virtually immune from criticism despite his dishonesty.[5] It is true that the problems in the Wardrobe went deeper than the irresponsibility of the master, but the first step toward correcting these would have been to apply the principle of accountability at the top.

Coke also served on a commission appointed to reform the ordnance office appointed in 1630 and renewed in 1633. This might have served as an opportunity for Coke to accomplish the reform he had been denied in 1620. The problems of the ordnance had not changed, including feuding among the officers and shoddy accounting practices. The new commission had made little headway against these problems, however, when, in 1634, the earl of Newport bought the mastership of the ordnance. After Newport's appointment, the ordnance commission was reduced to a powerless supervisory role, and for the next five years the earl exploited the office for as much personal profit as he could.[6]

As an adjunct to the work of the ordnance commission, Coke investigated the closely related, smaller office of the armoury. Here, too, little or nothing was achieved. Coke's report on the armoury is interesting, however, because it expresses some of his views on administrative reform with special clarity. Coke emphasized two familiar points in his assessment of the armoury: the need for more routine and rigorous financial accounts, and the need for a formal, binding exposition of each officer's responsibilities. Drawing on his experience in other departments, Coke observed that 'the same defects appear in this office which have been found in the office of the navy, of the ordnance, and other places – in all which, though a yearly account is or ought to be taken of the monies received and issued, . . . I find neither auditors appointed nor any order settled or directed for

[5] *Cowper MSS.*, I, 423; SP 16/153/62, 16/164/55, 16/259/26, 47; Aylmer, 'Administrative Reform', pp. 250-4; Aylmer, *The King's Servants,* p. 350.

[6] SP 16/179/60; Aylmer, 'Administrative Reform', pp. 242-6; Aylmer, *The King's Servants,* p. 231; *DNB*, II, 712. Coke's notes of the ordnance commission's meetings are SP 16/193/59, 16/259/35.

accounts'. Equally familiar was the lack 'of orders and instructions either for the general government of the office or for the particular duties of every officer in his place, so as no man knoweth his charge, and the master by this means disposeth all at his pleasure, and no comptrollment is kept of anything that is done'.[7]

Apart from the routine duties of the Secretaryship and numerous additional commissions, Coke's chief area of expertise and interest in the early 1630s continued to be the navy. In the navy, as in the Wardrobe and ordnance, a promising start was made in 1630. In October 1630, King Charles asked Coke to present an account of the navy's activities during the preceding year. Coke was pleased at this development and hoped it would mark the beginning of 'better government in sea affairs, by causing accounts from time to time to be delivered unto him [Charles] that he may understand the difference of profitable and unprofitable servants'.[8] Coke's seventeen-page report was highly critical of Sir Henry Mervyn, the admiral of the Narrow Seas, and of his old antagonists, the principal officers. Coke charged that the officers quarrelled among themselves, delegated their duties to inadequate deputies, and generally neglected their responsibilities. He accused them of meeting together scarcely once every three months when they should have met weekly. He noted that a room had even been rented in London to serve as an office for them, but 'the king payeth the rent and they make little or no use of it'.[9] Coke's recommendation that Mervyn be replaced as admiral of the Narrow Seas appears to have been followed.[10] The problem of the principal officers was more complicated, but Coke seems to have achieved some satisfaction in the following way. The Lord Admiral's office had been placed in commission after Buckingham's assassination. Coke was a member of this commission, although not in as strong a position as he had formerly enjoyed as Buckingham's right-hand man. Meanwhile, the principal officers had remained in charge of the daily operation of the navy ever since Buckingham had reinstated them at the beginning of 1628. What Coke needed was a way of checking on the activities of the principal officers that was more direct and reliable than his supervisory vantage point on the Admiralty commission. That way was worked out in October of 1630 when Sir Kenelm Digby was appointed a special, additional, principal officer.

[7]SP 16/179/65. See also 16/179/64, 66-9.

[8]SP 16/174/21.

[9]Coke MSS., packet 33, '1630. Octob. 30. Account for Sea Services.' For the charges against Mervyn, see also *Cowper MSS.*, I, 430-1 and Coke's notes on the subject in packet 34 of the Coke MSS. See also *CSPD*, 1629-1631, p. 338.

[10]*CSPD*, 1631-1633, pp. 37, 51.

Sir Kenelm Digby was the closest Coke ever came to having a protégé. Coke wrote the letter to the principal officers announcing Digby's appointment and ordered them to 'forthwith receive him unto your society, at your meetings and otherwise in all businesses concerning the navy'.[11] From the point of view of the officers, Coke had placed a spy among them. Their discomfiture was reported by one contemporary in the following words:

> The Kinge hath geven Sir Kellam Digby a pattente under the Broad Seale to bee Superviser, and a principall officer of the Navy. I redd the pattente. It is a new instituted office, and vexeth the Tresorer, Servayer, and Controwler of the Navey, and a thinge that Sir Kellam Digby never so mutch as once knew of, till the Kinge sente it to him by Mr. Secretary Cooke's servante, for which hee payed not one penny.[12]

Coke had another ally in Kenrick Edisbury, a naval clerk for whom he had shown a high regard as early as 1628.[13] Coke had need of these allies because two longstanding opponents had reappeared. Sir Robert Mansell was once again being consulted on naval matters, and Phineas Pett, a former colleague of Mansell, was again employed as shipwright for the navy.[14] For the time being, however, with Digby's assistance, Coke was more than able to counterbalance these adversaries. The ascendancy of Coke and Digby reached its apex in 1632. Coke's fellow Secretary, Dorchester, died in February of that year, and for the next four months he was not replaced. In the summer of 1632, Sir Edward Nicholas observed that: 'Mr. Secretary Coke is yet in effect sole Secretary, and Sir Kenelm Digby is the most potent man that I see with him.'[15] Then Sir Francis Windebanke entered the picture.

Coke wrote the letter on 12 June 1632 that officially informed Windebank he had been chosen to succeed Dorchester as the second Secretary of State.[16] The mere existence of two Secretaries was in

[11] Coke MSS., packet 33, Coke's draft of commissioners of the Admiralty to the officers of the navy, 13 Oct. 1630.

[12] HMC, *Various*, VII, 398.

[13] SP 16/106/31; Coke MSS., packet 50, Edisbury to Coke, 15 Aug. 1631; *Cowper MSS.*, I, 439.

[14] SP 16/220/16, 16/221/56, 16/223/21, 37; *CSPD*, 1629-1631, p. 533; 1631-1633, pp. 90, 313, 326, 328, 340, 373; R.T. Petersson, *Sir Kenelm Digby: The Ornament of England 1603-1665* (Cambridge, Mass., 1956), pp. 83-4; Oppenheim, *Royal Navy*, p. 209; *Cowper MSS.*, I, 403; Manwaring, *Sir Henry Mainwaring*, I, 220-4. Greville had clashed with Pett in the last years of Elizabeth. See Perrin, *Phineas Pett*, pp. lvi, 11, 15, 17-18.

[15] SP 16/220/44.

[16] SP 16/218/42, 45.

itself an invitation to jealousy and competition, but this latent problem had failed to materialize before Windebank's appointment. Both Conway and Dorchester had been agreeable partners for Coke. Windebank, by contrast, was a rival. Windebank's chief patron was William Laud, bishop of London and soon-to-be archbishop of Canterbury. Laud took perhaps too much credit for himself when he recorded in his diary: 'Mr. Francis Windebancke, my old friend, was sworn Secretary of State; which place I obtained for him.' In a personal letter to Windebank, Laud jokingly told the new Secretary that: 'The name of the parish is St. Troubles.' Laud had no idea how troublesome, indeed, his ambitious disciple would become. What Windebank did was to ally himself with Lord Treasurer Portland and Sir Francis Cottington, the Chancellor of the Exchequer. Laud saw this as a wholesale defection to the enemy who were sympathetic to Spain and to Catholicism. In October of 1635, Laud counted Windebank among his 'occasions of grief'.[17] It would be a mistake, however, to view the situation strictly through Laud's biased eyes. Windebank was a clever man who would have preferred to remain on friendly terms with Laud while at the same time cooperating with Portland and Cottington. It was Laud who insisted on a me-or-them attitude and branded Windebank's actions as betrayal. Furthermore, Laud's expression of betrayal in 1635 has tended to obscure the fact that Windebank allied with Portland and Cottington at a much earlier date.[18] In the summer of 1633, just one year after his appointment to the Secretaryship, Windebank was left behind in London when Coke accompanied King Charles on his progress to Scotland. At this time Cottington told Windebank that Portland wanted a cypher to use in their correspondence. Windebank sent Portland this cypher and, following further instructions from Cottington, conferred with the Spanish resident in London.[19] This is the first evidence of a league that became more formalized at the end of 1633 when King Charles specifically delegated Portland, Cottington, and Windebank to conduct highly secret negotiations with Spain.[20]

Windebank's appointment was not an immediate scourge for Coke. Despite the special relationship that developed between

[17]Laud, *Works*, II, 215; VII, 201. SP 16/218/46. Compare Hugh R. Trevor-Roper, *Archbishop Laud, 1573-1645* (London, 1940), pp. 129-30; *DNB,* XXI, 634.

[18]Trevor-Roper, *Archbishop Laud,* p. 223; Evans, *The Principal Secretary,* p. 97 n. 4.

[19]SP 16/239/71. Clarendon, Edward Hyde, earl of, *State Papers Collected by Edward, Earl of Clarendon, Commencing from the Year 1621* (3 vols., Oxford, 1767), I, 120-1. In 1634 Windebank also referred back to deliberations with Portland about Ireland which had occurred in the summer of 1633. SP 16/262/21.

[20]Gardiner, *History of England,* VII, 349-52.

Windebank, Cottington, and Portland, Coke was not entirely alienated from the latter two courtiers. Cottington described Coke as 'an honest and an able man', and Portland observed that Coke's allegiance was 'totally and solely English and for the king's service without relation to any parties'.[21] Portland and Coke had worked together as far back as 1618 on the naval commission under Buckingham. By 1628 Portland had enough respect for Coke's naval expertise to recommend that he be sent to salvage the fleet at Portsmouth. In the early 1630s Portland, as the most powerful member of the Admiralty commission, continued to work closely with Coke on naval matters. It is simplistic, therefore, to divide these men into two diametrically opposed factions, one Protestant and one Catholic. Further proof of this is the fishing company founded in 1632 and headed by Portland until his health failed in 1635. S. R. Gardiner said that the fishing company was founded 'by Portland and his Roman Catholic friends', but the man who wrote voluminously on the subject of fishing to promote and sponsor the company along with Portland was Coke.[22] Furthermore, Portland's biographer has said that during the Lord Treasurer's final months Coke was one of only two persons 'with whom Portland's relations were completely untroubled'.[23] While Portland lived, then, Coke was not completely cut off from the so-called Catholic faction at court.

The competitiveness that did arise from Windebank's appointment was most pronounced in the realm of foreign affairs. Coke had been given sole responsibility for the foreign correspondence after Dorchester's death; the secret negotiations of Windebank, Cottington, and Portland circumvented this official channel and had the effect of trivializing what Coke did. More serious than this, though, was the increasing intrusion of Windebank on his own into foreign affairs (a subject so complex and important that it has been set aside as the subject of the whole next chapter). Meanwhile, in domestic affairs the competition between Coke and Windebank was most noticeable in the reorganization of the postal system. Coke patronized and worked together with a man named Thomas Witherings, whereas Windebank took the part of Witherings's opponent, a man named William Frizell. Had it not been for Coke's protection, it seems certain that Witherings would not have survived. Witherings acknowledged his great debt to Coke and did something to repay him simply by leaving behind an

[21] SP 16/216/14, 16/222/11.

[22] Gardiner, *History of England,* VII, 349; Alexander, *Charles I's Lord Treasurer,* pp. 206-7. SP 16/152/57, 63, 64; 16/165/20; 16/188/72; 16/191/7; 16/203/53; 16/206/37, 46, 50; 16/221/1; 16/229/71-3, 76-84, 86, 92-4; 16/233/75.

[23] Alexander, *Charles I's Lord Treasurer,* p. 218.

accomplishment that can be justly associated with Coke's name. Indeed, the postal reform of Coke and Witherings has been hailed as 'one of the few authentic improvements achieved under the early Stuarts', and Coke has been praised for his 'enlightened policy' in this respect.[24]

Coke's work in the navy was not affected by Windebank's appointment as much as by other factors. The clerk favoured by Coke, Kenrick Edisbury, was appointed Surveyor of the Navy in October 1632. For a short while, therefore, Coke had two friends among the principal officers: Sir Kenelm Digby and Edisbury, whom Digby described as an 'honest and upright' man obsessed with improving the government of the navy.[25] Edisbury and Coke accused Phineas Pett and another officer of selling old cordage for their own profit, but, in Pett's own words, 'it pleased God that their malice took no effect, the King giving us a free discharge'. Pett as much as admitted his own guilt, however, when he added that afterward 'we repaid the moneys received for the commodity to the Treasurer of the Navy for his Majesty's use'. Pett referred to Coke as 'my professed enemy', and he noted with pleasure that Coke had no choice but to feign friendliness when in the presence of the two men King Charles expressed his continued support for Pett.[26] The amnesty afforded by Charles subverted good government, and Coke had further proof of this fact in the case of Sir James Bagg, who had been Sir John Eliot's old adversary and Buckingham's follower. Bagg was tried twice in the Court of Star Chamber in the mid-1630s on charges that boiled down to corruption. In the first case, Coke was among a small minority who voted against Bagg. In the second case a bare majority, including Coke, found Bagg guilty, but Charles intervened to let Bagg escape without punishment. Coke's consistent vote against Bagg, even when he was in a minority of four, confirms the suspicion that he did not particularly like Bagg. Back in the 1620s he had worked with Bagg because Buckingham had required it and because Bagg was Eliot's competitor. But there is no reason to suppose that he felt any natural affinity for a man who (because of his corruptness) was known to his

[24] Aylmer, *The King's Servants,* p. 369; Evans, *The Principal Secretary*, p. 282; SP 16/154/81; 16/206/89; 16/231/62, 63; 16/234/47; 16/239/50; 16/242/19; 16/273/18, 58; 16/297/15; 16/370/53; 16/479/20; *Cowper MSS.,* II, 6, 16-18, 47, 99-100, 119, 151, 163, 171-2, 195-6, 235-6, 254.

[25] A.W. Johns, 'The Principal Officers of the Navy', *Mariner's Mirror,* 14 (1928), 49; SP 16/223/21; Oppenheim, *Royal Navy,* p. 281. Oppenheim said Edisbury was 'perhaps the most observant and energetic' principal officer.

[26] Perrin, *Phineas Pett*, pp. 153-6.

contemporaries as 'bottomless Bagg'.[27] The most serious blow to Coke's work in the navy was the loss of Digby, who withdrew from his position as a principal officer when thrown into deep depression by the death of his wife in May 1633.[28] For the next two years, although Digby's work in the navy had ended, Coke remained on close terms with him. Near the end of 1635, Digby departed for France, still professing his affection and respect for Coke. In France, however, he converted to Roman Catholicism and drifted into Windebank's orbit.[29]

As long as it lasted, Coke's alliance with Kenelm Digby between 1630 and 1633 was a curious phenomenon. Digby was a man of many talents, a writer, experimenter, patron of learning, and philosopher. His family had long been associated with Catholicism, his father having been executed for complicity in the Gunpowder Plot, yet as late as 1636 Digby professed that Coke and Archbishop Laud were his two best friends. Coke's alliance with Digby was made all the more improbable by the fact that he was related to the earl of Bristol who had opposed Buckingham. Whatever the basis of their mutual respect, the world of learning was at least part of what drew Coke and Digby together. It is easy to lapse into thinking of Coke as only a dull bureaucrat and to forget his earlier, university, background. Coke was probably drawn to Digby as he had many years earlier been drawn to that other literary personality who figured so prominently in his life, Sir Fulke Greville. Coke, now nearly seventy years old, may also have seen in Digby a reflection of what he himself had once been – a man torn between scholarly pursuits and active political involvement. When the death of his wife drove Digby into solitary contemplation, Coke described him as a man who 'liveth amongst his books', and he expressed the hope that Digby would return to 'the stage of the world' where he could profit from 'a mixture of studies and employments'. Coke did not live to see Digby's return to the public stage during the Interregnum when, versatile and irresistible as ever, he became a friend of Oliver Cromwell while at the same time serving as the Roman Catholic chancellor to Queen Henrietta Maria.[30]

[27] Gardiner, *History of England,* VIII, 89-91; *DNB,* XIII, 556; SP 16/534/115; *Cowper MSS.,* II, 163-4.

[28] Johns, 'The Principal Officers', p. 48.

[29] *Cowper MSS.,* II, 64-5, 90, 92-3, 154; Petersson, *Sir Kenelm Digby,* pp. 102, 109-10; SP 78/99/fol. 135; 78/103/fols. 211, 264; 78/105/fols. 134, 211, 287, 373.

[30] *DNB*, V, 965-9; *Cowper MSS.,* II, 65, 154, 247. Coke MSS., packet 69, Coke to Digby, June or July 1633; packet 81, Coke to son John, 24 Aug. 1634. The first of these two letters is incorrectly assigned to 1639 in *Cowper MSS.,* II, 247.

Coke's final years as a naval administrator are his least edifying; he seems to have grown more quarrelsome and negative. This can be seen in his relations with the commanders of the ship-money fleets. Coke drafted the instructions for the first ship-money fleet in 1635 and soon after rebuked the commander of the fleet, the earl of Lindsey, for his inaction. Lindsey said that Coke 'dipped his pen in vinegar'. Coke had always shown an exaggerated faith in sea power and usually had unrealistically high expectations for the English fleets, but his excoriating letter to Lindsey makes him appear more querulous and ill natured than usual. On the other hand, there are explanations for Coke's behaviour in this instance. He may still have been nursing resentment over the fact that Lindsey had failed in the second attempt to relieve La Rochelle in 1628. One also suspects that Coke generally preferred captains like Sir John Pennington, Sir Henry Mainwaring, and Richard Plumleigh who came from common stock rather than ornamental captains from the nobility. Finally, although Coke reprimanded Lindsey with obvious sincerity, it is also true that he did so 'by his Majesty's direction'.[31] Of a more serious nature was Coke's attitude toward another nobleman, the earl of Northumberland, who in 1636 succeeded Lindsey as commander of the ship-money fleets. Northumberland was a far abler man, indeed the first admiral Charles selected from the nobility who was truly competent.[32] Northumberland was appalled at the state of the navy and set out to do something about it. The abuses he uncovered were for the most part the same that Coke had been battling with since the reign of Elizabeth. Coke should have been Northumberland's natural ally, but there is evidence that instead he resisted the earl's efforts. Again excuses can be found for Coke's behaviour. For example, the evidence of Coke's opposition is meagre, and the argument hinges on extrapolating from only two documented incidents. Furthermore, Northumberland was part of a faction which, as we shall soon see, conspired to oust Coke from office, so some friction between the two men is understandable. Nevertheless, we are left with the sad but apparent fact that Coke, after a lifetime of striving to reform the naval administration, in the end became an obstacle to reform. A clue to his behaviour can be found in a letter written by Lord Conway, son of the former Secretary. Writing to Lord Deputy Wentworth in Ireland, Conway explained:

> Mr. Secretary *Coke* is as ill satisfied with my Lord of Northumberland. . . At Sea he made two Officers, whom the Commissioners of the Admiralty turned out so soon as the Ships

[31] *Cowper MSS.*, II, 104; SP 16/291/58, 59; 16/293/39, 60, 61.

[32] Oppenheim, *Royal Navy*, pp. 237-8.

> came into Harbour; of which Injury he complained to the King at the Council-Table; the Secretary was Champion, and lost the Day. Since my Lord complained of some Abuses in the Admiralty, the other sought to make void the Complaint, but they were very evidently proved.

Conway gives the impression that Coke had grown defensive about the state of the navy and had come to feel a proprietary interest in it. Lord Deputy Wentworth thought this to be the case, too. In his reply to Conway, Wentworth expressed it this way: 'I used to tell Mr. Secretary Coke that the Admiralty is his mistress; nor doth he willingly admit any to come near, so as if the young earl be smackering about her, it is no wonder if the old man grow jealous.'[33]

As the preceding quotation suggests, Wentworth knew Coke well. Indeed, the relationship between Coke and Wentworth is one of the most interesting aspects of the Secretary's work during the 1630s. The friendship between these two men was based on mutual respect and common values. Of course Coke was not exactly Wentworth's equal, but the two men were kindred spirits in their deep regard for honesty, efficiency, and economy. These were the objectives that underlay the policy of 'Thorough' associated with Wentworth and Archbishop Laud, and they were the objectives that Coke pursued on a smaller scale throughout his life. Wentworth's respect for Coke was based on a recognition of this natural affinity. As Wentworth expressed it, Coke was 'a Servant that goes the same Way to my Master's Ends that I do'.[34]

Coke's relationship with Wentworth is amply illustrated in the latter's work as Lord Deputy of Ireland. Coke took a more enlightened view of Ireland than his visceral hatred of Roman Catholicism might lead one to expect. This was best displayed at the very beginning of Wentworth's rule when the question of financing the army in Ireland was raised. The earl of Cork, as Lord Treasurer of Ireland, had argued that the army should be supported entirely through the vigorous collection of recusancy fines. Indeed, he had already begun to follow this course before Wentworth's arrival, to the distress of Irish Catholics who saw it as a poor omen of the new Lord Deputy's

[33] SP 63/256/19; Knowler, *Strafforde's Letters*, II, 45; Arthur Collins, ed., *Letters and Memorials of State* (2 vols., London, 1746), II, 445; HMC, *De L'Isle and Dudley MSS.*, VI, 66; Aylmer, 'Administrative Reform', 237-40; SP 16/338/40. Windebank, trying to ingratiate himself with Northumberland, complained of 'My elder brother, Sec. Coke, not leaving me so much as a younger brother's portion in matters of business wherein I can serve you'. HMC, *Third Report,* appendix, p. 72.

[34] Knowler, *Strafforde's Letters,* I, 87.

régime.[35] Coke sharply differed with the earl of Cork over this policy, arguing that the burden could be borne more easily if spread among Protestants and Catholics alike, that it would attach a stigma of disloyalty to Catholics who were in fact law-abiding subjects, that it would drive the Irish away from conformity in religion, and that, in any case, it was not exactly brilliant to place the financing of the army in the hands of the very people against whom this policy would make it all the more likely that the army would have to be used. But Coke's primary argument against forcing the Catholics to support the army was more statesmanlike and deserves to be quoted:

> [It] would make a rent by forming two professed parties in the kingdom, whereof one should be free, and the other chargeable by an oblique way to raise an army in opinion against itself. This perhaps might be counsellable to the head of a party, but not to a king, who must endure no show of parties, but must govern all as one body, subject to equal justice and equal contributions for all public services.[36]

Coke was in perfect harmony with Wentworth, who successfully overruled the earl of Cork and his faction in Ireland, forcing the abandonment of the recusancy fines and the continuation of a voluntary subsidy instead.[37] After his arrival in Ireland, Wentworth reaffirmed this policy and arranged for the calling of an Irish Parliament to obtain a more permanent source of revenue – all of which Coke pronounced a political 'masterpiece'.[38]

Upon his appointment as Lord Deputy in 1632, Wentworth established certain rules that were approved by the king and Privy Council. One of these was that Wentworth's correspondence would be routinely handled by only one of the Secretaries of State, and this responsibility was assigned to Coke. Another rule was that no grants concerning Ireland should be allowed without Wentworth's prior knowledge and, preferably, approval.[39] Coke's conscientiousness with respect to these two rules would strengthen his bond with Wentworth. As the Lord Deputy prepared to leave for Ireland, he told Coke that it was 'not one of my least Comforts that I shall have the Means to resort to so wise and well affected a Friend to me, as I

[35] *Cowper MSS.*, I, 481, 483.

[36] Coke MSS., packet 51, Coke to the earl of Cork [Dec. 1632].

[37] Aidan Clarke, *The Old English in Ireland 1625-42* (Ithaca, New York, 1966), pp. 65-74.

[38] Knowler, *Strafforde's Letters*, I, 115.

[39] *Ibid.*, I, 65-7.

esteem yourself'.[40] This expectation was justified by subsequent events. Several months after his arrival in Ireland, Wentworth gratefully acknowledged Coke's 'clear and speedy Intelligence' and 'Excellent Dispatch', deeming it his greatest source of comfort in the burdensome office.[41] The following month, when Wentworth successfully managed his first Irish Parliament, he praised Coke's promptness in sending all the necessary papers as an example of 'the great Care and Judgment you shew in his Majesty's Service'.[42] Wentworth also appreciated Coke's fidelity to the rule controlling the flow of Irish grants and favours. On one occasion he wrote approvingly to Coke: 'The Course you hold for receiving of *Irish* Petitions is passing good, and will assuredly free his Majesty and ourselves from infinite Trouble and Vexation, which the breaking of that Rule will bring in upon us all. Therefore for love of God hold it still.'[43] On another occasion, when Coke held up a suit till Wentworth's opinion could be obtained, the Lord Deputy responded: 'I thank you for reserving yourself, till you heard thus much from me. And this I will say, that so long as I stay here, you shall never find me halting in one of these broken Businesses: And, as for Petitions preferred there, in Breach of the Rules already set by his Majesty, I shall so constantly second you, as we shall leave them little Heart.'[44] From England, Archbishop Laud reported to Wentworth that Coke was 'careful of all things that concern you' and 'very honest to you'.[45]

Windebank never succeeded in supplanting Coke in Wentworth's favour, but it was not for lack of trying. As one historian said, Windebank 'pried unceasingly into Irish affairs'.[46] Although Coke had been placed officially in charge of the Irish correspondence, he was also required, as the senior Secretary, to travel with the king whereas Windebank remained in London. Windebank cannot be censured simply for dispatching Irish business when Coke was out of town, but it is instructive to observe how he exploited one such opportunity early in 1634. In this instance, Wentworth, having written to several other persons, scrupulously confided in Coke: 'I have sent you the Duplicates of all my Dispatches to his Majesty and others, as you will find in the Pacquet this Bearer shall bring unto you;

[40]*Ibid.,* I, 87.

[41]*Ibid.,* I, 153. See also p. 133.

[42]*Ibid.*, II, 281.

[43]*Ibid.,* I, 152.

[44]*Ibid.,* I, 249. See also pp. 135, 160.

[45]Laud, *Works,* VII, 383, 486. See also Knowler, *Strafforde's Letters,* I, 271, 299.

[46]C.V. Wedgwood, *Strafford, 1593-1641* (London, 1935), p. 214.

only I desire you will be pleased not to take Notice thereof, unless it be brought unto you by some other Hand.'[47] As it turned out, since Coke was attending the king at Newmarket, these papers were transmitted to Windebank. Of course Windebank was only doing his job when he answered Wentworth's dispatch, but he was doing something else when he insinuated that he himself was chiefly responsible for the obtaining of Wentworth's desires and when he oddly omitted Coke's name from a recently appointed committee for Irish affairs.[48] Nor did Windebank shrink from openly criticizing Coke. Two months later he complained to Wentworth that only Coke knew what the king's pleasure was concerning the Lord Deputy's last communication. 'The main Dispatch, I am sure he hath concealed from me', Windebank said, 'and the rest of the Lords advow they had as little communicated to them, so strait-laced is my elder Brother to the rest for my Sake.'[49] Windebank deserves less sympathy than he is asking for here because, as we shall see, it was he who made a real fetish of secrecy, particularly where Coke was concerned and even after he had clearly gained the upper hand over Coke in foreign affairs. We shall also see that it was typical of Windebank to try to undermine Coke's position by openly criticizing him in this fashion. By contrast, Coke, who is supposed to have had far less tact than Windebank, never, so far as we know, stooped to demean his fellow Secretary in writing. All Windebank's efforts to insinuate his way into Wentworth's confidence met with minimal success at best.[50] Windebank sometimes used his sons to strengthen relations with ambassadors on the Continent, but even this device backfired in Ireland. Windebank was encouraged for a while by the way Wentworth employed one of his sons, but then the son and a friend got themselves into trouble over their choice of female companions in Ireland and had to be sent home.[51]

Although he received little encouragement from the Lord Deputy, Windebank nevertheless did intrude himself repeatedly into the conduct of Irish affairs. Wentworth particularly disapproved of Windebank's greater liberality in the matter of Irish grants. As

[47] Knowler, *Strafforde's Letters*, I, 202.

[48] *Ibid.*, I, 210. This incident was first recounted in Evans, *The Principal Secretary*, p. 98 n. 2. See also SP 16/262/21.

[49] Knowler, *Strafforde's Letters*, I, 256.

[50] I agree with Evans, *The Principal Secretary*, p. 98: Wentworth 'gave Windebank little encouragement in his attempt to obtain the control of Irish matters in the same insidious way as he had obtained that of foreign affairs'. For a quite different interpretation, see Patricia Haskell, 'Sir Francis Windebank and the Personal Rule of Charles I' (unpublished Ph.D. thesis, Southampton University, 1978), pp. 109-14.

[51] Knowler, *Strafforde's Letters*, I, 256; C.V. Wedgwood, *Thomas Wentworth First Earl of Strafford 1593-1641: A Revaluation* (New York, 1962), pp. 204-5.

Windebank gained increasing influence over Irish business at the end of the 1630s, one can plainly see Wentworth's mounting exasperation over this issue. In 1637 Wentworth pleaded with King Charles to scrutinize grants involving Ireland more carefully and to obtain the Lord Deputy's prior approval. It is clear that Wentworth thought ground was being lost, both figuratively and literally, and that Windebank deserved much of the blame. By contrast, said Wentworth: 'I must needs say, I have not seen one of these slip Mr. Secretary Coke, since I served in this Place, for which I value him very much.' Calling for a return to the arrangements that had been agreed upon in 1632, Wentworth advised Charles that 'one good Means it were to a Reformation, if (according as it was settled by your Majesty's Orders in the Time of my Lord *Dorchester*) all the Affairs of *Ireland* were solely put into the Hands of Mr. Secretary *Coke*'. Wentworth wished for this, he said, 'with all my Heart'. If, on the other hand, Charles insisted on letting Windebank continue to deal with Irish business, then Wentworth asked the king to at least instruct Windebank 'to observe your Establishment and Orders, and not thus early to engage and gain your Majesty's assent before he hath first communicated the Business with us'.[52] In 1638 Wentworth protested to Windebank with at least a hint of sarcasm that an order for payment of certain arrears 'however attested by you, yet I am persuaded hath sure been written and procured by some without your Privity, not well informed of these Affairs'.[53] Wentworth repeatedly had to block and try to reverse grants that had already been issued without his approval in England. In 1639 he told Windebank that 'too much is too much' and bemoaned the fact that he was 'forced to respite the Performance of so many Directions sent me under your Hand'. In a final, not-so-subtle gesture of despair, Wentworth sent Windebank a copy of the rules from 1632.[54]

Considering how stingily Wentworth guarded Irish grants, how much he praised Coke for supporting this policy, and how much he blamed Windebank for neglecting it, there is a marvellous irony in the fact that one grant involving 30, 000 acres of Irish land went to Coke. This occurred in 1635, when Charles asked Wentworth to find a suitable reward for Coke's long service to the Crown. Wentworth chose a tract of land near Dublin known as the Vartry which was estimated to be worth about £500 per annum. In fact, however, the recalcitrant Irish and the Civil War prevented Coke from ever

[52]Knowler, *Strafforde's Letters*, II, 83-4. See also SP 16/365/87.

[53]*Ibid*., II, 201.

[54]*Ibid*., II, 293; Wedgwood, *Strafford*, pp. 214-15.

actually taking possession. Coke would probably have been better off accepting Wentworth's offer of £1,000 cash in lieu of the land.[55] Far from protesting over this grant, Wentworth treated it as a reward that Coke genuinely deserved. Reporting his progress on this business to Charles, Wentworth lavishly praised Coke to the king: 'I have not indeed known since my coming to this Government any Thing pass his Hand in breach of the Instructions, or in the least against your Honour or Profit.' This, said Wentworth, was 'the Way of the highest Integrity' and 'the least private Benefit'.[56] There is no hint of insincerity in these words or in the words used by Wentworth in a letter written to Coke at about the same time. Remarking upon 'that uniform sincere Course I have always observed you to trade in', Wentworth vowed to Coke: 'I shall honour you all the Days of my Life.'[57]

There is another, less favourable way of viewing Coke's grant of Irish land: it was his share of the loot. One of Coke's chief occupations during the 1630s was to find additional sources of income for Charles's insolvent government, and Ireland was one of those sources. Coke's major contribution with respect to Ireland was in taking the Londonderry Plantation away from the City of London. It is true that the City's Irish Society had not entirely fulfilled the terms of their contract to establish settlers, buildings, and fortifications in Ireland, but this would probably have been overlooked if the English government had not been so desperate for money.[58] Sir Thomas Phillips, the governor of Coleraine, took the lead in gathering information against the City while Coke promoted the case at court. In August of 1630, Coke studied the 'load of writings' Phillips had provided him with and, after considerable effort, transformed these into a treatise against the City. Coke conceded that 'the Londoners are powerful and diligent and have many advantages', but he predicted that resolute prosecution of the case would break their resistance and bring profit to the Crown.[59] Coke used his treatise as much as possible to turn opinion against the Londoners. The best example of this tactic comes from Sir William Jones, who reported to

[55] *Cowper MSS.*, II, 111, 124, 132-3, 152, 155-7, 171, 246-7, 253, 286, 295. SP 63/256/18.

[56] Knowler, *Strafforde's Letters,* I, 492.

[57] *Ibid.,* I, 494.

[58] Robert Ashton, *The City and the Court 1603-1643* (Cambridge, 1979). pp. 158-60; Valerie Pearl, *London and the Outbreak of the Puritan Revolution: City Government and National Politics, 1625-43* (Oxford, 1961), p. 81; Richard Bagwell, *Ireland Under the Stuarts and During the Interregnum* (3 vols., London, 1909), I, 252-4.

[59] SP 16/172/72, 74; *Cowper MSS.,* III, 149.

Coke in October of 1630: 'I have, according to your honour's directions, diligently read and perused the treatise concerning the Londoners' Plantation in Ulster exquisitely and with great judgment compiled by your honour. I can add nothing thereunto; neither (as I think) can any man else.'[60] Jones was a judge of the Court of Star Chamber, where the case against the Londoners was pending. Jones's testimony is similar to that of a serjeant-at-law who argued against the City's Irish Plantation in a related case in the Court of Exchequer and who told Coke some years later that he had been 'directed and instructed in it by that painful and learned collection of yours in which you discovered the root and growth and proceedings of all their fraud, and made that most public which they by multiplying deceits had made most obscure and perplexed'.[61] While legal proceedings dragged on, a royal commission was sent to Ireland in 1631-2 to gather more information against the City. Phillips was again at the head of this effort, and Coke did all he could to assist him.[62] Phillips took Coke's treatise with him to Ireland and reported that it had converted many people to the king's side.[63] Much more time was spun out while the City and the government tried to make a deal whereby the City would be left in possession of its Irish lands in return for a cash payment. At the end of 1634, however, Coke observed that the king had at last taken the business to heart and 'howsoever this Service hath been coldly followed hitherto, I know not for what Respects, yet now it is carried on by his Majesty's own Resolution, and will come to a speedy, and, I hope, a good End'.[64] The case was now prosecuted in the Star Chamber and judgment delivered against the City in February of 1635. The City was ordered to surrender its Irish lands and pay a fine of £70,000, out of which Sir Thomas Phillips was supposed to get £5,000. There is no evidence, however, that Phillips received anything when the City finally did relinquish its lands in 1637 and paid a reduced fine of £12,000.[65]

The Londonderry Plantation was not the only asset of the City that the government coveted in the 1630s. In fact, the settlement of 1637 embraced and laid to rest several other disputes between the City and the Crown. Foremost of these was a charge that the City had

[60]Coke MSS., packet 33, Jones to Coke, 14 Oct. 1630.

[61]*Cowper MSS.,* II, 92.

[62]SP 16/197/7, 16/239/58; *Cowper MSS.,* I, 450-1, 454, 466.

[63]*Calendar of the State Papers Relating to Ireland*, ed. Robert Pentland Mahaffy (8 vols., London, 1900-10), I, 631, 643.

[64]Knowler, *Strafforde's Letters*, I, 340, 415; *Cowper MSS.,* II, 73.

[65]Pearl, *London,* pp. 82-7; *Cowper MSS.,* II, 99.

cheated the Crown and creditors in the way it disposed of royal land consigned to the City to cover loans it had raised for the Crown between 1617 and 1628. This charge was investigated by a royal commission in 1632, and a complaint was lodged against the City in the Court of Exchequer. The City was not as blameless in this case as it had been in the case of the Irish lands, but again it is doubtful whether the Crown would have been as aggressive in its prosecution if it had not needed the money so badly.[66] There is no proof that Coke played as prominent or leading a role in this case as he had with respect to the Irish lands, though of course his official position necessarily involved him in the business. As early as December 1629, Coke had obtained information against the City.[67] Later, when Lord Treasurer Portland reported on this subject to the committee for trade on 3 March 1631, Coke took careful notes, as he did again five days later when Attorney General Heath outlined the case against the City.[68] The only other evidence linking Coke to this business is a set of comments he wrote, apparently in response to the City's defence of its actions when it was being investigated by the royal commission in 1632. From these comments it is obvious that Coke assumed the same hostile and self-righteous attitude against the City on this subject as he had on the subject of the Irish lands, but there is no way of knowing what influence, if any, he had in this instance.[69]

An issue that was not resolved by the settlement of 1637 was the Crown's efforts to regulate building in the environs of London. Here, too, altruistic motives were probably not as strong as mercenary motives; and here, too, Coke played at least a marginal role. In November 1633, he drafted a long order from the Privy Council authorizing the commissioners for buildings to investigate irregularities in past building practices, prosecute violators in the Star Chamber, and curtail the licensing of new buildings. This order, which was approved by the king and Council, also suggested that the City should entertain the idea of incorporating new suburbs into the City by increasing the number of wards – a prospect that frightened the City aldermen because of its social and political implications. The Crown later proceeded to incorporate the suburbs without the City's co-

[66] Pearl, *London*, pp. 81-6; Ashton, *The Crown and the Money Market 1603-1640* (Oxford, 1960), pp. 142-53; Ashton, *The City and the Court,* pp. 160-1; Ashton, *The English Civil War* (London, 1978), p. 93.

[67] *Cowper MSS.,* I, 394-5.

[68] SP 16/186/21, 58.

[69] SP 16/220/65.

operation, and the legal wrangling over this issue continued until the Civil War.[70]

The Crown's harrassment, intimidation, and outright exploitation of the City for economic gain during the 1630s had the effect of alienating municipal authorities who would otherwise have had a natural affinity for the Crown. This was just as true of commercial interests in the City who in many cases comprised the same abused individuals.[71] An example of Coke's role in this comes from the records of the East India Company. Coke had already shown no compunction in extorting £10,000 from the Company back in 1624, and his other services to the Company were of dubious value, particularly the unsuccessful effort to get some retribution from the Dutch for the Amboyna massacre. One thing Coke had done on behalf of the Company was to support their request to manufacture gunpowder in 1625. The urgent requirements of war seemed to justify a relaxation of the gunpowder monopoly enjoyed by John Evelyn, but with the return of peace in the 1630s, Coke was again thinking about how to restore the monopoly and wring some profit from it. What he had in mind was apparently no more than renewing the contract that had been worked out with Evelyn after the abortive ordnance reform in 1620: the king would pay eight pence per pound for his own powder, surplus powder would be sold to the public at ten pence per pound, and the extra two pence per pound profit would go to the king.[72] The gunpowder monopoly was a genuine asset in a necessary commodity, and it was reasonable to expect it to be profitable. Coke's plan was a modest one that would at least defray the king's own expenses for powder and perhaps even yield a small annual profit; and the price the public was expected to pay was not exorbitant. Meanwhile, though, Evelyn had to be freed from the competition of the East India Company. Coke notified the Company near the end of 1630 that they were expected to cease their production of gunpowder, but they showed no eagerness to comply. Two years later the Company was required to appear before the Privy Council, and a nasty scene ensued when Coke and Lord Treasurer Portland accused them of reneging on a promise to cease their operations. This meeting ended with the understanding that the Company would get out of the gunpowder business, but Evelyn was not a clear winner.[73] In 1636, when

[70] *CSPD*, 1633-1634, p. 285; Ashton, *The City and the Court,* pp. 165-71.

[71] This is the central argument of Ashton's *The City and the Court*. See also his *The English Civil War,* pp. 92-7.

[72] SP 16/180/10.

[73] Court minute books, XII, 96; XIII, 61, 135.

Evelyn's last contract with the Crown expired, the monopoly was transferred to the men who had been running the mills of the East India Company. Unfortunately, there is no indication of what role, if any, Coke played in establishing this new monopoly. It would certainly be interesting to know if he had a hand in determining the new arrangement because it was radically different from any he had ever contemplated with Evelyn. Under the new arrangement, the king actually paid slightly less for his own powder, but the price to the public jumped to eighteen pence per pound. This is an excellent example of Charles's short-sighted pursuit of profit in the 1630s. Between 1636 and 1639 he sold 240,000 pounds of powder annually, reaping an annual profit of £10,500. But when war with Scotland broke out, he did not have the powder he needed to wage war; and when the Long Parliament met, the victims of his price-gouging were quick to abolish the monopoly.[74]

More important than the East India Company's right to make gunpowder was its basic monopoly of trade with the East, and the Crown actually infringed even this monopoly in the 1630s by supporting a rival company associated with Sir William Courteen. It was not Coke, however, but Windebank who knew what was going on in this case and obstructed the Company's protests, not least because he had a free £1,000 share in the Courteen company.[75]

The foregoing examples reinforce the view that if Charles had any underlying policy at all in the 1630s, it was a simple one: to raise by any means imaginable the revenue he needed to subsist without Parliament. Of course this policy left victims in its wake, and none more fascinating than Philip Burlamachi. Burlamachi had lent stupendous sums to Charles's government during the war years, and he disbursed even larger sums out of his own pocket to meet the Crown's obligations. While the war lasted, the Crown had a vested interest in maintaining Burlamachi's credit, but in 1633 his debts caught up with him, and the Crown did little to save him from bankruptcy. Coke was most unsympathetic to Burlamachi's plight. When Burlamachi pressed the Crown to honour its obligations to him in 1636, Coke wrote strongly worded letters to Archbishop Laud and Lord Treasurer Juxon to persuade them not to accept Burlamachi's accounts. Coke argued that those accounts were not based on 'legal and regular

[74]H.E. Malden, ed., *The Victoria County History of the Counties of England: Surrey* (London, 1905), II, 317-21; *Cowper MSS.*, II, 128; *CSPD*, 1637-1638, p. 96; 1639-1640, p. 340.

[75]*Calendar of the Court Minutes of the East India Company, 1635-1679*, ed. Ethel Bruce Sainsbury (11 vols., Oxford, 1907-38), I, xv-xix, 124, 231, 236-7, 295.

warrants' and accepting them would 'bring confusion into the revenue of the Crown'. Technically, of course, Coke was right, and his position in this case is consistent with his lifelong crusade for regular, responsible, verifiable financial records. But practically speaking there was no way that Burlamachi could have obtained legal warrants in advance for all his disbursements – just as there had been no way for Sir Fulke Greville and Coke always to get such authorization in advance when they were disbursing money for the Crown in Elizabeth's navy. In Burlamachi's case we see accentuated, then, the characteristics that appear in many of Coke's transactions in the 1630s: his sanctimonious identification with the financial interests of the Crown and his deadly earnestness where money was concerned.[76]

Coke's attitude toward Burlamachi is all the more unpardonable in view of the way he sedulously looked after his own financial interests. The fact is that public office made Coke a rich man – or, to phrase it more critically, Coke used public office to make himself rich. This wealth did not accrue from Coke's salary. The annual salary he received as a Secretary of State was the same he had received as a Master of Requests, only £100. Judged on the basis of salary alone, Coke's £300 allowance as chief commissioner of the navy, which he received until the commission was disbanded in 1628, was more impressive. It was not the salary but other allowances, fees, and gratuities that made the Secretaryship so lucrative. The single biggest allowance was £700 annually 'for intelligence and other secret services'. The next biggest allowance was the 'diet', a provision of ten dishes of food for the Secretary and his assistants, which by Coke's time was commuted into a cash payment of 'board wages'. These amounted to £577 annually. Of course a sizeable portion of the intelligence money and the board wages would have been spent for their allotted purposes, but there is no doubt that an appreciable balance remained for the Secretary's profit. Dividends and fees were another source of profit. Each Secretary received a share of the fees from the Signet Office and from two departments of the Chancery, the pettibag and hanaper, which were channelled through the Signet Office. The value of these dividends fluctuated wildly. In one year, for example, they amounted to £127 for each Secretary and in another they amounted to £265. Another fee was customarily paid to the Secretary for obtaining the king's signature. This varied from a standard £5 to as much as £40 for wealthy clients. In his earlier capacity as Master of Requests, Coke

[76] *Cowper MSS.*, II, 126-8, 131; Robert Ashton, 'The Disbursing Official Under the Early Stuarts: The Cases of Sir William Russell and Philip Burlamachi', *Bulletin of the Institute of Historical Research*, 30 (Nov. 1957), 167-73.

had already become acquainted with this fee and the many other kinds of inducements and rewards enjoyed by a man located so advantageously close to the king. For example, Coke's relationship with the East India Company continued to be a profitable one. On several occasions they paid him the routine £5 for the king's signature, they gave him an annual New Year's present of £55, and one year they 'ordered that Mr. Secretary Coke should have a proportion of spice over and above his present in gold, in respect of the many extraordinary good offices he hath done the Company'. It has been estimated that a Secretary's gratuities and fees amounted to at least £2,800 annually. Adding up all the foregoing sources of revenue and making deductions for the necessary expenses of the office, it seems reasonable to accept the traditional assumption that the net annual income of a Secretary of State must have been at least £2,000.[77]

Land was another source of income for Coke and another measure of his wealth. In 1628, when he sold Hall Court, the home he had shared with Marie prior to his regaining office, its purchase price was £3,000 and its annual rents were calculated to be £200.[78] By this time, however, Coke had already embarked on the acquisition of a new estate costing seven times as much as Hall Court and yielding at least seven times as much in annual rents. Coke wasted no time investing the profits of office. Less than six months after his appointment as Secretary, he purchased the manor of Baggrave in Leicestershire. The price, he told Sir Fulke Greville, 'will not be less than £8,000'.[79] Baggrave was not, however, the centrepiece of Coke's estate. In 1628 he purchased the manor of Melbourne in Derbyshire not far from his ancestral home of Trusley. Melbourne, which cost £6,600, was Coke's country home.[80] He set out to remodel the hall at Melbourne, drawing the plans and giving detailed instructions to the

[77] *Cowper MSS.*, I, 373, 397, 403, 463; Coke MSS., packet 32, Coke to Marmaduke Darrell, 7 March 1629. Coke's dividends from the Signet Office are recorded monthly in the PRO Signet Office docquet books. The sums I have calculated are from Index 6,807 and 6,808 for the years 1626 and 1628. East India Company court minute books, VIII, 353; X, 202; XI, 227; XIII, 144-5; XVII, 109, 122-3. Evans, *The Principal Secretary,* pp. 208-11; Aylmer, *The King's Servants,* pp. 205, 221.

[78] PRO, CP 43/180/membrane 18r. The purchaser was Dr. Samuel Fell, Lady Margaret professor of divinity and later dean of Christ Church, Oxford. *Cowper MSS.,* I, 374; *DNB*, VI, 1,162-3.

[79] *Cowper MSS.,* I, 231, 233-5; Coke MSS., packet 46, Coke to Greville, 6 Dec. 1625; PRO, Index 6,807 (Feb. 1626).

[80] *Cowper MSS.,* I, v, 339, 340, 354-5, 361. According to the editors of the *Cowper MSS.,* Coke bought a lease for three lives for Melbourne. At the bottom of Coke's account for Melbourne for the year 1628, including payments to the seller, Sir Francis Needham, Coke added, 'All since cleared as the acquittances show for the whole sum of £6,600.' Melbourne Hall muniments room.

carpenters, plasterers, glaziers, and other workers engaged in the task. He even directed the workers to salvage all the wood, brick, stone, lead and other building materials from dismantled parts of the old building to be used in constructing the new portions. Similarly, the major building material, stone, was taken from the nearby dilapidated castle. Coke's typical thoroughness and frugality are evident in this project, but there is also at least a hint that Melbourne represented the fulfillment of a dream for Coke, the younger son returning in triumph to his native county.[81] Between 1628 and 1634, Coke employed two different stewards. He meticulously examined their accounts and was not entirely satisfied with their work. In 1634, Coke's son, John, began to handle some of these financial affairs. In 1635 he settled permanently at Melbourne and assumed full responsibility for the stewardship of all his father's lands.[82] Melbourne was not the last of Coke's purchases. Near the beginning of 1631, he bought Overhaddon and the Wynlands in Derbyshire, paying apparently £4,424.[83] About 1634 he bought the manor of Donnington on the border between Derbyshire and Leicestershire for more than £1,400.[84] These were the principal lands owned by Coke, although there were also other smaller parcels. Adding the purchase prices of these major lands together, we arrive at a total of £20,424. This may not be a perfectly accurate figure, but it is very close to another valuation arrived at by other means. In 1655, Coke's royalist son, Thomas, had to pay a fine on the lands he had inherited. The fine was £2,200 and was supposed to be one-tenth the value of his estate. Thus his estate was valued at £22,000, which made him one of the richest men in Derbyshire.[85] It is therefore reasonably accurate to conclude that by the time Coke left office he had accumulated lands worth at least £20,000. Furthermore,

[81] Melbourne Hall muniments room. This information is taken from a folder of papers relating to the remodelling of Melbourne which was apparently compiled by taking papers from various packets of the Coke MSS. The major item in the folder is a thirty-two-page book of instructions by Coke dated 20 Nov. 1629.

[82] Coke's stewards were first Francis Astley and then a cousin, Henry Condey, who proved particularly unsatisfactory. Coke was writing to his son about business matters in the spring and summer of 1634. Accounts for Melbourne, 1628-33, in the muniments room; accounts and letters in the folder described in the preceding note; Coke MSS., packet 81, Coke to son John, 4 June 1635; Coke, *The Last Elizabethan*, pp. 170-3.

[83] Melbourne muniments room. Coke noted that his offer of £2,400 for the Wynlands was accepted and his offer of £1,400 for Overhaddon was under consideration. Coke also appears to have paid at least £624 to buy the reversions to additional Overhaddon leases. *Cowper MSS.*, I, 418.

[84] *Cowper MSS.*, II, 245.

[85] J. Charles Cox, 'Proceedings of the Derbyshire Committee for Compounding, and other Commonwealth Papers', *Journal of the Derbyshire Archaeological and Natural History Society,* 13 (1891), 144.

during the 1630s, Coke made additional cash outlays of at least £9,000 in the form of dowries for his three daughters from his first marriage.[86] Of course Coke's land, unlike these dowries, was a source of profit as well as expense. By piecing together the surviving financial accounts in the muniments room at Melbourne, we can say with reasonable certainty that Coke had an annual income from rents alone amounting to at least £1,500.[87]

In summary, then, Coke derived at least £2,000 from the Secretaryship and by the mid-1630s a further £1,500 from rents each year, giving him a total annual income of at least £3,500. This was no mean accomplishment for a man who had begun life with an annuity of less than £7. Two comparisons may help to put Coke's wealth in perspective. First consider the labourers who hauled stone from the ruined castle to Coke's home at Melbourne. Each of these men was paid eight pence per day and worked six days a week.[88] If one of these workers had been fortunate enough to find steady employment of this sort for fifty weeks of the year, then his annual income would have been £10 as compared to Coke's £3,500. In other words, Coke enjoyed an income at least 350 times as great as the income of the labourer who hauled stone for him at Melbourne. In fact, the labourer would have worked all year long to earn an amount which Coke could obtain simply by procuring the king's signature twice at the standard rate of £5 per signature. Indeed, when Coke procured the king's signature for a particularly wealthy client, he might be paid four times the labourer's annual wages in just one transaction. Second consider the sailors who returned from Cadiz in the winter of 1625-6. These wretched creatures, sick, starving, clothed in rags, returned to

[86]Coke MSS., packet 81, Coke to son John, 27 Feb. 1634; packet 83, Coke to son John, 20 Jan. 1637. Melbourne muniments room, Melbourne folder, Coke to son John, 23 May 1634. Trusley, Fane transcripts, Coke to son John, 10 Nov. 1636, 28 Jan. 1637, 12 Oct. 1637. Coke paid dowries of £3,000 each for Mary and Anne. The Fane transcripts at Trusley indicate he may have paid £3,500 for Elizabeth's dowry, which was a poor bargain because her husband lived only a few months. He died near the end of 1637, not 1633 as usually indicated.

[87]In various accounts, the rents from Melbourne are between £474 and £487, for Baggrave between £584 and £640, for Overhaddon and the Wynlands £369 which was increased to £435 by raising rents about the year 1636, for Donnington between £43 and £59. The rents for Melbourne are often given as near £535, but £45 of this had to be paid to the bishop of Carlisle, leaving a net of about £490. I regret not being able to give more specific citations for these papers. When I examined them in 1968-9, they were scattered chaotically around the muniments room. They have subsequently been sorted and placed in boxes which should make the work of future researchers easier and allow for more specific citations.

[88]This amount is specified in Francis Astley's accounts for 1629 located in the Melbourne folder in the muniments room. This was a common wage for summer work. At other times of the year the wage was commonly one penny per day less. Godfrey Davies, *The Early Stuarts 1603-1660*, 2nd ed. (Oxford, 1959), p. 296.

discover that in most cases they could not even hope to be paid for their suffering. Yet Coke at this very same time was paying £8,000 for Baggrave. And in the summer of 1628, while Coke worked at Portsmouth among men whose distress he himself compassionately recorded, he was paying £6,600 for Melbourne. Of course Coke cannot be personally blamed for the fact that he lived in a society marked by great disparities in wealth, and Parliament could be blamed just as easily as Coke and the other royal ministers for the desperate condition of the nation's fighting men. Still, there is something at least unseemly about Coke's huge land purchases during the war years. And, although there is no evidence that Coke was ever the least bit dishonest, neither is there any reason to doubt Clarendon's accusation that 'his most eminent infirmity [was] covetousness'.[89]

[89] *History of the Rebellion,* I, 81. Sir William Monson charged Coke with selling naval offices. But Monson's charge is unique, and there is no supporting evidence. Oppenheim, *Naval Tracts of Sir William Monson,* III, 366-7; IV, 138-40.

14

FOREIGN AFFAIRS IN THE 1630s

Sir Francis Windebank's rivalry with Coke is conspicuous in the foreign affairs of the period; evidence of that rivalry will be demonstrated in dealings with one country after another. Before turning to individual instances, however, it is important to have a general understanding of what was going on. When Windebank was appointed junior Secretary in June of 1632, Coke had already been a Secretary of State for seven years. During those seven years, foreign relations had never been shared between the two Secretaries. First Conway and then Dorchester had possessed nearly exclusive control of the foreign correspondence. Indeed, the chief authority on the Secretary's office has stated that 'during the Coke-Dorchester partnership there may almost be said to have been in existence a home office and a foreign office'.[1] When Dorchester died, Charles placed foreign affairs in Coke's hands. At the beginning of the correspondence between Coke and the English ambassador in Paris, for example, Coke referred to 'the charge committed unto me by his Majesty of his foreign affairs'.[2] This fact should be borne in mind as well as the fact that Coke was the sole Secretary for four months before Windebank's appointment. Coke did not expect to relinquish his sole control over the foreign correspondence when Windebank was appointed. It was not part of his experience for the Secretaries to share this correspondence. As he viewed it, he had inherited the exclusive charge of foreign affairs that had previously been Conway's and Dorchester's. The month following Windebank's appointment, when Jerome Weston was sent on a mission to the Continent, Coke wrote his instructions, including a passage directing him to 'make your dispatches from time to time to our Secretary who hath charge of foreign affairs'.[3] Nor was this just Coke's peculiar view of the situation. As late as January of 1634, the English agent in Paris explained that 'since my lord of Dorchester's death, I have made all my addresses to Mr. Secretary Coke, his successor (as I did conceive) in the sole direction of foreign affairs'.[4] Furthermore, the Secretaries together received an allowance of £1,400 annually to pay for foreign intelligence. When Windebank

[1] Evans, *The Principal Secretary*, p. 91.

[2] SP 78/91/fol. 121. See also SP 78/91/fols. 120, 122, 142; 16/222/11, 43; 16/231/62.

[3] SP 78/91/fols. 395, 405.

[4] SP 78/95/fol. 3.

was appointed, he obtained a privy seal for half this amount, but Lord Treasurer Weston believed that Coke deserved the full £1,400 to himself because he alone had charge of the foreign correspondence, and King Charles is said to have agreed.[5]

Officially, Coke retained this responsibility throughout the 1630s. He wrote the instructions for English ambassadors when they went abroad, he wrote countless letters to them after they arrived in foreign parts, and he received countless replies. He also presented the reports of ambassadors to the foreign committee of the Privy Council. Because Coke handled all this foreign correspondence, he was said to have charge of foreign affairs. We might say he 'conducted' foreign affairs. But he did not personally engage in foreign negotiations or shape foreign policy except through his membership of the foreign committee. After Coke resigned in 1640, responsibility for the foreign correspondence was divided between his successor and Windebank. The northern European, mostly Protestant, countries were assigned to Coke's successor and the southern European, mostly Catholic, countries were assigned to Windebank. This division was a formalization of what had developed quite unofficially in the preceding years. Charles could have officially divided the foreign correspondence between Coke and Windebank in the 1630s, but he did not choose to act so decisively and openly.

How and why, then, did Windebank intrude into Coke's conduct of foreign affairs, especially where Catholic countries were concerned? He did so partly for personal reasons. Correspondence with England's agents abroad seemed a source of status and influence. Windebank was a jealous and insecure man who, as we shall see, repeatedly implored and intimidated ambassadors to write to him. Because Coke had official charge of the foreign correspondence, secrecy was the only means by which Windebank could intrude into this realm, but there is also an unmistakable impression that Windebank genuinely delighted in secrecy. More important, though, was the simple fact that Charles chose to use Windebank this way. Charles used Windebank, Portland, and Cottington to conduct secret negotiations with Spain at the end of 1633. After this initiation, Windebank continued to engage in secret negotiations for the king. Throughout the 1630s, then, there were usually two sets of negotiations afoot: official ones conducted with the knowledge of all members of the foreign committee, and secret ones conducted in the early 1630s by Charles, Windebank, Portland, and Cottington, and in the later 1630s by just Charles and Windebank.

[5] *Cowper MSS.*, I, 463. Evans, *The Principal Secretary*, p. 213. It is not clear what the final disposition was.

Obviously the secret negotiators had the upper hand because they always knew about both sets of negotiations. By contrast, Coke and the other members of the foreign committee could only guess what Charles and his confidants were up to. This made a sham of the foreign committee, reduced Coke to the level of a paper-shuffler, and elevated Windebank to a position of special trust.

Why did Charles choose to operate in this fashion? It appears that he was forced into double-dealing by the existence of two competing groups at his court. The first group was the triumvirate of Cottington, Windebank, and, till his death in 1635, Portland. Historians used to assume this triumvirate could be described unhesitatingly as a pro-Spanish, Catholic faction. More recent authors, while not denying the Catholic sympathies of these men, have made them seem more moderate and pragmatic. They are portrayed not as active advocates of Catholicism and Spain but rather men who, because of their personal convictions, were better able and more willing than Charles's other councillors to explore friendlier relations with Spain if it was in England's interests to do so.[6] Charles's remaining councillors, including Coke, can be divided several different ways. For our purposes here, however, most of them can be crudely lumped together in a second group that was Protestant, hostile to Spain, and simply distrustful of the first group. The problem would appear to lie, then, not with Charles but with these divided councillors through whom he had to work. And the problem was caused not so much by Portland, Cottington, and Windebank, who would deal with anyone, as by Coke and the others who were too implacably opposed to Spain to deal reasonably with her. If Charles wished to explore all his diplomatic options, then presumably he had to operate behind the backs of the 'Protestant' group.

This interpretation may be true, but in Coke's case at least, it requires several qualifications. First, despite his deep-seated hostility, we shall see that Coke understood the strategic arguments in favour of negotiating with Spain. Granted that Coke would not have been the right man to involve in those negotiations, it is not clear that they positively had to be conducted behind his back. The fact that Charles chose to do so does not prove that he had no other choice. Secondly, let us not forget that all these men were above all else political animals. Religion was important to them, to be sure, but so was political power. Coke had shown under Buckingham that he would support his patron in practically any policy, even including the attempted Spanish match, that was necessary to retain his place at court. Likewise, Windebank

[6] Alexander, *Charles I's Lord Treasurer,* pp. 29-30, 183, 215-16; Havran, *Caroline Courtier,* p. 77; Haskell, 'Windebank', chapter 8.

was said by a contemporary to be 'so meane and fearfull, that he will not moue any Thing that shall be distastefull' to the king.[7] No matter how great the religious division among Charles's councillors, a less devious and more competent king might have forced them to cooperate in a common foreign policy or risk loss of office. Finally one must consider what would have happened if Charles had ever succeeded in his secret negotiations. Success would have made it necessary to transform secret negotiations into public, probably military action. Then Charles would have had to choose between informing the full Privy Council of what was going on or continuing to keep most of them in the dark through even greater subterfuge. We shall see that Charles faced such a choice in 1634 when he nearly allied with Spain against the United Provinces, and the course he chose on that occasion was to trick his Council into supporting him. Having made a bargain behind the back of his own Privy Council, Charles now had to trick his Council into honouring his part of the bargain. He was trapped in his own web of lies because he could not deal honestly with his Council at this point without revealing his deceit at earlier points.[8] For all these reasons, it is arguable that Charles both could and should have operated above board from the start.

On must beware of undue moralizing. Duplicity is a part, perhaps a necessary part, of diplomacy. Certainly it was commonplace in the seventeenth century; the foreign ministers Charles dealt with were hardly paragons of honesty, and they were happy to mislead him as much as he misled them. Charles's duplicity is questionable on purely pragmatic grounds, however. Abroad it is traditionally assumed to have undermined his reputation and credibility while gaining him nothing of consequence.[9] That is perhaps too facile a judgment, and will have to be reconsidered at the end of this chapter. For the moment, we are more concerned with the consequences of Charles's duplicity at home, and here the consequences are less debatable. One could conceivably argue that Charles was balancing competing factions at his court, but it seems more obvious that what he actually did was to exacerbate factionalism where he could have fostered cooperation, had deviousness not been so deeply ingrained in his

[7]Arthur Collins, ed., *Letters and Memorials of State* (2 vols., London, 1746), II, 615.

[8]Gardiner, *History of England,* VII, 367-8.

[9]J.R. Jones, *Britain and Europe in the Seventeenth Century* (New York, 1967), p. 22. See also his 'English Attitudes to Europe in the Seventeenth Century' in J.S. Bromley and E.M. Kossman, eds., *Britain and the Netherlands in Europe and Asia* (London, 1968), pp. 37-41.

nature. Certainly where Coke and Windebank were concerned, any chance that might have existed for the two men to function as partners was destroyed by the way in which Charles chose to employ Windebank.[10]

Coke's role in foreign affairs, his relations with English ambassadors on the Continent, and Windebank's ubiquitous competition can best be viewed from three vantage points. First is the Protestant United Provinces where Coke was left largely in charge and the ambassador, Sir William Boswell, proved a steadfast friend. Second is Catholic Spain and its tributary, Flanders, where Coke was kept largely in the dark and the English ambassadors treated him with a plain civility that barely disguised their contempt. Third is the far more complicated case of France where jealousies and machinations abounded and no one clearly gained the upper hand. We shall view the conduct of foreign affairs from each of these three vantage points and then draw some general conclusions. In all three places, our account makes more use of primary sources than is usually the case on this subject. This is particularly true of the foreign state papers in the Public Record Office, which are the fundamental primary source for the foreign affairs of Charles I but have tended to be neglected, probably because, unlike the domestic state papers, no printed calendar exists to guide the historian through them.

Coke was still the sole Secretary of State in March of 1632 when Boswell was sent to the Hague as ambassador to the United Provinces.[11] During his initial two and a half years there, Boswell wrote occasionally to Portland, Cottington, and Windebank, but the overwhelming majority of the letters in which he conducted the actual business of his office were directed to Coke. On two occasions when he did write to Windebank, Boswell scrupulously explained to Coke why he had done so and what he had said.[12] Windebank resented this exclusion and protested to Boswell in September of 1634 that he would respond 'whensoever you shall call upon me, which the sooner and more frequently you shall do by your letters, the more you shall concur with other his Majesty's ministers in foreign parts from whom I hear often'.[13] The following month Windebank wrote again to Boswell, this time adopting his most confidential tone and invoking the name of the king: 'His majesty hath commanded me to let you know a secret which

[10]Compare Evans, *The Principal Secretary,* pp. 92-5.

[11]For Coke's view of the Dutch, see SP 84/144/fol. 165; 84/147/fol. 222.

[12]SP 84/147/fols. 184-5; 84/148/fol. 43.

[13]SP 84/148/fol. 201.

you are to intimate to her Majesty [the queen of Bohemia] only and to none other upon your allegiance.' The secret Windebank imparted was that the king of Spain had suspended military action in the Palatinate as a way of demonstrating that he respected England and was willing to act as mediator with the Emperor. Windebank also announced that he would send Boswell a cypher because he might 'have like occasion hereafter to convey his Majesty's secret commandments to you'.[14] Windebank must have been sorely disappointed with the results of this overture. Boswell, obviously unimpressed, replied that as far as the secret was concerned, the queen of Bohemia 'had heard [it] about a month before'. And as for Spain mediating on her behalf with the Emperor, Boswell blankly replied, she did not trust Spaniards.[15] Through the balance of 1634 and beginning of 1635, Windebank made no further headway with Boswell. The king did authorize Windebank to deal exclusively with Boswell for redeeming the crown jewels that had been pawned in Holland during the war years. But Boswell continued to hold Windebank at arm's length, writing to him only about this particular business and keeping Coke informed of when and why he did write to him.[16] Windebank's avid desire to establish independent communication with Boswell was not based on any official need because he would have been routinely apprised of Boswell's activities at the meetings of the foreign committee.

Windebank's next opportunity to insinuate himself into Boswell's confidence came when Portland died in March of 1635. Windebank informed Boswell that the king had entrusted him with Portland's cypher. In June, Boswell thanked Windebank for this information and promised to use the cypher 'according to your Honour's directions as may be requisite', but he apparently did not find it very requisite.[17] By the beginning of 1636, Windebank was so exasperated that he scolded Boswell: 'You must give me leave to expostulate (not to quarrel) with you in a friendly manner that I have not had the happiness until these your last letters to receive any one word of advertisement from you since May last except in June or July somewhat concerning this business of the jewels. Whence this strange reservedness proceeds I understand not.' Windebank told Boswell that he was not 'ambitious of any man's correspondence' but was concerned only about 'the king's service and your good'. Besides, he added, 'there is not any of his Majesty's ministers in foreign parts (and some of their faces I

[14] SP 84/148/fol. 230.

[15] SP 84/148/fol. 274.

[16] SP 84/149/fols. 85, 89, 91, 150, 197.

[17] SP 84/149/fol. 256.

never saw) but holds fairer correspondence with me than you'.[18] It is interesting to compare this letter with one Windebank wrote only three months earlier to King Charles. In this Windebank explained why he had refrained from communicating certain advertisements out of France to the foreign committee: 'I perceived that Mr. Secretary Coke had not received the ordinary advice of that week, and I doubted, if I had produced them at the Committee, he might have been jealous, that your Ministers in foreign parts, held a straiter correspondence with me than him.' Windebank told Charles that such jealousy would be 'most unfit' because 'into whatsoever hand it fall, your Majesty's service is still the same'.[19] If Windebank truly believed these last words, then why did he repeatedly pester Boswell for closer correspondence? And who, indeed, actually exhibited signs of jealousy? And, finally, who in this incident is shown overty representing himself to the king as a more valuable servant and denigrating his colleague?

Through the remainder of 1636, Boswell continued to write infrequently to Windebank and to inform Coke when he did so.[20] Boswell's pronounced preference for Coke was probably based on religious sympathies but may also have had a more personal basis. Coke had known Boswell at least since 1623, and he often signed his letters to Boswell as 'old friend', not a closing that he commonly used. Boswell may also have been alluding to a more long-standing relationship when he told Coke in April of 1636: 'I have ever had access unto your Honour's wisdom for direction of the most important actions of my life; and it [is]. . . an effect of your Honour's love and mediation (for so I take it) that his Grace[Laud] vouchsafes me such affection and countenance.'[21] Nevertheless, during Coke's last three years as Secretary, Windebank was finally able to gain some of Boswell's attention if not affection. The vast bulk of his correspondence during this period still went to Coke, but letters to and from Windebank are also more evident. The chief subject of correspondence between Windebank and Boswell was a plan to sell fishing licences to the Dutch. This matter, unlike the earlier matter of the crown jewels which had also been entrusted to Windebank, was kept a complete secret from Coke. As Windebank explained in his initial letter to

[18] SP 84/151/fol. 1.

[19] Edward Hyde, earl of Clarendon, *State Papers Collected by Edward, Earl of Clarendon, Commencing from the Year 1621* (3 vols., Oxford, 1767), II, 214, hereafter referred to as *Clarendon State Papers*. Florence Evans said that Windebank wrote this letter with 'forced humility'. *The Principal Secretary,* p. 95 n. 3.

[20] SP 84/151/fols. 15, 221, 243.

[21] SP 92/14/fols. 145-6; 84/151/fol. 160; *Cowper MSS.,* I, 149.

Boswell on the subject: 'This you are by his Majesty's special commandment to carry with great secrecy and dexterity, and to give account to myself only of your proceeding from time to time herein.' The business of the fishing licences involved a third party, Balthasar Gerbier, the English agent at Brussels. Windebank instructed Boswell to 'hold a straight and most secret intelligence with Gerbier in this business'.[22] In fact it was the business of the fishing licences that initiated Windebank's own 'straight and most secret intelligence' with Gerbier.

Windebank established the sort of privileged relationship with Gerbier in Flanders that he was never able to achieve with Boswell in the United Provinces. From this, the second vantage point of Flanders and Spain, we see the extent to which Coke was disregarded and kept ignorant of the clandestine negotiations of the period. By the summer of 1638, Windebank and Gerbier were engaged in a piece of highly secret diplomacy. They had entered into talks in Flanders with the Princess Phalzburg who had put herself forward as a mediator, trying to strike a deal between England, Spain, and the Empire.[23] This fact had to be kept highly confidential because Charles had practically concluded a treaty with France and Sweden. He did not want these two nations to learn that he was simultaneously dealing behind their backs with the enemy. Coke knew nothing about the Windebank-Gerbier-Princess Phalzburg talks. On 5 August 1638, Gerbier wrote to Windebank that 'Princess Phalzburg was again hard at me I should make a step to England'. The princess wanted Gerbier to speak personally with Charles about her proposals. Gerbier explaind that if Charles agreed to his visiting England some pretext would have to be invented to forestall rumours and speculation about the true nature of his visit. One person in particular who had to be put off the scent was Coke. Gerbier proposed a way to fool Coke, and he gave Windebank two letters addressed to Coke containing a wholly spurious explanation for his visit. If the king approved of this duplicity, then Windebank was to give Coke these false letters. On 13 August, Windebank replied to Gerbier that 'for your coming hither his Majesty is very well contented, and I will send your letters . . . to be transmitted to Mr. Secretary Coke according to your desire'. On 14 August, Coke received them. On 17 August he discussed them with the king, who had to pretend of course that he was unacquainted with their contents and that he took them at their face value. After this meeting Coke

[22] SP 84/152/fols. 9, 108-10.

[23] Gardiner, *History of England*, VIII, 375-7; Henri Lonchay and Joseph Cuvelier, eds., *Correspondance de la cour d'Espagne sur les affaires des Pays-Bas au XVII siècle* (6 vols., Brussels, 1923-37), III, 238-9.

reported to Gerbier that the king 'hath commanded me to signify unto you his approbation of your speedy coming over'. Obviously Charles had played his role well. Following Gerbier's plan, he and Windebank had easily duped Coke.[24]

Two months later these secret negotiations provided another illustration of Coke's markedly inferior position. The Spanish resident in England, Alonso de Cardenas, wrote a letter in which he referred to these clandestine talks and alleged that actual treaty negotiations would follow in Flanders. Unfortunately for Cardenas and for Charles, this letter was intercepted and published on the Continent. When Coke received a copy, he showed it to the king, who of course was outraged. Charles had no choice but to indignantly deny the details of Cardenas's letter and hope that its central premise regarding negotiations with the Habsburgs would not be believed. Again Charles played his part well. As Coke reported it, Charles 'commanded me and my brother Secretary to send for Cardenas and demand of him whether he would avow the contents of such a letter as written by him'. Of course Cardenas disavowed the letter, but he was ordered to produce his original draft, and Charles found grounds for disapproval in it. Coke and Windebank were instructed to summon Cardenas again, to rebuke him, and to banish him temporarily from court. How much this was a charade and how far Charles and Windebank could participate in good conscience is admittedly open to question. Windebank told Gerbier that Cardenas's allegations could be denied without having to lie because 'you know there is no direct treaty at all between His Majesty and them, and that all that has been done hath been by way of proposition moving from that side and managed by second hands, His Majesty neither appearing nor being engaged nor obliged to anything'. It is true that there was no 'direct treaty' and that Charles conducted the talks through 'second hands', but it is not surprising that Windebank had to explain this hair-splitting distinction to Gerbier. After all, only two months earlier Gerbier had arranged to visit England at Princess Phalzburg's insistence to discuss her overtures with Charles. Unlike these other participants, Coke did not have to wrestle with his conscience because he was blithely ignorant of the kernel of truth in Cardenas's allegations. Coke was confident that 'any treaty remitted to Flanders with his Majesty's consent' was 'a fiction . . . without any truth or ground'. Seeing 'how clearly his Majesty hath proceeded with his man', Coke concluded that 'all his

[24] SP 77/28/fols. 442-3, 450, 472, 479, 481. I am grateful to Caroline Hibbard for these references. See also SP 16/397/59.

Majesty's friends may be fully assured of his real and royal intentions, and how free he is from treating underhand'.[25]

The Cardenas affair could not be so easily laid to rest, however. The treaty still pending with the French was obviously jeopardized by Cardenas's letter and the flurry of rumours it fostered. French confidence in Charles, which must never have been very high, plunged even lower. The French ambassador in England demanded reassurance that Cardenas's allegations were unfounded. Charles therefore arranged for another scene to be acted out, or as Coke described it: 'This moved his Majesty to call us his Secretaries and to require us to testify whether any admission of such a treaty at Brussels *or any other with the house of Austria,* had passed by our pens or knowledge since the treaty begun with France.'[26] Coke and Windebank naturally denied any knowledge of such dealings, but only in Coke's case was this the absolute truth. For further reassurance, Coke instructed the English ambassador in France to demand an audience to deny the existence of the alleged negotiations on 'the word of a king'. Unless Coke was a consummate dissembler, he honestly believed that Charles was free from 'treating underhand' and that his word was as good as 'the word of a king'. One could hardly imagine a better demonstration of Coke's appalling gullibility and his pathetically misplaced trust.

Obviously Coke lost substantial ground to Windebank in the late 1630s. In the case of Spain, however, Windebank had been the dominant Secretary almost from the start. As already mentioned, near the beginning of 1634 Windebank had the privilege of being included with Portland and Cottington in highly secret negotiations with the Spanish ambassador, Juan de Necolalde, in London.[27] One does not have to believe that Portland, Cottington, and Windebank were secret supporters of Catholicism and Spain to see that they were at least more interested in dealing with Spain than most other Privy Councillors, particularly Coke. Certainly no love was lost between Coke and Necolalde. In August of 1634, for example, when Necolalde wished to travel outside London, he asked Windebank for a passport 'to avoid occasion of suspicion; especially at Plymouth, in case I should light amongst some Holland Puritans, who instantly

[25] SP 84/154/fol. 255; Gardiner, *History of England*, VIII, 377-8, 378 n. 1. See also Coke's report of this incident to the earl of Leicester in Collins, *Letters and Memorials,* II, 574.

[26] SP 78/106/fol. 418. Italics mine. Charles himself revised some of the wording in this letter from Coke to the earl of Leicester. See also SP 78/108/fol. 19; *CSPV*, 1636-1639, pp. 489, 541, 553.

[27] *Clarendon State Papers,* I, 236, 243, 297; Gardiner, *History of England,* VII, 349-52.

would be ready to . . . deliver me into the hands of Coke, and he cry, Away with him to Martin [judge of the Admiralty Court]'.[28] Necolalde deserved a vacation at this time because he seemed well on his way to enlisting English naval power on the side of Spain. So long as Charles was absolutely determined to avoid being drawn into a land war, the only thing he could offer a potential ally was naval assistance. The Spanish were sorely in need of such assistance to protect their own forces and especially Flanders from the pincer-grip of the Dutch and French. An argument can be made that it was in the best interests of England to prevent the Dutch and French from overwhelming Flanders and dividing the west coast of Europe between themselves, even if this meant allying with Spain.[29] Apart from Portland, Cottington, and Windebank, however, Charles did not expect his Council to embrace this strategy willingly. What happened in the summer of 1634, therefore, was that Charles found it necessary to produce the fleet that he was holding out as bait for a Spanish treaty, but he shrank from telling his Privy Councillors that this fleet would be partially financed by Spanish money and chiefly used to protect Spain's hold on Flanders. After it was determined that ship money could be raised for support of the fleet, all that remained was to persuade the Privy Council that a fleet was necessary, but on grounds other than the true ones. To use S.R. Gardiner's word, Charles decided that the Council had to be 'hoodwinked', and again in Gardiner's words, 'No better instrument for this work of concealment could be found than Secretary Coke'.[30] Charles told Coke to persuade the Council that a fleet was necessary, and Coke carried out the task without the slightest suspicion that he was being made a fool of for the purpose of fooling others.

Coke's speech to the Council on 8 June 1634 bears an eerie resemblance to his speeches in Parliament during the previous decade on behalf of the war fleets. The argument Coke employed in his 8 June speech was that 'our ancient reputation and respect is not only cried down, but we submit ourselves to wrongs and indignities in all places, which are not to be endured'. Coke painted a picture of English humiliation from Constantinople and Russia in the east, throughout the Mediterranean, to England's own coastal waters where the Spanish, French, and Dutch showed no respect for English sea power. He advised Charles and the Council to 'consider of some speedy and powerful means to redeem us from this contumely and

[28]*Clarendon State Papers,* I, 235-6; *CSPV*, 1636-1639, p. 186.

[29]The best defence of Charles on this basis is Haskell's 'Windebank', chapter 6.

[30]Gardiner, *History of England,* VII, 356-7.

contempt'. Coke was indignant at the conduct of the Dutch, 'of whom as we have deserved best, so we suffer most', but his paramount concern was Spain. Summarizing the insolencies of the Spanish, he invoked the observation of Arthur Hopton, the English agent in Madrid, who said that 'you can expect no redress till you do it yourself by commanding your ships to drive them all from hence'. And in his parting exhortation to the Council, Coke returned to 'Mr. Hopton's good advice: That there is no hope left of obtaining justice but by doing it yourself'.[31] Coke had begun his speech by declaring that it was the duty of a Secretary 'to represent to his Majesty the truth in all affairs, how distasteful soever', but one can only imagine how surprising the real truth would have been to Coke if he had known that the secret object of this first ship-money fleet was to assist rather than chastise the Spanish.

The treaty with Spain was never concluded, and the English navy did not enter hostilities on the Spanish side. But the navy did give some protection to Spanish shipping, and the treaty negotiations meanwhile led to Windebank's control of the Spanish correspondence. In February of 1634, Windebank informed Hopton:

> I have now no more to add, but, by particular commandment from his Majesty to tell you, that this particular business, concerning Spain, he only communicates to my Lord Treasurer, Lord Cottington, and myself; and therefore you must be careful to preserve it in this secrecy, and to address your answers and despatches hereupon only to myself.[32]

Thereafter a system of dual dispatches was followed. Hopton continued to write his routine dispatches of 'general occurrences' to Coke, reserving matters of more consequence for his secret correspondence with Windebank.[33] When Lord Aston joined Hopton as ambassador at Madrid in 1635, he too wrote dual dispatches. Windebank again received the news of note, and Coke received pages of gossip, sometimes of the most frivolous sort.[34] One kind of business that Hopton and Aston did carry on with Coke related to the complaints of English merchants; indeed both men wearied of the endless complaints Coke forwarded to them.[35] How easily these dual

[31] SP 16/269/51. Hopton used similar words in a letter to Cottington. *Clarendon State Papers*, I, 171.

[32] *Clarendon State Papers*, I, 144, 150.

[33] *Ibid.,* I, 156, 197, 284, 309.

[34] *Ibid.,* II, 338-41, 443-50, 453-6; III, 328-32, 419-25.

[35] *Ibid.,* II, 111, 117, 389-90, 393; III, 88-9.

dispatches could generate jealousy and anxiety is revealed in a small misfortune that Aston encountered. He found that his letters to Coke had been sent on one ship and his letters to Windebank on another, so that it was entirely possible that Coke would receive his first. Aston worriedly apologized to Windebank 'lest, the one arriving before the other, the error of the merchant may be thought a neglect in me', and he arranged to avert this problem in the future.[36] On another, rare, occasion the shoe was on the other foot when Coke sent Aston a letter from the Prince Elector Palatine to be delivered to the king of Spain. Coke gave not the slightest hint regarding the letter's contents. This placed Aston in an awkward position, having to deliver the letter at the Spanish court, not knowing even if its contents were hostile or cordial. He complained to both Coke and Windebank about this treatment, and his complaint was a valid one.[37] Yet Aston was hardly in a position to pontificate about the horrors of secrecy while he and Windebank were keeping Coke thoroughly in the dark. Viewed thus, what looks like a piece of ineptitude on Coke's part could in fact have been a calculated act of petty revenge.

At about the same time as Aston went to Madrid, John Taylor was dispatched to Vienna. The adventures of Taylor and the disappointing mission of the earl of Arundel which followed lie outside the subject of this book, but it is appropriate to characterize very briefly Coke's role in these relations with the Holy Roman Empire. In general, Coke was not excluded from diplomacy with the Empire to the extent that he was with Spain. This is particularly true of the earl of Arundel's mission which was unusually above board. There is some scant evidence that Windebank may have wished to keep Arundel's mission more confidential, and the earl was somewhat friendlier toward Windebank than Coke, but Coke was fully engaged in the correspondence and aware of how the negotiations were proceeding.[38] On the other hand, where Taylor was concerned, the pattern was much more similar to Spain. Coke was involved at the outset, writing in fact five drafts of Taylor's instructions.[39] But Windebank soon enjoyed that sort of 'straight intelligence' with Taylor that he sought from all English agents abroad. In January of 1636, Windebank admonished Taylor: 'You must not forget to write more frequently to Mr. Secretary Coke; and especially if you have anything good, you may

[36] *Ibid.*, II, 443-4.

[37] *Ibid.*, III, 295, 297.

[38] *Ibid.*, III, 133, 221, 255; SP 80/9/fols. 105-14, 201-2, 207.

[39] SP 80/9/fols. 34-46; 16/294/65; 16/295/76.

communicate it to him; otherwise you are to keep your distance; and the most secret you are still to impart to myself only.'[40]

From our final vantage point, France, one can observe not only the familiar sparring between Coke and Windebank but also the larger network of alliances and rivalries that made the English court in the 1630s a house divided against itself. Coke had never possessed exclusive control over the correspondence with the English agents in France. The typescript lists of this correspondence (in the Public Record Office in London) seem to indicate that the English agents in France wrote almost exclusively to Coke, but these lists are wrong. Examination of the actual letters reveals that the two agents in France, René Augier and Henry de Vic, wrote joint dispatches to Coke, but both agents also wrote separately to Lord Treasurer Portland from 1633 till his death in 1635.[41] The fact that the agents in France wrote separately to Portland is a tribute to the Lord Treasurer's power, which included incidentally the power to see that England's agents abroad received their pay. Portland must have wanted this direct communication with the agents in France, but he was content to receive little more than copies of the official reports they sent to Coke. Windebank, by contrast, sought a closer alliance with one of the two agents. He established communication with de Vic in Paris only a few weeks before he did the same with Hopton in Madrid. Apparently Windebank was in an expansionist mood at the beginning of 1634. In the case of France, he had no secret mission to warrant his intrusion, but his importuning was persuasive. De Vic explained that he had been writing to Coke because it was Coke who sent him his instructions and who he thought had charge of foreign affairs. Now, he told Windebank: 'I am very sorry to have been wanting in anything your Honour may have expected from me, which had I known sooner, you had not stayed until now to have received that satisfaction which I will endeavour to give you hereafter.'[42] The following month, de Vic sent Windebank a cypher in order to communicate 'with more freedom and secrecy'.[43] In autumn 1634 Windebank, with Portland's assistance, cemented this relationship by procuring a reversion for de Vic to the Secretaryship of the French tongue. Windebank also helped de Vic avoid being recalled to England to discharge the duties of this new post in person. De Vic

[40] *Clarendon State Papers*, II, 381. See also pp. 327-30.

[41] SP 78/vols. 94-6. This analysis is based on the endorsements and occasional internal evidence (for example, SP 78/94/fols. 158, 304, 363).

[42] SP 78/95/fol. 3.

[43] SP 78/95/fols. 83-4.

thanked Windebank for 'preserving me the place whereof you had formerly procured me the reversion', and told him to 'make account of me as of one that is wholly yours'.[44] Meanwhile the other agent in Paris, Augier, drifted closer to Coke. From 1634 until Coke's dismissal in 1640, the rivalry between Coke and Windebank in England was mirrored in France by the rivalry between Augier and de Vic.

The plot thickened at the beginning of 1635 when it was decided to send an ambassador to France in the person of Viscount Scudamore. Coke officially notified Scudamore of his appointment, but Windebank's letter of congratulation promptly arrived the same day. Scudamore's personal reply to Windebank shows that they formed a close association from the outset.[45] Furthermore, when it came to deciding which of the two agents Scudamore should retain at the Paris embassy – Augier or de Vic – Coke naturally recommended the former and Windebank the latter. Scudamore accepted Windebank's offer of de Vic's services, saying: 'I take great contentment in knowing him to be such unto you as you style him . . . we may thus fasten presently together.'[46] One week later Scudamore declined Coke's offer of Augier's services.[47] When Scudamore arrived in Paris, he quickly allied with de Vic. Somehow, though, a stalemate had been reached because he also had a written order from Coke to continue Augier's employment.[48] Of course this did not prevent Scudamore from favouring de Vic and excluding Augier as much as possible. From June 1635 until May 1636, the cosy triumvirate of Windebank, Scudamore, and de Vic prevailed.[49] They relegated Augier to the sidelines and even concocted a plan for his total elimination.[50] When it seemed that the plan had been accomplished, Scudamore told Windebank: 'I am glad Augier is recalled. Your Honour hath done his Majesty good service therein.'[51] Even as Scudamore wrote these

[44] SP 78/96/fol. 252. See also fols. 108, 163, 226, 236-9, 252, 256, 258, 260, 302, 309, 311-12, 460.

[45] SP 78/97/fol. 24.

[46] SP 78/97/fol. 67.

[47] SP 78/97/fol. 99.

[48] SP 78/98/fols. 278-9.

[49] Scudamore wrote confidential letters to Windebank and routinely sent him copies of all his official dispatches to Coke. De Vic made a new cypher and also kept writing weekly to Windebank. See, for example, SP 78/98/fols. 124, 223, 245, 269-71, 293; 78/99/fols. 18-19, 38, 115, 135, 223, 245, 287; 78/100/fols. 37, 197.

[50] SP 78/99/fols. 89, 191-2, 276.

[51] SP 78/102/fols. 109-10. See also SP 78/101/fols. 236, 393.

congratulatory words, however, the more perceptive de Vic sensed that something had gone terribly wrong with the plan.[52]

What upset the plan to eliminate Augier was the dispatch to France of an ambassador extraordinary, the earl of Leicester, who was expected to be a more successful negotiator than Scudamore had been. The close, conspiratorial relationship that had existed during the preceding year between Windebank, Scudamore, and de Vic was abruptly jolted by Leicester's arrival in France in May 1636.[53] Leicester had specific orders from Coke to retain Augier, for whom he quickly developed a decided personal preference of his own.[54] De Vic observed that the new ambassador 'puts more trust, as far as I can see, in my colleague'.[55] He also noted that Augier was sending reports to Coke under the earl's cover.[56] Leicester himself described Augier as 'the most usefull Servant to his Majestye in this Countrye, of those that I have seen here'.[57] Windebank, by contrast, told King Charles that 'if Augier stay there, the chief stirrer of these differences, as I have been informed, will be continued, to the great discouragement and disadvantage of the Lord Scudamore'. Meanwhile, the foreign committee of the Privy Council considered the issue and reached the same stalemate in 1636 as had been reached in 1635: both Augier and de Vic were retained.[58]

In autumn 1636, then, it might seem that there were two opposing factions: on the one side Windebank, Scudamore, and de Vic; on the other Coke, Leicester, and Augier. One might also assume that the tables were now completely turned, with the latter faction having displaced the former in importance. There is some truth in this. Leicester was decidedly cool toward Windebank, Scudamore, and de Vic. He could hardly find words adequate to express his disgust for Scudamore. He told Coke that Scudamore 'is thought here to betray all that he knows unto the enemies of the Cause, to which I am confident you wish well, and so little the Lord Scudamore is esteemed here that it will be a great wonder if he spoil not his Majesty's service

[52] SP 78/101/fol. 334.

[53] For a good discussion of Leicester's embassy, see the 'Introduction' to the HMC, *De L'Isle and Dudley MSS.*, VI, xix-xxix.

[54] Collins, *Letters and Memorials,* II, 397, 405, 457-8.

[55] SP 78/101/fols. 232-3.

[56] SP 78/101/fol. 139.

[57] Collins, *Letters and Memorials,* II, 459.

[58] *Clarendon State Papers,* III, 291-2.

as far as he hath to do with it'.[59] In a letter to a confidant, Leicester called Scudamore a 'ridiculous Creature' who was pompous, conceited, inept, ineffectual, and spoke French 'as if he had learn'd it in *Herefordshire*, and would shew by that his good Breeding'.[60] Scudamore was now excluded from much of the embassy's business. He frequently protested to Windebank, complaining on one occasion that: 'My lord of Leicester continues in his wonted coldness and silence, so that I know from him little or nothing of any business whatsoever.'[61]

Despite these distinct divisions, there were other factors that militated against Coke, Leicester, and Augier ever becoming a tight-knit faction to the complete exclusion of Windebank, Scudamore, and de Vic. In the first place, King Charles was persuaded that the rivalry between Leicester and Scudamore was too acrimonious to be tolerated. Leicester received a command written in the king's own hand requiring him to communicate all his proceedings to Scudamore. Leicester surmised that the king had been put up to this by Windebank. As he explained to his brother-in-law, Henry Percy, the king's order had come 'enclosed in a Letter of Secretary *Windibanks*, by which you may imagine how this is come to pass. For I received not one line from *Cooke*, who gave me my Instructions, and who I beleeve knows not of this'.[62] On several other occasions, Coke did admonish both Leicester and Scudamore to cooperate, and, although he was carrying out instructions from the king, he seems to have been sincere.[63] This brings us, however, to another reason why Coke, Leicester, and Augier did not form an exclusive, tight-knit faction: Coke never developed the sort of close relationship with Leicester that Windebank enjoyed with Scudamore. Coke seems to have started out on good terms with Leicester, but he soon did several things that seriously damaged his relationship with the earl. In particular, Coke held up payment of Leicester's allowance and accused him of deviating from his instructions, a charge that Leicester vigorously and convincingly refuted.[64] Why was Coke so uncharitable toward

[59] SP 78/103/fol. 191. See also SP 78/101/fols. 137-8; 78/102/fol. 74; Collins, *Letters and Memorials,* II, 389, 490.

[60] Collins, *Letters and Memorials,* II, 387.

[61] SP 78/103/fols. 3, 361-4. See also SP 78/102/fols. 242, 254; 78/103/fols. 11, 53.

[62] Collins, *Letters and Memorials*, II, 387; SP 78/101/fol. 109.

[63] Collins, *Letters and Memorials,* II, 422-4, 503-4; SP 78/101/fols. 99-100, 307; 78/103/fols. 131, 419-20; 78/104/fol. 15; 16/337/71.

[64] SP 78/101/fol. 271. Collins, *Letters and Memorials*, II, 426, 428, 429, 432-6, 439-41, 448-50, 456. HMC, *De L'Isle and Dudley MSS.,* VI, 48, 51, 53-4. 57, 59, 65, 118.

Leicester? The earl's brother-in-law, Henry Percy, attributed it to Coke's quarrelsome temperament. Percy said that Coke's complaint was 'as malitious, as he is old'.[65] The countess of Leicester thought her husband had offended the 'old man' by criticizing him. She told Leicester that Coke was 'extreamlie malisious to you wich I beleeve you did not expect, but it seemes you have writen sumething of his obscure directions wich did displease him'.[66] The countess also mentioned another possibilitity: that Coke considered Leicester's financial demands exorbitant, an explanation that finds some support in the evidence on that subject. There may also have been an element of class tension. Coke may have resented a man like Leicester who by blood and marriage was part of the old nobility, who did not see how he could be expected to live in Paris on an allowance of only £400 per month, and who looked down his nose at people who spoke French as if they had learned it in Herefordshire, where Coke had lived for nearly twenty years.

Finally, to get at the root of the tension between Coke and Leicester and to understand generally what was going on between the Secretaries of State in England and the embassy in France during these years, one has to look at the larger nexus of relationships at the English court. Leicester was intimately related to a powerful faction that had coalesced around Queen Henrietta Maria. Leaders of that faction included the earl of Holland, the earl of Northumberland, and Henry Percy. The first of these was an avid supporter of Leicester and the other two were his brothers-in-law. Nor should the countess of Leicester be overlooked. She did everything in her power to link her husband's fortunes to these men and to enlist the aid of her sister, the countess of Carlisle, who was another confidante of the queen.[67] For his own part, Leicester professed himself the queen's 'slave'.[68] Now where did Coke fit into this scheme of things? Coke was alienated from this faction in numerous ways, including his views on war and government, his social class, even his age and personality. Henrietta Maria has been described as 'a gay and flirtatious woman' in her twenties who was attracted to men who were dashing, handsome, and young. Coke, in his seventies, hardly filled this bill. Moreover, the queen's friends tended to be peers and wealthy gentry, men who played at court politics as if it were a game they deserved to win by

[65] Collins, *Letters and Memorials,* II, 453-4.

[66] *HMC*, De L'Isle and Dudley MSS., VI, 67.

[67] Collins, *Letters and Memorials*, II, 387, 456, 463-4, 495, 506-9, 514, 516, 523, 539, 591, 597, 611, 618, 626, 629, 631, 634, 636; HMC, *De L'Isle and Dudley MSS.*, VI, 59-60, 62-4, 71, 85, 88, 92, 94, 106, 156, 192, 204, 211.

[68] Collins, *Letters and Memorials,* II, 387.

virtue of their breeding and their wealth. Her enemies, on the other hand, were usually the duller men of meaner birth who worked hard to make Charles's government as strong, solvent, and efficient as possible. Coke clearly belonged to the latter group, as did his two chief supporters, Wentworth and Laud.[69]

Laud was a pivotal figure in this network of relationships. Just as Leicester referred to himself as the queen's slave, so did the countess of Leicester refer to Coke as Laud's slave.[70] This in itself tended to put Leicester and Coke on opposite sides of the fence. Furthermore, Laud was a warm supporter of Scudamore.[71] When Scudamore was slighted by Leicester, he appealed to the archbishop for help.[72] The countess of Leicester reported that Laud resented the earl both for his criticisms of Scudamore and for his friendship with the earl of Holland, another member of the queen's faction.[73] This resentment was probably passed on from Laud to Coke. Indeed, on the issue of Leicester's allowance, Coke and another ally of Laud, Lord Treasurer Juxon, obstructed it while the earl of Holland was foremost in advancing it. Even Coke's accusation that Leicester deviated from his instructions fits this analysis because the queen's faction favoured war in alliance with France, and what Coke objected to was precisely that Leicester seemed too eager to engage England in war.[74]

And how did Windebank fit into this scheme of things? For a while he fitted no better than Coke. He was associated not only with Scudamore but also with a policy of friendship towards Spain which naturally estranged him from the queen's pro-French faction. But when the treaty with France failed to materialize as quickly as had been hoped and when Leicester's friends surveyed the court for additional supporters, Windebank began to seem more acceptable. In August 1637, Henry Percy advised Leicester to enlist Windebank as an ally.[75] Leicester, who only two months earlier had apologized to

[69]R.M. Smuts, 'The Puritan Followers of Henrietta Maria in the 1630s', *English Historical Review,* 93 (1978), 27, 31, 44. For Holland see Barbara Donagan, 'A Courtier's Progress: Greed and Consistency in the Life of the Earl of Holland', *The Historical Journal*, 19 (1976), 317-20, 342.

[70]HMC, *De L'Isle and Dudley MSS.,* VI, 77.

[71]SP 78/100/fol. 323; 78/101/fols. 161-2; 78/103/fols. 3, 11, 131, 264; 78/104/fols. 15, 49; HMC, *De L'Isle and Dudley MSS.,* VI, 83; Trevor-Roper, *Archbishop Laud*, pp. 62-3, 214-15, 375.

[72]SP 78/101/fol. 100.

[73]Collins, *Letters and Memorials,* II, 454, 463-4, 629; HMC, *De L'Isle and Dudley MSS.,* VI, 74, 157.

[74]Collins, *Letters and Memorials*, II, 432-6, 439-41, 448-50.

[75]*Ibid.,* II, 509. See also p. 507.

Windebank for writing so infrequently, now followed Percy's advice at least half-heartedly.[76] Of course the official correspondence between London and Paris regarding the treaty negotiations continued to be Coke's responsibility, but from this time onward Windebank and Leicester corresponded on other matters, which, if not more important, were more secret. One item of particular secrecy was a proposal for the Queen Mother to return to France. On this subject, Windebank told Leicester, the king 'commandes me to give your Lordship Order, not to communicat this Businesse to Mr. Secretary *Coke*, nor to give him the least Touch of it in any of your Letters'.[77] Some weeks later Leicester assured Windebank: 'For Secrecy, Diligence, and Fidelity, I will engage myself unto your Honour.'[78] During 1638, through Windebank's mediation, Leicester wrote letters to Charles and Henrietta Maria on their secret businesses.[79] There is evidence that Windebank still encountered some reticence on the earl's part. At the beginning of 1639, when Scudamore was recalled from Paris, Windebank thanked Leicester for 'honouring me with the acceptance of a particular straight intelligence', but in his draft he referred to this as 'a more particular straight intelligence than heretofore'.[80] Perhaps, then, Leicester never confided in Windebank quite as much as the Secretary would have liked.[81] Nevertheless, it is obvious that Leicester knew Windebank was impressively close to the king and queen, and he acted accordingly from 1637 to 1640. By contrast, Leicester's regard for Coke sank to the point of ridicule.[82]

The foregoing survey of foreign affairs in the 1630s amply illustrates two things: Charles's penchant for secrecy and double-dealing and, closely related to this, Windebank's active competition with Coke for control of the foreign correspondence. But was there a larger picture? Did Charles have any underlying foreign policy?[83] And, if so, what did Coke think of it?

[76] SP 78/103/fol. 341; Collins, *Letters and Memorials*, II, 511.

[77] Collins, *Letters and Memorials,* II, 517. See also SP 78/104/fols. 344-5, 374.

[78] Collins, *Letters and Memorials,* II, 524.

[79] *Ibid.,* II, 548-52, 558-9, 570-3, 579-81, 584-5, 596-7; HMC, *De L'Isle and Dudley MSS.,* VI, 143-9.

[80] SP 16/537/6. The calendar incorrectly assigns this letters to 1637.

[81] Religion was surely a point of difference between the two men. By early 1639 Leicester was growing wary of Catholic influence at the English court. Caroline Hibbard, *Charles I and the Popish Plot* (Chapel Hill, 1983), pp. 233-4.

[82] Collins, *Letters and Memorials*, II, 553-4.

[83] My interpretation of this subject is quite traditional. For a radical reinterpretation see Patricia Haskell's 'Windebank'.

The key to England's foreign policy and to Coke's view of it can be summarized in one word: peace. Despite the fact that Charles engaged in a bewildering series of treaty negotiations, he always shrank from outright war. What Charles was really looking for in his negotiations was not so much an ally as someone else who would do his fighting for him. And on this point, Coke and Charles were in agreement. As Coke phrased it when he wrote the foreign committee's report to Charles regarding certain French proposals in 1638: 'We think it not fit that your Majesty should be tied by them to assist your own nephew which your Majesty should rather require at their hands.'[84] The idea that England could persuade someone else to fight in her stead was unrealistic, even ludicrous, but it did tend to keep England at peace.

Of course the balance of power, especially between France and Spain, threatened to draw England into war. Coke knew, for example, that England should not allow France and the United Provinces to take Flanders away from Spain.[85] Where Flanders was concerned, he said, England had 'better reason to maintain the Spaniards there than to let the French in'.[86] Coke also knew that England was in an enviable bargaining position. In the beginning at least, she could negotiate with all parties on the Continent, playing one side off against the other in order to extract the best possible conditions. England's only concern, said Coke, was the restitution of the Palatinate, and 'for other quarrels or differences, as we are friends to all sides and enemies to none, so we will not tie ourselves to any neutrality which may hinder us from treating with any party that shall offer best conditions . . . we keeping the freedom and advantage to join with the best party, and till that shall appear, to keep both sides in suspense'.[87] In 1634 Coke observed that France wanted to negotiate with England, but 'if they shall insist upon unfitting conditions, the king of Spain was forward to draw his Majesty to their side, and the balance in probability may produce good effects'.[88] Similarly, in 1636 Coke instructed the earl of Arundel not to leave Vienna but to 'temporize' because the spectre of an Anglo-Imperial alliance might persuade the French to conclude on better terms.[89] This strategy could boomerang, however. In 1635, for example, Coke noted that France's temporizing with England put

[84] SP 78/99/fols. 40-1.

[85] SP 78/93/fols. 61-3.

[86] SP 78/92/fols. 207-8.

[87] SP 84/149/fols. 234-5.

[88] SP 84/148/fol. 229.

[89] SP 80/10/fol. 207.

France in a better bargaining position with Spain and the Empire.[90] In other words, the spectre of an Anglo-French alliance could benefit France more than it did England. More fatal to this strategy, however, was the fact that it could not be carried on indefinitely without losing effect. Eventually both Spain and France seriously doubted whether Charles would ally with anyone. They kept trying to lure him into the war, but it became increasingly apparent that the best they could hope for was England's continued neutrality.

Charles flirted dangerously with war, but he was unwilling or unable to pay the cost of admission. England's negotiators went to the Continent with only the haziest notion of what Charles was willing to offer England's prospective allies. Although Coke wrote voluminous instructions for these negotiators, they repeatedly expressed puzzlement as to what they were supposed to negotiate for and with. Lord Aston, the ambassador to Spain, admitted: 'I never have clearly understood what his Majesty for the present would be contented to accept of for satisfaction from Spain, nor what content to return them.'[91] The countess of Leicester was afraid that her husband would offend Charles because he was uncertain what Charles wanted him to do.[92] Sir Thomas Roe at Hamburg was afraid the Swedes would discover that he did not know what he was authorized to offer them.[93] This uncertainty arose not from the ambiguity of Coke's instructions but from the ambivalence of the king's intentions. Charles wanted to affect the outcome of the war and yet avoid war. What he wanted, in short, was to get something for nothing. The French finally pushed Charles to the point of paying for some mercenary soldiers, but this was hardly worth bargaining for even if Charles had been able to keep up the payments. The English navy was Charles's one great asset, and the Spaniards particularly wanted to enlist it on their side. But Charles largely disappointed them, most dramatically in 1639 when he abandoned the Spanish fleet in the Downs to a devastating attack by the Dutch.[94]

[90]SP 78/99/fol. 343.

[91]Edward Hyde, earl of Clarendon, *State Papers Collected by Edward, Earl of Clarendon, Commencing from the Year 1621*, quarto ed. (3 vols., Oxford, 1767-86), II, 2-3.

[92]HMC, *De L'Isle and Dudley MSS.*, VI, 101. See also Collins, *Letters and Memorials*, II, 417.

[93]Berkshire Record Office, Trumbull MSS., XX, no. 1.

[94]For Coke's view of the concessions made to the French, see SP 78/106/fol. 419; 84/152/fols. 15-16, 245; 84/154/fols. 254-5. Gardiner, *History of England,* IX, 58-69.

Charles resisted making the sort of concrete commitment that his prospective allies expected from him. Writing from Paris, the earl of Leicester tried to explain to Coke what Charles had to do. The French leaders, said Leicester, were not children 'and therefore will not be fedd with Shadowes, nor pleased with Babyes'. If England expected France to do anything, the earl explained, 'you must help them, or be assured they will doe nothing'. Driving his point home, Leicester observed that 'among the chief Statesmen here, there is very little Beleefe, that we will do any Thing'. What Leicester said was true, but so was Coke's reply:

> You say the *French* are no Children, to be frightened with Shadows, or pleased with Babies; for such you wil esteeme all the Offers we make unto them. But, my Lord, wee must on the other Side consider, not so much what pleaseth them, as what is fit for us to do in Reguard of our Interests . . . and uppon serious Consideration therof, I presume your Lordship would not advise me, to step one Foote forwarder then wee have donne.

Leicester would be doing his nation a great service, said Coke, 'if you can shew wherin wee may further complie without imbroiling our Estate, and drawing the Burden of the Warre uppon our selus'.[95]

Whether it was prudence or, more likely, poverty that kept Charles out of war, the benefits of peace were immeasurable. Apart from the savings in human life, neutrality conferred decided economic advantages on England. Perhaps most well-known of the commercial advantages was the arrangement whereby silver coming from Spain was diverted for safety's sake through England on its way to Flanders. Two-thirds of this silver was minted in England in return for bills of exchange, and the other one-third was re-exported to Dunkirk under English protection. This arrangement not only put more silver in circulation but, more importantly, brought with it a sizeable trade in other commodities, encouraged by preferential customs duties for goods re-exported on the Spain-Flanders route. The fact that Coke detested Spain did not prevent him from appreciating these commercial advantages, much as he had envied the prosperous Dutch trade with Spain during wartime back in the 1590s. England's advantageous position was enhanced even more when France entered the war against Spain in 1635, and when the fall of Breisach closed the land route known as the 'Spanish Road' in 1638, making the sea route called the 'English Road' the only remaining lifeline between Spain and Flanders. Merchants from all the warring nations found it advisable to send their goods by way of Dover to be re-exported on

[95] Collins, *Letters and Memorials,* II, 435, 440.

English ships, and the English carrying trade in general experienced tremendous growth. Meanwhile the English government raised revenues on this trade to augment the always inadequate royal income. It was a boom that only two developments could alter – peace on the Continent or war in England – both of which would shortly occur.[96]

Coke understood how valuable and how fragile peace was. In June 1636, he spoke at Oxford University urging acceptance of new statutes prepared for the university by Archbishop Laud. Naturally Coke used this opportunity to praise Laud and Charles ('our royal Justinian'), but it was on the subject of peace that for once he came close to eloquence and, unfortunately, prophecy. After describing in graphic terms the terrible destruction that war had caused on the Continent, Coke surveyed the happier condition of England:

> Now we by God's blessing are in a better case; we sit here in God's house thankful in true devotion for this wonderful favour towards us; we enjoy peace and plenty; we are like to those who resting in a calm haven behold the shipwreck of others, wherein we have no part, save only in compassion to help them with our prayers; which we all ought to do as interested in their sufferings, lest the like may fall on us.[97]

[96] Harland Taylor, 'Trade, Neutrality, and the "English Road", 1603-1648' and J.S. Kepler, 'Fiscal Aspects of the English Carrying Trade during the Thirty Years War', *Economic History Review*, 2nd series, 25 (May 1972), 236-83.

[97] Laud, *Works*, vol. V, part 1, p. 131.

15

DECLINE AND FALL

Coke was an old man in the 1630s; he turned seventy in 1633, the year of Windebank's appointment. This has made it tempting to assume that he was failing in mental acuity and physical stamina. One should beware, however, of age bias in descriptions of 'plodding old John Coke, honest, painstaking and slow'.[1] We cannot understand Coke in these final years simply by falling back on a negative and stereotypical view of old age. Age by itself proves nothing. The question must rather be, when and to what extent did age affect Coke's ability to perform the duties of his office? Granted that he clung to office beyond the point where his powers began to fail, Coke had nevertheless been a prodigious worker at the height of those powers, and we cannot blithely assume that as an old man he was physically or mentally inferior to the other officers of Charles I's court, who themselves were hardly youthful.

Prior to his last year in office, it is not easy to document Coke's decline. For one thing, he enjoyed remarkably good health. He did not fall prey to the 'agues' and 'stones' mentioned so frequently in the correspondence of the period, usually with an undertone of dread. He was spared, for example, the slow, excruciating sort of death experienced by Portland, who suffered from kidney stones. Back in 1626 Coke had missed seven weeks of Parliament because of illness, but so had many other members. In the 1630s, so far as we know, he was stricken by only one illness, an odd one of relatively short duration — a nosebleed that lasted intermittently for four days. Coke estimated he lost a frightening amount of blood before resorting to the king's physician 'who by stopping my nostril at which the blood issued hath changed the course into the natural passage by the veins'. Coke had the best physician in the world for a circulatory disorder: the king's physician was William Harvey who only eight years earlier had published his seminal work on the circulation of the blood. Coke noted that prior to this episode he 'enjoyed firm and entire health' and afterwards he found 'no debility nor prejudice to my health, which remaineth as before'.[2] This episode occurred in February 1636 and followed close on the heels of rumours that he 'should leave his

[1]C.V. Wedgwood, *The King's Peace, 1637-1641* (New York, 1956), p. 148.

[2]Coke MSS., packet 81, Coke to son John, 18 Feb. 1636. Coke mentioned Harvey by name. See also Knowler, *Strafforde's Letters,* I, 523.

Secretary's Place'.[3] The fact that Charles had obtained an estate for Coke in Ireland the preceding year may be more than a coincidence. Perhaps it was a hint that Coke should be thinking of retirement. If so, Coke failed to take the hint. The concern expressed by Charles and 'many of the greatest about him' at the time of the nosebleed episode convinced Coke that, to the contrary 'they are in no disposition to be weary of me'.

Coke, like the Roman Empire, did not just decline from within; he was also attacked from without. In 1637 there is no solid evidence that he was declining in ability, but there is ample evidence that he was declining in power. Northumberland was gaining ascendancy in naval matters, Windebank was substantially encroaching on the foreign correspondence, and there was a far more serious, direct attack mounted by the wife and friends of the earl of Leicester. Coke had obstructed payment of the earl's allowance as ambasssador to France and criticized his conduct of the negotiations. The countess consequently developed an intense dislike for Coke, vowing in her own colourful language that, 'it shall be parte of my letainie to deliver all my frends from embasies till Secretarie Coke be laid downe in pease'. Historians do not agree in their assessment of the ambition of the earl of Leicester, but there is no doubt about the glaring ambition of his wife. She saw her husband's embassy as a stepping-stone to higher things — to Coke's Secretaryship.[4] In early autumn 1637, Leicester's brother-in-law, Henry Percy, reported that their plot to replace Coke with Leicester had miscarried for the time being. The queen wholeheartedly supported the plan, but it was divulged too soon, allowing its opponents to organize resistance and angering King Charles because, as Percy said, 'our Master loues not to heare other People giue, what is only fitt for him'.[5]

Coke survived the setbacks of 1637, but toward the end of 1638 the forces of internal decay and external attack began to converge. The Secretary's job required the writing of an incredible number of letters, and before 1638 most of these are in Coke's own handwriting. Starting in August 1638, however, appreciably more of Coke's letters are in the handwriting of his clerks.[6] And Coke's own handwriting begins to seem stiffer and more laboured. Of course the Secretary did not have to write his own letters. Secretary Conway, for example, had

[3]Knowler, *Strafforde's Letters,* I, 507; *CSPV,* 1632-1636, pp. 515, 524, 527.

[4]HMC, *De L'Isle and Dudley MSS.,* VI, 62, 74.

[5]Collins, *Letters and Memorials,* II, 514, 516.

[6]This phenomenon is first apparent in SP 16/vol. 397 and continues through the domestic state papers until Coke's retirement.

preferred to employ a clerk for this purpose. But it is significant that Coke changed his practice in this respect in 1638. More significant is the fact that Coke's chief assistant, Rudolph Weckherlin, began to make approaches to the opposition. He had written to the earl of Leicester back in November 1637, offering to keep Leicester informed 'when I see or thinke Mr. Secretarie will not write'. But it was not until November 1638 that he succeeded in establishing regular, direct communication with Leicester.[7] Weckherlin was afraid for his job and was trying to gain the confidence of the man he expected to succeed Coke. His apprehension had no doubt been heightened by conversations with a friend of Leicester's named Sir William Temple. In the winter of 1638-9, Temple, convinced that Coke was on the verge of resigning, reported: 'I finde Mr. Secretary [Coke] somewhat discontented, and euen weary of his Imployment: The Businesse upon his Hands at this Time is euen beyond what his Age and Infirmities will admitt him to manage. He speakes how happy he should be in a retired Life.' Temple thought he had succeeded in persuading Coke to support Leicester as his successor. According to Temple, Coke had 'very lately euen of him selfe, wished with all his Hart, that his Lordship had his Place'. From what Temple observed at court, he was confident that now was 'the proper Time to moue in' because 'I finde such stirring now att Court, as I apprehend him [Coke] not long liued in his Place'. Temple was not entirely wrong about the shifting situation at court, but surely Coke had played upon his gullibility. The countess of Leicester remarked with less optimism but greater discernment: 'I have no opinion that the old man will quite his inploiment so longe as he can goe, which he yeet dose but verie weaklie.'[8]

In the winter of 1638-9 Coke knew that efforts were being made to ease him out of office. His wisest course would have been to yield to those efforts, but, as the countess of Leicester understood, he was too proud and too wedded to his job to relinquish it. There is an inglorious quality about Coke's last years in office caused not least by our awareness of the fact that he was clinging to an office even after he had lost the capacity to use that office in any original, meaningful, constructive way. F.M.G. Evans described Coke as 'reserved and

[7]HMC, *De L'Isle and Dudley MSS.*, VI, 135, 149-51, 154-5, 160. One might also surmise from Weckherlin's diary that he was assuming responsibility for much of Coke's work, but Coke probably always delegated a great deal of work to Weckherlin. Unfortunately the diary does not allow comparison with the earlier 1630s because it does not start in earnest until 1637. Berkshire Record Office, Trumbull MSS., miscellaneous correspondence, vol. LXI.

[8]Collins, *Letters and Memorials,* II, 591-2; HMC, *De L'Isle and Dudley MSS.*, VI, 157-8.

almost sullen', and those words aptly capture his mood in the later 1630s.[9] Despised by the self-seeking conspirators at court, susperseded in the king's and queen's confidence by Windebank, pushed aside in naval affairs by the earl of Northumberland, who in 1638 replaced the Admiralty commission when he was appointed the first Lord Admiral since Buckingham, and beleaguered by younger aspirants to his office like Leicester, Coke did not mellow in these final years; he soured. He was obviously in no position to rout these competitors, but there were still two things he could and did do. One was to deny them an easy victory by refusing to surrender his office. The other was to guard jealously what few vestiges of power he still possessed. Windebank, who had least right of all to complain about other people's secrecy, bemoaned 'my colleague's reservedness'.[10] Elaborating more fully in a letter to Leicester, Windebank explained that

> through the retentive faculty of my colleague I cannot expect that more shall pass to my knowledge than what he cannot keep from me, and that from him I seldom come to the understanding of anything of moment but at the foreign committee, which though his Majesty have [*sic*] commanded to meet every week, yet he husbands that likewise so thriftily that unless his Majesty call us upon some special occasion once in a month or six weeks, we never otherwise come together.[11]

Windebank volunteered this criticism of Coke in order to advance his own interests, and it is suspiciously similar to complaints he made to Wentworth in 1634 and Northumberland in 1636. Perhaps, however, it was more valid at the beginning of 1639. If Coke did behave this way, note that Windebank attributed it not to feebleness or forgetfulness but to conscious calculation. Note also that this crude tactic was evidently working. If Coke no longer had much prospect of implementing his own desires, he could nevertheless obstruct the desires of those he considered his opponents. Operating from a position of inferior strength, he could still worry them, keep them off balance, and at the very least delay their victory.

That he assumed this defensive posture in his later years was admitted by Coke shortly after his dismissal. He explained that he was dissuaded from retiring earlier by 'the persuasions of my friends that I must not abandon the public, whilst my being upon the stage might either advance some good, *or at least give interruption to the*

[9] *The Principal Secretary,* p. 86.

[10] SP 16/537/5.

[11] SP 16/537/6. This and the preceding letter are incorrectly dated in the calendar.

prevailing of some evil. . . though I knew how little I could prevail in either'.[12] Unfortunately, Coke did not spell out what he considered 'good' and 'evil' in this context. If good government was the criterion, then by 'good' he meant economy and efficiency, and the evil-doers would have been those who Coke thought would waste the Crown's resources and perhaps plunge it into war. If religion was the criterion, then 'good' meant ardently Protestant, and the evil-doers were people who in Coke's eyes were too sympathetic to Spain and Catholicism. This was probably the case because it squares with what Coke said in another letter written after his retirement. In that letter Coke complained that after the reign of Elizabeth the English clergy drifted away from the Protestantism of the Continent and the English court drifted in the direction of Spain. Coke recounted in particular an attempt to establish trade between England and the Barbary coast, an attempt he believed had been sabotaged by merchants protecting Spanish interests. From this event, he said, 'I found that it was in vain to strive in anything wherein Spain was so much concerned.'[13] Perhaps, then, Coke did intentionally obstruct the meeting of the foreign committee for the sake of spiting Windebank and depriving his other opponents of a forum. This was no more blameworthy than the behaviour of Charles and Windebank, who had shamelessly worked behind the back of that same committee since 1634, but it was no way to run a government, least of all a government perched on the brink of war — with Scotland.

The impending war weakened Coke's hold on the Secretaryship. Sir William Temple was probably not alone in believing that 'the Affaires of the King require a more actiue Man'.[14] Moreover, Coke was unenthusiastic about the war. According to Clarendon, Coke 'understood nothing that had been done in Scotland, and thought that nothing that was or could be done there worth such a journey as the King had put himself to'.[15] Nevertheless, Coke remained in office and was required to accompany Charles on the campaign to the north in the spring of 1639. Coke had been a young man almost twenty-four years old when Mary Queen of Scots was executed under Elizabeth. Now, at the age of seventy-six, he participated in the negotiations with the Scottish Covenanters.[16]

[12]*Cowper MSS.*, II, 250. Italics mine.

[13]Coke MSS., packet 65, Coke to son John [Dec. 1640]. This letter is erroneously attributed to 1641 in *Cowper MSS.*, II, 296-7. See also pp. 269-71.

[14]Collins, *Letters and Memorials*, II, 591.

[15]Knowler, *Strafforde's Letters*, II, 186; Clarendon, *History of the Rebellion*, I, 161.

[16]HMC, *Rutland MSS.*, I, 503, 506-9, 513-14.

Windebank and the remnant of the Privy Council left behind in London depended on Coke for information about the king's proceedings. Toward the end of April, Windebank complained to Charles that 'we are not at all advertised here of what passeth there; and my lords are many times troubled at sundry vulgar reports, and send to me to be informed of the truth, presuming that Mr. Secretary gives advice hither of what passeth there; but I am not able to give them the least satisfaction'. Windebank characteristically concluded this complaint by asking Charles 'not to interpret this as a complaint, nor to take notice of it as from me'. Two days later the whole Council in London wrote directly to Coke asking him for prompter communication.[17] There is no reason to doubt the legitimacy or the seriousness of these complaints. On the other hand, this does not appear to be another case of deliberate secretiveness. Coke did write more than twenty letters to Windebank during this period, and sometimes at least his tardiness could be attributed to the nature of the situation. On 22 June, for example, he explained: 'The reason why I gave you no account of our proceedings here in that time was the uncertainty thereof. For our treaty with the Scots standing all that while upon doubtful terms, I thought it not fit to write unto you or the lords, conjectures and suppositions, when every day promised more assurance the next meeting.'[18]

The official correspondence between Coke and Windebank during the First Bishops' War is not as revealing as what was going on behind the scenes. Here there were several signs of court conflict and, for Coke, impending defeat. Conflict is evident, for example, in the gossipy letters of Edward Norgate, a signet clerk associated with Windebank whom Coke had brought along in addition to his own clerks. Norgate complained first about too little work, then about too much work, but especially about the way Coke's clerks monopolized the lucrative work. As Norgate explained it, Coke 'permits his men Weckherlin, Poole, and May to seal letters at the signet, to take the fees, and never acquaint me with what passes, to the hindrance of the office and hurt of the subject, who inquire for copies of those things which are surreptitiously gotten and unduly concealed'.[19] Norgate was resentful; he had been a signet clerk for less than a year and was obviously anxious to make the office pay for itself.[20] Cutting away the

[17] *Clarendon State Papers* (quarto edition), II, 39; *Cowper MSS.,* II, 223.

[18] *CSPD,* 1639, pp. 11-12, 26, 30, 47, 65, 105, 112, 143-4, 154-5, 178-9, 188-9, 206, 247-9, 266-7, 277, 280, 340, 375, 388, 397. The 22 June letter is SP 16/424/47.

[19] SP 16/421/34; Aylmer, *The King's Servants,* pp. 154-5; *CSPD,* 1639, pp. 12, 59-60, 82, 116-17, 144-6, 180-1, 242-3, 269-73.

[20] SP 16/397/75.

bombast about secrecy and the welfare of the subject, we see from Norgate's letters how jealously the staffs of Coke and Windebank were pitted against each other. Windebank's clerks continued to be preoccupied with questions of who had more status, business, and fees even after Coke was replaced, but competition was probably more acute in 1639 because Coke's clerks must have known that his days in office and perhaps their own were running out.

Other signs of conflict during this period came from Lord Deputy Wentworth's effort to remove the Lord Chancellor of Ireland, Viscount Loftus. On 26 April, while the king was still encamped at York, the earl of Holland persuaded him to issue an order for Loftus's release from confinement in Ireland. Perhaps because of Coke's known allegiance to Wentworth, Holland 'prest the Kinge so stoutly in Loftes behalf as that he humbly desyred his Majesty Mr. Secretary Cooke might not draw the letter for his enlardgment, but that he might draw it himselfe for his present enlardgment'.[21] The Wentworth-Loftus contest touched Coke again in August when he was accused of having failed to write an official letter on the matter. Coke's assistant, Weckherlin, told him that 'ill offices were done against your Honour', and he interpreted this episode as part of the general intensification of court competition that occurred after the return from Scotland, 'seeing there are stout champions that have sustained the like and ruder assaults here than they did ever fear at the camp'.[22]

A further bad sign for Coke at this time involved his arch rival from the 1620s, Sir Robert Mansell. The commissioners of the navy had never approved all the accounts from Mansell's years as Naval Treasurer, accounts which they considered both inadequate and improper. The fact that Mansell had been denied approval for more than twenty years must surely have been Coke's responsibility. On the last day of May 1639, while Coke was still in the north with the king at Berwick, Juxon and Cottington back in London approved Mansell's accounts for the years 1614 to 1617. The accounts were as inadequate as ever and actually credited Mansell with a surplus in one year. At the end there was still a balance due of £665, but other expenses were found to eradicate this debt, so that Mansell 'resteth clearly discharged and quit'.[23] The symbolic significance of Mansell's belated

[21] HMC, *Rutland MSS.,* I, 509. For this subject in general, see Wedgwood, *Thomas Wentworth: A Revaluation,* pp. 239-45, 272 and Gardiner, *History of England,* IX, 71-2. See also *Cowper MSS.,* II, pp. 234, 238-9; HMC *Various Collections,* III, 161-2, 182, 186-7, 196-7, 208, 210.

[22] Coke MSS., packet 13, Weckherlin to Coke, 8 Aug. 1639.

[23] PRO, E 351/2, 252-5.

victory need hardly be emphasized. As Coke's career drew to a close, he was defeated in more ways than one.

There was a final sign of Coke's impending fall so blatant, so bald and unequivocal, as to be ludicrous: he had his lodgings at Whitehall taken away from him. Furthermore, they were assigned to the earl of Northumberland. Originally Coke seems to have been told that Northumberland would occupy his quarters only for the duration of the campaign against the Scots, but it was soon evident that Northumberland planned to move in permanently. Coke had left his keys with a cousin who procrastinated about surrendering them, knowing 'that my lord Northumberland shall forever keep them if you now part with them'. Coke's cousin reported that the court officer who asked for the keys 'was very smart with me. . . and told me he did once move you for your favour about a ship. . . and found you very strait in your office, and he knew no reason but that he should be so in his'. It was a sure sign of decline when a petty officer dared to act so impertinently. Northumberland eventually got the keys. In June, while Coke was still in Scotland, the earl asked him to instruct someone to remove the papers and trunks that cluttered two rooms. Coke replied that these papers were 'his Majesty's letters, treaties, negotiations with foreign princes and states, which are in my charge, and are of that weight that I neither dare nor can put them into any other hands'. Harbouring no hope of recovering his lodgings, Coke asked only for the earl's patience because 'the sorting and removing cannot be done in my absence nor in a short time'. It was now clear that if Coke planned to return from Scotland to Whitehall, he would have to find new lodgings. He was offered alternative accommodations, principally those of the earl of Ancram, but it is doubtful whether Charles had any serious intention of actually requiring Ancram to vacate his quarters for Coke.[24]

Coke did not proceed directly from Scotland to London. Instead he stopped at his home at Melbourne. We do not know precisely when this was, but we do know that he stayed there through the month of August and the first week of September. On 15 August, Weckherlin reported to Coke that the king had declared a vacation. Councillors were free to leave the court until Michaelmas, and those who stayed behind would meet only on Sundays. 'But all this notwithstanding', said Weckherlin, 'your Honour's presence is much desired and urged by the earl of Holland, whom I see daily, as also his Majesty, though

[24]Coke MSS., packet 13, John Leigh to Coke, 10 April 1639; Northumberland to Coke, 6 June 1639. Coke MSS., packet 69, Coke to Northumberland, June 1639. *Cowper MSS.,* II, 231, 234, 239-41.

I find no business, but only to talk of news.' It was an odd situation. Lord Treasurer Juxon had gone to Bath, others had gone elsewhere, and none were required to return till October. But Coke, who at the age of seventy-six must surely have needed a vacation as much as the others, was urged to return, though only 'to talk of news'. Meanwhile, Coke had no lodgings at Whitehall, and, as Weckherlin described it: 'All your Honour's stuff lieth in an old kitchen.' By 19 August, Weckherlin sounded desperate: 'I know not in what terms to express sufficiently how much your Honour's return is desired, and (without doubt) very necessary and requisite. Though I forbear to write the causes, which (God willing) I hope shortly to tell your Honour by word of mouth, hoping your absence will not be drawn out beyond the end of August.' On 4 September, Coke had still not returned, and Weckherlin implored again: 'Your Honour's return is so much desired and expected that his Majesty doth now daily. . . inquire after your coming, and hath again this morning commanded me to desire you from him to come unto him. . . as soon as possibly you can.'[25] Several explanations can be found for Coke's slow response to these pleas. One specific, verifiable explanation is that he was detained at Melbourne by the death of his older brother, Francis, which occurred at nearby Trusley on 16 August.[26] Coke hardly required this further reminder of his own impending end. There are two other explanations for his lingering at Melbourne which are more in the nature of suspicions. First, the Scottish campaign may have exhausted him and he was trying to recuperate. Secondly, he may have been postponing what he now knew to be the inevitable. As long as he lingered at Melbourne, he was still a Secretary of State. But why did Charles insist on his return to court? Coke may have been needed to conduct the work of the foreign committee. Archbishop Laud observed that there was no meeting of that committee between the king's return from Scotland and 8 September. He attributed this to 'Mr. Secretary's stay at his house in Derbyshire; and all the papers were in his hands'.[27] However, it would seem more plausible that Charles wanted Coke at court so that he could dismiss him in person from his office. But when Coke did finally return during the second week of September, what was plausible and inevitable did not yet happen.

Coke was given what amounted to a reprieve of a little more than four months. He assumed a brave countenance, explaining to his son: 'For myself (I thank God), I still enjoy good health and am settled to

[25]Coke MSS., packet 13, Weckherlin to Coke, 15 and 19 Aug. 1639.

[26]Coke, *Coke of Trusley,* pp. 13-14.

[27]Laud, *Works,* VII, 587.

my mind and find my friends as I left them. Here hath been a great expectation of changes, yet all things still move upon the same wheels, and for my part I fear not what the times may produce.'[28] By December, Coke was reported to be 'very little acquainted with the Affaires of this Court'.[29] On 12 December, Edward Nicholas observed: 'It will not be long after Christmas before we shall (as I hear) have a new Secretary of State in place of Sec. Coke, who is much decayed, and albeit I cannot commend him for anything, yet I wish we have not a worse in his room, for seldom comes the better.'[30] By December it was also apparent that the earl of Leicester would not be Coke's successor. As noted earlier, Leicester had several promoters, chief among them being the queen. In November, however, it was rumoured that Charles had peremptorily refused the queen's renewed plea to give Leicester the Secretaryship. The king's categorical rejection of Leicester was attributed to the fact that the earl had one great enemy at court, Archbishop Laud. The archbishop disliked Leicester for his low-church views and, more particularly, never forgave him for his disrespectful treatment of Scudamore.[31]

Leicester was ruled out, but no alternative had yet emerged when suddenly on 10 January the long-awaited blow was struck. As the earl of Northumberland described it, Charles sent Lord Treasurer Juxon to inform Coke 'that by Reason of his Age, he found him not able to discharge, as he ought to do, the Bussinesse incident to the Place he held; therefore, in plaine Tearmes, that he was resolved presently to make another Secritarie; and if without farther Trouble, he would willingly resigne, his Majesty should take it well at his hands'. Although Coke's dismissal had long been generally anticipated, when it actually happened it took some at the court by surprise. Wentworth was particularly unprepared for it. Northumberland reported that the king's request was 'immediately submitted vnto by the olde Noddie', but the next day Coke appealed to Wentworth for help.[32] It is impossible to know whether or not Wentworth would have defended Coke purely for his own sake, but certainly he spared no efforts to retain the Secretaryship for Coke when he learned that the intended successor was a personal enemy, the Treasurer of the Household, Sir

[28] Coke MSS., packet 84, Coke to son John [September 1639]; HMC, *De L'Isle and Dudley MSS.,* VI, 180, 183.

[29] Collins, *Letters and Memorials,* II, 621.

[30] SP 16/435/64.

[31] Collins, *Letters and Memorials,* II, 611, 618, 623, 629; HMC, *De L'Isle and Dudley MSS.,* VI, 182, 204, 208, 211.

[32] Collins, *Letters and Memorials,* II, 631.

Henry Vane. Wentworth and Vane were engaged in a personal feud at precisely this time. On 12 January, Wentworth received the earldom of Strafford and the barony of Raby. It was this subsidiary title that incensed Vane because he, as the owner of Raby castle, had wanted the barony for himself.[33] The fact that Coke was dismissed from his office two days before Strafford's official elevation is probably more than a coincidence. One of Leicester's correspondents explained that Strafford's 'taking away the Baronie of Raby' had caused Vane 'to seeke recompence this way'.[34] Strafford had two motives, then, for defending Coke. On the one hand, as Clarendon said, 'it was done with great reason and justice by the earl, on the behalf of an old fellow-servant and his very friend'. On the other hand, although Strafford acted 'out of some kindness to the old man, who had been much trusted by him and of use to him', the earl also acted 'out of contempt and detestation of Vane'.[35]

Coke held on for three weeks, even attending Privy Council meetings, while Strafford fought to retain him in the Secretaryship.[36] In view of the fact that Charles had already firmly demanded Coke's resignation, Strafford might have done better to abandon Coke and concentrate instead on promoting a candidate of his own choosing. But after the king's rejection of Leicester, Strafford had not fixed upon any other candidate. In this he was clearly outmanoeuvred by the queen who had promptly shifted to promoting Vane. Nor did Strafford receive any assistance in this cause from his usual ally, Laud. Laud supported Sir Thomas Roe, who was absent in Germany and quite unlikely to win. Strafford stood little chance of succeeding in this contest with the queen, but it was a hard-fought battle nevertheless. As one observer described it: 'The holding Coke in his place hath beene extreame earnestly solicited.' Clarendon likewise recorded that Strafford 'opposed the removal of Secretary Cooke with all the interest he could, got it suspended for some time, and put the Queen to the exercise of her full power'.[37] But Coke's removal could only be delayed, not prevented. Coke finally accepted defeat and surrendered the seals of his office to the king on the last day of January, the same

[33] *CSPD,* 1640, p. 436; HMC, *De L'Isle and Dudley MSS.,* VI, 207.

[34] HMC, *De L'Isle and Dudley MSS.,* VI, 224.

[35] Clarendon, *History of the Rebellion,* I, 166, 197.

[36] PRO, PC 2/51, pp. 244, 248, 251, 254, 261, 264. Coke missed just one meeting, on 15 Jan., then reappeared on 17, 19, 24, 26, and 29 Jan.

[37] HMC, *De L'Isle and Dudley MSS.,* VI, 225; Clarendon, *History of the Rebellion,* I, 166.

day on which exactly nine years later Charles I was executed.[38] Coke was succeeded in the Secretaryship, as expected, by Sir Henry Vane. 'The Queen was his means', Laud remarked, 'and very earnest.'[39]

Windebank was too minor a court figure to have played any part in Coke's dismissal. Much as he competed against Coke, it was not clearly to his advantage to have Coke replaced by a more youthful man who was likely to have more influence with the king and queen. In Windebank's letters, the references to Coke's dismissal are those of an interested but uninformed bystander. With Coke no longer constituting a danger, Windebank even referred to him charitably as the 'old gentleman'.[40] One of Windebank's clerks, Robert Read, was probably correct in thinking 'it is very indifferent to our Mr. Secretary whether he [Coke] stay in or no, for all we shall gain by it is at most but a diet which. . . must not be neglected for credit's sake'. Windebank and his clerks got the prestigious ten-dish diet they hoped for, but, as Read reported: 'I do not find that we have much more sign of seniority, Mr. Treasurer [Vane] having full as much of the foreign business as Mr. Secretary Coke had.'[41] Windebank and his clerks were disappointed not to have got more of the foreign business for themselves. Instead, Charles divided the foreign correspondence between Windebank and Vane, following a pattern that had been developing informally for years: Spain, Italy, Flanders, and Ireland went to Windebank; Germany, France, and the United Provinces went to Vane.[42] Even under this new arrangement, however, the division was not complete or mutually exclusive. Both Secretaries were supposed to receive copies of routine dispatches from all countries, a fact that Windebank emphasized in announcing the new arrangement to Sir Thomas Roe in Germany, which now lay outside his province.[43] The new arrangement also allowed for either Secretary to communicate secretly with any ambassador when the king so desired. Windebank could therefore continue to dominate foreign affairs just as he had in Coke's day. Two months after Vane's appointment,

[38]Berkshire Record Office, Trumbull MSS., miscellaneous correspondence, vol. LXI (Weckherlin's diary), 31 Jan. 1640; HMC, *De L'Isle and Dudley MSS.,* VI, 230; SP 16/444/36, 53.

[39]SP 16/445/35. See also Collins, *Letters and Memorials,* II, 634. For Coke's dismissal in general, see Trevor-Roper, *Archbishop Laud,* pp. 374-6; Wedgwood, *Strafford,* pp. 272-4; Brian Manning, 'The Aristocracy and the Downfall of Charles I' in Brian Manning, ed., *Politics, Religion and the English Civil War* (London, 1973), pp. 49-51.

[40]SP 16/442/101; 16/444/52; 78/109/fols. 15, 33.

[41]SP 16/441/119, 16/442/83, 16/443/31. The first of these is misdated. HMC, *De L'Isle and Dudley MSS.,* VI, 230.

[42]Evans, *The Principal Secretary,* pp. 102-5.

[43]*CSPD,* 1640, pp. 433-4.

in fact, Windebank was already writing secretly to Leicester in France, a country ostensibly assigned to Vane.[44] The fact that Vane retained two of Coke's former clerks, Weckherlin and Poole, makes things look even more familiar.[45] We will never know whether Windebank and Vane would have worked together more harmoniously than Windebank and Coke because events carried them away. In less than one year Windebank fled to the Continent to escape the wrath of the Long Parliament. And in less than two years Vane, who had finished his feud with Strafford by giving the most damaging testimony in Parliament against the earl, was removed by Charles from the other Secretaryship.

Reflecting now on Coke's dismissal, it is fairly easy to understand why it happened. The only novel explanation came from Clarendon, who claimed that Coke was used as a scapegoat for the humiliating conclusion of the First Bishops' War.[46] Less debatable is the fact that Coke finally fell victim to an aristocratic clique at court allied with the queen. Beyond both these political explanations, however, lies the even more certain, biological, fact that Coke had simply grown too old for the office. We have seen mounting evidence of Coke's physical decline beginning in 1637. The trip to Scotland in the summer of 1639 accelerated this decline and sealed Coke's fate. It is even possible that Charles was half expecting or hoping that Coke, at the age of seventy-six, would not survive the ordeal. The concurrent reassignment of Coke's lodgings to the earl of Northumberland certainly implies that for one reason or another Coke was not expected to need them in the future. Coke did survive, of course, but only just. He returned from the north a visibly weakened man ('much decayed', as Nicholas said). Even supposing that he was still capable of executing his routine duties as Secretary, there is no reason to think he was capable of representing the Crown in the forthcoming Parliament as he had done over a decade earlier. Coke's time had simply run out. His death or voluntary resignation had been generally expected at court for years. Indeed, the constant expectation that nature herself would conveniently eliminate him may have dissuaded the king from acting earlier. When Charles finally did demand Coke's resignation in January of 1640, it was not premature. If anything, it was overdue.

The real problem with Coke, as with the Roman Empire, is not to explain why he fell but how he managed to last as long as he did. Of course he had to have friends at court, but these are not easy to find in

[44]Collins, *Letters and Memorials,* II, 644.

[45]Coke MSS., packet 43, Vane to Coke, 4 Feb. 1640; SP 16/444/14.

[46]Clarendon, *History of the Rebellion,* I, 165.

the 1630s. At least three men helped to keep Coke in office. During the first half of the decade, as we saw, Portland worked agreeably enough with him and prevented him from becoming isolated. Coke must have been either more respected or more adaptable than his old friend, Sir Robert Naunton, who did become isolated in this period. After Portland's death, Coke's chief remaining support came from Laud and Strafford. For a supposed puritan, Coke got on remarkably well with Laud. Both Laud and Strafford saw Coke as an honest, hard-working man; and they had the same enemies — in particular the queen, Cottington, and Windebank. Of course, no one's support would have been sufficient to maintain Coke in office if King Charles had not wanted him there. The Secretaryship was held at the king's pleasure. It was not necessary to give an outgoing Secretary another post or a costly pension. In fact, Coke left the court without receiving his regular arrears of pay, much less any special recompense.[47] In general, Charles did not part quickly with the men who had suffered with him through the early years of the reign. Two good examples are Sir Thomas Coventry, who remained Lord Keeper until his death just weeks before Coke's dismissal, and Sir Edward Nicholas, the former naval secretary to Buckingham, who would go on to succeed Windebank as Secretary of State in 1641. Like these men, Coke was a living tie with the past, one of the dwindling number of courtiers who had actually served the duke of Buckingham. Charles had little respect for Coke, but he may have felt a sense of attachment to him. That at least would explain why he gave Coke every possible opportunity to leave office voluntarily, even through the inglorious final months of 1639, before at last demanding his resignation.

The final key to Coke's longevity at court must lie in the particular way he did his job. Coke was gullible and obsequious. He could be manipulated by Charles, and he could be expected to carry out his orders. All this is well known. Less appreciated is the fact that Coke was discreet. He occasionally blundered into an argument, but more generally he avoided confrontation. His voluminous correspondence in the 1630s contains precious little of the direct criticism and unguarded grumbling that abounds in the letters of other courtiers such as Northumberland, Laud, and Wentworth. Although ignorant of the details, Coke surely knew that Windebank was operating behind his back, yet it is Windebank, not Coke, who spiced his letters with peevish criticisms of his colleague. This is a handicap to the modern historian who would like to know Coke's view of the other personalities at court, but it was an asset at the time to Coke. Grander

[47]PRO 31/3/79/fol. 25 (Baschet's transcripts); *Cowper MSS.*, II, 277.

courtiers took grander risks. Coke did what he could in a quieter way and carefully went about his own business. As such, he was not likely to break into the foreground of court politics, but he was peculiarly able to persevere in the background. On the other hand, he did not simply plod along. He handled an enormous amount of work with uncommon ability. In the course of his career, too, he acquired experience which few other men could match. Even in January 1640, when Coke's dismissal was imminent, he was called upon to write a royal letter 'because the other [Secretary] knew not how'.[48] This, on balance, seems the most plausible explanation for Coke's long tenure. He was not so much a courtier liable to the vicissitudes of favour as a neutral functionary. In fact, through the 1630s, by virtue of his diligence and ability, he assumed the appearance of a fixture at court. Then, in 1640, Charles decided that Coke, at the age of seventy-six, had finally outlived his usefulness.

Coke spent most of his retirement from 1640 to 1644 at Melbourne. There he was spared from the direct attack of the Long Parliament, but he was not entirely free from danger. Parliament did inquire into his past actions in office and might still have censured or punished him if it had not been for the efforts of his son, Sir John Coke, who sat in the Commons as a member for Derbyshire and gravitated toward Parliament's side in the Civil War. Coke's other son, Thomas, also sat in the Commons but went over to the king's side. Meanwhile, life at Melbourne was far from tranquil. Coke's enclosures were destroyed, his mill was burned to the ground, soldiers occupied his home, he was repeatedly harassed, and he was forced several times to pay just to be left alone.[49]

Coke lived long enough to hear of Strafford's execution, Windebank's hasty flight to France, Henrietta Maria's flight to the Hague, Vane's dismissal and quick alliance with Parliament, and the defection of Northumberland and the navy to Parliament's side. He probably did not know that the Council had briefly considered employing Sir Robert Mansell to secure the fleet for the king, an idea which was rejected because Mansell, like Coke, was too old. The man appointed to command what remained of a royalist sea force was Sir John Pennington, the veteran captain who had commanded many

[48] SP 16/441/92.

[49] SP 16/459/36; Mary Frear Keeler, *The Long Parliament* (Philadelphia, 1954), pp. 137-8; *Cowper MSS.*, II, 257, 264-71, 294, 315, 328-30, 335-7, 340; Wallace Notestein, ed., *The Journal of Sir Simonds D'Ewes* (New Haven, 1923), pp. 35, 89, 90, 110, 132, 174, 412; W.H. Coates, ed., *The Journal of Sir Simonds D'Ewes* (New Haven, 1942), pp. 50-1.

ships in Coke's day, including those lent to the French in 1625. Pennington outlived Coke by only one year. In the topsy-turvy world of Coke's final years, one of the few remaining certainties was the inexorable advance of old age and death. Even the wealth that Coke had accumulated seemed as ephemeral as fame and power. Coke was brought to despair that 'I have lost all I had in this country and have no more here to lose'. Even the affection between Coke and his older son was strained by the turbulent times. Coke fell back on pious hopes for unity and peace that were not very different from those he had expressed in the 1620s. In what appears to be the last of Coke's letters, he described himself as living 'in the midst of daily dangers, hoping at length He will work us all into one heart and one way that the light of His countenance may again be turned towards us and I may depart in peace'.[50]

Coke did not live to see peace. He was eventually forced to leave Melbourne and take refuge in his wife's home at Tottenham. There he died on 8 September 1644, having lived, as his son recounted, '81 years, 6 months, 3 days, and about 4 hours'. Had he lived until 1647, he could have relished the fact that when Charles I was captured, one of the nine guards who had custody of the king was Sir John Coke.[51] Coke's death brings to mind words he wrote to Buckingham back in 1622 that can now serve appropriately as an epitaph. His words were coloured by self-deception, and of course he had no way of knowing how the rest of his life would turn out. But he left a clear statement of how at least he wanted to be remembered by posterity when he described himself to Buckingham as follows:

> . . . howsoever I am valued, my descent is not base. I was not bred in servile or illiberal trades; the university was my nurse. I have travelled many countries, where I saw peace and war. I am acquainted with books, and no stranger to the courts and affairs of the world. And though those know, who know me best, that I ever affected a private course of life, yet I never refused any service whatsoever to give God, my prince, and country a good account of my time, nor ever made the public a step to private ends, nor set profit or honour in the first place of my heart.[52]

[50] Coke MSS., packet 2, Coke to son John [*ca.* 20 Sept. 1642]; packet 90, Coke to son John [Jan. 1644].

[51] Coke, *Coke of Trusley,* pp. 61, 63-4. Coke MSS., packet 2, Sir John Hartopp to Mr. Husband, without date. Coke left no will. The letters of administration for his estate are recorded in the Prerogative Court of Canterbury as follows: Rivers (1644), fol. 1; AA 1,650, fol. 133; AA 1,663, fol. 69; AA 1,676, fol. 51.

[52] Coke MSS., packet 45, Coke to Buckingham, 12 Oct. 1622.

16

KINGS CANNOT BE SERVED

The road that led from the reign of Elizabeth I to the downfall of Charles I was not a straight and inevitable 'High Road to Civil War'. It was a long road, full of twists and unexpected turns, and the remarkable fact about Coke's life is that he travelled every mile of it. From the days of Elizabeth and Essex, through the era of Buckingham, to Strafford and Laud — Coke worked in the shadow of power and acquired no little power himself. He also acquired a range of experience in the English government that few men before or after him could equal. When he reached the end of the road, when he had abundant cause to ponder the meaning of his life and work, what must the old man have thought about it all?

One clue to Coke's attitude in these final years is the noteworthy fact that he did not support the king in the Civil War. G.E. Aylmer considered him a neutralist, and others have gone so far as to assign him to the parliamentary side.[1] The evidence that survives is ambiguous. There is, for example, the circumstantial evidence that Coke remained close to his older son, John, who sided with Parliament, while apparently ceasing to communicate with his other son, Thomas, who became a royalist. As we shall see in a moment, however, it is impossible to know how much John's parliamentarianism sprang from political convictions and how much from practical considerations of safety and property. In his father's case these practical considerations must have weighed even more heavily. Coke was too old and vulnerable to fight for either side even if he had wanted to. His overriding concern must have been simply to save his own skin for what little time he had left. This pragmatism, at least as much as genuine enthusiasm for the parliamentarians, was probably the common bond that held Coke and his elder son (and heir) together. There is also evidence that Coke was alienated from the king as a direct result of his expulsion from court. Coke left the court declaring that 'no offence is taken against me, and so much expression of good opinion and good will towards me both in Court and City that I would never withdraw myself with more favourable aspect'. He claimed to be entering retirement at Melbourne 'with as much quiet, and with as calm a mind, and with as little repining or complaining or spleen against any, as any servant from a Court to a country life, after so

[1] *DNB,* IV, 702; Russell, *Parliaments,* pp. 428, 434; Aylmer, *The King's Servants,* p. 365.

many and so long employments'.[2] Within a few months, however, this magnanimous resignation had turned to self-pity. Now he explained that: 'I endure with patience to be neglected and forgotten at the court as if I had never performed any acceptable service there.'[3] Coke was resentful, as he had been after his expulsion in 1604. On the other hand, resentment and alienation are hardly the same as rebellion. More concrete evidence is provided by two instances when Coke wrote expressions of support for Parliament. On one occasion he referred to 'my affection to the cause', and on the other occasion he said, 'my heart is faithful and my prayers assiduous for the prosperity of the Parliament, wherein consisteth the welfare of this church and state'.[4] In both these instances, however, Coke had reason to feign support for Parliament: he was appealing for relief from their ravaging military forces and their financial demands. Coke complained of Parliament's repeated extortion, and as Aylmer observed, 'he did not *voluntarily* subscribe money to either side'.[5] Granted that Coke inclined toward support of Parliament, it remains difficult to get at the root of that support, to determine how much he was motivated by conviction and how much by mere expediency.

One way to try to distinguish more precisely between conviction and expediency is to examine the attitude of Coke and his son to the attainder of Strafford. John had several serious qualms about the attainder. He did not like prosecuting a man for his alleged 'intentions', he thought Strafford's offences were being exaggerated, and he suspected that the case had become a vehicle for private ends.[6] John was absent from the Commons when the attainder came to a vote. Shortly thereafter, he wrote a letter to his father explaining this absence, apparently because his father had scolded him for it. Here is John's explanation:

> And for the process of the Earl of Strafford I most humbly desire you to suspend your judgment of me until I wait upon you; for I hope I shall never appear to have deserted my religion or my country, which are dearer to me than life. My absence from the vote I hope hath not deserved so severe a censure as it seems is laid upon me by some, especially when I may truly say that I

[2] *Cowper MSS.,* II, 250.

[3] Coke MSS., packet 44, Coke to Strafford, May 1640.

[4] Coke MSS., packet 69, Coke to unknown [Oct. 1643]; packet 2, Coke to 'Your Excellency' [the earl of Essex], 20 Sept. 1642. Coke signed this letter, 'Your Excellency's humble servant as he was your father's'.

[5] *The King's Servants,* p. 365.

[6] *Cowper MSS.,* II, 278-80.

> absented not myself but was casually away that evening, not expecting that vote in an afternoon so near night. But I never spake for him in my life. Whatever my scruples have been is more known to you than to any man living. For I have carefully observed the rule to keep myself from making a party of any side; I confess not considering that there was so much danger of disrepute in otioso silentio.[7]

What do these words from son to father show? First, it appears, though it is not certain, that Coke had expressed disapproval of his son's absence from the vote. Secondly, it appears that Coke favoured the attainder. This is curious in the light of his earlier, close relationship with Strafford, but there are plausible explanations. Coke may have thought that Strafford could have done more to save him the Secretaryship. There is also evidence that in his last, desperate days Strafford tried to pass some blame onto the former Secretary.[8] And, more than anything else, Coke may have turned against Strafford when the latter courted Catholics and Spain to rescue Charles's government. Thirdly, however, the most interesting conclusion to be drawn from this letter is that the rightness or wrongness of the attainder itself was not as much at issue as the political considerations that surrounded the vote. John had 'carefully observed the rule to keep myself from making a party of any side', but even this neutral ground was dangerous. At a later point in this letter, John said: 'I think I shall never go with any tide whilst I live.'[9] But clearly he had learned that it was imprudent to resist the tide — or even appear to be resisting it — in the case of Strafford's attainder. A year later, this same pattern repeated itself. John avoided being appointed one of Parliament's deputy-lieutenants for Derbyshire, and he expressed the desire 'to be absent if any clashing be either in Derby or Leicestershire betwixt the [parliamentary] Ordinance and the [royalist] Commission of Array'. Coke again advised against this studied neutrality, again making him seem more supportive of Parliament than his son, but practical concern for his own welfare and his son's could still have been his principal motive.[10]

If considerations of safety drove Coke further toward Parliament's side than he might otherwise have gone, this is nowhere more evident than in a letter he wrote in November of 1641 to William Lenthall, the

[7] Coke MSS., packet 86, son John to Coke, 25 May 1641.

[8] Notestein, *D'Ewes Journal,* p. 412.

[9] *Cowper MSS.,* II, 284.

[10] *Ibid.,* II, 310, 319; Anthony Fletcher, 'Petitioning and the Outbreak of the Civil War in Derbyshire', *The Derbyshire Archaeological Journal,* 93 (1973), 38.

Speaker of the House of Commons. The occasion of Coke's writing was a vote in the Commons (85 to 68) declaring him a delinquent and ordering him to be sent for.[11] Coke was pleading to be excused from this order, but he began his letter by casting a backward glance over the long course of his life. 'I have served now thirty years, three succeeding princes, in their affairs of honour and special trust', Coke wrote, 'and from them all received acceptance and marks of favour. I have also been a member of many Parliaments in their several reigns, without disrespect or disgrace in any.' When, at last, the infirmities of old age prompted Charles 'graciously to dismiss' him, Coke explained that he retired to the country so that 'after a laborious and long life I might have some free time to study my way to death'. Now, plagued by failing health and the threatening inquiries of Parliament, Coke deeply feared a summons to London. Begging to be left in peace, he appealed to Lenthall: 'I cannot conceive that I have been so ill-deserving of church and commonwealth that the hastening of my end by an impossible journey should be required to expiate an offence wherein no man can charge me to have been a mover or procurer of that which is objected.' Unfortunately, it is not clear what particular charge Coke was defending himself against. Nor is the issue illuminated by Coke's lame explanation: 'If my hand went with the whole Council board, it was the duty of the place I then held which bound me thereunto.'[12] Through this emotional appeal to Lenthall, through his reputation as a foe of Roman Catholicism, and not least through the efforts of his son, Coke managed to escape this parliamentary inquisition.[13]

From the foregoing letter it seems obvious that practical considerations of property and safety forced Coke to become as servile toward Parliament as he had once been toward the Crown. But the deeper question still remains: was this contrary to Coke's true convictions, or did he submit to Parliament more willingly because his loyalty to the Crown had already been eroded? Except for the scant evidence already cited, we could only guess at the answer to this question if it were not for the discovery of a previously unknown letter. Nearly one hundred years ago, Coke's papers were transcribed by William Dashwood Fane and published by the Historical Manuscripts Commission. Fane's transcripts were phenomenally accurate, and very few of Coke's letters were overlooked, but among those few which were overlooked, one is a gem. The letter was written by Coke at the

[11] Coates, *D'Ewes Journal*, pp. 50-1.

[12] Bodleian Library, Tanner MSS., vol. 66, fol. 194.

[13] *Cowper MSS.*, II, 290-1, 294-5; Coke, *The Last Elizabethan*, pp. 293-4.

end of 1640. He had just learned that an old friend, Sir Robert Pye, had told the House of Commons that 'no man in England understood the Navy and Office of the Ordnance so well' as Coke. Pye thought it would be absolutely necessary for Parliament to have Coke's assistance in reorganizing the government's finances.[14] Coke knew that he was too old to embark on another effort at reform. 'Reformation in any kind must be a work of love', Coke told his son, 'and therefore it were not only folly but madness for me at fourscore within three to meddle therewith in any kind.' Coke implored his friends:

> not to hurry me up to London where I must now appear less than I was before I came from thence, and cannot now with courage undertake a service which is now beyond my power and to me can have no other issue but the loss of all my comforts here at home, the shortening of my days, and ruin of my estate... and all to do I know not what.

Although Coke had no desire to participate in new enterprises, Pye's suggestion prompted him to reflect on his lifetime of experience and to distill what advice he could from it. Having had 'more experience than many others in reformation of sundry parts of the king's estate', Coke advised against 'any sudden undertaking of all at once'. Given the two choices of either increasing revenue or decreasing expenses, Coke strongly preferred the latter because he was wary of 'what the kingdom can endure'. Although he thought reducing expenses was the wiser course to follow, he did not think it would be easy. As he warned: 'This you will find the most necessary and most difficult part which will take up all your time if you sit not months but years. Sir Robert Pye can tell you how long we sat about the commission for revenue and how little good we did.' Regarding the Household, Coke noted that he had been on two commissions. The second of these made some improvement but 'left all the rest in as ill case as we found it'. Then Coke turned to the area of his special concern: 'For the commission of the navy, wherein I with eleven others of far greater sufficiency laboured many years, though we brought something to pass which remaineth upon record, yet when the state fell into action, all we had done was by other counsels overthrown.' Coke's magnanimous praise of the other commissioners was twenty years late, and his reference to 'other counsels' looks suspiciously like an effort to divert the blame away from himself. On the more positive side, though, he did explicitly acknowledge that reform of the navy was wrecked by war 'when the state fell into action'. And it is conceivable that by

[14] *Cowper MSS.*, II, 270. The existence of Coke's reply is merely noted on page 296, where it is misdated. The letter itself is in packet 65 of the Coke MSS.

'other counsels' he meant not just Sir Robert Mansell, or the Council of War, or a stingy Parliament, but Buckingham. Next Coke noted that he had also served on commissions for the ordnance 'and what was done and undone the record will declare'. Finally, looking back over this whole lifetime of fruitless efforts, Coke tried to summarize what the moral of his long career had been. 'Now by all these and such other employments', he concluded, 'I have been taught that which the archbishop of Canterbury said often: that kings cannot be served against their wills.'

Coke omitted much from his letter. He did not mention several underlying obstacles to good government (for example, venality, corruption, and the lack of an adequate, professional bureaucracy). He did not acknowledge his own complicity in the ruinous adventures of Buckingham. He did not explain how court rivalries had led him to cooperate in destroying the greatest early Stuart reformer of them all, Cranfield. He did not recognize that he had failed to share responsibility and to develop the leadership abilities of others who might have preserved his work. He did not understand that biases of class and religion, including his own, had prevented the committees of the 1630s from operating more constructively. But he concluded by laying the ultimate blame at the feet of the monarchy, and that is where it belonged. More and more, we are discovering that the courtiers of James I and Charles I worked harder and more honestly than previously assumed, but they worked for monarchs who squandered their talents.

Influence was stronger than merit at court. Coke and Greville failed to achieve naval reform in 1604 because they could not enlist enough influence on their side. Even before that event, Coke had observed that a man's reputation at court was something 'which no worth can uphold. . . without an adherence'.[15] Royal favour was the only force at court powerful enought to overcome influence. It was royal favour, however, that kept Sir Robert Mansell in office and immune from prosecution. Conversely, it was royal favour that made naval reform possible in 1618, but this was due much less to the merit of the project than to the influence that Buckingham had acquired over James, and within another decade that same influence wrecked what it had managed to achieve. Coke then learned — as Linda Peck has said of the earl of Northampton — that reform could be overturned by 'the same set of patronage relationships which created his own

[15] Coke MSS., packet 69, Coke to Sir Robert Naunton [*ca.* March 1599].

position'.[16] Of course James and Charles did sometimes recognize and reward merit. G.E. Aylmer has shown that although patronage was the most important asset for acquiring an office under Charles, qualifications and ability became at least equally important in determining whether a man achieved further promotion.[17] But patronage always loomed large, and to say that Charles rewarded his servants for their ability is not to say that he utilized their ability to much good purpose. One has only to recall the mountain of foreign correspondence written by Coke in the 1630s to no point whatsoever because Charles was often as not pursuing a contrary policy behind Coke's back. In the end, neither Coke nor Windebank had anything to show for all those countless hours of committee meetings and letter writing. Even peace, the one undoubted achievement of the 1630s, was at last thrown away.

The tragedy of Coke's life, then, was that he did not serve better masters.[18] This is not to imply that, given better masters, he could have single-handedly reformed the whole English government. But the exception of 1618 — when the king supported him and Buckingham protected him — shows that Coke had more than just blind obedience to offer. His efforts need not have been wasted, but they were, because he served masters who lacked both the will and the intelligence to govern responsibly. Coke had returned to court in 1618 believing that public office was 'a stage to do good'. And in 1622 he had told Buckingham that he would not 'dispose of my life for wages'. But in the end, what good had Coke achieved, and what did he have to show for his efforts except wages?

To conclude that kings cannot be served against their wills, Coke had to distinguish between the true service that he thought kings should desire and the false service that in practice they did desire. In other words, Coke had come to realize that the interests of the king and the interests of the kingdom were not necessarily identical. It is impossible to know precisely when Coke arrived at this realization, especially since he was too discreet to put such thoughts in writing before 1640, but a review of its causes may give some clue to its timing. Coke's servility might have persisted till the very end of his life if he had not been expelled from office. Reevaluation of the monarchy was forced upon him by his physical removal from the court, when he suddenly found

[16]'Patronage, Policy and Reform at the Court of James I: The Career of Henry Howard, Earl of Northampton' (unpublished Ph.D. thesis, Yale University, 1973), p. 253.

[17]*The King's Servants,* pp. 92-3, 274-7.

[18]Compare Rebholz, *Fulke Greville,* p. 322.

himself 'neglected and forgotten at the court as if I had never performed any acceptable service there'. The climate of critical opinion generated by the Long Parliament no doubt drove him further along this path. On the other hand, Coke had taken the first, tentative steps along it well before 1640. The religious and foreign policies of the Stuarts had always worried him. He wanted the king to stand firmly opposed to Roman Catholicism and to Spain. Charles's dealings in this respect, mostly secret, mostly through Windebank, in the 1630s were deeply repugnant to Coke, as his recollection of the Barbary trade dispute attests. One can only surmise how much he was driven further away from Charles by the king's continued association with Catholics, especially in 1640. Injured pride and religious prejudice, hardly laudable motives, were not the only grounds for Coke's estrangement from the monarchy. It must be remembered that his only direct criticism of the monarchy followed his recapitulation of a lifetime of failed efforts at administrative reform. From the triumph of Mansell in 1604, through countless commissions for the navy, the ordnance, and other departments, to the belated approval of Mansell's accounts in 1639, Coke had been learning the lesson of his life: that the greatest obstacle to economy, efficiency, and honesty in the king's service was the king himself. Servility had been the price of Coke's service to the Crown. That same servility, Coke came in time to realize, had made it impossible to go to the root of the problem, had made his lifelong service to the Crown worthless. Coke was an accountant; he knew what the balance sheet of his life revealed. After serving for 'thirty years, three succeeding princes, in their affairs of honour and special trust', he saw little in his long career but a sorry story of repeated failures. Somewhere along the way, then, Coke rejoined that disappointed generation of aspiring Elizabethans described by Anthony Esler. For his use of that phrase — 'that kings cannot be served against their wills' — shows that Coke ended up after all, like the other members of that generation, with a taste of ashes in his mouth.

BIBLIOGRAPHY

I. Manuscript Sources

Berkshire Record Office, Reading
Trumbull MSS.

Bodleian Library, Oxford
Tanner MSS.

British Library, London
Additional MSS.
Harleian MSS.
Lansdowne MSS.

Hatfield House
Cecil MSS.

Kent County Archives, Maidstone
Cranfield MSS.

Lambeth Palace Library, London
Shrewsbury MSS.

Melbourne Hall, Derbyshire
Coke MSS.

Orbit House, London
Court minute books of the East India Company

Public Record Office, London

AO 16	Audit Office, miscellaneous
C 66	Chancery, patent rolls
CO 77	Colonial Papers, East Indies
CP 43	Common Pleas, enrolled deeds
E 351	Exchequer, declared accounts, pipe office
INDEX 6,807-11	Signet Office docquet books, Charles I
INDEX 16,787-94	Indexes to the patent rolls, Charles I
PC 2/51	Privy Council Register, 1639-40
PRO 31/3	Baschet's transcripts
REQ 1	Court of Requests, orders and decrees
SP 14	State Papers, domestic, James I
SP 16	State Papers, domestic, Charles I
SP 39	Warrants, King's sign manual
SP 63	State Papers, Ireland, Elizabeth I to George III

SP 77	State Papers, foreign, Flanders
SP 78	State Papers, foreign, France
SP 80	State Papers, foreign, Germany: The Empire
SP 84	State Papers, foreign, Holland
SP 92	State Papers, foreign, Savoy and Sardinia

Somerset House, London
Prerogative Court of Canterbury, wills and letters of administration

Trusley, Derbyshire
'The Family Chronicle'
Fane's transcripts

Yale University, Beinecke Library
Osborn MSS.

Yale Centre for Parliamentary History
Typescript of Sir William Spring's diary for 1624
Typescript of Edward Nicholas's diary for 1624
Typescript of Nathaniel Rich's diary for 1626
Typescript of Bulstrode Whitelocke's diary for 1626

II. Printed Primary Sources and Calendars

Acts of the Privy Council of England. Edited by J.R. Dasent. 32 vols. London, 1890-1907.

Ball, W.W. Rouse and Venn, J.A., eds. *Admissions to Trinity College, Cambridge.* 5 vols. London: Macmillan and Co., 1911-16.

Berington, Joseph, ed. *The Memoirs of Gregorio Panzani.* Westmead, England: Gregg International Publishers Limited, 1970.

Birch, Thomas, comp. *The Court and Times of Charles I.* 2 vols. London: Henry Colburn, 1849.

______ *The Court and Times of James the First.* Edited by R.F. Williams. 2 vols. London: Henry Colburn, 1848.

______ *Memoirs of the Reign of Queen Elizabeth.* 2 vols. London: A. Millar, 1754.

Calendar of the Court Minutes of the East India Company, 1635-1679. Edited by Ethel Bruce Sainsbury. 11 vols. Oxford, 1907-38.

Calendar of State Papers and Manuscripts Relating to English Affairs Existing in the Archives and Collections of Venice. Edited by Rawdon Brown, G.C. Bentinck, H.F. Brown, Allen B.

Hinds. 38 vols. London, 1864-1940.

Calendar of State Papers, Colonial Series: East Indies, China and Japan. Edited by William Noel Sainsbury. 5 vols. London, 1862-92.

Calendar of State Papers, Domestic Series, of the Reign of Charles I (1625-1649). Edited by John Bruce and W.D. Hamilton. 23 vols. London, 1858-97.

Calendar of State Papers, Domestic Series, of the Reign of James I (1603-1625). Edited by Mary A.E. Green. 4 vols. London, 1857-9.

Calendar of State Papers Relating to Ireland Preserved in the Public Record Office, 1625-1670. Edited by Robert Pentland Mahaffy. 8 vols. London: 1900-10.

Clarendon, Edward Hyde, earl of. *State Papers Collected by Edward, Earl of Clarendon, Commencing from the Year 1621*. 3 vols. Oxford: Clarendon Printing House, 1767.

______ *State Papers Collected by Edward, Earl of Clarendon, Commencing from the Year 1621.* 3 vols. Oxford: Clarendon Printing House, 1767-86. Quarto edition.

Coates, Willson Havelock, ed. *The Journal of Sir Simonds D'Ewes from the First Recess of the Long Parliament to the Withdrawal of King Charles from London.* New Haven: Yale University Press, 1942.

Collins, Arthur, ed. *Letters and Memorials of State.* 2 vols. London: T. Osborne, 1746.

Cosin, John. *The Works of the Right Reverend Father in God John Cosin, Lord Bishop of Durham*. Edited by J. Sansom. 5 vols. Oxford: John Henry Parker, 1843-55.

Eliot, John. *An Apology for Socrates and Negotium Posterorum: By Sir John Eliot.* Edited by Alexander B. Grosart. 2 vols. London: Earl St. Germans, 1881.

Ellis, Henry, ed. *Original Letters Illustrative of English History.* 3 vols. First series. London: Harding, Triphook, and Lepard, 1824.

Elton, G.R., ed. *The Tudor Constitution: Documents and Commentary.* Cambridge: Cambridge University Press, 1965.

Gardiner, S.R., ed. *Debates in the House of Commons in 1625*. Camden Society, new series, vol. 6. Westminster, 1873.

______ ed. *Documents Illustrating the Impeachment of the Duke of Buckingham in 1626.* Camden Society, new series, vol. 45. London, 1889.

______ ed. *The Fortescue Papers*. Camden Society, new series, vol. I. London, 1871.

______ ed. *Letters and Other Documents Illustrating the Relations Between England and Germany at the Commencement of the*

Thirty Years War. 2 vols. Camden Society, vols. 90, 98. Westminster, 1865, 1868.

_____ ed. *Notes of the Debates in the House of Lords Officially Taken by Henry Elsing, Clerk of the Parliaments, A.D. 1624 and 1626.* Camden Society, new series, vol. 24. Westminster, 1879.

Goodman, Godfrey, comp. *The Court of King James the First.* Edited by John S. Brewer. 2 vols. London: Richard Bentley, 1839.

Hardwicke, Philip Yorke, second earl of, ed. *Miscellaneous State Papers from 1501 to 1726.* 2 vols. London: W. Strahan and T. Cadell, 1778.

Hill, Lamar Mott, ed. *The Ancient State Authoritie, and Proceedings of the Court of Requests by Sir Julius Caesar.* Cambridge: Cambridge University Press, 1975.

Historical Manscripts Commission. *Buccleuch and Queensbury MSS.* 3 vols. London, 1899-1926.

_____ *Cowper MSS.* Twelfth Report, appendix, vols. 1-3. London, 1888-9.

_____ *De L'Isle and Dudley MSS.* 6 vols. London, 1925-66.

_____ *Portland MSS.* 10 vols. London, 1891-1931.

_____ *Rutland MSS.* Twelfth Report, appendix, vols. 4, 5. London, 1888-9.

_____ *Salisbury MSS.* 24 vols. London, 1883-1976.

_____ *Third Report.* London, 1872.

_____ *Various Collections.* 8 vols. London, 1901-14.

Howell, T.B. ed. *Cobbett's Complete Collection of State Trials.* 33 vols. London: T.C. Hansard, 1809-26.

Jamison, C. *A Calendar of the Shrewsbury and Talbot Papers in the Lambeth Palace Library.* Revised by E.G.W. Bill. Vol. 1. London: Historical Manuscripts Commission, 1966.

Johnson, Robert C.; Cole, Maija Jansson; Keeler, Mary Frear; and Bidwell, William B. *Commons Debates 1628.* 4 vols. New Haven: Yale University Press, 1977.

Journals of the House of Commons. 81 vols. London, 1742-1826.

Journals of the House of Lords. 31 vols. London, 1767-77.

Kenyon, J.P. *The Stuart Constitution.* Cambridge: Cambridge University Press, 1969.

Knowler, William, ed. *The Earl of Strafforde's Letters and Dispatches.* 2 vols. London: William Bowyer, 1734.

Laud, William. *The Works of the Most Reverend Father in God, William Laud, Sometime Lord Archbishop of Canterbury.* Edited by James Bliss and William Scott. 7 vols. Oxford: John Henry Parker, 1847-60.

Leadem, I. S., ed. *Select Cases in the Court of Requests 1497-1569*. Selden Society, vol. 12. London, 1898.

Lonchay, Henri and Cuvelier, Joseph, eds. *Correspondance de la cour d'Espagne sur les affaires des Pays-Bas au XVII siècle.* 6 vols. Brussels, 1923-37.

McClure, Norman E., ed. *The Letters of John Chamberlain.* 2 vols. Philadelphia: American Philosophical Society, 1939.

McGowan A.P., ed. *The Jacobean Commissions of Enquiry 1608 and 1618.* Navy Records Society Publications, vol. 116. London, 1971.

Manwaring, G.E., ed. *The Life and Works of Sir Henry Mainwaring.* Navy Records Society Publications, vols. 54-5. London, 1920-2.

Naunton, Robert. *Fragmenta Regalia.* Edited by Edward Arber. English Reprints, no. 20. Westminster, 1895.

______ *Fragmenta Regalia . . . A New Edition with Notes and a Memoir of the Author.* London, 1824.

Nicholas, Edward. *Proceedings and Debates in the House of Commons in 1620 and 1621.* Edited by T. Tyrwhitt. 2 vols. Oxford, 1766.

Notestein, Wallace; Relf, Frances; Simpson, Hartley; eds. *Commons Debates, 1621.* 7 vols. New Haven: Yale University Press, 1935.

Notestein, Wallace and Relf, Frances, eds. *Commons Debates for 1629.* Minneapolis: University of Minnesota, 1921.

Notestein, Wallace, ed. *The Journal of Sir Simonds D'Ewes from the Beginning of the Long Parliament to the Trial of the Earl of Strafford*. New Haven; Yale University Press, 1923.

Oppenheim, Michael, ed. *The Naval Tracts of Sir William Monson.* Navy Records Society Publications, vols. 22, 23, 43, 45, 47. London: 1902, 1912-14.

Perrin, W.G., ed. *The Autobiography of Phineas Pett.* Navy Records Society Publications, vol. 51. London, 1918.

Returns of Members of Parliament. 2 vols. London, 1878.

Rushworth, John, ed. *Historical Collections.* 7 vols. London: G. Thomason, 1659-1701.

Rymer, Thomas. *Foedera.* Edited by Robert Sanderson. 20 vols. London: J. Tonson, 1704-35.

Scott, Walter, ed. *The Secret History of the Court of King James the First.* 2 vols. Edinburgh: John Ballantyne and Co., 1811.

Spedding, James, ed. *The Letters and the Life of Francis Bacon.* Vol. 6. London: Longman and Co., 1872.

Tanner, Joseph R., ed. *The Historical Register of the University of Cambridge.* Cambridge, 1917.

______ ed. *Two Discourses of the Navy 1638 and 1659 by John Holland, Also A Discourse of the Navy 1660 by Sir Robert*

Slyngesbie. Navy Records Society Publications, vol. 7. London, 1896.

Venn, John, ed. *Grace Book Delta Containing the Records of the University of Cambridge for the Years 1542-1589*. Cambridge: Cambridge University Press, 1910.

Warner, George F., ed. *The Nicholas Papers: Correspondence of Sir Edward Nicholas.* Camden Society, new series, vols. 40, 50, 57, and 3rd series, vol. 31. London, 1886-1920.

Wheatley, Henry B., ed. *The Diary of Samuel Pepys.* 9 vols. London: G. Bell and Sons, 1893-9.

III. Secondary Sources

Adams, S.L. 'Foreign Policy and the Parliaments of 1621 and 1624.' In *Faction and Parliament,* edited by Kevin Sharpe, pp. 139-72. Oxford: Oxford University Press, 1978.

Akrigg, G.P.V. *Jacobean Pageant: The Court of King James I*. New York: Atheneum, 1967.

Albion, Gordon. *Charles I and the Court of Rome.* Louvain: University of Louvain, 1935.

Alexander, Michael Van Cleave. *Charles I's Lord Treasurer: Sir Richard Weston, Earl of Portland.* London: The Macmillan Press Ltd., 1975.

Allsebrook, W.B.J. 'The Court of Requests in the Reign of Elizabeth.' M.A. thesis, University of London, 1936.

Ashton, Robert, *The City and the Court 1603-1643.* Cambridge: Cambridge University Press, 1979.

_____ *The Crown and the Money Market 1603-1640*. Oxford: Oxford University Press, 1960.

_____ 'The Disbursing Official Under the Early Stuarts: The Cases of Sir William Russell and Philip Burlamachi.' *Bulletin of the Institute of Historical Research,* 30 (Nov. 1957), 162-74.

_____ *The English Civil War: Conservatism and Revolution 1603-1649*. London: Weidenfeld and Nicolson, 1978.

Aylmer, G.E. 'Attempts at Administrative Reform, 1625-40.' *English Historical Review*, 72 (April 1957), 229-59.

_____ *The King's Servants: The Civil Service of Charles I, 1625-1642.* Rev. ed. London: Routledge and Kegan Paul, 1974.

_____ Review of A.P. McGowan, *The Jacobean Commissions of Enquiry 1608 and 1618. English Historical Review,* 90 (April 1975), 440-1.

——— *The State's Servants: The Civil Service of the English Republic 1649-1660*. London: Routledge and Kegan Paul, 1973.

Bagwell, Richard. *Ireland Under the Stuarts and During the Interregnum.* 3 vols. London: Longmans, Green, and Co., 1909.

Ball, J.N. 'Sir John Eliot and Parliament, 1624-1629.' In *Faction and Parliament*, edited by Kevin Sharpe, pp. 173-207. Oxford: Oxford University Press, 1978.

——— 'Sir John Eliot at the Oxford Parliament, 1625.' *Bulletin of the Institute of Historical Research*, 28 (Nov. 1955), 113-27.

Barker, G.F. Russell and Stenning, Alan H., comps. *The Record of Old Westminsters.* 2 vols. London: Chiswick Press, 1928.

Beaven, Alfred B. *The Aldermen of the City of London.* 2 vols. London: E. Fisher and Company Limited, 1908-13.

Bone, Quentin. *Henrietta Maria: Queen of the Cavaliers.* Urbana: University of Illinois Press, 1972.

Bonner, Robert Elliott. 'Administration and Public Service Under the Early Stuarts: Edward Viscount Conway as Secretary of State, 1623-1628.' Ph.D. dissertation, University of Minnesota, 1968.

Briggs, John J. *The History of Melbourne in the County of Derby.* 2nd ed. London: Whittaker and Co., 1852.

Bullough, G. 'Fulk Greville, First Lord Brooke.' *Modern Language Review,* 28 (Jan. 1933), 1-20.

Charnock, John. *An History of Marine Architecture.* 3 vols. London: R. Faulder, 1800-2.

Clarendon, Edward Hyde, earl of. *The History of the Rebellion and Civil Wars in England.* 3 vols. Oxford, 1707.

——— *The History of the Rebellion and Civil Wars in England Begun in the Year 1641.* Edited by W. Dunn Macray. 6 vols. Oxford: Clarendon Press, 1888.

Clarke, Aidan. *The Old English in Ireland 1625-42*. Ithaca: Cornell University Press, 1966.

Clarke, Samuel. *Martyrologie.* London, 1652.

Coke, Dorothea. *The Last Elizabethan: Sir John Coke, 1563-1644*. London: John Murray, 1937.

Coke, John T. *Coke of Trusley, in the County of Derby, and Branches Therefrom: A Family History.* London, 1880.

Corbett, Julian S. *England in the Mediterranean.* 2 vols. London: Longmans, Green, and Co., 1904.

Cox, J. Charles. 'Proceedings of the Derbyshire Committee for Compounding, and other Commonwealth Papers.' *Journal of the Derbyshire Archaeological and Natural History Society,* 13 (Jan. 1891), 132-73.

Davies, David W. *Elizabethans Errant: The Strange Fortunes of Sir*

Thomas Sherley and His Three Sons. Ithaca: Cornell University Press, 1967.

Davies, Godfrey. *The Early Stuarts 1603-1660.* 2nd ed. Oxford: Oxford University Press, 1959.

Devereux, Walter B. *Lives and Letters of the Devereux, Earls of Essex.* 2 vols. London: John Murray, 1853.

Dietz, Frederick C. *English Public Finance, 1558-1641.* 2nd ed. New York: Frank Cass and Co. Ltd., 1964.

Donogan, Barbara. 'A Courtier's Progress: Greed and Consistency in the Life of the Earl of Holland.' *The Historical Journal,* 19 (1976), 317-53.

Dugdale, William. *The Antiquities of Warwickshire.* 2 vols. 2nd ed. London: J. Osborn and T. Longman, 1730.

Dyer, George. *History of the University and Colleges of Cambridge.* 2 vols. London: Longman, Hurst, Rees, Orme, and Brown, 1814.

Esler, Anthony. *The Aspiring Mind of the Elizabethan Younger Generation.* Durham, North Carolina: Duke University Press, 1966.

Evans, Florence M.G. *The Principal Secretary of State: A Survey of the Office from 1558 to 1680.* Manchester: Longmans, Green, and Co., 1923.

Farmer, Norman. 'Fulke Greville and Sir John Coke: An Exchange of Letters on a History Lecture and Certain Latin Verses on Sir Philip Sydney.' *Huntington Library Quarterly,* 32 (May 1970), 217-36.

Fisk, Fred. *The History of Tottenham.* Tottenham: Fred Fisk, 1913.

Fletcher, Anthony. *A County Community in Peace and War: Sussex 1600-1660.* London: Longman Group Ltd., 1975.

______ 'Petitioning and the Outbreak of the Civil War in Derbyshire.' *The Derbyshire Archaeological Journal,* 93 (1973), 33-44.

Foster, Joseph, ed. *Alumni Oxonienses: The Members of the University of Oxford, 1500-1714.* 4 vols. Early series. Oxford: Parker and Co., 1891-2.

Fuller, Thomas. *The History of the Worthies of England.* Edited by P. Austin Nuttall. 3 vols. New ed. London: Thomas Tegg, 1840.

Gardiner, Leslie. *The British Admiralty.* London: William Blackwood and Sons, Ltd., 1968.

Gardiner, S.R. *History of England from the Accession of James I to the Outbreak of Civil War, 1603-1642.* 10 vols. London: Longmans, Green, and Company, 1883-4, 1894-6.

______ *A History of England Under the Duke of Buckingham and Charles I, 1624-1628.* 2 vols. London: Longmans, Green, and Company, 1875.

Grosart, Alexander B. *The Friend of Sir Philip Sidney.* The

Elizabethan Library. [Chicago], 1894.
_____ ed. *The Works in Verse and Prose Complete of the Right Honourable Fulke Greville, Lord Brooke*. The Fuller Worthies' Library. 4 vols. [Edinburgh], 1870.
Haskell, Patricia. 'Sir Francis Windebank and the Personal Rule of Charles I.' Ph.D. dissertation, Southampton University, 1978.
Havran, Martin J. *Caroline Courtier: The Life of Lord Cottington.* London: The Macmillan Press Ltd., 1973.
Heidenheimer, Arnold J. *Political Corruption: Readings in Comparative Analysis.* New York: Holt, Rinehart and Winston, Inc., 1970.
Hibbard, Caroline. *Charles I and the Popish Plot.* Chapel Hill: University of North Carolina Press, 1983.
Hill, Christopher. *Puritanism and Revolution.* New York: Schocken Books, 1958.
_____ *Society and Puritanism in Pre-Revolutionary England.* New York: Schocken Books, 1967.
Hill, Lamar Mott. 'The Public Career of Sir Julius Caesar, 1584-1614.' Ph.D. dissertation, University of London, 1968.
Hulme, Harold. *The Life of Sir John Eliot, 1592-1632: Struggle for Parliamentary Freedom.* New York: New York University Press, 1957.
_____ 'Sir John Eliot and the Vice-Admiralty of Devon.' *Camden Miscellany,* vol. 17. London: Royal Historical Society, 1940.
Hurstfield, Joel. 'Political Corruption in Modern England: The Historian's Problem.' In *Freedom, Corruption and Government in Elizabethan England*, by Joel Hurstfield, pp. 137-62. London: Jonathan Cape, 1973.
Innes, H. McLeod, comp. *Fellows of Trinity College Cambridge.* Cambridge: Cambridge University Press, 1941.
Johns, A.W. 'The Principal Officers of the Navy.' *Mariner's Mirror,* 14 (1928), 32-54.
Jones, J.R. *Britain and Europe in the Seventeenth Century.* New York: W.W. Norton and Company Inc., 1967.
_____ 'English Attitudes to Europe in the Seventeenth Century.' In *Britain and the Netherlands in Europe and Asia,* edited by J.S. Bromley and E.M. Kossmann, pp. 37-55. London: Macmillan, 1968.
Keeler, Mary Frear. *The Long Parliament.* Philadelphia: The American Philosophical Society, 1954.
Kenny, Robert W. *Elizabeth's Admiral: The Political Career of Charles Howard, Earl of Nottingham, 1536-1624.* Baltimore: Johns Hopkins Press, 1970.
Kenyon, J.P. *Stuart England.* Harmondsworth: Penguin Books, Ltd., 1978.

Kepler, J.S. 'Fiscal Aspects of the English Carrying Trade during the Thirty Years War.' *The Economic History Review,* 2nd series, 25 (May 1972), 261-83.
Lake, Peter. 'Robert Some and the Ambiguities of Moderation.' *Archive for Reformation History,* 71 (1980), 254-79.
Lewis, C.T. and Short, S., eds. *Harper's Latin Dictionary.* New York: Harper and Brothers, 1879.
Lloyd, David. *State Worthies.* 2 vols. London: J. Robson, 1766.
Lloyd, Howell A. 'Corruption and Sir John Trevor.' *The Transactions of the Honourable Society of Cymmrodorion,* Sessions 1974 and 1975, pp. 77-102.
Lockyer, Roger. *Buckingham: The Life and Political Career of George Villiers, First Duke of Buckingham, 1592-1628.* London: Longman, 1981.
McGowan, A.P. 'The Royal Navy Under the First Duke of Buckingham, Lord High Admiral 1618-1628.' Ph.D. dissertation, University of London, 1967.
Malden, H.E., ed. *The Victoria History of the Counties of England: Surrey.* London: Archibald Constable and Company Limited, 1905.
Manning, Brian. 'The Aristocracy and the Downfall of Charles I.' In *Politics, Religion and the English Civil War,* edited by Brian Manning, pp. 37-82. London: Edward Arnold Ltd., 1973.
Marcus, Geoffrey J. *A Naval History of England.* Vol. 1. Boston: Little, Brown and Co., 1961.
Mathew, David. *The Jacobean Age.* London: Longmans, Green, and Co., 1938.
Morgan, Edmund S. *The Puritan Family.* New York: Harper and Row, 1966.
Morgan, Irvonwy. *Prince Charles's Puritan Chaplain.* London: George Allen and Unwin Ltd., 1957.
Newton, Arthur Percival. *The Colonising Activities of the English Puritans.* New Haven: Yale University Press, 1914.
Nicholas, Donald. *Mr. Secretary Nicholas (1593-1669): His Life and Letters.* London: The Bodley Head, 1955.
Nichols, John Gough. 'The Discovery of the Jesuits' College at Clerkenwell in March 1627-8.' *Camden Miscellany,* vol. 2, no. 4. London: Camden Society, 1852.
Ollard, Richard. *The Image of the King: Charles I and Charles II.* New York: Atheneum, 1979.
Oppenheim, Michael. *A History of the Administration of the Royal Navy and of Merchant Shipping in Relation to the Navy.* London: The Bodley Head, 1896; reprinted: The Shoestring Press, Inc., 1961.

Pearl, Valerie. *London and the Outbreak of the Puritan Revolution: City Government and National Politics, 1625-43*. Oxford: Oxford University Press, 1961.

Peck, Linda Levy. 'Corruption at the Court of James I: The Undermining of Legitimacy.' In *After the Reformation: Essays in Honor of J.H. Hexter,* edited by Barbara C. Malament. Philadelphia: University of Pennsylvania Press, 1980.

______ 'Patronage, Policy and Reform at the Court of James I: The Career of Henry Howard, Earl of Northampton.' Ph.D. dissertation, Yale University, 1973.

______ 'Problems in Jacobean Administration: Was Henry Howard, Earl of Northampton, a Reformer?' *The Historical Journal,* 19 (1976), 831-58.

Penrose, Boies, *The Sherleian Odyssey.* London: Simpkin, Marshall, Ltd., 1938.

Petersson, R.T. *Sir Kenelm Digby: The Ornament of England 1603-1665*. Cambridge: Harvard University Press, 1956.

Prestwich, Menna. *Cranfield: Politics and Profits Under the Early Stuarts*. Oxford: Oxford University Press, 1966.

Rabb, Theodore K. *Enterprise and Empire: Merchant and Gentry Investment in the Expansion of England, 1575-1630*. Cambridge: Harvard University Press, 1967.

Rebholz, Ronald. *The Life of Fulke Greville, First Lord Brooke.* Oxford: Oxford University Press, 1971.

Rees, Joan. 'Greville's Epitaph on Sir Philip Sydney.' *Review of English Studies,* new series, 19 (Feb. 1968), 47-51.

Rex, Millicent B. *University Representation in England, 1604-1690*. Norwich: George Allen and Unwin Ltd., 1954.

Ruigh, Robert E. *The Parliament of 1624.* Cambridge: Harvard University Press, 1971.

Russell, Conrad. *The Crisis of Parliaments: English History 1509-1660.* London: Oxford University Press, 1971.

______ ed. *The Origins of the English Civil War.* New York: Harper and Row Publishers, Inc., 1973.

______ 'The Parliamentary Career of John Pym, 1621-9.' In *The English Commonwealth 1547-1640,* edited by Peter Clark, Alan G.R. Smith, and Nicholas Tyacke, pp. 147-66. Leicester: Leicester University Press, 1979.

______ 'Parliamentary History in Perspective, 1604-1629.' *History,* 61 (Feb. 1976), 1-27.

______ *Parliaments and English Politics 1621-1629*. Oxford: Oxford University Press, 1979.

Schreiber, Roy E. *The Political Career of Sir Robert Naunton 1589-1635*. London: Royal Historical Society, 1981.

Sharpe, Kevin, ed. *Faction and Parliament: Essays on Early Stuart History.* Oxford: Clarendon Press, 1978.

Smuts, R.M. 'The Puritan Followers of Henrietta Maria in the 1630s.' *English Historical Review*, 93 (Jan. 1978), 26-45.

Stearns, Stephen J. 'Conscription and English Society in the 1620s.' *Journal of British Studies,* vol. 11, no. 2 (May 1972), 1-23.

Stephen, Leslie and Lee, Sidney, eds. *Dictionary of National Biography.* 22 vols. London: Oxford University Press, 1921-2.

Stephens, Edgar, comp. *The Clerks of the Counties, 1360-1960.* Newport, England: Society of Clerks of the Peace of Counties and of Clerks of County Councils, 1961.

Stone, Lawrence. *Family and Fortune.* Oxford: Oxford University Press, 1973.

——— *The Family, Sex and Marriage in England 1500-1800.* New York: Harper and Row, 1977.

——— 'The Inflation of Honours, 1558-1641.' *Past and Present,* 14 (1958), 45-70.

Students Admitted to the Inner Temple, 1547-1660. London: William Clowes and Sons, 1877.

Tawney, Richard H. *Business and Politics Under James I: Lionel Cranfield as Merchant and Minister.* Cambridge: Cambridge University Press, 1958.

Taylor, Harland. 'Trade, Neutrality, and the "English Road", 1630-1648.' *The Economic History Review,* 2nd series, 25 (May 1972), 236-60.

Thompson, Christopher. 'The Origins of the Politics of the Parliamentary Middle Group, 1625-1629.' *Transactions of the Royal Historical Society,* 5th Series, 22 (1972), 71-86.

Thompson, I.A.A. *War and Government in Habsburg Spain 1560-1620.* London: The Athlone Press, 1976.

Tillyard, E.M.W. *The Elizabethan World Picture.* London: The Macmillan Company, 1943.

Trevor-Roper, Hugh R. *Archbishop Laud, 1573-1645.* London: Macmillan and Co. Ltd., 1940.

——— 'The General Crisis of the Seventeenth Century.' In *Crisis in Europe 1560-1660*, edited by Trevor Aston. Garden City, New York: Doubleday and Company, Inc., 1965.

Turner, Edward R. *The Privy Council of England in the Seventeenth and Eighteenth Centuries.* 2 vols. Baltimore: Johns Hopkins Press, 1927.

Tyacke, Nicholas. 'Puritanism, Arminianism and Counter-Revolution.' In *The Origins of the English Civil War,* edited by Conrad Russell, pp. 119-43. New York: Harper and Row, 1973.

Venn, John and Venn, J.A., eds. *Alumni Cantabrigienses.* 4 vols.

Cambridge: Cambridge University Press, 1922-7.

Walton, Isaac. *The Lives of Dr. John Donne, Sir Henry Wotton.* Edited by Thomas Zouch. York, 1796.

Wedgwood, Cicely V. *The King's Peace, 1637-1641*. New York: The Macmillan Company, 1956.

——— *Strafford, 1593-1641*. London: Jonathan Cape, 1935.

——— *Thomas Wentworth First Earl of Strafford 1593-1641: A Revaluation*. New York: The Macmillan Company, 1962.

Willson, David H. *King James VI and I.* London: Jonathan Cape, 1956.

——— *The Privy Councillors in the House of Commons, 1604-1629*. Minneapolis: University of Minnesota Press, 1940.

Young, Michael B. 'Illusions of Grandeur and Reform at the Jacobean Court: Cranfield and the Ordnance.' *The Historical Journal,* 22 (1979), 53-73.

Zaller, Robert. *The Parliament of 1621*. Berkeley: University of California Press, 1971.

INDEX

List of volumes in this series

19 La Rochelle and the French Monarchy: Conflict and Order in Seventeenth-Century France — *David Parker*

20 The Purchase System in the British Army 1660-1871 — *A. P. C. Bruce*

21 The Manning of the British Navy during The Seven Years' War — *Stephen F. Gradish*

22 Law-Making and Law-Makers in British History — *Alan Harding (ed.)*

23 John Russell, First Earl of Bedford: One of the King's Men — *Diane Willen*

24 The Political Career of Sir Robert Naunton 1589-1635 — *Roy E. Schreiber*

25 The House of Gibbs and the Peruvian Guano Monopoly — *W. M. Mathew*

26 Julian S. Corbett, 1854-1922: Historian of British Maritime Policy from Drake to Jellicoe — *D.M. Schurman*

27 The Pilgrimage of Grace in the Lake Counties, 1536-1537 — *S. M. Harrison*

28 Money, Prices and Politics in Fifteenth-Century Castile — *Angus MacKay*

29 The Judicial Bench in England 1727-1875: The Reshaping of a Professional Elite — *Daniel Duman*

30 Estate Management in Eighteenth-Century England: The Building of the Leveson-Gower Fortune — *J. R. Wordie*

31 Merchant Shipping and War: A Study of Defence Planning in Twentieth-Century Britain — *Martin Doughty*

32 Faith by Statute: Parliament and the Settlement of Religion, 1559 — *Norman L. Jones*

33 Britain, Greece and the Politics of Sanctions: Ethiopia, 1935-1936 — *James Barros*

34 Heresy and Reformation in the South-East of England, 1520-1559 — *John F. Davis*

35 John Talbot and the War in France 1427-1453 — *A. J. Pollard*

36 Law, Litigants, and the Legal Profession — *E.W. Ives & A. H. Manchester (eds.)*

37 'Agrarians' and 'Aristocrats' Party Political Ideology in the United States, 1837-1846 — *John Ashworth*

38	Caesar's Due: Loyalty and King Charles 1642-1646	*Joyce Lee Malcolm*
39	T.P. O'Connor and the Liverpool Irish	*L. W. Brady*
40	Law and Social Change in British History	*J. A. Guy & H. G. Beale (eds.)*
41	The Road to Sedan: The French Army 1866-70	*Richard Holmes*
42	The *Parlement* of Poitiers	*Roger G. Little*
43	Britain and Palestine during the Second World War	*Ronald W. Zweig*
44	The Right-Wing Press in the French Revolution	*W. J. Murray*